BUSINESS ETHICS
& COMMON SENSE

BUSINESS ETHICS & COMMON SENSE

EDITED BY
Robert W. McGee

QUORUM BOOKS
Westport, Connecticut • London

Library of Congress Cataloging-in-Publication Data

Business ethics and common sense / [edited by] Robert W. McGee.
    p. cm.
  Includes bibliographical references and index.
  ISBN 0–89930–728–0 (alk. paper)
  1. Business ethics. 2. Social responsibility of business.
I. McGee, Robert W.
HF5387.B8765 1992
174′.4—dc20   92–9568

British Library Cataloguing in Publication Data is available.

Library of Congress Catalog Card Number: 92–9568
ISBN: 0–89930–728–0

First published in 1992

Quroum Books, 88 Post Road West, Westport, CT 06881
An imprint of Greenwood Publishing Group, Inc.

Printed in the United States of America

The paper used in this book complies with the
Permanent Paper Standard issued by the National
Information Standards Organization (Z39.48–1984).

10 9 8 7 6 5 4 3 2

Copyright Acknowledgment

Grateful acknowledgment is made for permission to reproduce Dominick T. Armentano,
"The Ethics of Anticompetitive Practices," *Mid-Atlantic Journal of Business* 27, 1 (1990):
67–80.

Contents

Preface

Many business ethics books take a basically collectivist approach to the subject. They speak in terms of collective rights and interests, the "public interest," "social" justice, the greatest good for the greatest number, and so forth. If individualism is mentioned at all, it is mentioned disparagingly. This book takes a different approach. Although some contributors to this volume take some of these popular approaches, many of them do not. Thus, this book offers a more balanced presentation of business ethics than that found in most books on the subject.

The book is divided into four parts. Part I covers the philosophical foundations of business ethics. Tibor Machan points out some of the obstacles that must be overcome when teaching business ethics when the audience has preconceived notions that anything to do with business is somehow unethical. Antony Flew discusses the philosophical concepts of selfishness, exploitation, and the profit motive from a business ethics perspective. Douglas Rasmussen discusses the relationship between capitalism and morality, as does James Chesher. Jerry Kirkpatrick applies the philosophy of Ayn Rand to the ethical foundations of business. Roger Koppl discusses the concept of the public interest.

Part II addresses business ethics issues that involve the relationship of the corporation to outsiders. D. T. Armentano points out that some so-called anticompetitive practices may not always be unethical and that individuals who enforce the antitrust laws may be acting unethically because they violate the rights of individuals. George Benson and Douglas Den Uyl discuss the concept of corporate duty and social responsibility from different perspectives. Robert Gordon addresses some environmental issues from a business ethics perspective.

Part III discusses some issues regarding the responsibility of the corporation to insiders. Robert McGee points out some of the ethical issues involved in acquisitions and mergers. Rosalyn Berne and R. Edward Freeman take a managerial approach to ethics and affirmative action. Bevars Mabry discusses ethical behavior in labor relations. Robert McGee and Walter Block focus on some of the ethical issues involved in insider trading.

Part IV covers some of the ethical responsibilities of employees and the corporation. George Benson discusses conflicts of interest. William Grollman and Joan Van Hise point out some of the ethical dilemmas of management accountants. Riva Bickel discusses the ethics of computer activities. Leo Ryan writes about codes of ethics.

This book includes most of the major issues in business ethics and presents some of the issues in a manner not found in most other business ethics books. I hope that it stimulates thought, conversation, and enjoyment regardless of the reader's philosophical views.

Part I

Philosophical Foundations of Business Ethics

1

Teaching Business Ethics in an Academic Environment of Mistrust

TIBOR R. MACHAN

This chapter explains some of the practices of the teaching of business ethics within academe. It argues that much of that activity denigrates the profession of business, following the widespread conviction that the goals of this profession—namely, to earn a profit or to achieve prosperity for shareholders, investors, executives, etc.—are found to be demeaning morally.

The main source of this attitude is identified as the dualistic conception of human nature in terms of which each person is divided into two selves, one base and one noble, with the body and its satisfactions declared base and spiritual pursuits identified as noble. Business tends to seek the satisfactions of the body and thus is not deemed a respectable, morally upright profession.

This attitude is presented here as a serious problem for Western capitalist-inclined societies, especially when the practical failure of noncapitalist systems has become obvious. An alternative notion of human nature—that persons are whole natural entities with the responsibility to serve all aspects of their selves, not mainly the spiritual—is sketched and supported. In this view, the moral contempt for the profession of business no longer holds sway, and capitalism itself is seen in a far more positive light from the moral perspective.

Some time ago *Newsweek* ran a "My Turn" column[1] by Professor Amitai Etzioni of George Washington University, who taught a term of business ethics at the Harvard Business School. The author, who has written, among other works, a book[2] highly critical of neoclassical economics, spent the entire piece lamenting the meager interest his MBA students showed in the subject he was trying very hard to explain to them.

Etzioni's main complaint in the *Newsweek* piece is that he "clearly had not found a way to help classes full of MBA's see that there is more to life than money, power, fame and self-interest." More specifically, the MBA students were disappointingly fond of business, including advertising. Some endorsed the idea of "consumer sovereignty," meaning that consumers pretty much have the chance to make up their minds as to what they will purchase, even in the face of the persuasive efforts of advertisers. Our author complained in the face of this belief, "But what about John Kenneth Galbraith's view [which] argues that corporations actually produce the demand for their products, together with whatever they wish to sell— say male deodorants." The implication was that the idea of consumer sovereignty is a myth— people are made to buy things by advertisements, not by their own considered judgments as they encounter the advertisements' messages.

Another complaint advanced by Etzioni was that the Harvard MBAs didn't wholeheartedly welcome his "ethical" criticism of corporate political action committees (PACs). He notes that "scores of corporations encourage their executives to form political-action committees, and use the monies amassed to influence both Congress and state legislators. . . . One student said he liked PACs: 'Last summer, I worked for a corporation that has one. Its PAC allowed me to advance my economic interest. And I could use my vote in the ballot box, to support those who agree with my international ideas.' "

After he informs us of all these horrible goings-on, Etzioni asks, "So it's OK for corporate executives to have, in effect, two votes, while the rest of us have one?"

We could consider Etzioni's substantive criticism of business and its executives, of course, and find that they aren't very telling. For example, although our professor never mentions it, there is a famous response to Galbraith's debunking[3] of the consumer sovereignty doctrine. In a now well-known piece, only rarely used in business ethics texts, F. A. Hayek has argued[4] that while in a certain sense desires are of course created, this is not any different from what occurs with all innovations—artistic, scientific, religious, or whatnot. When a new symphony is written, it "produces" a demand. People take note of it and often find it preferable to what else they might listen to. Certainly, a new service or product is introduced on any front with the hope that it will meet the desires of someone who will see its point and judge it as having merit for him. Indeed, even male deodorants—a product Etzioni snidely denigrates in his piece as an obvious case of trivial consumption—may have a point for some of us who are not, perhaps, as lucky as our sweet professor.

No doubt some consumers will buy things for poor reasons and even waste their money on what is positively bad for them. As against the neoclassical economist's protest, this much needs to be granted to Galbraith and Etzioni—market failures, that is, wrongs, can occur within the system of free exchange. But one may doubt Galbraith's or even a business ethics teacher's general competence to judge better than we ourselves whether it is the right thing for us to buy what we buy. Such a judgment would be especially hard to make from Harvard or George Washington University's ivory towers.

Consider also the PAC case. What about the well-respected U.S. public policy—part and parcel of any functioning democracy—that people "petition the government for redress of grievances" (such as repealing the double taxation involved in the corporate capital gains tax or being singled out as the bad guys in the fight for a clean environment)? Where does Professor Etzioni's lament leave all the special interest groups that eagerly lobby in Washington for such noble causes as the protection of the snail darter, defense of animal rights, and the vigorous redistribution of the "nation's" wealth? What about all the Naderite public interest research groups (PIRGs) and the Sierra Club's constant pleading. Why should we decry PACs without also noting that essentially these kinds of organizations, lamentable or not, are by no means unique to efforts by businesses to participate in the democratic process?

Judging by the author's own account of how he went about teaching his business ethics course, it is no wonder that his students responded with little enthusiasm. Evidently, what the professor did was not to teach business ethics but to engage in that familiar academic pastime, business bashing.

But the main point to be made in response to this outcry by a teacher of business ethics is not that this approach to teaching the subject is biased but that it does not even cover the topic that names the course. What is going on here is not teaching of business ethics but the bashing and attempted taming of business.

Etzioni's approach to teaching "business ethics" is, sadly, not atypical. It is prevalent throughout the country's universities wherever such courses are taught. Such courses, all too often and rather ironically—considering that "truth in labeling" is one of those public matters urged during such courses—mislabeled as business ethics, are essentially concerned not with the subject matter of ethical conduct within the profession of business but with the denigration of the profession and the advocacy of public policy to reform it.

In medical ethics—and educational, legal, or engineering ethics—the objective is to take general and mostly familiar ethical theories and show how they might be made applicable to problems that have to be tackled within these special disciplines. What would utilitarianism say about surrogate motherhood or the problem of honest communication in the case of fatal diseases? How do we apply the tenets of Christian ethics or those of ethical egoism to the problems of risk aversion in the building of high-rise apartments or automobiles?

These are what may fairly be construed as the problems of some branches of applied ethics. Any such field presupposes that people want to be decent human beings in the conduct of their various professions and in the different roles they play in their lives and that all they need is some enlightenment about what the special problems in these areas might require of them. This amounts to showing the implications of the general ethical precepts or principles they should live by and have usually already assimilated into their lives for these special areas. That is what properly taught professional ethics courses are about. The professor does not simply take a side and try to badger students into believing that way. Rather he or she airs the tenets of the major ethical systems and shows their different implications for the special areas of human conduct being explored.

Of course, at a more advanced level of teaching, a professor would not need to be coy and could air his or her own convictions and even defend them, but here students may be assumed to be reasonably prepared to think things out for themselves and to take issue. At the same time the professor would help them do so despite his or her own convictions, not because there are no right ethical answers but because in a university setting a teacher's job is not to indoctrinate but to make familiar, to explain, to give a just treatment to major viewpoints on vital topics. A bit of the ethics of education would bring this home to teachers of so-called business ethics.

Yet business ethics is taught entirely differently in most courses and textbooks with that name affixed to them. Business ethics courses, as taught in most places, involve demonstrating to students that the very objective of the profession is something shady. Notice how eagerly Professor Etzioni recalls his student's justification of joining a PAC organization: it "allowed me to advance my economic interest." This, one may gather, had no ethical significance for the professor, who is well known as a severe critic of any kind of consequentialist ethics, the sort where good and right are identified by reference to some valuable results. For such philosophers and ethicists the pursuit of prosperity is by itself simply amoral. Never mind that there is a long tradition of ethical teaching wherein such pursuit could well be construed as a species of prudence, a trait of character that has, after all, been construed as the first of the cardinal virtues.

Instead of being seen as the institutional expression of this virtue—the good deeds people engage in by carrying out economically prudent endeavors—business itself, as a profession, is mostly distrusted and denigrated. By implications, of course, the only way to be ethical in business is essentially to abdicate. Short of that, which most people won't quite volunteer to do, one is at least required to wash one's hands after one has left the executive suite.

Is it any wonder that Harvard's MBA students were not jumping for joy when this kind of business ethics was taught to them, in terms of which their professional future instantly came under a moral cloud? As business ethics is conceived of in many classrooms and in most textbooks, a decent, moral person in this profession must basically demonstrate to others in the culture that he or she is not really serious about this business stuff after all. The only reason some people must carry forth in the field is that, sadly, it turns out to be a necessary precondition for doing some really good things in life. But a decent person in business is one who pays attention not to making money or earning a good return on investment but to rectifying social ills and being responsible socially.

Consider that most teachers and authors in this field view corporate commerce in the tradition of mercantilism: Corporations are entities created by the government to serve some public purpose. Richard DeGeorge, who has authored numerous texts and articles in business ethics,[5] adheres to this view, which is shared by, of all people, that great friend of business Ralph Nader. Both see people in the business world as entrusted with some public purpose and not with achieving economic success. They also ignore the point, made in reply by Robert Hessen,[6] that the idea of business corporations as entities created by the state harks back to a conception of the state within the feudalist and mercantilist tradition wherein citizens were viewed as subjects and thus as lacking sovereignty. This attitude needs to be seen for what it is, an unjustified elevation of some people to a superior status over others. The inference to be drawn from the "government-created entity" view of business corporations is that citizens are essentially servile, even in their economic endeavors. The argument against this idea is that business corporations are better understood as voluntary associations. People employ some professionals to perform various economic tasks from which to reap profit, that is, as a means by which to prosper.[7]

Admittedly, when business ethicists who denigrate commerce look to economists as the moral defenders of the institution and profession of business, they find, apart from a very few texts, little that is of moral substance. No wonder: As students of commerce, economists seek a technical understanding of the workings of business. They make a few assumptions about what generates business life in the first place, and they do not dwell on moral issues. In this, they are not at all unlike other social scientists who are trying with all their might to remain value-free and what they take to be scientific about their subject. (Some, unfortunately, extrapolate these assumptions to the rest of human life and thus pretend that their arid "science" can render all of human affairs fully understandable. But moral philosophers should not take advantage of that, and they usually do not when it comes to other social sciences of whose politics and ethics they do not despair.)

Instead of looking to the economists to say why business might indeed be an honorable activity, business-bashing ethicists should look to fellow ethicists, ones who see in business activity a perfectly legitimate form of prudential behavior, aiming at the prosperity of the agents or their clients. They should then try to come to terms with the arguments that try to establish the moral propriety of such prudential conduct.

Instead, what business ethicists tend to do, in the main, is to argue with those in a different field, with people really not prepared to debate the fine points of moral philosophy. Accordingly, these business ethics teachers find it a simple matter to discredit the moral foundations of bona fide business, making it appear that the field is nothing but an arena of naked greed and thus of sheer vice.

As noted earlier, most business ethics courses and textbooks are preoccupied with the notion that we need to tame business by government intervention, regulation, or litigation. This is done by inventing a host of new rights that consumers and workers are supposed to have, rights that then are owed government protection (as indeed basic rights are viewed in our type of government).[8] First, it is necessary to defend workers' rights to decent wages, wages based on comparable worth (by some intuited standard), fairness, job security, safety and health protection on the job, and so forth. (It does not matter much what the market, that is, the freely choosing consumers and the existing supply of goods and services, including labor, enables the employer to pay and do or what workers agree to do of their own free will.) Next, business ethicists are ready to advocate a deluge of regulatory measures that require people in business to comply or go under. Is there any wonder, then, that PACs have become vital to the business community?

All this implies that what people in business are after, namely, profit or, to use a less-tainted term, prosperity, is really not a very honorable objective. We simply shouldn't let people run free when they want to accomplish that objective. They need to be kept under severe supervision and stringent controls. This is what is accomplished by establishing innumerable government regulatory bodies at the federal, state, county, and municipal levels of government. Never mind that often this means stifling what little real chance human beings have for economic solvency. After all, because no real moral merit can be found in the pursuit of profit, in case of even the slightest moral demand upon those in the field, their professional objectives must be sacrificed. No doubt, as most teachers and writers in the field will admit, solvency is of some concern—but certainly let's not be preoccupied by that.

Now I'm painting a rather bleak picture. There might be some who teach this course with a different perspective who would be more balanced in their approach than those I have been focusing on. Yet, if we consider the literature in the field, including major scholarly books and articles as well as textbooks, the picture that emerges is very close to how I have been painting it.

I edited and contributed to a book on business ethics,[9] and the epilogue is called "Recent Work in Business Ethics: A Survey and Critique." (It appeared independently in the *American Philosophical Quarterly*.[10]) This piece chronicles what the various major business ethics books and business ethics writers have been saying, backing up thoroughly all that I have argued here.

For example, in discussing employment the major objective of most business ethics authors and professors is to demonstrate that there shouldn't be *employment at will*. Employers ought to be constrained forcibly, by government regulation or litigation, in their judgment as to whom they hire or fire or promote or advance in their endeavors. Nor can employees make certain kinds of decisions, such as to work at higher risk than, say, at the federal government level OSHA (the Occupational Safety and Health Administration) has allowed. Those who might wish to take the risk for higher pay are forbidden to do so by the government's imposition of certain standards on every business, however new and in need of some initial cost-cutting it might be.

In another area, the major objective of most business ethics professors tends to be to show how the role of subordination of most employees ought to be changed and how so-called employee rights should diminish if not annihilate the position of management. The employer is viewed as a tyrant, an oppressor, and an exploiter, which needs to be countered with some effective legislation and court decisions.

It does not matter that some employees may prefer working for others who take the bigger risks and are thus expected to reap the greater returns. Never mind that different business establishments might require different types of organization and that in some there may not be much room for shared management roles if the business is to run efficiently. All this is subordinated to the will of the state, with the fervent approval of many who teach our college students the ethics of business.

Clearly, then, we have in the academic community a fairly sustained attack on the profession of business. What ought to be an attempt to guide students preparing for the profession into some of the particular ethical difficulties of their field, based on a study of the various classic ethical positions, and an attempt to help them in their thinking by presenting them with problems, turns instead into a message to prospective members of the business community that their chosen profession is no good.

The question is, Why is this such a prevalent phenomenon in university departments of philosophy, even in business schools? Why is it that business has such a very bad press?

A lot of people propose answers to this question. Among them are those who say it has to do with envy. That is probably the most prevalent analysis produced by those who observe the phenomenon and want to understand it. Some others talk about the dislike and distrust of economic power that can be used to exploit innocent and helpless folks. Others claim that members of the business profession have brought all this upon themselves by not relying on the rules of the free market to play the game of commerce but instead calling upon the state to help them in times of hardship, for example, as Lee Iacocca asked the federal government to bail out Chrysler when it experienced economic problems.

I am not at all convinced by such explanations. The envy premise does not explain very much because in many areas of life people are excellent or outstanding and reach success and are not so confidently and righteously envied and denigrated as they are in the business world. People win Nobel Prizes or become top singers, actors, or actresses; while there may be some shameful envy associated with this, most people recognize legitimate accomplishment and tend to honor them, flock to the movies where they appear, or go to their concerts, rather than badmouth them with indignation and try to drag them down. As to the economic power, here the problem is that power has many sources, some more and some less popular. When we lament economic power we are already confessing our distrust of economics. If power comes from being a celebrity or very beautiful or a great prose writer or an artist or a magnificent television commentator, we seem not to have very much trouble with that. Concerning business's willingness to turn to the state, these days practically everyone runs to government with a pet project. If government advances ecological interests, this is deemed to be an honorable project, indeed. If artists are given support, the ethicists in our society seem not to mind very much—nor are they themselves disdainful about taking a few thousand dollars in support of their next ethics book (e.g., from the National Endowment for the Humanities).

There is a more fundamental reason that business has gotten such a bad rap. This is really, at least at the level of ideas, a very ancient reason, one that comes from some of the most honored philosophers—Plato in particular, and to some extent Aristotle.[11] Indeed, many of the major philosophical figures in the history of Western philosophy must take the blame. The basic intellectual underpinning of hostility to business is a form of dualism or, more particularly, a form of idealism.

Idealism in philosophy means, roughly, that the most important reality is ideas and not nature. Put differently, it is the spiritual realm, not the natural, that is of primary significance.

Dualism tends to mean that there are two major elements of reality, the natural or material and the spiritual or intellectual element. In the history of philosophy many of the major thinkers, when they did embrace a form of dualism of two basic substances in the world, chose the intellectual or spiritual as the high substance, as the more important one. To the extent they believe that human beings are composed of these two elements, these philosophers usually select for special treatment and honor the intellectual element of human life.

Indeed, in Aristotle's ethics—not entirely noncontroversial yet quite explicit—the truly happy life is the life that is lived entirely in terms of one's intellect.[12] This is the contemplative life. From Plato's philosophy, in his ethics as well as his politics, one gets the impression that people who specialize in the use of their intellect—who excel in that respect in their lives—are the more worthwhile people. These then are the people who are excellent and who ought to be accorded the role of leadership and guidance in society.[13]

Plato's view of the intellectual or theoretical people contrasts with how we should view those who are mostly concerned with mundane matters, including trade and business. Following this philosophical viewpoint, subsequent Western theology fell into line. This in part makes sense of why the biblical claim that sooner will the camel go through the eye of a needle than the rich man gain entrance into the kingdom of heaven has been taken to mean a denigration of wealth-seeking per se. In this context, Jesus's extreme anger and even violence toward traders using his church also makes good sense. One may be sure that churches were used by other professions, yet we don't know of Jesus ever resorting to violence against their members.

These popular religious readings tend to denigrate seeking prosperity and wealth. The institution of usury, one that characterizes the tasks of most banking and lending establishments, was for centuries denigrated and found to be unnatural for human beings. This view was and continues in some circles to be a normative point, namely, that if individuals are to be loyal to their true selves they ought not to engage in it.

Generally speaking, the only time in Western philosophy that we escaped this kind of thinking was during a very radical and almost extreme swing toward the other side of the pendulum, with Thomas Hobbes's complete materialism. Hobbes in the sixteenth century, following his enthusiasm with Galilean physics and science in general (itself sanctioned through the reintroduction of Aristotle's work in Western culture by St. Thomas Aquinas), basically denies the spiritual or intellectual realm.[14] For Hobbes and his followers everything is matter-in-motion, and the whole world can be pretty much understood in terms of physics. Hobbes's philosophy, more or less braced by many others of that era (e.g., Francis Bacon), was a kind of a reaction, swinging from idealism or dualism over to pure materialism.

Suppose now that we find reality as well as human beings divided into two spheres, and suppose that we designate one sphere to be divine or spiritual, that is, a higher level of reality. It is then clearly not surprising that those who are concentrating their attention and work on supplying our natural needs and wants, the basis for our earthly existence—our worldly joys, pleasures, happiness—will not be highly honored and may even be held in moral suspicion lest they divert our attention from what is truly important to us. This goes hand in hand with the kind of suspicion that has been shown toward human sexuality throughout the ages. It is a base sort of activity of human beings, necessary but not noble. It is certainly not deserving of honor or respect and not to be held up as something unambiguously respectable.

I think that a goodly portion of the attack on business is ultimately to be traced to this attitude, except that in our time there is an additional factor. This is that, given the brief swing to the opposite extreme via the materialist philosophy of Hobbes and his followers, including the political economists of classical liberalism, in actual fact business has made some gains, at least on the practical fronts and in those disciplines concerned with practical matters such as politics and economics. In short, commerce has at least become legitimized. Some of the more severe disdain toward it, which had once issued an outright ban on much of what now passes for business, is no longer institutionalized. Instead, what remains is a moral or ethical suspicion toward business that, however, feeds into the legal mechanism and has by now helped the institution to descend nearly to its earlier disreputable status.

Interestingly, with this attitude toward business the West has lost the ability to teach the newly emerging Eastern European countries how they might recover from the horrors of socialist economic mismanagement. The moral high road for capitalism has been abandoned, and only a half-hearted support can be heard from the likes of George Bush and other Western leaders.

Yet none of this is new. It's not just today's *Newsweek* or tomorrow's episode of "Dallas" or next term's business ethics courses that support this half-hearted attitude, a mixture of fascination and disdain. It is, as I have been suggesting, the fundamental confusion that human nature can be divided. Accordingly, one part of human nature is far more noble than the other. The other one is lamentable, and we are waiting to get rid of it until we fully realize ourselves into wholly spiritual beings.

In a way Socrates put the theme of this fundamental confusion very well by saying that all of life on this earth is really just a preparation for death and that death is when we join our truly spiritual selves and will have abandoned our material or natural selves.[15]

In that kind of dominant intellectual atmosphere it should not be surprising that those who concentrate on making a prosperous, successful, material, natural living possible for most of us—those who serve us in shopping centers, not in churches, not at universities, not in laboratories— would not be honored, not be respected.

It is interesting to notice, finally, some of the practical policy consequences of the widespread scorning of business. Just consider how throughout history the people who have been alien to a culture and therefore couldn't participate in their own traditions often had no alternative but to join the business or financial class. Very often in Europe these were Jews, though elsewhere other ethnic groups played the same role. These aliens were at first demeaned and later, when the practical value of their work could no longer be denied, became the object of envy. In some cases in the end they were liquidated.

In any case, this is what I take to be one serious way to understand why business is treated so shabbily in our culture, not only by the Left but also by the Right. Although other reasons may be involved, I would probably argue that they are not so fundamental as those I have been discussing. And there are also at least some apparent difficulties with the position I have advanced. For instance, one might be tempted to argue that the Left's major contemporary doctrine, namely, Marxism, is an exception to my analysis; after all, isn't Marxism a materialistic philosophy, and doesn't it at the same time nevertheless denigrate business?

First of all, Marxist materialism is a peculiar kind, namely, dialectical materialism. It still abides by the notion of a firm hierarchy of nature. Even in Marxism the top of the hierarchy in human social life tends to be the intellectuals, especially in Marxism-Leninism. Those engaged in intellectual labor are regarded to be of a higher caliber than those who merely do menial work. One of the functions of capitalism in Marxist philosophy is eventually to do away with menial labor and to make us ready for pure intellectual labor in a communist society.

Furthermore, according to Marxism, until in the future humanity will be rewarded for its labors, most of us are supposed to wait around and act pretty servile. When that future has arrived, one of the rewards to humanity will be that most of our generalized work will be intellectual, while the tedious and harsh work will be done by machines created in the capitalist phase of human history. Marxism, furthermore, holds that capitalists, who are producing for the masses what the masses ignorantly want and thus engender market anarchy rather than a rational economic order, are unhappily willing to offer to people what they want and desire. But a rational order would produce what is right, namely, aside from basic necessities, goods and services arising from our intellectual talent such as musical composition and philosophical criticism.

Now, I am not going to criticize the thesis underlying the denigration of business at great length. My aim was to pinpoint the intellectual source of this attitude and the institutions stemming from it, including how business ethics is treated at our universities and colleges. Some of my criticism is already implicit in what I have said.

Yet, let me put myself on the record, anyway, by stating that I think the fundamental mistake is to divide human beings into separate selves and not to recognize that they are of one cloth and that, if they are important, they are important in all respects. A human being is an integrated entity, and the entirety of this entity needs to be cared for and honored, not just some special part of it.

Now that is an exaggeration; our nails at this time of human history are not as important as our eyes. But certainly from an ethical point of view to be prudent or conscientious about one's life involves also taking good care of one's material well-being: Clearly, this is acknowledged to some extent when we are prepared to care—and gain credit for caring—about our health. But as one grants the health professions an honorable standing, probably as a kind of derivative theoretical science, the same reasoning should apply in granting the business professions an honorable standing.

Professionals in business are clearly attending to some of the legitimate purposes of human life, namely, the securing of prosperity, of a pleasant, happy, spirited, and in the last analysis robust human life. Although they may not be the main contributors to a full-quality life, they are surely very important to it and their work ought to be respected. Their profession deserves all the honors given to educators, doctors, scientists, lawyers, and politicians.

When we teach business ethics to students who will probably enter that profession, we ought to teach them not to abandon their task, feel ashamed about it, set out merely to tame it, denigrate it, and consider themselves freaks. Rather they should be guided in how to do this entirely honorable task in a way fully compatible with living up to all of the basic moral requirements of a human life. It should be made clear to them that when some moral point of view appears to denounce their profession, this is not necessarily the end of the story. The moral point of view might be in error. Let them figure out how to handle it, rather than try to indoctrinate them to believe that business must be at fault. (This might be viewed along the lines of presenting the pacifist morality to military cadets—let them come to terms with this on their own. After all, Socrates, our model of the good pedagogue, was a gadfly, not a drill instructor.)

There is nothing peculiar about telling people that yes, while you are a businessperson, you probably also have the responsibility, in most normal cases, to be concerned about how to be a good father or mother or citizen. That doesn't denigrate business. But it does to tell them, "Well, you may carry on with the profession of business only because it's something we need, but it is too bad you have to. And if you can do anything else, please don't hesitate, but do it." This is just the message communicated to us all the way from TV sitcoms to the classrooms of the Harvard Business School. That's the kind of cultural moral atmosphere we live in.

Now perhaps it will be noted that other professions often also are ridiculed and lambasted in our culture. Why then make special note of business's bad press? Yet while doctors, lawyers, politicians, and others do receive some friendly drubbing—at the hands of comics, Hollywood, and the like—the business community is smeared and maligned outright. The frequency with which it turns out to be someone trying to make a buck who holds the smoking gun in cheap or even expensive dramas, from detective novels to complex PBS mysteries, is staggering. Although Samuel

Johnson may have believed that "A man is seldom so harmlessly employed as when he is making money," this is not at all the viewpoint of those like Arthur Miller in *Death of a Salesman* or the screen writers of "Wall Street," who all seem to agree that people in commerce are "money-grubbing scum."

All this has yet another result: It is very difficult to induce people in business to behave themselves properly, given how utterly confused they must by now be concerning moral issues. It is as if we were trying to teach ethics to professional hit men. Once we have declared an activity to be categorically wrong, as necessarily under moral suspicion, to start to up-grade it is nearly impossible. It amounts to trying to perform a contradictory mission. We have driven the profession of business basically into the moral underground, and in this moral underground it is no wonder that even those in the profession find themselves confused as to how to lead an upstanding professional life.

Those in business, as many of them will admit—usually to their children who then report it in the classroom—are virtually schizophrenic about their profession. They can't be proud of what they do when they discuss it at home; they are not able to tell their children, as a doctor or as an educator is able to do, that they are engaged in something honorable outside their home and that the culture respects them for it.

No, business or commerce is a kind of shady thing always under attack. People in academe—as well as too many artists, politicians, movie producers and, oddly enough, members of the business community itself—tend to sanction this reputation of business. After all, programs such as "Dallas" are being sponsored by corporations, as are all the sitcoms in which, for example, someone might be making a decision as to whether to become an elementary school teacher or business executive and the entire half hour is devoted to a humorous but biting exploration of how rotten a decision it would be if it turned out to favor joining the profession of business.

All this is, of course, quite tragic. It is probably debilitating in many more ways than I have suggested—psychologically, morally, and culturally.

We are a society in which pages and pages of each daily newspaper are devoted to business. It is deemed a most important aspect of our lives on the one hand. On the other, however, the very people who are playing the role, the drama, in those pages, cannot take full human pride in their activity in the way other professionals can.

When I teach business ethics, in contrast to Etzioni's experience at the Harvard Business School, I discuss all these issues. I find that I don't meet with the response Etzioni and, one may assume, many of his colleagues have encountered. I don't find my MBA students hostile to ethics because basically I treat their profession as fully capable of being honorable. It is with that assumption that we then discuss various problems of ethics that might arise in it. They don't see anything untoward in raising the possibility of unjustified dishonesty in advertising, in unjust discrimination in employment and promotion, in some of the problems and injustices of nepotism or the moral complications involved in trading with foreign colleagues who adhere to standards that seem to be morally insidious. They find none of this objectionable, even when it is suggested that often in life the bottom line, so called, isn't the bottom line at all.

But it is no surprise to me that MBA students at Harvard found Etzioni's approach to teaching business ethics objectionable. His message was that what you're doing is from the ground up contemptible, a lamentable activity that we somehow must engage in but if we could only get away from it we could go out and live a decent, respectful, human life. This quasi-Marxist notion, that capitalism is just some nasty period of humanity's existence that simply cannot be avoided but will, fortunately, soon be overcome, with the capitalist class promptly liquidated when the time is ripe, has overtaken our universities, not consciously but because sadly a goodly portion of Western intellectual history plays right into its hand.

NOTES

1. Amitai Etzioni, "Money, Power & Fame," *Newsweek,* September 18, 1989.
2. Amitai Etzioni, *The Moral Dimension: Toward a New Economics* (New York: The Free Press, 1988).
3. John Kenneth Galbraith, "The Dependence Effect," in *Ethical Theory and Business,* ed. T. L. Beauchamp and N. E. Bowie (Englewood Cliffs, N.J.: Prentice-Hall, 1983), p. 360.
4. F. A. Hayek, "The *Non Sequitur* of the 'Dependence Effect,' " *Ethical Theory and Business,* ed. T. L. Beauchamp and N. E. Bowie (Englewood Cliffs, N.J.: Prentice-Hall, 1983), p. 508.
5. Richard T. DeGeorge, *Business Ethics* (New York: Macmillan, 1982).
6. Robert Hessen, *In Defense of the Corporation* (Stanford, Calif.: Hoover Institution Press, 1979).
7. For a more detailed analysis of the profession of business and of commerce in general along these lines, see the various contributions in Tibor R. Machan, ed., *Commerce and Morality* (Totowa, N.J.: Rowman and Littlefield, 1988). Essentially, the idea is that commerce is one manifestation of prudential conduct in large social systems, and the profession of business emerges as the institutional result of such prudential conduct.
8. For a good collection of essays debating the issue of workers' rights, see Gertrude Ezorsky, ed., *Moral Rights in the Workplace* (Albany: State University of New York Press, 1987). See, for a detailed defense of the workers' rights view, Patricia Werhane and H. Persons, *Rights and Corporations* (Englewood Cliffs, N.J.: Prentice-Hall, 1985). For a detailed bibliography of books and essays in the now-burgeoning field and subfields of business ethics, see Donald G. Jones and Patricia Bennet, eds., *A Bibliography of Business Ethics 1981–1985* (Lewiston, N.Y.: The Edwin Mellen Press, 1986).

9. Machan, *Commerce and Morality*.

10. Douglas J. Den Uyl and Tibor R. Machan, "Recent Work in Business Ethics: A Survey and Critique," *American Philosophical Quarterly,* April 1987, pp. 107–24.

11. Many would argue that it is Plato's and Aristotle's explicit questioning of the merits of wealth—and, indeed, commerce itself—that should in part be held responsible, as given expression in Plato's *Republic* and Aristotle's *Nicomachean Ethics*. That seems to me a minor source of lamentation about these issues. What is far more important is Plato's (wholesale) and Aristotle's (at least partial) denigration of the kind of human life that seeks the kind of happiness that is achievable on earth. Both philosophers, not to mention subsequent followers, especially in theology, seem to consider success in a merely natural life either base or not significant enough. The source of the belittling of commerce and the business profession is the topic of my forthcoming book, *Business Besmirched: Why We Malign Commerce*.

12. Aristotle, *Nicomachean Ethics,* Book X, 7, 1177b. 18–21.

13. This, of course, is the general substance of Plato's *Republic,* as ordinarily interpreted.

14. The history of this is widely discussed. See, for example, Wallace I. Matson, *A New History of Philosophy* (San Diego, Calif.: Harcourt Brace Jovanovich, 1987).

15. See Plato's *Apology*.

2

Selfishness, Exploitation, and the Profit Motive

Antony Flew

> Besides, there is nothing so plain boring as the constant repetition of assertions that are not true, and sometimes not even faintly sensible; if we can reduce this a bit, it will be all to the good.
>
> —J. L. Austin[1]

There can be few more compelling examples of the sort of thing that the implacable Professor J. L. Austin hoped to reduce a bit than the constantly reiterated assertion that, because supposedly they are driven by the profit motive, competitive capitalist economies must be—as compared with the socialist command alternative—peculiarly and intrinsically selfish.

Thus R. H. Tawney, to go no further back, in his first prophetic book immediately after World War I excoriated what ever after he was to view as a "system in which industry is carried on, not as a profession serving the public, but for the advantage of shareholders." He therefore wanted "to release those who do constructive work . . . to apply their energies to the true purpose of industry, which is the provision of service." He reflected with satisfaction, "Over a considerable field of industry the Cooperative Movement has already substituted the motive of communal service for that of profit."[2]

A few years later these thoughts were echoed by the then once and future British Prime Minister Ramsay MacDonald: to transform "capitalism into socialism . . . industry must be converted from a sordid struggle for gain into a cooperative undertaking, carried on for the service of the community and amenable to its control."[3] Much later still, a few months before his death, Albert Einstein was quoted in *Socialist International Review* as saying: "The economic anarchy of capitalist society . . . is the

main cause of our evils. Production is carried on for profit, not for use."
And so it goes on, it seems, without end.

For in the summer of 1972, under the headline "Waiting for a Sign from
the Egoists," the *Times* of London reported that Archbishop Camara of
Brazil had asked a meeting of members of both Houses of Parliament,
"Why do you not help to lay bare the serious distortions of socialism such
as they exist in Russia and China? And why do you not denounce, once
and for all, the intrinsic selfishness and callousness of capitalism?" Today
Professor Raymond Plant—notwithstanding that he is often credited with
having striven valiantly and with rare persistence to come to terms with
the now no longer deniable failures of "actually existing socialism"—still
admits only most grudgingly, "There *may* well be a place for markets in
a humane society" (emphasis added), while nevertheless strongly insisting
that these must be tightly confined, "because they encourage some forms
of behaviour rather than others, viz. egoism over altruism, and rational
calculation of advantage over trust."[4]

To the archbishop's second question, the best first reply is another question: "Why is it that we never hear of the rent motive or the wages motive?"
Perhaps the classical distinction between profit and rent is obsolete. But,
if it is proper to speak of a profit motive, it should be equally proper to
speak of a wages motive. By parity of reasoning we shall then have to
admit into our new economic psychology the fixed-interest motive, the top-
price motive, and the best-buy motive. Of course, if it is proper to argue
that those who are paid wages must be stirred by the wages motive, then
it has to be not merely proper but positively refined to say that those whose
wages are paid at longer intervals and are called a salary or even compensation are inspired by, respectively, the salary motive and the compensation
motive.[5]

The purpose of this immediate counterquestion is to provoke two
thoughts. First: that it is misguided to insist on applying to psychology a
system of categories originally developed in, and appropriate to, economics. To insist on doing so is rather like postulating a set of chess motives,
distinguished one from another by reference to those similarities and differences that have been found relevant to the interests and purposes of
chess theoreticians, and then labeling these factitious postulations with
expressions drawn from the technical vocabulary of chess—the knight's
move motive, the fool's mate motive, the queening motive, or what have
you.

It may perhaps be of interest to compare here a classic example of making
a misguided move of this sort. For in *A Treatise of Human Nature,* David
Hume contrived to discover that "a man, who desires a thousand pounds,
has in reality a thousand more desires, which, uniting together, seem to
make only one passion; tho' the composition evidently betrays itself upon

every alteration of the object, by the preference he gives to the larger number, if superior only by an unite.''[6] Noticing that suggestive ''or more,'' we may be tempted to go on to urge that before decimalization the desire for a thousand pounds was—''in reality''—two hundred and forty thousand old penny desires, and that now it has proliferated to a hundred thousand new pence hankerings.

The second thought that should be provoked by that immediate counterquestion is that, if you are going thus to introduce any member of some set of distinctively economic or distinctively chess concepts into your psychology, then it is altogether arbitrary to introduce one only without the others—to speak of the knight's move motive without the queening motive, for instance, or of the profit motive without the wages motive.

A second line of response to the challenge presented by Archbishop Camara is to insist that no one has any business simply to assume that the desire to make a (private) profit is always and necessarily selfish and discreditable, notwithstanding that the corresponding desires to obtain a wage or a salary or a retirement income are apparently not.

It is, no doubt, true that all these various desires are interested, in the sense that those who are guided by them are, in the immortal words of Damon Runyon, the Balzac of Broadway, ''doing the best they can''! But, Precisely because this does apply equally to all, we can find no ground here for condemning one and not the others.

This neglected fact is awkward for the denouncers. For no one, surely, is so starry-eyed as to believe that any kind of economic organization can dispense with all such interested motives. ''Every economic system devised for ordinary human beings,'' we may read even in a tract otherwise devoutly socialist, ''must have self-interest as its driving force.''[7] If, therefore, one such system is upon this particular ground to be condemned as ''intrinsically selfish and heartless,'' then, by the same token, all must be. Yet that, of course, is not what is wanted by those who thus denounce capitalism root and branch while tolerantly discounting, as merely somewhat ''serious distortions,'' whatever faults they can bring themselves, however reluctantly, to recognize in countries already fully socialist.

There is a further and fundamental mistake here, and one that surely ought not to have been made by anyone with pretensions to act as a moral and spiritual guide. For, though selfish actions are perhaps always interested, only some interested actions are also selfish. To say that a piece of conduct was selfish is to say more than that it was interested. Selfishness is always and necessarily out of order. Interestedness is not, and scarcely could be.

For example: When two healthy children eagerly eat their dinners it would presumably be correct to say that each is pursuing his or her own interest; if any choices were involved, no doubt the economist would describe them as thereby maximizing their utilities. Yet this is no sufficient reason to start reproaching them. Time for that after brother has grabbed and eaten sister's dinner, too, or perhaps in some less flagrant way refused duly to consider others and respect their proper claims. Even when my success can be won only at the price of someone else's failure, it would be inordinately austere to insist that it is always and necessarily selfish for me to pursue my own interests. Is anyone prepared to say that rival candidates competing for some coveted position are culpably selfish in not withdrawing in order to clear the way for others?

The upshot, therefore, is that it will not wash to dismiss any one economic system as "intrinsically selfish and heartless" simply because that system depends upon and engages interested motives or even simply because it allows or encourages people to pursue their own interests in certain situations of zero-sum conflict. If there is something peculiarly obnoxious about wanting to make a (private) profit, it will have to be something about making a (private) profit rather than something about just wanting to acquire some economic good to even about competing to acquire scarce economic goods in any zero-sum conflict situation, as such.

That it is indeed essentially scandalous to make a profit and hence somewhat scandalous to wish to do so is an idea as old as the classical Greek philosophers. Consider what was said by the one who has had and who, albeit mainly through Aquinas and Hegel, continues to have by far the greatest influence.

Paradoxically the economic thought of Aristotle is found mainly in the *Politics*. One characteristic is that he accepts as normative whatever he believes to be, as it were, the intention of Nature. For those inclined to follow this lead, it should be salutary to discover where it took Aristotle:

Now if Nature makes nothing purposeless or in vain, all animals must have been made by nature for the sake of men. It also follows that the art of war is in some sense a natural mode of acquisition. Hunting is a part of that art; and hunting ought to be practised, not only against wild animals, but also against those human beings who are intended by nature to be ruled by others and refuse to obey that intention. War of this kind is naturally just.[8]

No one after reading this will be surprised to find that the ideal universal provider envisioned by Aristotle is Nature, and not, as it would be today, the state. His position is thus oddly reminiscent of that of those contemporaries, both clerical and lay, who assume that all wealth, in the form of immediately marketable goods and services, was directly created by God and is therefore available, free of any legitimate prior proprietorial claims, for radical redistribution in accordance with the putative principles of "social justice"[9]

On a general view, as we have already noticed, a supply of property should be ready to hand. It is the business of nature to furnish subsistence for each being brought into the world; and this is shown by the fact that the offspring of animals always gets nourishment from the residuum of the matter that gives it its birth.[10]

It is significant that, after this high-minded classical formulation of the shabby familiar doctrine that the world owes us a living, Aristotle emphasizes acquisition rather than production:

The natural form, therefore, of the art of acquisition is always, and in all cases, acquisition from fruits and animals. That art . . . has two forms: one which is connected with . . . trade, and another which is connected with the management of the household. Of these two forms, the latter is necessary and laudable; the former is a method of exchange which is justly censored, because the gain in which it results is not naturally made, but is made at the expense of other men.[11]

One point made here is that such exchange (trade) is in essence exploitation. Aristotle believes that the acquisitions of any trader must be made at the expense of that trader's trading partner, whereas the only creditable acquisitions are those achieved from nonhuman nature direct. Shorn of these notions of what is and is not in accord with the intentions of Nature, Aristotle's is the same thesis, and the same misconception, as that we find in *Unto This Last*: "Whenever material gain follows exchange, for every plus there is a precisely equal minus."[12]

This win-lose viewpoint has for centuries been, and still remains, a popular misconception, perhaps now especially in a form referring particularly to all trade in labor (power). For instance, an author who reveals no other Marxist cloven hoof tosses off, as if it were the most uncontentious of truisms, the remark that "the mystique of capitalism . . . disguises the transfer of benefits from worker to employer under the form of an equal exchange of values, through the device of a free contract of employment."[13]

Aristotle's seminal mistake here provides an always welcome occasion to quote a poet-scholar's rebuke to a rival scholar's lapse: "Three minutes' thought would suffice to find this out; but thought is irksome and three minutes is a long time."[14] The crux is that trade is a reciprocal relationship. If I am trading with you, it follows necessarily that you are trading with me. Trade is also, for both parties, necessarily voluntary. Nothing that you may succeed in seizing from me by force can, by that token, be either acquired or relinquished in trade. If any possible advantage of trade to the traders could be gained only at the expense of some corresponding disadvantage to trading partners, it would appear that in any commercial exchange at least one party must be a fool, a masochist, or a gambler.

But, as all must recognize when not either by theory or by passion distracted, the truth is that sellers sell because, in their actual situations, they would rather receive the price than retain the goods while buyers buy because, in their actual situations, they would rather pay the price than be without the goods. Ruskin was therefore wrong. It is of the essence of trade not that any advantage for one party can be achieved only at the expense of the other but that no deal is made at all unless both parties believe, whether rightly or wrongly, that they stand to gain thereby or unless at least both prefer the deal actually made to any available alternative deal and to no deal at all.

Certainly one of the trading partners, or even both, may be mistaken or in some other way misguided in the decision to deal. Certainly too the actual situation of either party, the situation in which it seems better to make the deal than not, may be in many ways unfair or unfortunate. But all this is contingent and hence irrelevant to the present question, which is: "What is and is not essential to the very idea of trade?" Mutually satisfactory sex is a better model here than poker played for money. For in the former the satisfactions of each depend reciprocally upon those of the other, whereas the latter really is a zero-sum game in which your winnings precisely equal, because they are, my losses.

One temptation to conclude that trade necessarily involves a zero-sum confrontation lies in the fact that both buyers and sellers would often, if they had to, pay more or accept less than they do. Obviously it is in such a situation possible to regard either the more that might have been gotten or the less that might have been given as an advantage forfeited by one trading partner to the other. While this may often be the case, certainly it is not so always. Both buyer and seller may be, and I imagine typically are, simultaneously in similar situations with regard to such possible but unachieved advantages. It cannot be correct to infer, as a general conclusion, that all the gains of trade must always be achieved by one trading partner at the expense of the other.

Another less intellectual but in practice more powerful temptation lies in the unappealing human inclination rather to attend with eager jealousy to the gains of others than to find a modest contentment in one's own, to forget that the deal was to your advantage in order to resent that it was to his also. Surely he would not, as you so ungraciously insist, "have made his profits out of you," had it not also been the case that you saw some advantage to yourself in your dealings with him? Yet how true it is that "Few men can be persuaded that they get too much by those they sell to, how extraordinary soever their gains are; when at the same time there is hardly a profit so inconsiderable, but they'll grudge it to those they buy from."[15]

Aristotle's next contribution, equally unfortunate, has been equally important. The last passage quoted continues:

The trade of the usurer is hated most, and with reason.... Currency came into existence merely as a means of exchange; usury tries to make it increase. This is the reason why interest is called by the word we commonly use [the word tokos, which in Greek also means offspring]; for as the offspring resembles its parent, so the interest bred by money is like the principal which breeds it, and it may be called "currency the son of currency." Hence we can understand why, of all modes of acquisition, usury is the most unnatural.[16]

"Usury" is now, thanks first to Aristotle and still more to his medieval successors, such a bad word that we may at first fail to realize to what he is objecting. It is not only to those very high rates of fixed interest that would nowadays be condemned as usurious. Nor even is it only to all fixed interest as such, which, as we shall soon see, was the prime target of those medieval successors. No, Aristotle's objection here is to any money return upon any money investment. It is, he thinks, against nature for money to breed money.

The moment Aristotle's point is appreciated, it becomes quite clear that both his objection and his supporting reason are superstitious and muddled. For a sum of money is the convertible equivalent of any of the goods or collections of goods that it might buy. There can, therefore, be nothing obnoxiously unnatural about receiving a money return upon an investment in money, unless it would be equally obnoxious and unnatural to ask for some return either in money or in kind for the use of the goods themselves.

Three corollaries may be drawn from this explication of the essential nature of money—corollaries the drawing of which makes these further references to Aristotle of more than merely antiquarian interest. First, it has to be entirely unilluminating psychologically to speak of any money motive and, by the same token, still more unilluminating to try to develop a complete economic psychology upon a basis of a series of economic distinctions between various mercenary motives. For that someone wants to make a profit or earn a wage tells us nothing of what he wants the money for. Almost any desire can take the form of a desire for money. It is obvious that this is a necessary consequence of the essential nature of money as a conventional instrument of exchange. Aristotle himself elsewhere makes this point about the nature of money. Nevertheless, as we have just seen, he fails to appreciate its present application.

The second corollary is that it has to be wrong to hope that the abolition of money or even a reduction of the range of desired goods which money can buy might by itself reduce greed and competition. Certainly it is tautologically true that the profit motive, the fixed-interest motive, the wages motive, and all the other factitious economic motives so far listed or suggested are mercenary. All, that is, may be defined in terms of the acquisition of money. It might therefore seem that totally to abolish money or to reduce its importance as a means of acquisition must be to abolish or at least to weaken all mercenary motives.

In an appropriately empty sense no doubt this is true. Yet, unless these changes happened to be accompanied by something quite different, an enormous transformation of present human nature, people would presumably continue to pursue, and to compete for, whatever it was that they had always wanted but that money could not now buy. In a word: if cars are not on sale for money but are available as a perquisite of public office, then this will by itself tend only to intensify the competition for such privileged official positions, a result long familiar to close observers of the Soviet-type economies (STEs) of Eastern Europe. To abolish money would save us from being mercenary merely in the same empty way in which the substitution of the word *gender* for the word *sex* saves us from sexist sin. For by itself, and short of the aforesaid total transformation of human nature, the abolition of money could not and would not so much as begin to make us either less materialistic or less competitive.

The third corollary is that money and the extension of the range of goods and services that money can buy are sovereign instruments of choice. If rewards are offered not in money but in kind, then recipients are precisely not allowed to choose: whoever fixes the rewards then determines not only their sizes but also what they are all to be. And if and to the extent that, for instance, health, education and welfare services are monopolistically provided by the state, then the citizens will be deprived of any direct and individual choice of what quantity and quality of such services they wish to consume.[17]

In his *A Critique of the Gotha Programme,* Karl Marx proclaimed a distributive ideal that many have found appealing: "From each according to their abilities, to each according to their needs." Few, it seems, have caught the sinister overtones both of authoritarianism and of austerity in that slogan. (Perhaps these were missed even by Marx himself.) But necessities are most typically and naturally contrasted with luxurious superfluities; and although we are all of us the best experts about our own *wants,* it is others who are so eager to tell us that what we really *need* is altogether different, and usually disagreeable.[18] How too, save by compulsion, is it to be ensured, after all individual incentives have been eliminated, that all will labor at their prescribed tasks to the limits of their abilities?

Aristotle maintains, as quoted above, that trading exchanges are always essentially exploitative. In the same passage he makes a tricky and precarious distinction between two forms of the art of acquisition, acquisition for household use and acquisition for financial gain. This must surely be the first forefather of an evergreen antithesis, that is, the antithesis, between production for use on the one hand, and production for the satisfaction of human needs on the other hand.

Though it is an evergreen, a moment's thought should show this antithesis to be false. Producers for a market cannot expect to make any profits at all save insofar as other people are able and willing to purchase their products. Presumably those others—that is, we ourselves—propose in some way to use whatever we buy, judging that it is needed to satisfy some of our wants. What is most emphatically not guaranteed is that what ordinary people are able and willing to pay for will be what liberal intellectuals, preening themselves upon their egregious superiority to the unenlightened, vulgar, rule that we truly and properly need.[19]

The true antithesis here is, of course, that between a market and a command economy. In the former, producers produce what they believe they can find people able and willing to buy. In the latter, what is produced is whatever the actual power elite commands shall be produced, which is likely to be some combination of what they want for themselves with what they decide is all that the rest of us really need. In the last few years, and especially in recent months, more information than ever before has become available about the preference structure of the actual power elite in the USSR. What—to borrow General Lee's phrase for describing Union armies—"those people" have most greedily wanted for themselves has been, in order to maintain and to extend their power, enormous and efficiently equipped military and police forces.[20] What they have considered to be sufficient to meet the needs of the rest of the Soviet people is, by the standards of contemporary democratic capitalism, simply wretched.[21]

There is a final fatal flaw in the assertion that, because supposedly they are driven by the profit motive, competitive capitalist economies must be, compared with the socialist command alternative, peculiarly and intrinsically selfish. It is that it depends upon an invalid form of inference. This invalid form of inference proceeds from propositions about the purposes attributed to institutions and to the people establishing these institutions to conclusions about the actual operative motives of the future managers and employees of these institutions.

There is no disputing that the management of any firm that wants to stay in business and has no access to any openended subsidy has to pay constant attention to the bottom line. Yet, from this fundamental and undisputed fact about private business we are most emphatically not entitled to infer that to obtain and to maximize profits is necessarily and throughout all working hours the exclusive and overriding concern of that management, much less that that must be the predominant or indeed any very noticeable concern of all the employees.

To keep profitable is in the long run a necessary condition of staying in business. But that is by no means a sufficient or indeed any sort of good reason for insisting that the only motive that anyone can or does have for going into or staying in business is to obtain for themselves the maximum possible profit. Furthermore, not only is the argument to this cynical conclusion invalid but the conclusion itself is also in fact false. For very few of us ever manage to be so utterly single-minded about anything. Many, too, have had occasion to rue the fact that such a single-minded profit orientation was far from characteristic of some firms in which they themselves have invested. Everyone must, surely, have had plenty of experiences of friendly and considerate treatment that was quite obviously not motivated by a pure and exclusive pursuit of financial gain?

Nor, of course, is the fact that some productive enterprise is a state-owned monopoly or that some other organization was specifically established to serve the public interest any guarantee that those employed in their operation will either already be or by these facts be encouraged to become not only more altruistic and less egoistic but also more trusting and less given to any "rational calculation of advantage" than the rest of us.

If Professor Plant does sincerely believe that it *is* a guarantee, then it is very difficult to prescribe and hopefully effective remedy. Nevertheless some introductory readings might help: technical readings in the economics of public choice[22] and/or some more agreeably entertaining readings of *Yes Minister*.[23]

The uncomfortable inquiry that should be pressed upon Professor Plant and upon all those others who share his intrusive interest in the motives of economic agents is simply, "Why?"—or, more aggressively, "By what right?" If people sell me satisfactory products at competitive prices, then it is surely no business of mine to pry into their motives for first making or otherwise acquiring these products and then selling them to me and to anyone else able and willing to pay the prices charged?

Such intimate investigations are properly left to their chosen spiritual advisers, if any. The most salutary example here for all of us is that of Queen Elizabeth the First of England. She used to insist that she wanted no windows into men's souls. It was enough for that most talented and liberally inclined ruler that her subjects, whatever their private motives and beliefs, should behave always as loyal and obedient subjects.

In general, and it is a reflection that has wide relevance, economic arrangements are best judged by results. Concentrate on the price and quality of the product. Do not officiously probe the producer's purity of heart. It is difficult to avoid diagnosing this eagerness to pursue such irrelevant and intrusive probings as springing from anything but a stubborn refusal to accept that socialism has most decisively failed the test of judgment by results, combined with a desperate hope that it might still be saved by an appeal to its supposedly altruistic intentions.

Where questions about motives are out of place, however, questions about interests may be very much to the point. For even the most minimally prudent persons must always hope, and try to ensure, that their suppliers have some interest in supplying them to their satisfaction; and this quite irrespective of whether or not these interests provide the main or sole operative motives of the suppliers. You do not need to be the total cynic to feel anxious about the quality and reliability of supply where the suppliers have no interest in giving satisfaction and where their clients have to depend on the universal presence and strength of "the motive of communal service"—one of the goods that is notoriously almost always and everywhere scarce. The author of the first and greatest classic of development economics was, as usual, both humane and realistic when he wrote:

It is not from the benevolence of the butcher, the brewer, or the baker that we expect our dinner, but from their regard for their own interest. We address ourselves, not to their humanity but to their self-love, and never talk to them of our own necessities but of their advantages. Nobody but a beggar chooses to depend chiefly upon the benevolence of his fellow citizens.[24]

NOTES

1. J. L. Austin, *Sense and Sensibilia* (Oxford: Clarendon, 1962), p. 50.

2. R. H. Tawney, *The Acquisitive Society* (London: G. Bell, 1921), pp. 140, 150, 152.

3. Quoted at p. 136 of S. H. Beer, *British Politics in the Collectivist Age* (London: Routledge, 1972).

4. K. Hoover and R. Plant, *Conservative Capitalism in Britain and the United States: A Critical Appraisal* (London: Routledge, 1989), p. 232.

5. The aptest comment on such prissy synonyms for the monosyllabic "wages" and "pay" is made by Bernard de Mandeville in *The Fable of the Bees*, edited by P. Harth (Harmondsworth: Penguin, 1970), p. 66:

> And when folks understood their cant
> They changed that for "emolument";
> Unwilling to be short or plain,
> In any thing concerning gain....

6. David Hume, *A Treatise of Human Nature* (Oxford: Clarendon, 1978), I (iii) 12: p. 141.

7. W. A. Lewis, *The Principles of Economic Planning* (London: Fabian Society, 1949), p. 7.

8. Aristotle, *Politics*, in R. McKean, ed., *The Basic Works of Aristotle* (New York: Random House, 1941), 1256B 20–26, p. 1137. It is perhaps worth emphasizing that while some ancient Greeks argued that only barbarians (i.e., non-Greeks) ought to be enslaved, no one in those days ever suggested that this fate should be reserved solely for non-Caucasians.

9. It is, in Robert Nozick's happy phrase, "manna from heaven." Compare "God's Creation, Wealth Creation and the Idle Redistributors," in D. Anderson, ed., *The Kindness That Kills: The Churches' Simplistic Response to Complex Social Issues* (London: SPCK, 1984); also Ronald Nash, *Poverty and Wealth: The Christian Debate over Capitalism* (Westchester, Ill.: Crossway, 1986).

10. Aristotle, *Politics*, 1258A 33–36, pp. 1140–41 in McKean.

11. *Ibid.*, 1258A 37–1258B 2, p. 1141 in McKean.

12. John Ruskin, *Unto This Last* (London: G. Allen, 1899), p. 131. This fiercely anticapitalist work greatly influenced both Mahatma Gandhi and most of the founding fathers of the British Labour Party.

13. David Miller, *Social Justice* (Oxford: Clarendon, 1976), p. 204.

14. A. E. Housman, *Juvenales Saturae*, rev. ed. (Cambridge: CUP, 1931), p. xi.

15. Mandeville, *Fable of the Bees,* p. 113.

16. Aristotle, *Politics*, 1158B 2–8, p. 1141 in McKean.

17. Compare, for instance, F. A. Hayek, *The Road to Serfdom*, rev. ed. (London and New York: Routledge and Kegan Paul and University of Chicago Press, 1976) Chap. 7; Ralph Harris and Arthur Seldon, *Over-ruled on Welfare* (London: Institute of Economic Affairs, 1979); and Arthur Seldon, *Charge* (London: Temple Smith, 1977).

18. Compare, for instance, chapter 5, "Wants or Needs: Choice or Command?" in my *The Politics of Procrustes* (Buffalo, N.Y.: Prometheus, 1981).

19. See, for instance, J. K. Galbraith, *The Affluent Society* (Boston: Houghton Mifflin, 1958).

20. Compare, for instance, Henry Rowen and Charles Wolf, eds., *The Impoverished Superpower: Perestroika and the Soviet Military Burden* (San Francisco: Institute for Contemporary Studies, 1990).

21. See, for instance, Nick Leberstadl, *The Poverty of Communism* (New Brunswick, N.J.: Transaction Books, 1988).

22. A good short starter is William C. Mitchell, *Government As It Is* (London: Institute of Economic Affairs, 1988).

23. Jonathan Lynn and Antony Jay, *The Complete Yes Minister* (New York: Harper and Row, 1988).

24. Adam Smith, *An Inquiry into the Nature and Causes of the Wealth of Nations,* ed. A. S. Skinner and W. B. Todd (Indianapolis: Liberty Press, 1981).

3

Capitalism and Morality: The Role of Practical Reason

Douglas B. Rasmussen

And insight is of ultimate things in both directions; for insight and not reasoning is of the primary bounding principles and of ultimate things, and insight, *in demonstrations,* is of immutable bounding principles, whereas insight, *in matters of action,* is of the ultimate and of the contingent and of the minor premise.

—Aristotle, *Nicomachean Ethics*

INTRODUCTION

In evaluating the morality of capitalism, I want to examine the role that *phronesis* or practical reason plays in the very operation of this economic and social system. However, it is first necessary to understand what is meant by the term *capitalism*.

The economic and social system I shall call "capitalism" is in its very conception tied to a special moral claim. The term refers to a set of economic and social arrangements that presuppose a certain ethical perspective. For example, "Murder Incorporated" would not be regarded in a capitalist economic system as a business firm but as something criminal that must not be allowed to operate. Similarly, the term *profit* does not mean merely a return on an exchange that is over costs; it also involves a certain type of exchange, namely, a free or voluntary exchange. For example, the gunman's offer, "Your money or your life," is not considered a free or voluntary exchange—even though one would prefer remaining alive to losing one's money. The problem with such an "exchange" is, of course, that the gunman does not have a right to demand from you either your life or your money in exchange for the other.[1] In order to understand the ethical perspective from which the terms capitalism and profit derive their particular meaning, the notion of "rights" should be considered.

Capitalism is an economic and social system based on the recognition of individual rights. "Rights" are a moral concept, but they are different from other moral concepts. They have a unique function. Their function is not directly to secure the moral well-being of individuals but rather to protect the self-directedness or autonomy of individual human beings and thereby secure the social condition under which individual human moral well-being can occur.[2]

Rights provide guidance in the creation and interpretation of a legal system that protects individuals from being used by others for purposes to which they have not consented. Rights are used to determine what ought to be a law. They provide the normative basis to law, but they do not, like the virtues, provide individuals with guidance regarding what choices to make in the conduct of their daily lives.

The idea that "no one's purposes of goals take moral precedence over the purposes and goals of any other person in a way that would justify the complete or partial subordination of any individual to any other individual or to any group of individuals"[3]—more simply put, that there are no natural moral slaves or sovereigns—is expressed in the claim that individuals have rights. To have a right in this sense legally obligates others to abstain from physical compulsion, coercion, or interference. Generally speaking, only the government may take such actions, and then only against those who initiate physical compulsion, coercion, or interference.[4]

It should be emphasized that the protection against being used for purposes to which one has not consented is understood to include the non-consensual use of the product of one's labor. As Robert Nozick has said:

Seizing the results of someone's labor is equivalent to seizing hours from him and directing him to carry on various activities. If people force you to do certain work, or unrewarded work, for a certain period of time, they decide what you are to do and what purpose your work is to serve, apart from your decisions. This process whereby they take this decision from you makes them *part-owner* of you; it gives them a property-right in you. Just as having partial control and power of decision by right over an animal or object would be to have a property right in it.[5]

Government's function is to implement and enforce laws that protect the lives, time, and resources of persons from being used without their consent.

It will be against the backdrop of a legal system based on individual rights that the role of *phronesis* or practical reason in the activities of creating wealth and exchanging goods and services—what Nozick called "capitalist acts between consenting adults"—will be assessed. However, it is necessary first to make clear what kind of enterprise the moral life is and what role *phronesis* or practical reason plays in it.

THE MORAL LIFE AND PRACTICAL REASON

If we take an Aristotelian approach, the goal of the moral life is the self-perfection[6] of the individual human being. Aristotle calls this goal "eudaimonia." The attainment of this goal requires that one live intelligently, acting not from impulse and habit but from knowledge and understanding. Such a way of life is not merely a matter of employing intelligence or reason to achieve whatever ends one happens to desire. Rather, this way of life prescribes or determines the ends one should desire and thus involves the satisfaction of *right* desire. These ends in turn constitute "eudaimonia," or what many philosophers now call "human flourishing."

Human flourishing is the overall end or goal of human life. It is an "inclusive" end. In other words, it is "the most final end and is never sought for the sake of something else because it includes all ends."[7] Thus, human flourishing is not some end that competes with such basic ends as health, wealth, friendship, and knowledge. It does not dominate these ends and reduce their value to that of mere instruments. Nor does it require a preset weighting or evaluative pattern of the ends that constitute it. That is something that is left to the individual to work out for himself.[8] Finally, this is not an end that treats moral virtues such as pride, courage, temperance, and integrity as merely external means. Instead, the moral virtues are valuable in themselves. They are, as we shall see shortly, expressions of human flourishing.

It is important to understand that human flourishing does not consist in the mere possession and use of the ends or goods required for successful living. Flourishing or living well is not the same as having what it takes to live well. In fact, the basic goods would not exist as goods for a human being if they were not objects of his effort. If a person is to flourish, he must direct himself to the attainment of these goods as best as the circumstances will permit. Human flourishing consists in a person taking charge of his own life in order to develop and maintain those virtues for which he alone is responsible and that in most cases will allow him to attain the goods his life requires.

It is also important to understand that human flourishing is attained only through choices that necessarily involve the particular and the contingent. Knowledge of the moral virtues and human goods may tell all of us what, abstractly speaking, we ought to do; but in the real world of individual human conduct, where all actions and goods are concrete and where human flourishing takes a determinate form, what the moral virtues and human goods involve cannot be determined from the philosopher's armchair. This is why *phronesis* or practical reason, that is, the use of reason by the individual person to determine what ought to be done in the concrete situation, is the cardinal virtue. Determining what moral virtue and goods call for in terms of concrete actions in specific circumstances can vary from person to person, and certain virtues can have larger roles in the lives of some persons than others. Determining the appropriate response for the situation faced is therefore what moral living is all about.

A successful moral life is by its very nature something that is highly personal. For example, a career, an education, a home, friends, and medical care are goods that, considered from an abstract perspective, are good or appropriate for all human beings. They ought to be created or achieved. Yet, this claim is not too helpful in providing guidance to the individual in a concrete situation. None of these goods exists in the abstract. How are they to be created or achieved? What kind of job, education, home, and medical care does one need? Who will be one's friends? To what extent and in what amount are these to be pursued? How is the achievement of one of these goods to be related to the achievement of other goods? What is the proper balance or mix? These questions can only be answered by a consideration of the unique needs and circumstances of the individual, and the insight of the individual himself is crucial to determining the proper answer. Practical reason is needed in the achievement, maintenance and enjoyment, and coherent integration of these basic human goods.[9]

This is, of course, not to say that any choice one makes is as good as the next, but it is to say that the choice must be one's own and involve considerations that are unique to the individual. One person's flourishing cannot be exchanged with another's. The good-for-me is not, and cannot be, the good-for-you. Human flourishing is something objective, self-directed, and highly personal. It is not something abstract, collectively determined, or impersonal.

Practical reason is concerned with action. It is concerned with action attaining its goal here and now. Practical reason, however, does not function apart from the moral virtues. We are not rational *beings*; we are rational *animals*. Desires move us to action, toward objects of apparent benefit and away from objects of apparent harm. Yet our desires can be mistaken. If practical reason is to succeed at the task of achieving, maintaining and enjoying, and coherently integrating the multiple basic human goods in a manner appropriate for us as the individuals we are, then the use and control of desires, that is, the creation of rational dispositions, is pivotal to the process. Moral virtues broadly define the boundaries of proper desire. This is illustrated by Henry Veatch's vivid account of the doctrine of the mean:

To begin with, consider the ordinary run of human responses and feelings with respect to typical situations in which men find themselves—confidence and discouragement, enthusiasm and indifference, cautiousness and carelessness, appreciativeness and scornfulness, friendliness and hostility, worry and unconcern, dissatisfaction and complacency. Now there is no doubt that some of us all the time, and perhaps all of us some of the time, allow ourselves to worry overmuch about our affairs, or else not to worry enough; to be excessively dissatisfied with our lot, or else to be lazy and complacent; to be friendly and a hail-fellow-well-met toward everybody, or else churlish and disagreeable; to be ridiculously cautious and careful, or else reckless and by no means careful enough; to be blinded to everything of worth and value except what is dictated by an all-consuming ambition, or else shiftless and lethargic with no get-up-and-get at all; to be an eternal optimist, indiscriminately sanguine about everything, or else the gloomy pessimist with no sure judgment about even those chances and opportunities that are genuine. Nor is there any doubt that the more sensible behavior would be one which managed to observe the just mean between such extremes.[10]

The moral virtues enable a person to have the qualities of character, that is, the rational dispositions, needed for the appropriate integration and enjoyment of goods, if and when they are achieved, regardless of the situation faced. They represent the conditions under which the possession of basic human goods make sense for a particular person.[11] They are thus that through which an individual's flourishing is expressed.

It must be stressed, however, that what the moral virtues require in terms of concrete action is, as already noted, something that is relative to the individual. As Aristotle says, virtue lies in a mean *relative to us* (*Nicomachean Ethics* 1107a1) and as Veatch has observed, "The whole point of the doctrine of the mean is that in the very nature of the case it will be related to the particular situation, the principle being that how we feel and react to a situation should not be a mere uncritical and undisciplined response, but rather the sensible and intelligent reaction which the particular situation calls for."[12] Practical reason is needed, then, not only for the creation of the moral virtues but for their continued refinement and application to changing circumstances. Further, the exercise of practical reason is completed only at the time of action, when the individual determines for himself what it is concretely that moral virtue requires.[13] One does not follow moral virtues as one follows a recipe in cooking a meal.

What, then, may be said of the practically wise person who has made moral virtue "second nature"? Ideally, we may say interchangeably of this individual either that "He is where he wants to be, doing what he wants to do," or that "He is where he must be, doing what he must do."[14] Thus, if Aristotle is right, we have within our power the ability to make our own soul; and what we make of it is reflected through the "mix" of goods we have either intelligently or unintelligently pursued.

THE MORALITY OF CAPITALISM

Does the system I have called "capitalism" encourage virtue or vice? What may be said of the morality of persons who produce and exchange goods and services in a capitalistic system? One typical charge against the morality of persons in a capitalistic system is that they tend to display such vices as lust, greed, selfishness, and materialism.[15] The typical reply,[16] however, is that this charge confuses what is permitted with what is encouraged. Capitalism may permit many vices, but it does not follow that it encourages vices. Further, if the consequences of such shortsighted hedonic behavior cannot be passed on to others, if an individual must bear the costs of his vices and is not subsidized by governmental programs—that is, if we are talking of capitalism and not some version of the "mixed economy" or socialist welfare state—it is unclear how capitalism can be charged with encouraging them. Capitalism requires that a person take responsibility for his life. Finally, if, for the sake of the argument, it is admitted that capitalism tends to encourage some of these vices, it must also be admitted that it tends to encourage certain virtues. Capitalism could be said to encourage honesty, independence, thrift, and diligence,[17] not to mention, as the works of F. A. Hayek have shown, the values of order and cooperation.

Another common accusation against the morality of persons in a capitalistic system, a possibly stronger charge, is that they tend to ignore certain virtues, particularly those associated with the attainment of "higher" goods, for example, the development of one's mind, the pursuit of artistic excellence, and the nurturing of true friendships. The capitalistic system allows people to use their resources according to their most valued uses, which allows people to be insufficiently appreciative of "higher" goods. Furthermore, in a capitalistic system these "higher" goods are forced to compete alongside other goods, and goods that appeal to the lowest common denominator in society tend to command a larger share of resources than "higher" ones. Mediocrity thus tends to characterize the lives of people in a capitalistic system.

As already noted, and as must be emphasized again, there is a difference between what a capitalistic system (1) allows or permits people to choose and (2) what it encourages or discourages them to choose; and point (2) cannot be legitimately inferred from point (1). It cannot be justifiably claimed that capitalism encourages ignoring "higher" virtues or discourages their pursuit. Rather, it lets the valuations of persons be reflected in the market. If the values of people were to change, then so would the ways resources are used. Nothing in capitalism precludes the pursuit of "higher" goods.

Nonetheless, there still seems to be a sense in which capitalism might be said to encourage mediocrity, for in permitting people to place greater weight or value on "lower" goods, such as pleasure and wealth, than on "higher" goods, such as intellectual and artistic development, it treats "higher" goods as if they were not more valuable than "lower" ones, which seems to put capitalism in direct conflict with the moral ideal of satisfying right desire. In fact, many see capitalism as rejecting an ethics of human flourishing and endorsing a desire-based ethics in which the ruling principle is "De Gustibus Non Est Disputandum."

This interpretation of capitalism is, however, too quick. Capitalism need not be interpreted as endorsing a desire-based ethic. The charge that capitalism encourages mediocrity can be met if a more careful examination of human flourishing is made. Although it is certainly true that a life that involves no pursuit of intellectual and artistic excellences or friendships based on lasting and significant values is a life that is less than it could and should be, it by no means follows that the proper weighting or valuation that is to be placed on such basic human goods can be determined by an abstract analysis of human flourishing. Nor does it follow that there is nothing ethically relevant to the weighting or valuing that the individual himself provides. The fundamental problem, then, with the accusation that capitalism encourages mediocrity is that it is based on a flawed conception of human flourishing.

As already noted, human flourishing is an inclusive end. It is not some single end that dominates over basic human goods, and it does not require a preset evaluative pattern for the goods that make it up. Rather, human flourishing is individualized, that is to say, individuative features that are neither included nor implied by an abstract account of human flourishing determine the weighting, the valuation, the pattern or balance of the basic human goods. In other words, human flourishing achieves determinate form, that is, becomes something real, only in light of needs and circumstances that are unique to the individual. The maxims of Greek ethics, "Know thyself" and "Become what you are," thus have force in terms of both what and who one is.

The accusation that persons in a capitalistic system fail to value "higher" goods as they should becomes most problematic once the diversified character of human flourishing is recognized. Obviously, people who give no weight to intellectual and artistic pursuits or to achieving and maintaining true friendships are failing to live as they should; just as obviously, people who do not achieve the proper balance for them of basic goods are similarly lacking. But this does not mean that there is some preset weight or pattern that everyone should have if they are to flourish. Human flourishing is not a Platonic *eidos*. The accusation that in a capitalistic system people generally fail to sufficiently value "higher" goods is without support, for there is no way a moralist can determine from his armchair what the proper weighting or valuation each and every person should give to "higher" goods.

The fundamental point, however, is not merely that critics of capitalism do not have sufficient knowledge to make such a general moral criticism of the activities of persons within a capitalistic system. The point is more radical, and it involves a positive assertion about the relationship between capitalism and human flourishing. The highly individualized and self-directed character of human flourishing requires that practical reason be the central virtue of the moral life, but practical reason occurs only through an individual's confronting the contingent and particular facts of his concrete situation and determining at the time of action what is in that situation truly good for him. Only an economic and social system that permits and protects such conduct in creating and exchanging goods and services will be justifiable in terms of human flourishing. Only such an economic and social system will be consistent with the central role that practical reason plays in the moral lives of persons. The economic and social system I have called "capitalism" is such a system, and it seems to be the only such system.

CAPITALISM AND THE ROLE OF PRACTICAL REASON

The role that practical reason[18] plays in a capitalistic system can be grasped by understanding the type of knowledge that is necessary for the competitive forces of capitalism to work. A brief examination of the works of F. A. Hayek, particularly his famous 1945 essay, "The Use of Knowledge in Society,"[19] will make clear what type of knowledge is crucial to the operation of capitalism and the role that practical reason plays in its use.

Hayek argues that the dispute between advocates of socialism and advocates of capitalism is not a dispute about whether planning is to be done or not. Rather, the conflict is over who will do the planning: Will planning be done centrally, by one authority over the entire economy, or will it be divided among many individuals?[20] Which form of planning, centralized or decentralized, can more effectively coordinate men's economic activities? Hayek argues that the answer to this question depends on which system can make a fuller use of existing knowledge and this, in turn, ultimately depends on:

whether we are more likely to succeed in putting at the disposal of a single central authority all the knowledge which ought to be used but which is initially dispersed among many different individuals, or in conveying to the individuals such additional knowledge as they need in order to enable them to dovetail plans with those of others.[21]

Economic planning, whoever does it, requires knowledge; and the first problem to be handled, if economic activities in a society are to be coordinated, is communicating to the planner knowledge that is given not to him but to someone else.

Which method of coordination of economic activities more effectively communicates the necessary knowledge upon which people base their economic plans? This depends on the type of knowledge that is necessary for economic coordination of activities. So far as scientific knowledge is concerned, a suitably chosen group of experts seem to be in a better position to command the best of the scientific knowledge available than ordinary persons. Hayek admits that we may be more likely to succeed in putting the necessary scientific knowledge into the hands of experts having ultimate authority than into the hands of many different individuals dispersed throughout the economy. Hayek claims, however, that scientific knowledge is not the sum of all knowledge and that another type of knowledge must be considered when determining which economic system makes a fuller use of existing knowledge.

A little reflection will show that there is beyond question a body of very important but unorganized knowledge which cannot possibly be called scientific knowledge in the sense of knowledge of general rules: the knowledge of particular circumstances of time and place. It is with respect to this that practically every individual has some advantage over others, in that he possesses unique information of which beneficial use might be made, but of which use can be made only if the decisions depending on it are left open to him or are made with his active cooperation. We need to remember only how much we have to learn in any occupation after we have completed our theoretical training; how big a part of our working life we spend learning particular jobs and how valuable an asset in all walks of life is knowledge of people, of local conditions and special circumstances.[22]

Further, knowledge of this type is crucial to economic decision making:

To know of and put to use a machine not fully employed, or somebody's skill which could be better utilized, or to be aware of a surplus stock which can be drawn upon during an interruption of supplies, is socially quite as useful as the knowledge of better alternative techniques. The shipper who earns his living from using otherwise empty or half-filled journeys of tramp steamers, or the estate agent whose whole knowledge is almost exclusively of temporary opportunities, or the *arbitrageur* who gains from local differences of commodity prices are performing eminently useful functions based on special knowledge of circumstances of the fleeting moment not known to others.[23]

Knowledge of the concrete situation[24] in which economic decisions are made is not knowledge that we are likely to succeed in making available to the central planning authority.

The problem of making knowledge of the concrete situation available to the central planning authority is even more difficult than initially appears. The circumstances that constitute the concrete situation in which economic decisions are made do not stand still. They change, and they often change in a moment's notice. It might seem, however, that such changes could be followed by the central planners' computers if they are fed the vital statistics. Yet this forgets that statistical aggregates are arrived at "by abstracting from minor differences between the things, by lumping together, as resources of one kind, items which differ as regards location, quality and other particulars."[25] Yet it is just the differences that abstraction ignores that are crucial to adjusting one's plan for how to use his resources. Indeed, to anyone familiar with the daily economic decisions of, for example, a plant manager in a competitive industry or to anyone who reflects on his own daily economic decisions, it must seem that only "rationalistic hubris" could make one believe that central authorities, without direct knowledge of concrete circumstances, could keep track of such changes by use of statistical aggregates. The problem of communicating the necessary information to the central planning authorities is not technological, but epistemological.

The epistemological problem faced by a centrally planned economy does not, however, end here. How can there be effective communication of changes in relevant economic factors that are beyond the horizon of the immediate knowledge of an economic decision maker? How can changes in the concrete situations of other economic actors and their resulting decisions be communicated? How will the plant manager know, for example, if other uses have been found for the raw material his plant uses or if its supply has been eliminated, and thus how will he know that he should economize its use? The manager does not need to know *why* these changes have occurred at this time. His concern is not with scientific knowledge. Rather, he needs to know how much more or less difficult it has become to procure the raw material. It is "a question of the relative importance of the particular things with which he is concerned, and the causes which alter their relative importance are of no interest to him beyond the effect on those concrete things of his own environment."[26] Information of this kind is, of course, revealed in the price of the raw material in the market; but if the price for the raw material is instead set by the central planning authorities, knowledge of the relative importance of the raw material will not be available to the plant manager, who will then fail to coordinate his economic plans with that of others. Central planning seems, then, incapable of communicating the knowledge necessary for the efficient allocation of resources.[27]

Hayek sees the system of free prices in capitalism as the very device for communicating the type of knowledge necessary for economic decision making. He is critical of theoretical accounts of capitalism that assume knowledge of relevant economic factors, for example, the cost of a certain method of producing a good, to be "given." Such accounts misconstrue the true function of a system of free prices. These accounts assume to exist what it is that they are supposed to explain, namely, the ability of a system of free prices to communicate the decisions of others regarding the relative importance of resources. Hayek observes that

what is forgotten [by many economic theories] is that the method which under given conditions is the cheapest is a thing which has to be discovered, and to be discovered anew, sometimes almost from day to day, by the entrepreneur, and that, in spite of the strong inducement, it is by no means regularly the established entrepreneur, the man in charge of the existing plant, who will discover what is the best method. The force which in a competitive society brings about the reduction of price to the lowest cost at which the quantity salable at that cost can be produced is the opportunity for anybody who knows a cheaper method to come in at his own risk and to attract customers by underbidding the other producers.[28]

Entrepreneurial insight that discovers opportunities for profit in knowledge of the concrete situation is that upon which the efficiency of a capitalistic system depends.

Hayek's recognition of the role of entrepreneurial insight in the use of concrete knowledge is important when it comes to examining the role that practical reason plays in the operation of a capitalistic system. In order that a concrete situation can be "seen" as affording an opportunity for a more efficient use of resources and the necessary action taken, the practical reason of an individual must be exercised. A particular situation that could be otherwise must come to be recognized by an individual as a way to achieve the goal of efficiently allocating his resources. Knowledge of ways to achieve a more efficient use of a resource is not provided like manna awaiting distribution to the cognitively hungry. Such knowledge does not exist prior to or apart from the alertness and insight of persons who are acting in their own concrete circumstances to efficiently allocate their resources.

It should be realized that entrepreneurial insight in attaining practical knowledge of the concrete opportunities for economic exploitation and the use of practical reason in the creation and maintenance of a morally worth-while life are not separate activities. They go together. The insight necessary for someone to see an opportunity for profit in the concrete knowledge he possesses is an act of practical reason; and while this is not the only insight needed for a person to flourish, it is a necessary part of the self-perfection process.

It is often forgotten that "apart from the pathological case of the miser, . . . there is no 'economic' motive but only economic factors conditioning our striving to other ends. What in ordinary language is misleadingly called 'economic motive' means merely the desire for general opportunity, the power to achieve unspecified ends."[29] There is no such thing as the "economic side" of a person's life that exists in splendid isolation, separate and unrelated to the rest of a person's life. Although economic activities do not (and should not) exhaust human action, economic factors affect everything a person does. There can be no pursuit of human flourishing that does not involve the exercise of practical reason in the creation, maintenance, and use of wealth. Furthermore, the valuations or weightings that people give basic human goods involve the use of their time and resources, so they can be expressed in economic terms. A system of free prices thus expresses the valuations or weightings people have made of basic human goods.[30] Prices are the result of the exercise of practical reason by persons regarding how to use their time and resources so as to attain the goods and services their flourishing requires. Although it is true that some of these judgments of practical reason can be mistaken, it is also true that human flourishing could not exist in an economic system that did not allow practical reason to play a central role in its operation. As Hayek notes,

Economic control is not merely control of a sector of human life which can be separated from the rest; it is the control of the means for all our ends. And whoever has sole control of the means must also determine which ends are to be served, what values are to be rated higher and which lower—in short, what men should believe and strive for.[31]

NOTES

I wish to thank Douglas J. Den Uyl and Marie George for their helpful suggestions.

1. It has been noted that the gunman generally is not offering an exchange of life for money: if you give up your life, he does not refuse to take the money. This is, of course, true, but does not change the point that has been made. Even if the gunman refused to take the money after you gave up your life, that would not be considered a "free" exchange within a capitalist economic system.

2. See Douglas B. Rasmussen and Douglas J. Den Uyl, *Liberty and Nature: An Aristotelian Defense of Liberal Order* (La Salle, Ill.: Open Court, 1991) for a defense of individual rights.

3. Eric Mack, "The Ethics of Taxation: Rights Versus Public Goods," in *Taxation and the Deficit Economy,* ed. Dwight R. Lee (San Francisco: Pacific Research Institute for Public Policy, 1986), pp. 489–90.

4. Fraud is a way of violating individual rights—specifically, property rights. "Fraud involves cases where one party to an agreed-upon exchange deliberately refuse to fulfill his part of the contract. He thus acquires the property of another person but he sacrifices either none of the agreed-upon goods or less than he agreed upon." Murray Rothbard, *Man, Economy, and State,* vol. 1 (New York: Van Nostrand Company, 1962), pp. 157–58. The person who engages in fraud acquires the property of others on terms to which they did not consent. Fraud is, however, not merely breaking a promise (which is generally a moral wrong but not a rights violation). There needs to be a contract, a legally sanctioned agreement. Yet, to be more precise, fraud involves the deliberate acquisition of another's property by misleading the other person into exchanging a good or service for something you have no intention of exchanging. A refusal to fulfill a contract, but without the intentional misrepresentation of a material fact, constitutes a breach of contract and is usually remedied, as the lawyers say, by applying the law of damages.

5. Robert Nozick, *Anarchy, State and Utopia* (New York: Basic Books, 1974), p. 172.

6. Self-perfection is not a static state, but an activity. *Omne ens perficitur in actu*: flourishing is to be found in action.

7. J. L. Ackrill, "Aristotle on Eudaimonia," *Essays on Aristotle's Ethics*, ed. Amelie O. Rorty (Berkeley and Los Angeles: University of California Press, 1980), p. 23.

8. "Aristotle may be criticized for assuming that there is an answer to the question 'what is the best life for man?'—as opposed to the question 'what is the best life for *this* man or *that* man?' He certainly does think that the nature of man— the powers and needs all men have—determines the character that any satisfying human life must have. But since his account of the nature of man is in general terms the corresponding specification of the best life for man is also general. So while his assumption puts some limits on the possible answer to the question 'how shall I live?' it leaves considerable scope for a discussion which takes account of my individual tastes, capacities, and circumstances." J. L. Ackrill, *Aristotle's Ethics* (New York: Humanities Press, 1973), pp. 19–20. Whether this interpretation is actually *the* one that can be found in Aristotle's writings is a controversial matter, but this need not concern us. "Aristotelian" is used in this essay to indicate a general approach to ethics that takes its inspiration from Aristotle. This approach is more schematic than historical, more argumentatively based than textual.

9. This point, among many others, was made clear to me by Douglas J. Den Uyl. See his excellent book, *The Virtue of Prudence* (New York: Peter Lang, 1991), especially chapters 11 and 12.

10. Henry B. Veatch, *Rational Man* (Bloomington and London: Indiana University Press, 1962), pp. 92–93.

11. See Den Uyl, *Virtue of Prudence,* chap. 12.

12. Veatch, *Rational Man,* p. 93.

13. See Fred D. Miller, Jr., "Aristotle on Rationality in Action," *The Review of Metaphysics* 37 (March 1984): 499–520.

14. David Norton, *Personal Destinies* (Princeton: Princeton University Press, 1976), p. 222. Norton observes that the term *must* is used here in a moral sense, that is, it stems from a person's own choice and reason.

15. Competition is usually cited as the factor responsible for these vices. Competition is seen as the law of the jungle applied to social life. Yet, this is a total misunderstanding of the nature of competition; competition is actually a form of cooperation. "Competition is not a zero-sum game where someone wins and someone loses, such that there is no overall gain between parties. Competition is rather a method of coordinating activities in which those who are most efficient at utilizing a given resource are in a position to do so. A kind of human ecological balance is promoted by the market." Douglas J. Den Uyl and Douglas B. Rasmussen, "Capitalism," in *The Philosophic Thought of Ayn Rand,* ed. Douglas J. Den Uyl and Douglas B. Rasmussen (Urbana and Chicago: University of Illinois Press, 1984), pp. 174–75.

16. The following replies to this charge are found in Douglas Rasmussen, "Economic Rights versus Human Dignity: The Flawed Moral Vision of the American Catholic Bishops," Douglas Rasmussen and James Sterba, *The Catholic Bishops and the Economy: A Debate* (Bowling Green, Ohio: Social Philosophy and Policy

Center, and New Brunswick, N.J. and London: Transaction Books, 1987), pp. 77–83, and also in Douglas J. Den Uyl, "Freedom and Virtue Revisited," in *Man, Economy, and Liberty: Essays in Honor of Murray N. Rothbard,* ed. Walter Block and Llewellyn H. Rockwell, Jr. (Auburn, Ala.: The Ludwig von Mises Institute, 1988), pp. 195–213.

17. See "Commercialism, Friendship, and Liberty," chapter five of *Liberty and Nature* for a discussion of this issue.

18. Examining this topic was first suggested to me by an essay of Fred D. Miller, Jr., "Rationality and Freedom in Aristotle and Hayek," *Reason Papers* 9 (Winter 1983): 29–36.

19. This essay can be found in Friedrich A. Hayek, *Individualism and Economic Order* (Chicago: University of Chicago Press, 1948).

20. Regarding the logical middle between these two alternatives, Hayek notes: "The halfway house between the two, about which many people talk but which few like when they see it, is the delegation of planning to organized industries, or, in other words, monopolies." Ibid., p. 79.

21. Ibid.

22. Ibid., p. 80.

23. Ibid.

24. Lon L. Fuller has also noted the importance of knowledge of the concrete situation. See "Freedom—A Suggested Analysis," *The University of Chicago Law School Conference on Jurisprudence,* Conference Series #15, 1955, pp. 50–52.

25. Hayek, *Individualism and Economic Order,* p. 83.

26. Ibid., p. 84.

27. See Daniel Shapiro, "Revising the Socialist Calculation Debate: A Defense of Hayek against Lange," *Social Philosophy & Policy* 6 (Spring 1989): 139–59. Shapiro makes it most clear that Hayek was not using a model of perfect competition or the Pareto-optimality standard of efficiency in his criticism of socialist planning.

28. "Socialist Calculation III: *The Competitive 'Solution,' "Individualism and Economic Order,* p. 196.

29. Friedrich A. Hayek, *The Road to Serfdom* (Chicago: University of Chicago Press, 1944), p. 89.

30. This is not to say that the price of a good or service in the market necessarily reveals one's personal evaluation of that good or service. The market price of a good or service reflects the valuations of others, as well as one's own.

31. Hayek, *The Road to Serfdom,* p. 92.

4

Business: Myth and Morality

JAMES E. CHESHER

> It is not the business of business
> to do good.
> But when business tends to business,
> it results in good.
>
> —ancient American proverb

It is beyond dispute that the reputation and image of business as a profession does not compare well with that of law, medicine, and teaching. Whereas the other professions enjoy varying degrees of public respect, business is quite commonly the object of criticism, scorn, and disrespect. It is not generally held to be an honorable profession, much less a "calling" or vocation. This finding hardly requires proof, but a simple armchair survey of common attitudes and language will bear out the claim.

We hear of the evils of the "profit motive"; the unholy alliance between big business and government; business controlling public policy through economic pressure; politicians being "bought" by business bribes or blackmail; the employer as a heartless tyrant; industry destroying the environment; "buyer beware"; (the love of) money being the root of all evil; the exploitation of the worker; consumers being gouged, ripped off; unfair tax breaks for corporations; business "creating demand" for useless products rather than responding to needs; the "planned obsolescence" of products; the need for "consumer protection" and a consumer bill of rights; the psychosocial dangers of advertising and thus the need for truth in advertising; high-pressure sales; cost productivity over human lives; the complaint that medicine is "becoming another business" (and thus we ought to "socialize" it).

This image is perpetuated in the mass media, from television and movie scenarios to popular songs and current jokes. Business itself buys into the image by refusing to respond to the charges, by assuming a collective professional guilt, by paying for advertising to support the very media programs that depict business as ignoble and the enemy of the consumer and worker, and, of course, by occasionally acting in just those ways that the image portrays. Nor is this view of the untrustworthiness of business confined to the common man, whose opinions are typically unreflective. Christopher Stone, a professor of law responding to Milton Friedman's claim that the only business of business is to seek profits, argues that law and morality are not always sufficient to keep business in check and cites Ralph Nader's desire that corporate directors be publicly elected as a possible solution to corporate abuse.[1] This is hardly a vote of confidence; neither is it a minority sentiment among intellectuals.

Not only is the image of business as ignoble well entrenched, it is also deeply grounded historically, going back at least to the early modern period. Notwithstanding, the image is a myth of staggering proportions, a myth worth exploring, worth exploding, for on analysis it will emerge that business does not deserve this ill repute, but rather quite the opposite. It is a vicious myth, on a logical par with racial and sexual prejudice. Until it is understood and disabled, unnecessary social division and undeserved blame and criticism will continue. The myth is, in the end, a matter of justice and one of the great ironies of modern times: we are, so the expression goes, biting the hand that feeds us.

SOURCES OF THE MYTH

Economic

The prejudice against commerce has no single source, but rather a number of related causal factors that include religious, economic, political, and social dimensions. These factors were clearly at work at the end of the Middle Ages, which saw the beginning of the demise of church power and the beginnings of secular power in the form of nation-states. This period of Western history, from the end of feudalism (circa fifteenth century) to the birth of modern science (seventeenth century) is unprecedented in terms of fundamental and dynamic changes at all levels of human activity. A central and catalytic element of change was economic, with a shift from the medieval system of relatively independent estates that borrowed and traded on a barter system to the modern system, which relies heavily on the use of money in commercial exchanges. Among the effects of this shift were the emergence of a new socioeconomic class based on wealth from trade and the economic-political partnership between this class and the monarchs. The church, formerly the center of economic and political power, was clearly by threatened.

One source of the prejudice against commerce is precisely that the advent of commercialism came at the expense of the church, which could hardly be expected to accept challenge without resistance. Prior to the modern era, the church was the source of values and was formative in the development of attitudes concerning the behaviors, personal characteristics, and activities that were regarded as ideals. The church was thus responsible, in large measure, for prevailing attitudes regarding everything from education to money. Prior to the modern era, the attitude toward money and money-lending was decidedly negative. It was thought that profiting from the lending of money was ignoble; additionally, money-lending was associated with the Jews, the favorite and perpetual scapegoat of endangered majorities. Shakespeare's *The Merchant of Venice* is a vividly dramatic illustration of this prejudice. Near the end of the drama, to save himself from ruin, Shylock is forced to forfeit the bulk of his possessions and made to promise that he will become a Christian! Furthermore, in contrast with the ideals of chivalry, dominant at the time, the values of trade and commerce were thought to be unworthy. Thus arose the long-standing tradition, both social and religious, against "usury," which originally meant any lending of money for interest or profit. Gradually, given the necessity of credit for economic exchange, the church softened its position and forbade only the charging of "excessive" or "exorbitant" rates of interest.

Chivalry

Though attitudes toward money and commerce today are considerably different from those of the fifteenth century, there remains the undercurrent of medieval belief that the values of commerce are inferior to those of chivalry and nobility. The chivalric code suggests a much wider scope of human life than we typically learn in high school, where the knight is associated with courtly love and romance. Though the lance and the sword are things of the past, the values of knighthood have survived to the present day, values far more profound than simply enduring the unrequited love of a fair maiden. In his poem "Guinevere," Tennyson has King Arthur describe the ideals of knighthood as follows:

> To reverence the King, as if he were
> Their conscience, and their conscience as their King,
> To break the heathen and uphold the Christ,
> To ride abroad redressing human wrongs,
> To speak no slander, no, nor listen to it,
> To honor his own words as if his God's,
> To lead sweet lives in purest chastity,
> To love one maiden only, cleave to her,
> And worship her by years of noble deeds,
> Until they won her.

In these few lines we have the portrait of obedience to authority, self-sacrifice, and altruism. No mention of personal gain, individual vision, or self-realization. The ideals point ever away from self. The medieval scholar F. J. C. Hearnshaw observes of chivalry that "Above all, it inculcated an ideal of social service; *service without remuneration*; service, however humble its nature, free from degradation or disparagement; service of the weak by the strong; service of the poor by the wealthy; service of the lowly by the high"[2] (emphasis added). Hearnshaw argues that the chivalric ideal has had an influence profoundly greater than the actual practice of the institution in medieval times. He points out that "In England, particularly, it set that tone which has been perpetuated in the great Public School tradition."

Altruism

Needless to say, the values of chivalry and nobility are in striking contrast to those of commerce. The knight in shining armor and the man in the gray flannel suit are worlds apart. The knight has vowed allegiance to the church; the entrepreneur, to his entrepreneur, to his enterprise; the knight seeks to better the condition of others in the world, the entrepreneur seeks to better his own lot; the knight risks life and limb for the greater good of others, the entrepreneur risks capital (often not his own) for greater personal wealth. The knight has heart and mind turned toward the highest light, the entrepreneur is single-mindedly calculating his own advantage. In short, the knight seems to be standing on high moral ground; and everything he represents, from intention to consequence, seems opposed to the ideals of the entrepreneur. The ideals of chivalry are basically altruistic and in this sense consistent with the ideals of Christianity, thus supporting the preservation and popular appeal of the idea of the knight in shining armor. Chivalry proceeds from service to others; commerce, from the seeking of profit. Profit is seen as though coming at another's expense and is egoistically, rather than altruistically, motivated. Thus the stigma against profit-seeking, against business.

Competition

A related source of the myth of business as ignoble comes from the element of competition inherent in market activity. It is generally understood that, in a free economy, persons can and do engage in commercial transactions with an eye toward getting the most for their money or getting the most money for their goods or services. Thus, a "smart" deal from, say, the buyer's point of view exists when a purchase is made for a good or service at below market price, below the "going" rate of exchange; a "smart" deal from the seller's point of view is when the sale is above the market rate. When prices are not fixed, there is a tendency for buyers to seek out the lowest price and for sellers to seek command of the highest price. On occasion buyer and seller may even negotiate on the price, but even when this is not explicit, there is almost always upward pressure on prices from the seller's side, and downward pressure from the buyer's side. Thus, market phenomena are competitive by nature: seller competing with seller for the buyer's money; buyer competing with seller for the cost of goods and services; buyer competing with buyer for goods and services in demand. The competitive nature of commerce seems to suggest that people engaged in commercial transactions are at odds, in conflict, seeking gain at the expense of the other: The better the deal for the buyer, the poorer the deal for the seller, and vice versa. Market activity is likened to the jungle (a dog-eat-dog world), where only the strong survive and where survival depends upon cunning ("wheeling and dealing") and cold indifference to the needs and desires of others. Thus arises the market imperative, "Caveat emptor," buyer beware! There are dangers in the market place, and the weak are bound to suffer. Where there is competition there is a power struggle, and everyone knows that power corrupts. At the very heart of commerce, then, is the tendency toward corruption. Competition favors the strong at the expense of the weak. The very spirit that drives commerce is itself morally suspect, given the ideal of altruism and the demands of chivalry.

Industrialism

As we move from the beginnings of capitalism to the early industrial era, the myth of commerce as ignoble gets fleshed out with images of sweatshops, tyrannical employers, and overworked, underpaid, and shamefully exploited workers. The working conditions of late eighteenth and early nineteenth century England, in particular, were generally horrible, as dramatized by Charles Dickens's *Hard Times*. These deplorable conditions led to the passionate response of philosophers such as Jeremy Bentham, the father of utilitarianism, and Karl Marx, father of socialism. Additionally, there emerged the Romantic movement in literature, with such writers as Thomas Carlyle in England and Rousseau in France denouncing industrialism and science and championing a "return to nature," to a life of greater spirituality and less materiality. There were clearly strong artistic, social, political, and philosophical pressures at work against technology, industrialism, and the new money-based economy of capitalism and entrepreneurship, pressures that continue to this day. Indeed, the recent phenomenon of the environmental movement, with its suspicion of science, technology, and industry and its dream of returning to a preindustrial state, is an extension of the Romantic spirit into the twentieth century. It is relatively easy to recognize the parallels between today's

"Green" movement and the ideals championed by the works of Carlyle (England), Rousseau (France), Thoreau (the United States), and Goethe (Germany). In general, we see in both the Green movement and in Romanticism a certain suspicion of reason and logic and an emphasis on intuition and emotion, a belief in "nature" as opposed to "civilization," and an aversion to private property, which Rousseau regarded as the source of man's fall from his natural state of goodness.[3]

The horrors of the industrial era to which the Romantics responded are underscored by the great social reforms of the nineteenth century, reforms that began in England and spread throughout Europe and America. In 1819, the first Factory Act was passed. This act established numerous restrictions on employers, including a limit of twelve hours to the nominal working day of employees, and prohibited the employment of children under the age of ten in factories. That such legislation was necessary suggests a widespread abuse of workers and a general insensitivity of employers. Though not an industrialist, Dickens's Ebenezer Scrooge nonetheless typifies the nineteenth-century employer as a greedy, stingy, insensitive taskmaster. Indeed, the name "Scrooge" is now synonymous with greed and lack of charity. This further advances the view that business is ignoble.

Consumerism

Needless to say, contemporary working conditions are vastly improved. The negative attitude toward business and industry has since shifted focus from the worker to the consumer. It is a commonplace that business needs to be regulated by government in a variety of ways so as to protect the consumer (and the environment). Without such controls, it is argued, commerce will abuse the consumer for the sake of profit, going so far as to risk the safety and lives of people in order to save production costs. A classic example, it is observed, took place when the Ford Motor Company knowingly produced and sold millions of defective Pintos. The gas tank assembly was of an inferior and dangerous design, but the additional cost to correct it was deemed more valuable to the company than the lives that would be lost. It was a "calculated risk." Not until after a tragic accident, a lawsuit, and public exposure did Ford recall the Pinto. Such is the mentality and the morality of profit-seeking enterprises. Without government regulation of commercial enterprises, the public will be easy prey to greedy entrepreneurs. The savings and loan disaster of 1990 is cited as further evidence of what happens when government controls are relaxed.

Marxism

All these practical arguments against business and the capitalistic system that propels it get impressive theoretical backing from the philosophical work of Karl Marx, who is doubtless the most respectable intellectual voice against capitalistic commerce. Marx gave specific social application to Hegel's idea that human history operates according to an internal logic: an inexorable process of forces in opposition (thesis/antithesis) that results in a new and better condition (synthesis) containing elements of the earlier opposites. This process, striving always toward the ideal, produces an increasingly better human community. For Marx, the envisioned ideal was a "classless society," an egalitarian society where individuals share equally in the labors and rewards of the community. The ideal society is thus radically egalitarian in that its citizens would be socially, economically, and politically indistinguishable from one another. One may of course have a different conception of the ideal human community, but what is of significance here is that, given Marx's concept and his analysis of historical development, capitalism (including private property, competition, and profit-seeking) is a flawed system, doomed to give way to the next step, in which the workers/citizens/state own the means of production and the state controls the economy for the greater good of the community. The stage of development that we call "business" (capitalism) is flawed in principle according to Marx, because it does not operate with the ideal or goal of egalitarianism. Indeed, in actual practice, if not in principle, business stands opposed to equality. This is, on analysis, a moral flaw: Business by its very nature is ignoble.

FLAWS IN THE MYTH

Economic

The feudal system of the Middle Ages, which came to be replaced by the modern money-based economy, was essentially a hierarchical, rigid, and static arrangement clearly designed to preserve the status quo and protect the interests of those at the top:

Groups of peasants were bound to a lord in three senses alike—financial, legal, and military. The lord himself, with many of his fellows, was probably similarly bound to a greater noble; the greater noble again to his count or his duke; and the count or duke still owed service and obedience, if only nominal, to the sovereign . . . in theory, it kept up collectivism. It was highly centralized; it was an elaborate network leading inevitably upwards towards the sovereign. . . . Feudum, or fee, or fief, is land (or office, or revenue) held in dependence upon any person . . . every man owes homage and service, especially military service, to the man from whom he holds land. Thus, he stands to that man not only as tenant to landlord, but as vassal to over-lord.[4]

The nostalgia about simple peasant life notwithstanding, the collapse of the feudal system, due in large measure to the growth of trade and the importance of money in commercial transactions, was a step in the direction of economic and personal freedom for the common person. It is no co-incidence that individualism came on the heels of the death of feudalism and, with individualism, greater pressure for economic, religious, and political freedom. Whereas the myth that business is ignoble views the worker and consumer, the "common man," as something of a slave or victim to the entrepreneur, quite the opposite is true: The growth of trade, com-merce, and the importance of money saw a corresponding growth in in-dividual freedom. The emerging modern economy, in contrast to feudalism, made it possible for individuals to radically alter their station and class in life.

One reason for the church's stand against charging interest for loans was the belief that only the lender profits from the arrangement. The idea here is that the person seeking a loan is in need, and the lender is somehow "taking advantage" of the needy person by charging him for assistance. This of course contradicts the demands of charity. Further, during the Middle Ages, there was very little need for money, as the economy op-erated on a barter system. Thus, having money was like having a hammer or a plow that one was not using: It ought to be loaned without charge, because it is not of any present use to the owner.

First, it should be noted that the borrower does indeed profit from the loan of money, that he believes himself to be better off by borrowing than by not borrowing, otherwise he would not borrow. Depending upon how he uses the borrowed money, his life may be improved, perhaps even dramatically transformed. Second, the money is not, like the unused ham-mer, of no use to the lender. For one thing, the money represents the owner's capacity to enhance his own life in a variety of ways: to purchase desired goods and services; to provide security against the ravages of fate; to see to the well-being, education, and future of his family; to invest in enterprises that may result in the creation of greater wealth; to help others in need; to promote causes in which he believes, and so on. The idea that the entrepreneur's motive to realize a profit on his investment is somehow base and immoral is equivalent to claiming that a worker's motive to earn the highest possible wage for his labor is base and immoral. Profit is what the sale of goods or services yields over and above the costs of producing and marketing the goods and services. In other words, profit is to the businessperson what a wage is to the worker. No one argues that workers are too concerned with wages or that workers are corrupted by the "wage motive" or that employers are being exploited as workers demand and receive higher wages. Nor is it the case that a businessperson can seek a profit without regard to the needs, desires, interests, rights, or concerns of others, as seems to be the view of those who think that profit-seeking is base and immoral. To begin with, the goods or service that the business offers must, if the enterprise is to succeed, be such as to satisfy a need, desire, interest, or even whim (the "pet rock") of the consumer. Anyone selling a service or commodity that no one wants or needs, or at a price no one can afford, or of such a quality that no one is interested is bound to fail. The fundamental truth here is so obvious that it sounds trivial when expressed, yet the "profit motive" critics fail to realize it: To seek a profit intelligently is to act so as to accommodate certain needs and desires of others. Furthermore, the businessperson, as a person, is always under the general obligation to behave morally. This puts clear restraints on business activity regarding the rights and interests of others. Of course, these restraints are sometimes ignored by individual businesspersons and occasionally the moral rules or principles are stretched for the sake of profit, but these faults are due to the imperfections of human beings, not to any inherent baseness in seeking a profit. Occasionally, too, a doctor will act irresponsibly or immorally in her capacity as a doctor; so also an attorney or a teacher. Individual failures ought not be generalized, nor ought these failures to be attributed to the profession to which the individual belongs.

Chivalry

It is interesting to observe that the code of chivalry assumes the helplessness of others. The knight in shining armor is a hero just to the extent that he extricates others from circumstances that they are unable to transcend. He slays the dragon that threatens the frightened and frail peasants; he subdues the tyrannical usurper lord; he protects the innocent against the heathen invader. In all cases, the knight is able to succeed as a knight where, and because, others fail. He is their last hope, and they will be eternally grateful to him, their benefactor and their savior.

In contrast, the entrepreneur must find a way to appeal to others. He cannot assume that he will be welcome; he expects to be subject to evaluation and critical review; he must proceed in his dealings with others by recognizing their autonomy, as they are free to go elsewhere and will certainly do so if they believe they are being poorly dealt with. In short, whereas the code of chivalry elevates the knight and demeans others, commerce strives to gain the confidence and respect of others and can do so only by extending respect. Of course, individual businesspersons may act disrespectfully, may act dishonestly, or may treat others as less than persons, but they do so to their own detriment. Another obvious truth: in business, as in life generally, one succeeds with others by respecting them, not by abusing them. Chivalry gets most of its reputation from the fact that it seems to operate on the basis of altruism, service to others, but commerce performs services of its own, without assuming a position of superiority.

Altruism

Altruism is the moral theory that the good consists in doing whatever brings about the welfare of others. We are thus under an obligation to promote the welfare of others, even if it means sacrificing our own welfare. Indeed, the ideal of altruism is to sacrifice oneself for others. On its face this appears to elevate others, to put them at higher value. In fact, it presumes that one can accomplish for others what they cannot accomplish for themselves, namely, to provide for their own welfare. Further, it assumes that one can know what is good for others and that one ought to do what one perceives is in the best interest of others despite how others themselves might perceive things. Looked at this way, altruism has a tendency toward paternalism. Admittedly, people often are in circumstances where they require assistance, but, more often than not, in those circumstances what they require is not that others solve their problems for them or that others protect them or that they be treated as children. Such dealings with others is fundamentally demeaning, for it denies their autonomy. So it is that the knight rides into the troubled land to set things right because the people are unable to do so themselves. So it is that consumers need to be protected, that commerce needs to be regulated, for people cannot be trusted to do this on their own.

"Buyer beware!" is typically understood to mean something like, "The seller is out to cheat you." A proper understanding of "Caveat emptor!" is that, in the marketplace, as in life, one must act intelligently in order to realize one's goals. In other words, it is up to the individual herself to think, to reason, to deliberate, to choose, to decide, to ask questions, and to seek assistance when appropriate. If someone else does this for us, we are not acting autonomously, we are not acting on our own, we are not acting as mature adults. Altruism and its corollary, paternalism, hope to save people from pain, but they do so by sacrificing autonomy and independence, which are the grounds of self-esteem. The presupposition of the marketplace is that people can think for themselves and can make proper decisions when it comes to their own welfare.

Competition

It is, of course, impossible to be altruistic and competitive at the same time. This makes altruists suspicious of market activity, which is inherently competitive. One cannot sell or trade anything in the marketplace without stating or implying the worth (price) of the goods or services in the transaction. Unless the price is fixed, for example, by law, someone else is free to exchange at terms more favorable to the other, that is, someone else is free to ask a lower price. Now, it may seem that this feature of commerce, its competitive nature, guarantees that someone will lose, just as athletic events have losers. What is overlooked is that, in the end, everyone gains. This is what Adam Smith called the "Invisible Hand" at work: As sellers compete with one another in the activity of satisfying consumers' needs and desires, pressure is created to produce quality goods and services at lower prices. Since every one is a consumer, everyone benefits from this feature of the economy. Even those who fail at commercial endeavors still enjoy a more favorable condition as consumers because of the lower prices that competition produces. If the buyer does beware and the seller knows this, there will be that much more reason for the seller to deal honestly and respectfully with the buyer. Where corruption and dishonesty exist in commerce, the cause is not competition but human failing. Competition exists in sports, in music, in scientific research, in the courtroom, in the classroom. In each of these, at their best, there is honor, honesty, dignity, courage, and integrity. So, too, in the marketplace.

Industrialism

Technology, with its commercial child, industry, has its downside: pollution and dangers to health and safety on a global scale. Industry has been blamed for threatening ecological failure through global warming, for polluting the atmosphere and the oceans, for introducing synthetic carcinogens, and for holding mankind hostage to the fear of nuclear holocaust.

Without denying the gravity of these danger (though there is still debate about their nature and extent), one may yet suggest that technology is adequate to the solution of these problems. There have been significant advances in pollution abatement, in energy and conservation, and in research on alternative energy sources and waste management. The benefits of technology and industry are evident in literally every aspect of contemporary life in modern societies. We need only compare the standard of living of people in developed nations with those of the Third World to see that this claim is beyond dispute. There is little need to elaborate on this point. As to the deplorable working conditions of the early industrial era there is also little dispute, though a few important observations should be made.

It is a matter of historical fact and a feature of any developmental or evolutionary process that the early stages, in comparison to the more developed stages, lack the sophistication and refinement that the lessons of time and trial and error eventually produce. Consider, for example, the first automobiles or airplanes or televisions or computers. Imagine what the early wheel must have been like. The industrial era came upon the world almost suddenly, after centuries of virtual stagnation. Neither the means nor the knowledge of health and safety available today existed then. There existed no fire extinguishers or alarm systems; little knowledge of the effects of chemicals on human biology; crude lighting, heating, and ventilating systems; and nothing in the way of scientific, organized response to industrial emergencies and disasters. There were no standards of health and safety specific to industrial conditions, nor could there be, because those conditions were unprecedented. To put this in perspective, consider that at the time doctors performed operations without so much as washing, let alone sterilizing, their hands and equipment; neither did they use anesthetics. They were not brutal or careless or insensitive; they were simply, and innocently ignorant. Similarly, much of the horror—the accidents, deaths, and disasters—of the early industrial period were due to ignorance and lack of remedies rather than solely to the irresponsibility of insensitive and greedy industrialists, as the popular myth would have it.

This is not to say that there were no callous factory owners or harsh managers or greedy, uncharitable Scrooges: the point is that callousness, insensitivity, and greed are features of individual persons, not of professions or trades or careers. It is not inherent in industrialism that workers are mistreated. Mistreatment of human beings has existed throughout recorded history and can be found, in varying degrees, in every form of political and social institution, in every way of life. The case of child labor is particularly interesting here in that the existence of child labor is not peculiar to the industrial era. Child labor has been a fact of human communities for as far back as recorded history:

> Peoples are perhaps too apt to write of the industrial revolution as though it led to the enslavement and overworking of poor children who had hither been happy and free. But this misinterprets history. From the very beginnings of civilization the little children of the poor had always been obliged to do whatever work they could do. But the factory system gathered up all this infantile toil and made it systematic, conspicuous, and scandalous.[5]

Given the labor-intensive nature of preindustrial economies, children were an important element of production. One reason that underdeveloped nations have such high population rates is that children are needed to help in the fields. Once farming technology is introduced and the standard of living rises, the birthrate begins to fall.[6] There seems to be evidence, then, that industry and technology reduce the need for human labor and thus ease the pressure for child labor. During the early industrial era, the age-old practice of child labor persisted, but the children were subjected to the new hazards and dangerous conditions of what in retrospect can only be seen as crude means of production. Add to this the fact that social conscience was evolving, largely, no doubt, because of greater general education and communication through newspapers, parts of the benefits of technology. A dramatic irony in connection with this is that one of the great leaders of social reform, particularly in regard to improving conditions for factory workers, was the industrialist Robert Owen (1771–1858), who made a fortune in the cotton-spinning industry. Owen took it upon himself to improve the working conditions of his employees and to establish improved employer-employee relationships. During the first two decades of the nineteenth century, Owen made substantial progress in this direction, providing unemployment pay, training and education, and safer working conditions for his employees. Owen publicly campaigned for social reform and vigorously supported the famous Factory Acts of the early nineteenth century. It simply cannot be plausibly argued that industrialism is the enemy of the working class. Much of the reform and improved working conditions came from within industry itself, as a result of evolving social conscience and the realization that worker productivity is profoundly affected by working conditions. It is hardly in the best interest of an employer to abuse his workers; those who do are shortsighted and unenlightened. Although Scrooges exist in all walks of life, so do generous people. We need to remember that, in the end, Ebenezer does see the light, being transformed into a pleasant, warm, and generous man, yet he continues to be an employer. Stinginess and hatefulness are states of character; they are not occupational prerequisites.

Consumerism

The positive side of consumerism is the message that individuals must take some responsibility for their economic lives and have a good measure of control and power with the intelligent spending of money. By making their concerns, desires, needs, and fears known through individual initiative (letter writing, phone calls, product boycotting) and through consumer advocacy groups, people are able to exercise significant moral and economic pressures on commerce and industry. The negative side of consumerism is the assumption that business and consumers are in an adversarial relationship and that, if the buyer does not beware, he or she will likely be shortchanged in one way or another. The idea here is that anyone motivated by profits is morally suspect. This of course goes back to the medieval distrust of money and of those who deal in money. A moment's reflection will show that the entrepreneur is in general no more interested in making money than the consumer is in saving money. It is sheer prejudice to assume that the entrepreneur is predisposed to lie and cheat, to deal dishonestly with his customers. Even though consumers are motivated to save money, this does not predispose them to steal from the store. In the vast majority of cases, consumer and store-owner enage in mutually satisfactory transactions. The consumer may be aware that she could find the same pair of shoes, say, for two dollars less at another store, but the other store is in a congested part of the city and its service is much poorer. In purchasing the shoes where she does, she is making a statement about what she values and prefers. Similarly, the store owner could ask a higher price for his shoes but is unwilling to run the risk of making no sales or of acquiring the reputation of being overpriced.

Part of the negative view of consumerism involves the notion that commerce and industry are so interested in profits that they pay insufficient regard to safety and quality, sometimes risking the health and safety of consumers in order to save on production costs. Without doubt, Ralph Nader's "safe" automobile could be produced, but few people could afford it. In general, a Pinto is less safe, less comfortable, and less reliable than a Volvo; for these reasons it is comparably cheaper to produce and market. The question is not whether a product, for example, an automobile, could be made safer, for it certainly can in a variety of ways. The question is whether it meets acceptable standards of safety as determined by safety engineers. These standards are based partly on the existing conditions, on consumer needs, demands, and abilities, and on the availability and cost of required materials and labor. To claim that automobiles ought to be made as safe as possible regardless of cost is to ignore reality altogether. In the celebrated case of the Ford Pinto, safety standards were in fact met. Paul H. Weaver, in a book exposing the failure of corporate America to defend itself against unjust attacks, describes the frustration of being a public affairs staffer for Ford during the Pinto controversy. He makes the following observations:

The charge that the Pinto was particularly susceptible to fuel-tank rupture or fire in rear-end collisions was a bum rap. The design of the car's fuel system was essentially the same as that of other cars of its size and generation. Unsurprisingly, early model Pintos had about the same rate of injury and death from fire due to rear-end collisions as other cars of their generation and size, according to data from the government's Fatal Accident Reporting System (FARS). In short, there was nothing unusual about the Pinto and no good reason for believing that Ford was significantly negligent in designing the car.[7]

Nonetheless, the Ford Motor Company submitted to a public whipping in the press without defending itself, evidently fearful that doing so would work against its already tarnished reputation. Those at Ford in charge of public relations decided to say nothing, suffer the consequences, and hope that the trouble would soon pass.

But we didn't tell the truth about the Pinto. We did issue a bland denial of the charge that the fuel system was unsafe, but essentially we said nothing.

We did not explain the point about the Pinto's design. We did not tell people about the FARS data. We did not explain how the public's impression that Pinto was unsafe was created by aggressive lawyers and adversary journalists making tendentious use of internal documents and testimony by ex-Ford safety engineers who had developed a new, safer fuel-tank design.

Above all, we did not act on the basis of the truth. We did not fight to vindicate ourselves, we did not go hither and yon making speeches and running issue ads explaining why we were taking a bum rap, we did not act like an innocent person who is wrongly accused.

To the contrary, we acted the part of a person who has done something wrong but can't bring himself to admit it. Under pressure from private lawsuits and government regulators, we recalled the car to rebuild a fuel system that was no different from those in millions of Ford cars we weren't recalling. We settled many lawsuits out of court on condition that the plaintiff not disclose anything about the settlement. In short, we acted guilty.[8]

The consequence, of course, was the dramatic and devastating plummet in sales of the Pinto, Ford's best-selling car. Worse, the reputation of the Ford Motor Company reached an all-time low. This case illustrates the negative effects of the adversarial nature of consumerism and the extent to which business contributes to its own flogging by refusing to fight back even when it has truth on its side. It is sometimes the case that corporations are victims of public ignorance and prejudice.

Marxism

It is impossible to discuss Marxism adequately in brief, much less to argue against Marx's philosophical views in a short essay. What needs to be said here in regard to Marx's ideal of total equality and his attack on capitalism is that political freedom without economic freedom is impossible and that economic freedom and inequality are inevitable, given the differences in human abilities, needs, and desires. Marx no doubt was aware of these facts and so argued that capitalism (which requires political and economic freedom) falls short of the ideal of total equality. In other words, given the ideal of total equality, capitalism with its prerequisite of freedom and its consequence of economic inequality is flawed. But as the ideal of total equality requires severe limitations on individual freedom, one wonders why it is held as an ideal, especially when it can be argued that the capitalist system produces a society where the worst-off have a better standard of living than members of societies with controlled economies and egalitarian ideals.

Furthermore, it can be argued that where it makes sense to argue for human equality, namely, political equality or equality under the law, equality and capitalism are quite compatible. Democratic-capitalist societies such as the United States operate with the ideal of political equality, an ideal that guarantees greater freedom and autonomy to the individual than does the Marxist ideal of total equality, which must be engineered, regulated, and imposed. Where political equality exists and where social and economic inequalities are the result of choices that individuals have made in the absence of fraud and coercion, commerce can hardly be blamed for the inequalities. Nor are the inequalities inherently bad: That others make more money than I do does not diminish my personhood, though it may, depending upon my psychoemotive condition, threaten my sense of self-esteem. The latter is a purely individual matter, revealing more about the frailties and complexity of human psychology than the failings of economic freedom.

Everywhere one looks there are human inequalities. The question is whether those inequalities are unjust or inherently harmful. Generally speaking, in a marketplace free of fraud and coercion, the inequalities that arise as a result of market forces depend upon the talents and choices of individuals. If I decide not to buy an item because I believe I can get a better deal later or elsewhere, and it turns out that I am wrong in this and suffer as a result, my suffering cannot be called unjust; no one has done me wrong or deprived me of any rights. Additionally, though I am near the bottom of the socioeconomic ladder and not enjoying the benefits of greater wealth, so long as the system gives me the opportunity to provide for my basic needs and to advance economically by means of intelligence, diligence, and perseverance, the harm of the inequality will clearly depend upon individual psychological and emotional factors, not upon something inherent in the inequality itself.

Over a period of time, given adequate resources and political freedom, even those at the bottom of the social ladder may enjoy a relatively comfortable life. Such is the vision of the democratic-capitalist, who believes that everyone benefits from the unregulated free exchange of goods and services. The relationship between participants in the marketplace, between employer and employee, seller and buyer, lender and borrower, is voluntary, mutually advantageous, and generally open to negotiation and to contractual arrangements. There is room for abuse; there is the possibility of fraud and coercion; there are an indefinite number of ways that things can go wrong in the marketplace, as in life. This would be true of any imaginable economic system. It seems safe to say that, generally speaking, human beings fare much better in a climate of freedom and autonomy than under conditions of regulation and external control.

The view that businesses lie and cheat in order to make profit and that businesses operate as though consumers were objects to be manipulated cannot be held seriously by any reflective thinker. Admittedly, some businesses operate unethically, as do some teachers, doctors, lawyers, carpenters, clerks, psychologists, gardeners, bakers, and mechanics. The point is that business in general does not operate outside of the customary moral and legal bonds of the human community, because if cannot: discovery of the fact that a business is irresponsible or unreliable or otherwise untoward will incline consumers to its competitors. It is generally in the best interest of business, as it is of individual persons, to behave honestly, reliably, and in good faith. As Weaver says of the Ford Motor Company in response to its refusal to tell the truth about its innocence regarding the Pinto,

We should simply have told the truth about the car. We had nothing of substance to be ashamed of—and in product safety issues, manufacturers should always level with customers, no matter what. Failure to do so is a guarantee of disaster, and acting with a punctilious regard for customers' safety is the honorable and effective thing to do, as Johnson & Johnson later showed with its Tylenol product. The minute it appeared that someone was poisoning Tylenol capsules, J&J immediately removed the product from the market. That action made it possible for the company not merely to reintroduce Tylenol but to regain its original industry-leading market share once poisoning concerns were resolved.[9]

Given that honesty is both honorable and effective in human activities, it is reasonable to assume that business owners realize this and act accordingly. To assume otherwise is to maintain that business owners do not act in their own best interest and do not act intelligently, neither of which are plausible assumptions.

Business as Noble

If we approach the morality of commerce from the viewpoint of any of the major moral normative schools—utilitarianism, Kantian duty theory, divine command, Hobbesian egoism, or intuitionism—we discover nothing unique or distinctive about commerce. That is, from each of these points of view, agents and persons of all activities ought to behave in ways established by the general rules given in that theory. Thus, from a utilitarian point of view, what anyone ought to do and what any activity ought to promote is the general happiness; from the divine command perspective, one ought to obey God's commands; according to Kant, one ought to act in ways that are universalizable; according to Hobbesian egoism, one ought to satisfy individual desires; according to intuitionism, one ought to do what one's unclouded moral sense dictates. The task with each of these schools, at the level of applied ethics, is to show how the normative principles operate in real life situations. In every case, the person, situation, or activity is related to the principle, becoming, so to speak, an instance of the principle. And so debate is endless about what one ought to do, because debate is endless about which normative school is best.

It may be more fruitful to try another approach, from a classical Aristotelian perspective, which focuses on the goals that people strive for and that make sense of the actions they engage in. Aristotle does not offer a set of rules or a theory of morality. Rather, he offers what he takes to be a simple description of human behavior and attempts to make sense of what humans do in terms of the goals and purposes inherent in their activities. Aristotle observed that the goals of an activity establish the standards of evaluation proper for that activity. He further observed that human beings are unique in that we have the capacity to act intelligently in pursuit of our goals and that intelligent action is required to realize our highest goal, wellness of being or happiness. Put another way, we are being our best (our "being" is best) when we act rationally.

In classical Greek, the word *arete* means both "excellent" and "virtuous." For Aristotle, virtuous action, human excellence, defined the moral dimension. Because human excellence and the realization of our highest nature require reason, morality becomes a rational activity, a matter of making intelligent choices consistent with our highest goal. No matter what activity we are engaged in, we have the choice of acting intelligently or recklessly, thoughtfully or carelessly; and what counts as intelligent or rational behavior is defined by the goals of the activity. For Aristotle, then, morality is at once a very commonsensical and rational affair: commonsensical in that virtually anyone can discover the goals inherent in various activities and rational in that the choices one makes can be determined by or evaluated in terms of the standards and principles presupposed by those goals.

The question "What is a (morally) good businessperson?" is not significantly different from "What is a (morally) good parent or teacher or lawyer or mechanic?" Morality has to do with how people ought to live their lives; it is concerned with what is right and wrong in human conduct and with what is good for human beings as persons and what is bad for them as persons. Thus, morality applies to each and every person. To know what kinds of creatures human beings are, to know what persons are, is the first step in understanding what is good and bad for us. It is no coincidence that a mechanic understands how an automobile works, or that a doctor knows about human physiology, or that a gardener understands what soil conditions are suitable for which plants. Knowing what is appropriate for anything requires understanding that thing, knowing its nature.

Similarly, knowing what is proper in human conduct, knowing what is right and wrong, requires knowing what kinds of things persons are. The question "What is a person?" is a matter of considerable discussion and debate among philosophers. For the purposes of this essay, it is sufficient to observe that persons are the kinds of entities who must exercise choice even in order to survive, let alone flourish. Choice presupposes alternatives, survival presupposes that some alternatives are better than others; flourishing presupposes that some alternatives are optimal for human beings. Choice that favors survival and flourishing is intelligent choice, and intelligent choice requires the use of reason. Thus, human beings are the kinds of creatures whose nature consists in the capacity to make intelligent choices, to exercise reason in order to live life, and to exercise reason in order to realize the ideal of living life well. Given that it is our nature to use reason to make intelligent choices, it follows that living life well consists in living intelligently. Put another way, to refuse to live intelligently is to act in a way counter to our very nature. We seem to be the only creatures capable of violating their own nature. To repeat, we have the capacity to act intelligently; although living life well requires that we use this ability, we do not do so necessarily or automatically; we must choose to do so. Morality, then, is a matter of choosing to live rationally. This of course is a very general characterization. What counts as living rationally, what principles of conduct apply when and where, are questions that make up the body of study known as moral philosophy or ethics.

Making intelligent choices requires that there be principles we can appeal to and standards that we can apply; otherwise our choices would be random and fanciful. Put another way, we justify and explain our actions and choices by appealing to relevant principles. In turn, principles arise from or are grounded in the goals that persons pursue. For example, given the very general goal of living intelligently and rationally, the principle arises that one ought to favor truth over falsehood. This principle suggests yet other principles, and so on. What does all this have to do with business and morality?

Every human activity (medicine, law, parenting, science, or art) arises because of, and is definable in terms of, certain goals peculiar to that activity. Medicine, for example, has the goal of health; law, of justice; parenting, of independence; and so on for all of the human activities. Provided that the goals are consistent with the general requirements of morality, the specific rules governing the morality of an activity and the standards of evaluating behavior within that activity are determined by the goals of the activity. For example, given the physician's goal of health and our knowledge of what promotes health, a physician can be evaluated as a physician in terms of how well or poorly he realizes that goal. The same holds for the lawyer and the goal of justice, for the teacher and the goal of student growth, for the mechanic and the goal of maintaining an efficiently operating machine.

The question, "What is a (morally) good businessperson?" raises the question, "What are the goals of commerce and business?" The nature or purpose or function of business is to provide the public with goods and services in exchange for a return greater than the cost of providing the goods or service. The goods and services can be anything from food to pet rocks, or from entertainment to open-heart surgery. If the goods and services are offered on a nonprofit basis, either as a charitable offering or as state-provided welfare, then the activity does not count as a commercial venture, as a business. Of course, one can operate a business without making a profit, but this is either an exception or a failing enterprise. One can, for instance, have a "business" as a hobby, using money from other sources to sustain it, or one can have a business that is not profitable but continue to support it with other sources of revenue in the hope that it will eventually become profitable.

If the function or goal of business is to provide goods or services for a profit, people must be willing to pay for the goods or services, or the business will go bankrupt. It follows from this that the business must pay at least some attention to what people want or need and to what people are willing to pay for what they want and need. Very generally, commerce concerns itself with the wants and needs of people, with what people perceive as necessary or desirable in life. Of course, not every perceived want or need is an actual or a healthy or a desirable want or need, nor does business aim to satisfy all human wants and needs. Business does provide for the satisfaction of an indefinite number and variety of human wants and needs. Furthermore, it provides good and services that individuals could not possibly provide for themselves. Thus, commerce is directly and centrally involved in the human pursuit of happiness, arguably the highest of human goals. Looked at this way, commerce has a truly noble function in assisting people to realize what they perceive to be the good life. The fact that a business earns a profit for doing this is no less noble than the fact that a doctor or attorney or psychologist or teacher or mechanic or laborer earns money for her skill and labor. Indeed, given that consumers have options in a free and competitive market, the more profitable a business, the likelier it is that the business is indeed satisfying the wants and needs of people.

The goal of commerce, then, to provide goods and services at a profit establishes a standard of evaluation: If the goods and services offered are not perceived by buyers to be desirable (either in quality or in price), then, unless changes are made in quality or price, the goods and services will not sell, there will be no profit, and the business will fail. There is almost always market pressure to provide high-quality affordable goods. So long as businesses have to respond to consumer demands and are free to respond to those demands, consumers have a decisive voice in determining quality and price. A business owner may ask twice the price for the same quality goods as his competitor or may ask less than cost. Obviously if she does either over a long enough time, the business will fail.

Consider what is required, in general, to operate a successful (in Aristotle's terms, an excellent or virtuous) business. In the absence of fraud or coercion, a successful business, in comparison with its less successful or failed competitors, has satisfied its customers in terms of quality, price, and service. The business has stood behind its product or service to the general satisfaction of its customers. It has honored its word, kept its promises, and been punctual, efficient, respectful, knowledgeable, patient, resourceful, honest, and reliable. Insofar as the entrepreneur has taken risks—and in some cases the risks are considerable—she has acted courageously. The net result in noneconomic terms is what is known as the "reputation" of the business, on a logical par with the reputation or character of a person. Businesses, just like persons, "earn," protect, and sometimes lose their reputations. They do so exactly as individual persons do, by acting consistently with the common moral ideals recognized by peoples everywhere. In short, business, no less than medicine, teaching, or law, is a noble and honorable profession, worthy of admiration and esteem. That some entrepreneurs are a disgrace to their profession should be taken for the exception that it is, rather than unjustly generalized into a prejudice against an entire group of individuals whose work greatly benefits all members of society.

NOTES

1. Stephen Satris, *Taking Sides: Clashing Views on Controversial Moral Issues,* 2nd ed. (Guilford, Conn.: The Dushkin Publishing Group, Inc., 1990), p. 281.

2. G. G. Coulton, *Medieval Panorama* (Cleveland, Ohio: The World Publishing Co., 1962), p. 235.

3. Rod W. Horton and Vincent Hopper, *Backgrounds of European Literature* (New York: Appleton-Century-Crofts, Inc., 1954), pp. 356–60.

4. Coulton, *Medieval Panorama,* pp. 50–52.

5. H. G. Wells, *The Outline of History* (New York: Doubleday & Co., 1961), p. 771.

6. For a brief discussion of this theory, see Peter Singer's essay on world hunger in *Taking Sides: Clashing Views on Controversial Moral Issues,* 2nd ed. (Guilford, Conn.: The Dushkin Publishing Group, Inc., 1990), pp. 332–33.

7. Paul H. Weaver, "Mugged by Reality" in *Reason,* March 1988, p. 24.

8. Ibid.

9. Ibid.

5

Ayn Rand's Objectivist Ethics as the Foundation of Business Ethics

JERRY KIRKPATRICK

The purpose of this chapter is to present the essence of Ayn Rand's theory of rational egoism and to indicate how it is the only ethical theory that can provide a foundation for ethics in business. Justice, however, cannot be done to the breadth and depth of Rand's theory in so short a space as this chapter; consequently, I have provided the reader with a large number of references for further study. At a minimum, Ayn Rand's theory, because of its originality and challenge to establishment theories, should be included in all business ethics courses and discussions of business ethics.

TWO ERRORS IN DISCUSSIONS OF BUSINESS ETHICS

Two errors are commonly committed in today's courses on, and discussions of, business ethics. One error is the failure to include ethical theory at all. This occurs in the typical case course in which an ethical problem is somehow identified, analyzed, and solved by a consensus of the discussants; this, in fact, although seldom acknowledged in practice, is an expression of the pragmatist theory of ethics, which holds that there are no universally valid ethical principles, only situational guidelines that may change as a new situation arises. (For a critique of the business case method of teaching, as an expression of pragmatist relativism, see Kirkpatrick 1987.)

The other error committed is the discussion of ethical issues in the context of only one ethical theory, while ignoring other viewpoints as if they do not exist. Discussions of a business's social responsibility is the most common form of this error. Social responsibility, however, is rooted in the ethical theory of altruism, the doctrine that one should always value others above oneself; this is, of course, the Judeo-Christian ethics of self-denial and self-sacrifice. Various forms of it are popular today, ranging from the strict duty-oriented ethics of Immanuel Kant to the egalitarianism of John Rawls to the traditional defense of capitalism based on Jeremy Bentham's "greatest happiness" principle known as utilitarianism. (For a discussion of how these three ethical theories, along with Rand's, can be used to form the core of business ethics courses and discussions, see Kirkpatrick 1989.)

The doctrine of social responsibility, however, has been criticized. In his famous essay, Milton Friedman (1970) took the social responsibility dilemma—how can a selfishly motivated, profit-seeking business be socially responsible?—by its horns and argued that the "social responsibility" of business is to make as large a profit as possible. And Theodore Levitt (1958) charged that the doctrine could lead to nothing less than fascism or "a new feudalism!" A spirit of openness and a willingness to consider all viewpoints, I think, should call for the inclusion of Ayn Rand's theory of egoism. Her theory cuts off at its roots the often-heard cynical remark about ethics in business: "Business ethics—isn't that a contradiction in terms?" Ayn Rand's answer to that question, in substance if not also in style, might be: "It damned well is not!"

THE LEGITIMACY OF AYN RAND AS A PHILOSOPHER

Ayn Rand is the author of such best-selling novels as *The Fountainhead* and *Atlas Shrugged*; it was in these novels that she first presented her theory of egoism. Throughout the 1960s and 1970s, she wrote many non-fiction articles elucidating her philosophy, which she named "objectivism." Her most important work on ethics is *The Virtue of Selfishness*.

To be sure, Ayn Rand's ideas today are controversial, and the philosophy profession has been slow to recognize their value. Nevertheless, this situation is changing. For example, a scholarly organization called The Ayn Rand Society now exists within, and has been granted full recognition by, the American Philosophical Association. Her ideas are starting to appear in introductory philosophy textbooks (see Roth and Sontag [1988, pp. 314–22]). "Man's Rights," one of her essays in *The Virtue of Selfishness* (Rand 1964d), has been used in a moral reasoning core course in the Harvard undergraduate school. And the California-based Ayn Rand Institute, the nonprofit educational "Center for the Advancement of Objectivism," has been promoting Rand's ideas among students and professionals since 1985.

The primary reason, however, that Ayn Rand should be taken seriously as a philosopher is the breadth and depth of her system; her philosophy is a fully integrated system with answers, like those of all great philosophers, to all of the traditional questions of philosophy, from metaphysics right through to esthetics. (Her prose, however, unlike that of most great philosophers, is eminently readable.) In ethics, Rand does not begin, as many moral philosophers in the past have begun, by asking what values man should pursue. She asks: "Why does man need values at all?" The result is an objective proof of the necessity of ethics. The essentials of her highly original theory are (1) that man's life is the standard of moral value and (2) that each individual has the moral right to his own life and therefore to his liberty and property. This last provides the moral foundation, on egoistic grounds, for capitalism and profit-seeking business activity; specifically, it is a defense of laissez-faire capitalism as the only moral social system because it allows each man to selfishly seek his own happiness, neither sacrificing himself to others, nor others to himself.

THE OBJECTIVIST ETHICS

The traditional goal of a valid scientific ethics is the establishment of objective, universal value judgments, that is, normative or evaluative propositions that are true and apply to all human beings. These evaluative statements are validated by reference to a standard that serves as the supreme good or supreme value. All lesser judgments are seen as contributing to or deriving from the supreme good. Negative value judgments, or judgments of badness or immorality, clash with or contradict the supreme good. Consequently, ethical behavior is that behavior which is consistent with the standard of value; unethical behavior works against it. Ethical theorists disagree over what the supreme good is. Kant argues that it is duty; Bentham says it is pleasure; Rawls thinks it is social justice— "justice as fairness." For Ayn Rand, the standard of moral value is man's life.

Life, the Source of Values

As mentioned above, however, Rand does not begin by asking, "What particular code of values should man accept?" She asks, "Does man need values at all—and why?" (Rand 1964a, p. 13). That is, what in reality gives rise to the idea of value or ethics? She begins by observing that a value is "that which one acts to gain and/or keep" (p. 15) and that the concept is not an irreducible primary; it presupposes two conditions: (1) a valuer, or beneficiary of the action, which means an entity capable of acting to achieve a goal, and (2) action in the face of an alternative, which means that the kind of action taken to achieve a goal makes a difference to the entity that is acting, that is, the action can result in success or failure.

Living organisms, Rand observes, are the only entities that meet these two conditions. Life, as a process of self-generated, self-sustaining action, is conditional; and living organisms face only one fundamental alternative: existence or nonexistence, life or death. Inanimate matter such as rocks, tables, and mountains does not face this alternative; it may change its forms but it never goes out of existence. Living organisms, on the other hand, must take specific actions if they are to remain alive, or they will die. Consequently, life—as Ayn Rand was the first to identify—is the source in reality of values. "It is only the concept of 'Life' that makes the concept of 'Value' possible. It is only to a living entity that things can be good or evil" (1964a, pp. 15–16). Ayn Rand was the first to provide an objective defense of values, based on what to some may seem to be an obvious fact.

Life, the Standard of Value

Thus, whatever is required for the maintenance of a specific organism's life is a value for that organism and, therefore, is good for it; whatever threatens or destroys it is bad or evil. In other words, the nature of what a specific organism *is*—the organism's life—determines what the organism *ought* to pursue, that is, what is of value to it. Values, consequently, are *objective*—they are a special kind of fact (Rand's ethics, consequently, is known in philosophy as a theory of ethical naturalism).

Life, Rand concludes, is not just the source in reality of values but also the standard of value—the supreme good, ultimate value, or end in itself—for all living organisms. Plants, she observes, require food from the soil and sunlight in order to survive. Animals require locomotion to obtain the values they need for their survival; the higher animals that possess consciousness must use their perceptual faculties in order to guide their actions; and man, the highest animal of them all, possesses a *con*ceptual faculty, reason, and consequently must use his reason if he is to survive. Thus, "A plant can obtain its food from the soil in which it grows. An animal has to hunt for it. Man has to produce it" (1964a, p. 18).

The Objective Necessity of Ethics. The fundamental difference in this context between man and the lower animals is that man has no automatic, preprogrammed code of values. Animals, in effect, have "wired-in" a means of automatic knowledge of what is good or bad for them. "An animal has no power to extend its knowledge or to evade it. In situations for which its knowledge is inadequate, it perishes . . . " (1964a, p. 19). Man, however, must discover what is good for him and what is evil. The vegetative functions in man work automatically, as they do in plants and the lower animals. Man's senses automatically provide him with perceptual awareness of reality, but they will not tell him which of two species of mushroom is food and which is poison, or whether honesty is a virtue. This, man must discover through a process of reason or conceptualization. And he must initiate this process by choice.

"Man, the highest living species on this earth—the being whose consciousness has a limitless capacity for gaining knowledge—man is the only living entity born without any guarantee of *remaining* conscious at all. Man's particular distinction from all other living species is the fact that his consciousness is *volitional*" (1964a, pp. 19–20). The objectivist theory of free will holds that man is free at any given waking moment to focus his mind on reality, by initiating a process of thought, or to evade reality, or to allow his mind to wander aimlessly and become susceptible to chance influences. A "volitional consciousness," in other words, is one that must choose to be conscious; man must choose to exercise his distinctive mental capacity, reason, in order to sustain his life.

Man, consequently, by failing to acquire the knowledge required for his life, can act as his own destroyer; animals cannot. Man can improve his life, by choosing to learn how to rearrange the elements of his environment for his own benefit, or he can destroy his life, by attempting to live at the perceptual level of animals. Animals, Rand points out, are often at the mercy of their environments, where, for example, they die when their automatic knowledge is insufficient to cope with such hazards as fires and floods. But the knowledge, the values, required for man's survival must be volitionally discovered and defined by man. This, Rand says, is why man needs a code of values to guide his choices and actions. This is why man needs ethics.

Man's Life the Standard of Moral Value. Man's life is the standard of moral value in the objectivist ethics.

Since reason is man's basic means of survival, that which is proper to the life of a rational being is the good; that which negates, opposes or destroys it is the evil.

Since everything man needs has to be discovered by his own mind and produced by his own effort, the two essentials of the method of survival proper to a rational being are: thinking and productive work. (1964a, p. 23)

Human parasites of either the moocher or the looter type can survive only by sucking the lifeblood out of those men who choose to think and produce. Such moochers and looters are the ones who attempt to live at the perceptual level of animals, living on the range of the moment, spending their time stalking prey. "Man has to be man by choice—and it is the task of ethics to teach him how to live like man" (1964a, p. 25).

Man's life is the standard of moral value, but each individual's life is his own moral purpose. The standard provides the abstract principle that guides the individual to select concrete values necessary for his own happiness. The three cardinal values of the objectivist ethics are reason, purpose, and self-esteem; the corresponding virtues are rationality, productiveness, and pride.

Rationality is the source of all other virtues; it is "the recognition and acceptance of reason as one's only source of knowledge, one's only judge of values and one's only guide to action" (1964a, p. 25). Man's major vice, consequently, is the abandonment of reason, whether through lethargy or willfull evasion. Productiveness is the virtue of applying reason to the acquisition of material values; material values are the means by which man's physical survival is maintained and enhanced, but their creation must be guided by reason. Productiveness—with wealth-creation—is the virtue that business people today exhibit superlatively and are least appreciated for (see Rand 1983). Pride is the moral ambitiousness to "acquire the values of character that make [man's] life worth sustaining" (1964a, p. 27); it is the virtue of holding oneself as one's own highest value.

Egoism. Because life is an end in itself and reason is an attribute of the individual, so also is every individual's life an end in itself, not a means to the ends of others. Rand emphatically rejects any form of altruism or code of self-sacrifice—sacrifice meaning the act of giving up a higher value for the sake of a lower value or a nonvalue. Each individual, as the beneficiary of his own actions, has the moral right to live for his own sake and his own happiness. (Rand's theory of rational egoism, which emphasizes the consequences or goals of action, is known in philosophy as a theory of teleological egoism.) Rational egoism calls for the end of human sacrifices because no one has the right to sacrifice anyone to anyone, neither oneself to others *nor others to oneself.*

Individual Rights. The means by which rational men deal with one another in a social setting, according to Rand, is through the principle of trade, "the only rational ethical principle for all human relationships, personal and social, private and public, spiritual and material. It is the principle of *justice*" (1964a, p. 31). All relationships between rational men result from voluntary agreement; all values acquired from others are traded via voluntary consent.

Consequently, the basic political principle of the objectivist ethics is that no one—man, society, or government—has the right to initiate physical force against anyone else; each individual has the moral right to his own life, the moral right to be free from the coercion of others to acquire the values and property he thinks are necessary to sustain and enhance his life, provided he does not initiate physical force against others in the process of acquiring these values and property. Rights, in other words, assert as a social principle that no man may be sacrificed to others nor may others be sacrificed to oneself. Rights, according to Rand, are moral principles derived from the nature of man, not privileges granted and subject to withdrawal or regulation by God or society; the source of individual rights is man's rational nature and that, Rand points out, is why they are "inalienable" (1964d).

Rights are violated, as Rand was the first to make explicit, only by initiating physical force against others, that is by bypassing the rational judgment and consent of the person who is being coerced. "To interpose the threat of physical destruction between a man and his perception of reality, is to negate and paralyze his means of survival; to force him to act against his own judgment, is like forcing him to act against his own sight" (Rand 1961, p. 134). Individual rights are the means by which the government is subordinated to morality, the means by which political power is taken out of the hands of the politicians. This is the intent and meaning of the original American system of government. The only legitimate use of physical force by the government, which operates as an agent or "night watchman" for the citizens' self-defense, is in retaliation and only against those who have initiated physical force (Rand 1964d).

In today's context, it must be mentioned that, according to Rand, the right to life applies only to actual human beings, not to potential ones, that is not to fetuses. Rand accuses the antiabortionists of wanting to violate women's rights by turning them into breed animals. In addition, the right to life does not apply to animals, who have no power of reason or power to recognize rights. Animal rights advocates, true to their altruistic principles, would sacrifice man and all his achievements upon the altar of animals, and some even upon the altar of inanimate matter.

Capitalism. The moral purpose of government, then, is the protection of individual rights by using retaliatory force against those who initiate force. The only legitimate functions of government are the provision of a police, to protect men against internal criminals; a military, to protect men against foreign, criminal nations; and a system of law courts, to settle disputes among men according to objective law. This severely limited government defines a political and economic system of laissez-faire capitalism, a system in which business and government are completely separated, in the same way and for the same reasons that the church and government are now separated. Rights, productiveness and trade, and justice rule supreme; each person earns rewards for his successes and penalties for his failures. Capitalism, in other words, is the only moral social system possible because it is the one that acknowledges and protects the conditions of man's survival as a rational being: It recognizes individual rights by banning the initiation of physical force (Rand 1964f).

APPLICATION TO ETHICAL ISSUES IN BUSINESS

Many of the issues that fall under the rubric of business ethics today revolve around the virtue of honesty. Some of these issues are so simple as not to require serious discussion, such as whether it is moral for an employee to take home from the office a box of pencils for his own personal use, or whether a sales representative should stretch the truth by telling a client that his order is "on the truck" when in fact it is still in the warehouse, or whether the boss who does not want to talk to a particular customer should have his secretary lie for him by telling the customer that the boss is not in. Other issues are quite complex, often requiring additional discussion of political as well as economic theory in order properly to evaluate the situation. Five of these more complex issues will be discussed below: bribery, trading with morally questionable countries, environmentalism, deceptive practices, and monopolistic practices.

Suffice it to say that Ayn Rand considers honesty to be a derivative of the virtue of rationality; it means "that one must never attempt to fake reality in any manner" (1964a, p. 26). Honesty, as with all of her virtues, is not an unconditional, deontological "commandment" or duty. Honesty is conditional on the rational context of dealing with other men through voluntary cooperation. When force is initiated against an individual, however, all bets are off, or, as Rand puts it, "Force and mind are opposites; morality ends where a gun begins" (1961, p. 134). Whether it is a thief or the Internal Revenue Service who initiates the force, the individual has the moral right to lie his head off in self-defense; he has the moral right to use any retaliatory force necessary to subdue a violent attacker and to regain the values he has lost or was about to lose. (This last is not an advocacy of vigilantism. Further, Rand's statement that "morality ends where a gun begins" means only that morality cannot advise anyone when being coerced; Rand paid her income taxes because she did not want to go to jail, but not paying one's taxes would be equally moral or, rather, outside the province of morality).

The principle "morality ends where a gun begins" also applies to invasions of privacy, which often are indirect means of coercing information out of a person who has no obligation to so divulge the information. This applies to nosy mothers and other relatives ("What color is your roommate?"), nosy bosses ("Where were you at lunch today, a job interview?"), nosy customers ("Tell me honestly, now, how much will you really take for this product?"), and nosy competitors ("I hear you're about to launch a revolutionary new product; is that right?"). The victims of this snoopiness have no obligation whatsoever, according to the objectivist ethics, to divulge their position to anyone who has no right to it; and the people in these examples have no right to the information they are requesting. The biggest and most threatening snoop of them all, of course, because it can and does initiate direct physical force against business people, is the government.

Understanding this issue should make it clear that business does not "bluff ethical," nor is business a game. Supposedly, according to Carr (1968), business people "bluff" when answering the question about the rock-bottom price and consequently feign a moral stand. Further, business people supposedly lie to and deceive their competitors just as a poker player bluffs and deceives his playing partners; business, after all, asserts Carr, is just a poker game in which the rules allow some dishonesty. Carr's article has received much attention in business ethics discussions and textbooks (see Wokutch and Carson 1981, for example). This is unfortunate because his article is badly mixed, primarily because he does not distinguish the two ethical theories underlying his analysis, which are Kantian altruism and utilitarianism; and of course he fails to consider another possible theory, Ayn Rand's.

As indicated above, moral business people do not "bluff ethical" when asked inappropriate questions; they pronounce moral judgment against the invaders of privacy, or they speak if silence could be construed as consent. Business is not a game because the goal of business is to excel at producing and marketing goods and services that meet the needs and wants of consumers, not to defeat the competition; competition is a by-product of production (Rand 1971, p. 4; see also Rand 1966b; Reisman 1968; cf. Mises 1966, pp. 273–79).

Preliminaries

Applying an abstract ethical theory (or any theory, for that matter) to concrete situations is a challenging and difficult task. It requires, first, a thorough understanding of the theory; second, a thorough grasp of the facts comprising the concrete situation to be analyzed; and finally, an ability that might be called "subsumption," the mental skill of sifting through the myriad detail of the situation and deciding which set of facts is united and explained by which principle of the theory. Application is, essentially, a skill in deductive reasoning, not unlike that of Sherlock Holmes, in which new concrete facts are assigned to, or subsumed under, a known generalization. It is the skill of identifying a particular fact as being an instance of a general principle.

The simplest example of this, perhaps, would be the diagnosis and cure of a disease by a doctor. A patient comes to the doctor with a number of symptoms. The doctor's task is to identify the underlying cause of the symptoms. To identify the nature of the disease in this one patient, the doctor must call upon his previously acquired general knowledge of diseases. After reviewing the causes and symptoms of several known diseases, the doctor deduces that this particular case is an instance of, say, the measles; the doctor, in other words, applies his general knowledge about diseases to this one instance by subsuming it under the category "measles."

Dig for the Facts. The task of application, again, becomes quite challenging when attempting to apply broad principles to complex factual situations. The task today in business ethics is made even more challenging when the facts themselves are difficult to ascertain, as when, especially, certain political pressure groups have a vested interest in distorting or ignoring facts that are necessary for making sound ethical decisions. Sources of information, such as the press, that conflict with one another over just what the facts are do not help the analysis. Consequently, the first question to ask oneself, when applying ethical principles to a concrete business situation, must be: Do I have the facts? Have I dug deep enough to find all the relevant facts? Many alleged ethical dilemmas and ethical conflicts in business today can indeed melt away, if the participants have all the relevant facts.

The Legal versus the Moral. As should be apparent from Ayn Rand's theory of ethics, what is currently legal is not necessarily moral, for example, interventionist regulation of business; further, what is immoral should not necessarily be made illegal, for example, prostitution. Rand's basic political and legal principle is: Acts that initiate physical force must be banned; acts that result from the mutual consent of adults—whether moral or immoral—should be legal. Today's political and economic system, however, is not laissez-faire capitalism, it is a "mixed economy," a system that mixes freedom with controls. It mixes acts based on the mutual consent of adults with acts that initiate physical force.

Today, it is the government, in the form of laws and regulations, that initiates the physical force, under the basic political and legal principle: Acts (and products) that are intrinsically harmful must be regulated. But it will be shown below that, according to Rand's theory, this principle is false and that all laws and regulations that initiate physical force must, on *moral* grounds, be repealed.

Untangling Bribery

Many of the issues that come up in business ethics can be discussed using a pro-and-con format based on the above two contrasting principles: "acts that initiate physical force must be banned" constitutes one side of the issue, whereas "acts that are intrinsically harmful must be regulated" constitutes the opposite. Bribery, however, is one issue on which both sides agree that the act is wrong but disagree over the reasons and interpretation. The common view is that bribery is an intrinsically harmful act that must be regulated, whereas, according to Rand's ethics, bribery is an act that initiates physical force through a basic dishonesty. The trouble with current discussions of bribery is that adherence to the facts is seldom practiced by the discussants. So, what are the facts?

First, the press and others who discuss the issue seem to have a penchant for failing to distinguish the metaphorical use of the term "bribery" from the literal. Giving candy to a crying child, for example, is said to be a bribe; so also is any payment by U.S. businessmen to officials of foreign governments. The former, however, is metaphor; the latter may or may not be.

Second, no one bothers to provide the correct legal definition of the term "bribery." In law, a bribe is the covert undermining of a relationship of trust (Gifis 1984, p. 54); a payment, for example, given in secret to a purchasing agent in exchange for the agent's business is a basic dishonesty, because the salesman and agent together cheat the owner of the agent's business. Rand's theory of ethics would accept this legal definition and hold that the owner of the business could sue under civil law for damages, because physical force had been initiated against the owner by cheating him out of money or higher-quality products. (The salesman and agent also would be guilty of criminal fraud, under an objective definition of fraud.)

Third, other forms of payment made to others are seldom considered in today's discussions of bribery. For example, a perquisite is something "extra" that is expected or considered a normal part of one's job, such as a tip to a waiter or maître d'. Expensive luncheons, Christmas gifts, and company cars—if known and approved by the owner of the business—are perks, not bribes. I say "owner of the business" because if a salesman offers a payment to the owner of the business (i.e., a sole proprietor), then fundamentally the payment becomes a price concession or discount. The status of the persons being influenced and allegedly cheated is paramount in deciphering whether or not a bribe actually has occurred.

Fourth, the terms "grease payment" and "extortion" need also to be considered, especially when payments to government officials are made. This is because government intervention in the workings of a free-market economy always breeds corruption: regulation always violates the rights of some for the sake of others, which provides an incentive for those offended to go beyond the law to secure satisfaction. And unscrupulous bureaucrats are given the incentive to provide the satisfaction, for a price. This is why socialist economies are shot through with corruption and black markets; indeed, the citizens of such economies would not survive were it not for the black markets (cf. Mises 1944).

Because bureaucrats are exempt from the market discipline that is imposed on private businesses, the less scrupulous ones among them find it lucrative to demand money under the table to "lubricate" the bureaucratic machinery, that is, to get the bureaucrat to perform his normal duties. When bureaucrats are performing jobs that in a free economy would be performed by private businesses, they now, as representatives of government, wield the power of physical force over any citizen who must deal with them. (Governments, of course, and their agents, hold the legal monopoly of the use of physical force.)

Hence, if government officials, such as those of the Japanese government in the 1970s, demand payments from the Lockheed Corporation in exchange for granting a contract, de facto extortion has occurred. Extortion is a form of robbery in which something is obtained through a threat of harm or future harm. Government officials hold the gun; private businessmen do not. Lockheed, according to Rand's ethics, should feel no guilt over making those payments, no more than the victim of a mugging should feel guilt for having to give the mugger money in exchange for his life. The principle here, according to the objectivist ethics, is "morality ends where a gun begins." At the point of the Japanese gun, Lockheed, in addition to the covert payments they did make, might have chosen to refuse payment and then go into receivership, or it might have chosen to make the covert payments and then expose the corruption in the U.S. press. Any of these options would have been moral according to Rand's ethics. (The one thing in the Lockheed affair that Rand's ethics would emphatically denounce is Lockheed's attempt to defend itself on utilitarian grounds; see Kotchian 1977.)

Thus, bribery is not a simple payment of money; it is a complex concept that applies only in a carefully defined context, and facts are the crucial elements that define the context. (The above discussion of bribery, I should point out, is my own application of the objectivist ethics to the issue; Rand never discussed bribery.)

Trading with Morally Questionable Countries

Current wisdom holds that it is moral to trade with such countries as Russia and China, but immoral to trade with South Africa. Ayn Rand's ethics leads to the opposite conclusion. Rand's principle is that it is not moral to trade with a dictatorship, whether of the socialist or fascist variety, because dictatorships are outlaw nations and trading with such a country would be the equivalent of aiding and abetting a criminal. But the question of fact is, What is a dictatorship and which countries fit that definition?

A dictatorship, holds Rand, has four characteristics: "one party rule—executions without trial or with a mock trial, for political offenses—the nationalization or expropriation of private property—and censorship" (1964e, p. 105). China certainly fits this definition; Russia, *glasnost* and *perestroika* notwithstanding, still does, for the most part. South Africa does not. South Africa has, and has always had, multiparty rule; it does not execute for political offenses (Nelson Mandela was jailed, not executed, for acts of terrorism, not the advocacy of communism); it has private property and a thriving market economy, albeit hampered by considerable regulation—it is a mixed economy; and it has minimal censorship. South Africa, indeed, is the freest, most prosperous country in all of Africa.

It does have serious racial problems, and historically it has had severe codes of racial discrimination. These codes of racial discrimination, however, were supported and established in the 1920s by the socialist labor party to quell the rising black middle class that was being brought into existence by the then free-market elements of the country (Williams 1987, pp. 175–78). But, keeping to the facts, these codes are racial discrimination against the blacks and coloreds, not slavery. Every person today living in the People's Republic of China is a slave. "The man who produces while others dispose of his product, is a slave," says Rand (1964c, p. 94). Trading with a country like China, she might add, is the equivalent of trading with the commandant and guards of a concentration camp, which in fact is what China amounts to today; occasionally, a few crumbs are thrown to the inmates.

South Africa is a mixed economy, as are most of the other semifree countries of the world, including the United States. If mixed economies violate the rights of some for the sake of others, how can it be moral to trade even with these mixed economies? Rand's answer is that these mixed economies openly recognize the principle of individual rights but fail to implement it consistently in practice. Russia and China, however, have never accepted the principle of individual rights; they openly denounce it. For these reasons, according to Rand, one cannot trade with such countries and remain moral, anymore than one can remain moral by trading with a known criminal. (For more detail on the objectivist position on South Africa, see Schwartz 1986.)

Environmentalism

There is no better illustration of the principle that "acts that are intrinsically harmful must be regulated" than in the issue of environmentalism. The environmental movement is the ultimate expression and consequence of altruism, because it places intrinsic value on nature at the expense of man. Man, according to the environmentalists, is the villain who is destroying this intrinsically valued nature. Consequently, man's activities must be curtailed; man must sacrifice his comfort-producing material values for the sake of snail darters and redwood trees. Science, technology, progress, and all the other values of Western civilization, especially capitalism, say the environmentalists, have hit a dead end. Man, now, if he is to survive, must learn how to live in concert with nature.

This is not a caricature of the environmental movement. As the Vietnam War was winding down twenty years ago, the leaders of the environmental movement were stating their goals explicitly as attacks on reason, individualism, competition, science, and technology ("The Next Decade" 1969; "The Ravaged Environment" 1970). Today, the leaders are even more explicit—and irrational—valuing "wildness for its own sake" and openly hoping for a virus to come along to rid the earth of perhaps a billion men. Environmentalists, says one writer, "are not interested in the utility of a particular species or free-flowing river, or ecosystem, to mankind. They [the species, river, or ecosystem] have intrinsic value, more value—to me—than another human body, or a billion of them. . . . Until such time as Homo sapiens should decide to rejoin nature, some of us can only hope for the right virus to come along." Man, this writer asserts, is not a part of nature, but a cancer and "plague upon ourselves and upon the Earth" (Graber 1989).

Aside from the fact that man's life expectancy continues to increase year after year despite the alleged decline in the quality of life due to alleged environmental plagues; aside from the fact that the automobile has reduced pollution and disease from horse manure, urine stains and stench that would not go away, and decaying horse carcasses; and aside from the fact that the industrial revolution and capitalism in Western cultures have wiped out the precapitalistic pollutions of pestilence, often caused by open raw-sewage ditches, and famine; according to Ayn Rand, *there is no such thing as intrinsic value*. Nature does not have intrinsic value, nor does man.

Values, for Ayn Rand, are *objective*, not intrinsic (or subjective). The objective theory of value "holds that the good is neither an attribute of 'things in themselves' [the intrinsic theory] nor of man's emotional states [the subjective theory], but *an evaluation* of the facts of reality by man's consciousness according to a rational standard of value. (Rational, in this context, means: derived from the facts of reality and validated by a process of reason.) The objective theory holds that *the good is an aspect of reality in relation to man*—and that it must be discovered, not invented, by man" (1966a, p. 22, emphasis in original). The objective theory of value always keeps in mind the questions: of value to whom? and for what purpose? According to the objectivist ethics, man ought always to be the beneficiary of his own actions, not snail darters and kangaroo rats.

Objects of nature, consequently, have *no value at all* when man has no relationship to them. Iron ore, when lying buried in the ground, is worthless until man mines it and turns it into steel. Indeed, trees in parts of nine-teenth-century America were hostile obstacles to man's survival, that is, until they were removed to allow for farming. Most of nature, when left to its own devices, is hostile to man's well-being. But it is man's unique achievement, through reason, to be able to tame the hostility of nature and to adjust his environment to his own benefit. In fact, all capitalist production is an act of rearranging the elements of the environment for the benefit of man. And there are *no* shortages of natural resources, as the environmentalists so falsely proclaim, only a shortage of the political freedom that science and technology need in order to pursue the resources (Reisman 1979, pp. 15–20).

The environmentalists, Rand states, would reduce us all to the level of jungle animals that must compete with one another in a survival of the fittest contest for a fixed amount of food; man, however, especially over the last two hundred years under the influence of Western culture, has risen well above the wars of the jungle to provide us all not just with abundant food but with enormous varieties, quantities, and qualities of material values to increase our "quality of life" (Rand 1975).

It should be pointed out that the principle "acts (or products) that are intrinsically harmful must be regulated" is a prescription for dictatorship. If something is intrinsically wrong, why should not force be used to correct the wrong? This, in essence, is the justification for the regulation of business that we now have in mixed economies, but the principle can easily be seen to operate in socialist dictatorships. If we modify the principle to read "Jews who are intrinsically harmful . . . ," we can see how the Nazis justified their atrocities (cf. Peikoff 1982). And if we modify the principle to read "*ideas* that are intrinsically harmful . . . ," we can see how easily censorship can be justified.

The concept of intrinsic value must ultimately result in violence because there is no rational way to justify why some acts or objects have intrinsic value and others do not; something is valuable, it is alleged, because it is good "in, by, and of itself," not because it is good for someone or for some purpose. It takes the special "intuition" or "insight" of a saint—or Führer—to know which act or object possesses the intrinsic value. The conflict arises because saints and Führers disagree over which objects have intrinsic value. Ultimately, force is the only solution to settle the dispute. (Zealots and terrorists, of course, are all advocates of the intrinsic theory of value.) It is this whole pseudodebate over which objects have the intrinsic value that Rand's theory cuts off at its roots.

Objective values are values freely chosen by man—by individual men, each according to his own needs and context. It is capitalism and the free market, according to Rand, that makes this free choice possible. Indeed, a product's economic value under capitalism is neither subjective, as many economists today maintain, nor intrinsic; it is what Rand calls "socially objective value." For more detail on this and the whole issue of the intrinsic-subjective false alternative, see Rand (1966a, pp. 21–27).

In addition to this "intrinsic value of nature" argument, environmentalists also use the "argument from uncertainty." It runs as follows: "How do you know we won't discover in the future that some allegedly safe chemical causes cancer or pollution? We can't take the risk; it's better to be safe than sorry. So, we have regulate or ban it." Aside from the factual question of the causal connection between chemicals, cancer, and pollution, this argument asks the scientists to prove a negative, which is the logical fallacy *argumentum ad ignorantiam* (Ruby 1960, p. 141). It is impossible to prove a negative and no one, in reason, is obliged to do so. If there is no evidence even for the *possibility* of something, then we have every logical right to assume that the something does not exist. This argument has the same epistemological status as the assertion that "it is possible that gremlins exist," that is, it is utterly arbitrary and not worthy of further consideration by rational people (Peikoff 1981; see also Rand 1988a).

Other Issues in Business Ethics

The brevity with which the following issues are discussed does not mean that they are minor issues in business ethics or that they require minimal analysis. Space prevents a detailed analysis. For that matter, the analysis of the above three issues could be continued at some length. The application of broad principles to concrete situations requires a great deal of context-setting before the proper principles can be applied. Nevertheless, here is a brief analysis of two additional issues in business ethics indicating how Ayn Rand's theory of rational egoism might apply.

Deceptive Practices. Deception, of course, is dishonesty, and Rand's ethics opposes it in the pursuit of a value. Deceptive sales and advertising practices, if they are truly deceptive, would be immoral, according to the objectivist ethics. The question is, are they truly—factually—misleading and deceptive? One fact apropos of this issue is that the so-called social criticisms of advertising are laden with philosophic, economic, and psychological principles with which objectivism disagrees. For an application of the objectivist ethics to a discussion of the "social" criticisms of advertising, see Kirkpatrick (1986).

Are the statements of salesmen and advertisers any more misleading and deceptive than the headlines of newspaper articles that do not accurately describe the articles' content? Are they more misleading than the statements of many politicians, teachers, and parents? These questions are asked, not to justify misleading or deceptive statements but to keep a perspective on the much-maligned field of marketing; salesmen and advertisers do not hold a monopoly on the practice of making misleading statements. Indeed, it is the egoistic, profit-motivated nature of marketing that, according to Ayn Rand's ethics, deserves praise, not harassment and condemnation. It is the ethics of altruism and today's widespread hostility to capitalism and capitalistic activities that generate and support the many attacks made on salesmanship and advertising.

According to Rand's ethics, the only relevant political issue here concerning deceptive practices is that fraud—the indirect initiation of physical force—must be banned from human relationships. For fraud to occur—fraud, in the common-law sense of the term—several stringent conditions must be met; there must be a statement of a false material fact by the deceiver, reliance upon the truth of the statement by the victim, intent by the deceiver that the statement will be relied upon, and objective injury or damages to the victim (Gifis 1984, pp. 194–95). Mere sophistry, in other words, is not fraud. Without these stringent conditions, freedom of speech would indeed be vulnerable. Censorship, it must be pointed out, is always a government action to restrict the flow of information within society, never a private action. Falsely yelling "fire" in a crowded theater is not an expression of free speech; it is criminal assault. For more on this, see Rand (1964d; 1966d).

Big Business and Monopoly. Big business, according to Rand, does not rule America, but big government does, and nothing could be more unethical than the allegedly procompetition, antimonopoly laws called antitrust. The antitrust laws were passed because of the so-called market failures of capitalism that allowed the formation and growth of giant trusts, cartels, and monopolies. But the proper meaning of "monopoly" is "government-granted privilege" (Reisman 1979, pp. 74–76, 95–98); historically, all of the harmful effects normally associated with the term "monopoly" have been caused by government intervention into the operation of a free-market economy, that is, by a privilege granted by the government to some private businesses (Rand 1966c). That means that the government has initiated physical force against some people, violating their rights, in order to grant privileges to others.

The antitrust laws do not acknowledge these historical facts or the proper definition of monopoly. Further, they obliterate the distinction between political power, which is the power of the government's guns, and economic power, the power of a business to satisfy the needs and wants of consumers (cf. Folsom's distinction between political and market entrepreneurs, 1987), and charge big businesses de facto with political power (whether or not the businesses in question were acting under the influence of any government-granted privileges). Further, the antitrust laws themselves are so confused and contradictory and applied so arbitrarily that businesses today can (and are) charged with anything and everything; the antitrust laws, according to Ayn Rand, amount to ex post facto law that, she points out, is not supposed to exist in a free country and applies in the Unites States only to businessmen. For this reason, she calls big business "America's Persecuted Minority" (1966b; see also Rand 1988d; Greenspan 1966).

The antitrust laws apply not just to big businesses in general but also to many specific business practices such as advertising. The so-called economic criticisms of advertising charge advertising with monopoly power, which must be regulated. As with the "social" criticisms of advertising, the "economic" criticisms are laden with philosophic and economic principles with which objectivism does not agree. For a defense of advertising against the charges of monopoly power, based primarily on the writing of the "Austrian" school of economists but also on some of Rand's philosophical principles, see Kirkpatrick (1991).

CONCLUSION—"PEACE IN OUR TIME"

There are, of course, other issues in business ethics that I have not discussed, and new ones will arise in the future as fashions change. The concretes of the moment do not determine what is right and wrong; only a theory can illuminate the specific facts of any given business situation. It is ethical principles that give understanding to business people when they are confronted with the many complex situations in which ethical decisions must be made; it is ethical principles that give guidance to these same people when they must decide what to do. The premise of this chapter is that Ayn Rand's theory of rational egoism is the system of ethical principles that can provide the best understanding and guidance in business situations, because her theory is based on the facts—the nature of man and the nature of reality. The application of her principles without compromise should lead one to happiness or, at least, lead the way to happiness.

This last brings to light one final application of the objectivist ethics to business that must be mentioned. To compromise one's principles even a little, according to Ayn Rand, is to give up one's principles entirely and to accept the opposite principles. After all, she asks, who stands to gain from a compromise? "In any compromise between food and poison, it is only death that can win. In any compromise between good and evil, it is only evil that can profit. In that transfusion of blood which drains the good to feed the evil, the compromiser is the transmitting rubber tube . . . " (1961, p. 173; see also Rand 1964b; 1966e; and Peikoff 1989). The compromiser, according to Rand, thus grants to evil what it needs and desires the most, "the sanction of the victim" (Rand 1961, p. 165; 1988b; 1988c). The most vivid historical example of compromise and of the horrible consequences that follow is Neville Chamberlain's sacrifice of the principle of national sovereignty for Czechoslovakia to Hitler's principle of armed aggression.

If there is one thing that business people today have a penchant for, it is the compromise of moral principles. Or, to be more specific, business people are experts at appeasement and apology. When companies run full-page advertisements talking about the "social benefits" of their products and their "low" profits or, lately, how environmentally "green" their products are, they are trying to make peace with their enemies, as Chamberlain attempted, and they are apologizing for doing what business must do by its nature, that is make profits.

Such behavior, however, is doomed to failure, because it gives the critics the moral high ground. It makes business look like it is taking something out of the public till, which the critics, especially the Marxists, have been saying for decades. It grants the premise that business has done something wrong and ought to be apologizing for it. The critics, after all, are advocates of altruism and socialism (the former implies the latter), and appeasement and apology are the worst acts a businessperson could commit. Such compromises give the critics the admissions of "intrinsic harm" they are looking for; now, they say, that you have admitted to committing intrinsic harm, we must pass new regulations to control your harmful, selfish behavior.

But the proper response to the critics is, "Yes, we pursue egoistic profits, and large ones at that. We market products that meet the egoistic needs and wants of consumers, and we expect to be paid for the effort. We have earned our profits and are proud of every penny. We are not about to apologize for anything that free-market businesses do. We are the ones who are moral, acting in the only human way possible. If you have any rational arguments, demonstrating that our actions are harmful to man's life as a rational being, then bring them forth; otherwise, kindly take your coercive hands off our businesses." Rand's principle here is not "Judge not, lest ye be judged," but "Judge, and be prepared to be judged" (Rand 1964c).

Such a response would give business the moral high ground and the critics would be on the defensive. The only way, however, ultimately to fend off the many criticisms of business is to acquire a thorough understanding—a thorough internalization—of the theory of ethics that says it is good and moral to pursue selfishly motivated profits. The reason business people today cannot speak up to defend themselves is that they have internalized the ethical theory of altruism, which is incompatible with capitalism. Altruism paralyzes business people when they are confronted with charges of pursuing "selfish profits," which according to altruism is evil, and it drives them to a policy of appeasement (Rand 1988b).

To fight these attacks, business people must acquire the conviction that the pursuit of selfish profits is morally right. As Ayn Rand puts it:

In spite of all their irrationalities, inconsistencies, hypocrisies and evasions, the majority of men will not act, in major issues, without a sense of being *morally right* and will not oppose the morality they have accepted. They will break it, they will cheat on it, but they will not oppose it; and when they break it, they take the blame on themselves. The power of morality is the greatest of all intellectual powers—and mankind's tragedy lies in the fact that the vicious moral code men have accepted [altruism] destroys them by means of the best within them (1982, p. 81).

Business people must recognize that the attacks on business are attacks on their virtues—on their productiveness and on the pride that follows every achievement. The conviction of being "morally right" can only be acquired by a thorough understanding and application to business issues of Ayn Rand's theory of rational egoism, the objectivist ethics. Only then will "peace in our time" for business people be achieved.

BIBLIOGRAPHY

Carr, Albert. 1968. "Is Business Bluffing Ethical?" *Harvard Business Review* (January/February). Reprinted in Thomas Donaldson and Patricia H. Werhane, eds., *Ethical Issues in Business: A Philosophical Approach*, 3rd ed. Englewood Cliffs, N.J.: Prentice-Hall, Inc., 1988, pp. 69–76.

Folsom, Burton W., Jr. 1987. *Entrepreneurs vs. the State: A New Look at the Rise of Big Business in America, 1840–1920*. Reston, Va.: Young America's Foundation.

Friedman, Milton. 1970. "The Social Responsibility of Business Is to Increase Its Profits." *New York Times Magazine* (September 13). Reprinted in Thomas Donaldson and Patricia H. Werhane, eds., *Ethical Issues in Business: A Philosophical Approach*, 3rd ed. Englewood Cliffs, N.J.: Prentice-Hall, Inc., 1988, pp. 217–23.

Gifis, Steven H. 1984. *Law Dictionary*, 2nd ed. Woodbury, N.Y.: Barron's Educational Series, Inc.

Graber, David M. 1989. "Mother Nature as a Hothouse." Review of *The End of Nature*, by Bill McKibben. *Los Angeles Times Book Review* (October 22), pp. 1, 9.

Greenspan, Alan. 1966. "Antitrust." In Ayn Rand, *Capitalism: The Unknown Ideal*. New York: New American Library, Inc., pp. 63–71.

Kirkpatrick, Jerry. 1986. "A Philosophic Defense of Advertising." *Journal of Advertising* 15, 2 (June): 42–48, 64. Reprinted in Roxanne Hovland and Gary B. Wilcox, eds., *Advertising in Contemporary Society: Classic and Contemporary Readings on Advertising's Role in Society*. Lincolnwood, Ill.: NTC Business Books, 1989, pp. 508–22.

———. 1987. "Why Case Method Teaching Does Not Make Good History." In Terence Nevett and Stanley C. Hollander, eds., *Marketing in Three Eras*. East Lansing: Michigan State University, pp. 201–4.

———. 1989. "Ethical Theory in Marketing." In Doug Lincoln and Jeffrey Doutt, eds., *Marketing Education: Challenges, Opportunities and Solutions* (Proceedings of the Western Marketing Educators' Association Conference), pp. 50–53.

———. 1991. "An 'Austrian' Refutation of the Monopoly Power Arguments against Advertising." *The Mid-Atlantic Journal of Business*.

Kotchian, A. Carl. 1977. "The Payoff: Lockheed's 70-day Mission to Tokyo." *Saturday Review* (July 9). Reprinted as "Case Study—The Lockheed Aircraft Corporation," in Thomas Donaldson and Patricia H. Werhane, eds., *Ethical Issues in Business: A Philosophical Approach*, 3rd ed. Englewood Cliffs, N.J.: Prentice–Hall, Inc., 1988), pp. 11–20.

Levitt, Theodore. 1958. "The Dangers of Social Responsibility." *Harvard Business Review* (September–October), pp. 41–50.

Mises, Ludwig von. 1944. *Bureaucracy*. New Haven, Conn.: Yale University Press.

———. 1966. *Human Action: A Treatise on Economics*, 3rd rev. ed. Chicago: Henry Regnery Company.

"The Next Decade: A Search for Goals." 1969. *Time* (December 19), pp. 22–25.

Peikoff, Leonard. 1981. " 'Maybe You're Wrong.' " *The Objectivist Forum* 2, 2 (April): 8–12.

———. 1982. *The Ominous Parallels: The End of Freedom in America*. New York: New American Library.

———. 1989. "Why Should One Act on Principle?" *The Intellectual Activist* (February 27): 2–6.

Rand, Ayn. 1961. "This Is John Galt Speaking." In *For the New Intellectual: The Philosophy of Ayn Rand*. New York: New American Library, Inc., pp. 117–92.

———. 1964a. "The Objectivist Ethics." In *The Virtue of Selfishness: A New Concept of Egoism*. New York: New American Library, pp. 13–35.

———. 1964b. "Doesn't Life Require Compromise?" In *The Virtue of Selfishness: A New Concept of Egoism*. New York: New American Library, pp. 68–70.

———. (1964c). "How Does One Lead a Rational Life in an Irrational Society?" In *The Virtue of Selfishness: A New Concept of Egoism*. New York: New American Library, pp. 71–74.

————. 1964d. "Man's Rights." In *The Virtue of Selfishness: A New Concept of Egoism*. New York: New American Library, pp. 92–100.

————. 1964e. "Collectivized Rights." In *The Virtue of Selfishness: A New Concept of Egoism*. New York: New American Library, pp. 101–6.

————. 1964f. "The Nature of Government." In *The Virtue of Selfishness: A New Concept of Egoism*. New York: New American Library, pp. 107–15.

————. 1966a. "What Is Capitalism?" In *Capitalism: The Unknown Ideal*. New York: New American Library, pp. 11–34.

————. 1966b. "America's Persecuted Minority: Big Business." In *Capitalism: The Unknown Ideal*. New York: New American Library, pp. 44–62.

————. 1966c. "Notes on the History of American Free Enterprise." In *Capitalism: The Unknown Ideal*. New York: New American Library, pp. 102–9.

————. 1966d. "The Property Status of Airwaves." In *Capitalism: The Unknown Ideal*. New York: New American Library, pp. 122–29.

————. 1966e. "The Anatomy of Compromise." In *Capitalism: The Unknown Ideal*. New York: New American Library, pp. 144–49.

————. 1971. "The Moratorium on Brains." *The Ayn Rand Letter*, 1, 2 (October 25). Excerpt reprinted in Harry Binswanger, ed., *The Ayn Rand Lexicon: Objectivism from A to Z*. New York: New American Library, 1986, p. 80.

————. 1975. "The Anti-Industrial Revolution." In *The New Left: The Anti-Industrial Revolution*. 2nd rev. ed. New York: New American Library, pp. 127–51.

————. 1982. "Faith and Force: The Destroyers of the Modern World." In *Philosophy: Who Needs It?* Indianapolis, Ind.: The Bobbs-Merrill Company, Inc., pp. 71–93.

————. 1983. "The Money-Making Personality." *The Objectivist Forum* (February), pp. 1–9. Excerpt reprinted in Harry Binswanger, ed., *The Ayn Rand Lexicon: Objectivism from A to Z*. New York: New American Library, 1986, p. 307.

————. 1988a. "Who Is the Final Authority on Ethics?" In *The Voice of Reason: Essays in Objectivist Thought*. New York: New American Library, Inc., pp. 17–22.

————. 1988b. "Altruism as Appeasement." In *The Voice of Reason: Essays in Objectivist Thought*. New York: New American Library, Inc., pp. 32–39.

————. 1988c. "The Sanction of the Victims." In *The Voice of Reason: Essays in Objectivist Thought*. New York: New American Library, Inc., pp. 149–57.

————. 1988d. "Antitrust: The Rule of Unreason." In *The Voice of Reason: Essays in Objectivist Thought*. New York: New American Library, Inc., pp. 254–59.

"The Ravaged Environment." 1970. *Newsweek* (January 26), pp. 31–47.

Reisman, George. 1968. "Platonic Competition." *The Objectivist* (August and September).

————. 1979. *The Government against the Economy*. Ottawa, Ill.: Caroline House Publishers, Inc.

Roth, John K., and Frederick Sontag. 1988. *The Questions of Philosophy*. Belmont, Calif.: Wadsworth Publishing Company.

Ruby, Lionel. 1960. *Logic: An Introduction*, 2nd ed. Chicago: J. B. Lippincott Company.

Schwartz, Peter. 1986. "Untangling South Africa." *The Intellectual Activist* 4, 4 (January 20). Reprinted as "A Capitalist Solution to Apartheid" and distributed by the Ayn Rand Institute, Marina Del Rey, California, 1986.

Williams, Walter. 1987. "The War against Capitalism" and "The Solution." In *All It Takes Is Guts: A Minority View*. Washington, D.C.: Regnery Books.

Wokutch, Richard E., and Thomas L. Carson. 1981. "The Ethics and Profitability of Bluffing in Business." *Westminster Institute Review* 1, 2 (May). Revised 1986 and reprinted in Thomas Donaldson and Patricia H. Werhane, eds., *Ethical Issues in Business: A Philosophical Approach*, 3rd ed. Englewood Cliffs, N.J.: Prentice-Hall, Inc., 1988, pp. 77–83.

6

What Is the Public Interest?

ROGER KOPPL

INTRODUCTION

The Utilitarian Framework of the Analysis

The term "public interest" may seem suspicious to individualists. Surely it is the individual and not "the public" that has interests. The individualist may suspect that talk about the public interest is just a smoke screen for different attempts to get a favor from government. When someone says, for instance, "It is in the public interest to install wheelchair ramps in public buildings," he may really mean, "I like wheelchair ramps and I want other people to pay for them."

I will argue that such suspicions are not always appropriate, that there is such a thing as the public interest, and that it consists in the interests of individuals. The public interest is a matter of getting the best social institutions available. Getting the best social institutions means getting the institutions that afford the best tradeoff between maximizing the chances a randomly chosen individual has of achieving his goals and improving the quality of the goals that individual may be expected to adopt.

My argument draws heavily on the utilitarianism of Leland Yeager (1984/85; 1985). Yeager's position, as I understand it, is more or less a restatement of John Stuart Mill's utilitarianism in the light of F. A. Hayek's social theory. But labels can deceive. John N. Gray (1983) calls this position "indirect utilitarianism" and contrasts it with "rule" and "act" utilitarianism. Hayek, on the other hand, adopts the same ethical position but criticizes "utilitarianism" for its "constructivism" (1976, pp. 17–23). Whether or not Yeager's position is "really" utilitarianism, it is nothing like the crude "act-utilitarianism" often imputed to Jeremy Bentham. I will make my argument without resorting to the troubled vocabulary of utilitarianism. A few remarks on utilitarianism may be welcome anyway.

The utilitarian argument is that "actions are right in proportion as they tend to promote happiness" (Mill 1863, p. 18). This argument does not tell us what human happiness is. Utilitarianism gets bad press when critics assume that the terms *utility* or *happiness* denote some sort of crude hedonism. The utilitarian argument as such does not tell us that happiness is sensual pleasure. It does not tell us what happiness means. But different individual utilitarians have specified different meanings of happiness.

Philosophers have distinguished among utilitarians according to the specific meaning they give to the term "happiness." "Hedonistic utilitarians" identify the good with "pleasure." "Ideal utilitarians" hold that love, knowledge, friendship, and pleasure are all intrinsically good and that pleasure is not a necessary condition of goodness (see Smart 1956 and Ferm 1956, pp. 313–14). According to Smart, Mill might be called a "quasi-ideal utilitarian" (1956, p. 196) because he distinguishes higher and lower pleasures.

Plan of the Chapter

In the next section, I use Hayek's theory of society as a spontaneous order to argue against a "teleological" conception of the public interest and to argue for the idea that the public interest consists in the well-being of the randomly chosen individual. I later argue that the randomly chosen individual's welfare consists of both his chances of achieving the goals he sets for himself and the nature of the goals he chooses to pursue. Finally, I illustrate my argument with a few applications.

DEFINITION OF THE PUBLIC INTEREST

Possible Meanings of the Term *Public Interest*

The Term Public Interest *Is Ambiguous.* The word "interest" denotes one's benefit or advantage. To have an "interest" is to have a goal or end that one does or should wish to achieve. If there is such a thing as the public interest, it would seem to consist in the goals or ends of the public. But to speak of the goals or ends of the public masks an ambiguity. On the one hand, the goals of the public may consist in some social end that exists independently of the goals of any individual. On the other hand, the goals of the public may consist somehow in the goals of individuals.

The Teleological View of Society Differs from the Liberal View. The view that there is some social end that exists independently of individual interests is the teleological view of society. It is the view that society as such has a "teleology" or final end toward which things are moving. If there is some grand teleology at work in society, its fulfillment is, presumably, the highest moral aim an individual could set himself. This is the sort of position Marx argued for. History is driving us inevitably toward a proletarian revolution, the withering away of the state and the emergence of communism. Goodness and wisdom consist in helping history along.

If the teleological view is rejected, then the public interest must be composed, in some way, of individual interests. This is the individualistic or the liberal view of society. In this sense a liberal may be a nineteenth-century liberal who favors laissez faire or a modern liberal of the sort who sees the market as the cause of social injustice. In either case, the liberal's concern is not with any grand social dynamic but with the welfare of individuals. For the liberal, individuals are ends in themselves, not the means to serve the ends of others. The individualist is concerned with protecting the dignity and autonomy of the individual. For the liberal who does not reject the term public interest, the word "public" denotes the role of social institutions and public policy in the pursuit of individual ends.

I Reject the Teleological View. Society, I believe, is not governed by any grand teleology. There is no great social end "out there" whose fulfillment constitutes our collective destiny. Only individuals have interests. There are no ends, or interests of society as such. My argument on this point is borrowed from F. A. Hayek.

Society as a Spontaneous Order

Society was not planned. Society, according to F. A. Hayek (1973), is a "spontaneous order." The social institutions that allow us to cooperate with each other were not, for the most part, designed. They emerged, Hayek argues, as the unintended consequence of individual actions. To be sure, there has been plenty of planning about social institutions in Western history. One thinks, for instance, of the U.S. Constitution as a particularly dramatic example of a well-planned social institution. Nevertheless, according to Hayek, the overall social order is far too complex to have been the issue of any planning committee or solitary genius.

Hayek's Argument Is Counterintuitive. Hayek traces his argument back to eighteenth-century Scottish thinkers such as David Hume and Adam Smith. In spite of the argument's grand pedigree, however, it is very counterintuitive. In this age of scientific progress, we are accustomed to thinking of rational, scientific thought as the source of all social and material progress. Planning is good, anarchy is chaos. But I believe that it has more intuitive appeal than appears at first blush. I illustrate this claim with a brief look at the evolution of language.

The Example of Language. The claim that many of our social institutions emerged through a kind of evolution in which no one foresaw the ultimate result is, as I have said, counterintuitive. But in the case of language, a little reflection seems to show that this claim is the only reasonable view. The attempt to deny that human language evolved as unintended consequences of individual actions seems to land us in absurdities. Imagine that in the depths of man's prehistory there came a great genius who had invented language when his (or her) fellow humans were still grunting and thumping. This already is a difficult matter. It may be that reason cannot function without language. Leaving this rather difficult philosophical point aside, however, we still encounter difficulties. What is our genius to do? Shall he *tell* his fellow humans about his invention? As they know no language, he cannot tell them anything. Then how shall he proceed? He cannot. If we are to imagine such a great inventor, we must imagine him as one of the most tragic figures of the species.

If language could not have been the invention of a great genius, it must have emerged through some sort of evolutionary process. How might this have happened? Humanity inherited from its subhuman ancestors a kind of protolanguage in the form perhaps of different grunts and shrieks to indicate pleasure, anger, alarm, and so on. Over time each noise is ramified by individual acts of communication. The shriek that once meant simply "danger!" becomes two distinguishable shrieks, one meaning "near danger," the other meaning "far danger." The distinction emerges through concrete attempts by individuals to communicate in moments of danger, not from some plan thought through beforehand. (A more detailed account of how such a division might occur "spontaneously" is relegated to a footnote.[1]) Over time, such ramifications multiply and a structured language emerges without anyone even realizing that they are in fact using language. Language is an unintended consequence of individual action.

Considering the case of human language helps us to see that there can be social institutions that emerge as unintended consequences of individual action. It may then seem less surprising to claim that the whole of society is a spontaneous order, the result of human action, but not the product of human design. Let us turn now to this somewhat larger claim.

The Meaning of "Spontaneous Order" Is Explained. Our quick look at language has shown us that it is possible for social institutions to emerge by a kind of evolution in which actions aiming at particular purposes generate regularities in people's behavior that were not the purpose of those actions to bring about, or even imaginable to those whose actions brought them into being. Our quick look at language has not, however, shown us what it means to claim that society is a "spontaneous order."

To say that society is a spontaneous order is to say that there are regularities in the actions and interactions of individuals, rules that are the result not of planning but of the sort of "evolution" we saw at work in the emergence of language. It is to say further that these regularities are not confined to a few known institutions such as the rules of grammar and, say, the rules of common courtesy. In Hayek's vision, society is a complex system of rules governing individual actions. Some of these rules were designed by legislators and imposed from above. But most of them emerged as the rules of grammar did, as an unintended consequence of individual action. Just as children follow the rules of grammar even though they do not know what those rules are, we follow the evolved rules of the spontaneous social order even though we are not consciously aware of these rules.

Three Characteristics of Spontaneous Orders. We are now ready to see why it matters to my argument on public interest that society is a spontaneous order. Hayek identifies three "distinguishing properties" of a spontaneous order by contrast with designed systems. Designed orders

are relatively *simple* or at least necessarily confined to such moderate degrees of complexity as the maker can still survey; they are usually *concrete* in the sense . . . that their existence can be intuitively perceived by inspection; and, finally, having been made deliberately, they invariably do (or at one time did) *serve a purpose* of the maker. None of these characteristics necessarily belong to spontaneous order. . . . Its degree of complexity is not limited to what a human mind can master. Its existence need not manifest itself to our senses but may be based on purely *abstract* relations which we can only mentally reconstruct. And not having been made it *cannot* legitimately be said to *have a particular purpose*, although our awareness of its existence may be extremely important for our successful pursuit of a great variety of different purposes. (1973, p. 38)

It is the third property that is of interest here. If society is a spontaneous order, then it "cannot legitimately be said to have a particular purpose," but its existence is certainly of the highest moment for "our successful pursuit of a great variety of different purposes." From this perspective it would seem that there is no grand teleology propelling us forward to some supra-individual end. Society is a spontaneous order and has no end or goal. The public interest, therefore, cannot be society's interest. It must consist somehow in individual interests. We shall see presently that the distinguishing properties of spontaneous orders give us some insight into how we might seek to combine individual interests to form something we call the public interest.

How Public Policy Can Affect the Public Interest

The public interest, I have argued, is really just a combination of individual interests. This conclusion seems to follow from Hayek's social theory. Hayek himself, naturally enough, did not fail to see this same point. The general welfare, he argues, consists in the preservation of "that abstract order of the whole which does not aim at the achievement of known particular results but is preserved as a means for assisting in the pursuit of a great variety of individual results (1976, p. 5)." The good society, according to Hayek, is the one "we would choose if we knew that our initial position in it would be decided purely by chance" (1976, p. 132).

Hayek's reasoning goes something like this. Society has no overall purposes. It is instead the vehicle for the achievement of many individual purposes, some of which are bound to be in conflict. This state of affairs is impossible to change; the effort to transform society from a "spontaneous order" into a "made order" is sure to fail. The only legitimate meaning, therefore, which a phrase like "the public interest" can receive is the promotion of the well-being of the randomly chosen individual.[2] This is the meaning of public interest that we will accept, that the public interest consists in promoting the well-being of the representative individual.

We may distinguish two components to the well-being of the representative individual. On the one hand, the well-being of the representative individual is promoted by increasing his chances of achieving the particular goals he has set for himself. On the other hand, the well-being of the representative individual is promoted by inducing him to select his goals wisely.

The first of these two components of one's well-being is perhaps self-evident. The second may be less so. My concern with the wisdom of the representative individual's goals reflects my Millian preferences in moral theory. "It is quite compatible with the principle of utility," Mill argued, "to recognize the fact that some kinds of pleasure are more desirable and more valuable than others" (1863, p. 19).

Human beings have faculties more elevated than the animal appetites and, when once made conscious of them, do not regard anything as happiness which does not include their gratification. . . . No intelligent human being would consent to be a fool, no instructed person would be an ignoramus, no person of feeling and conscience would be selfish and base, even though they should be persuaded that the fool, the dunce, or the rascal is better satisfied with his lot than they are with theirs (1863, pp. 18–19).

Pigs and people are different. We should recognize this truth when considering the public interest. If we wish to promote the well-being of the representative individual, we must not rest content with institutions that promote his chances of achieving the goals he may set himself. We had better try to find the institutions that might deliver him from foolishness, ignorance, and greed. It is in the public interest to do so.

Our interest in the wisdom with which the representative individual chooses his goals does not imply statism. If, say, Robert Nozick's nightwatchman state is the best available, it is because such a state gives the representative individual his best combination of success in achieving goals and wisdom in selecting them. If "liberty" should lead people to act like swine, liberty be damned. The facts of the case, however, seem to favor liberty. As Mill argued in *On Liberty*, a person is more likely to develop his faculties when he is free than when he is in chains. Thus it is that men are endowed with certain inalienable rights and that among these are life, liberty, and the pursuit of happiness.

Some Examples of Arguing on the Basis of the Public Interest

Let us now turn to some examples to see how the principles I have argued for translate into arguments for and against specific public policy proposals. I look first at measures that are desirable, or not, principally because of their effect on the representative individual's ability to fulfill his goals, whatever they might be. Then I will consider some measures that are desirable, or not, principally because of the influence they have in encouraging the representative individual to select his goals wisely. My discussion of each issue will be skeletal. My object is not to decide any particulars, but to show how one goes about arguing on public policy issues from the perspective I have outlined above.

EXAMPLES OF PUBLIC POLICY HELPING TO IMPROVE THE CHANCES EACH INDIVIDUAL HAS OF ACHIEVING HIS ENDS

The Rule of Law

A standard argument of social theorists in the traditions from which Hayek draws is that preservation of the "rule of law" must be one of the state's central functions. If society is a spontaneous order of the sort Hayek describes, then the fulfillment of individual purposes is possible because we can form reliable expectations about the general features of other people's actions. Such reliable expectations cannot be formed, they argue, if our actions are not constrained by the rule of law. Thus, we must not capitulate to our otherwise noble impulse to redistribute wealth in response to special calamities.[3]

If the juries in personal liability cases should always dip into the "deep pockets" of the nearest corporate bystander, then firms will be less able to formulate reliable expectations and thus they will be less able to gear their actions to the economic realities they encounter.

If judges should decide civil disputes on the basis of their judgments about which disputant had greater moral courage or sensitivity, the meaning of every contract would be greatly attenuated. Such corruptions of the rule of law must be avoided if the chances of the representative individual to achieve his goals are to be maximized.

Social Insurance

Social insurance schemes are proposals to use the state to effect society-wide risk pooling. From the indirect utilitarian perspective I have adopted, if such schemes are desirable, it is because they help the representative individual to achieve his goals. Each of us faces certain risks. Illness, accident, or natural disaster may disrupt the pursuit of our goals. Risk pooling transforms this risk into a cost. Such a transformation then improves our long-run prospects of achieving our ends. Unless a strong counterargument can be found, indirect utilitarianism would seem to imply the desirability of social insurance. Of course, counterarguments do exist. One might argue that, because the state is sheltered from market competition, it is sure to pool risks inefficiently. Private insurance will do the job better, and so on. Whatever may be the best argument, the indirect utilitarian wants the issue to be judged by its implications for the representative individual's ability to achieve his or her goals.[4]

EXAMPLE OF PUBLIC POLICY HELPING TO IMPROVE THE NATURE OF THE ENDS EACH INDIVIDUAL PURSUES

I turn now to the example with which my chapter began, wheelchair ramps. Can one really argue for them on the basis of "public interest"? I believe that one may indeed argue for them on just such a basis, and I do so below. Before doing so I wish to deny that the arguments I present are definitive.[5] My point will be made if the reader is persuaded that such arguments are perfectly legitimate and can be made by individualists. I am content to show that we must, after all, consider the public interest when weighing proposals such as the installation of wheelchair ramps in public buildings.

The installation of wheelchair ramps in public buildings is certainly in the interest of those who use wheelchairs. If this were all that one might say in their favor, then one might oppose them or at least argue for a special wheelchair tax to defray the costs of their installation. How might one argue that they are in the public interest (and should thus be paid for out of general revenues)? Wheelchair ramps and similar facilities "mainstream" the handicapped.[6] They allow those who are confined to a wheelchair to participate in public life and thereby ennobles them. But for the same reason wheelchair ramps tend to ennoble those who do not use them. When the wheelchair-bound are "mainstreamed," each ambulatory person is induced to treat them with the same respect and consideration with which he or she treats the rest of the ambulatory population. The handicapped "count" fully. They do not somehow "count less" than others on account of the accident that they are confined to wheelchairs. This refines the "higher faculties" we saw Mill discuss earlier. Wheelchair ramps encourage in us all "feeling and conscience." They discourage the "rascal" in us. Thus, wheelchair ramps help us to choose our goals wisely and humanely. They are in the public interest.

CONCLUSION

My purpose in this chapter has been very restricted. I have attempted to show that an individualist need not suspect that "the public interest" is always a smoke screen for special interests. I have used an "indirect utilitarian" argument, which I interpreted as a restatement of John Stuart Mill's utilitarianism in the light of Hayek's social theory.

I have not constructed a blanket defense of every form of government action. The social theory of Hayek upon which I have built my argument warns us against the hubris of an excessive confidence in our ability to legislate all the social goals we happen to like. If society is a spontaneous order, then we do not and cannot have very much knowledge of how society really works. We cannot hope to exercise detailed control of society. Drug laws provide a good example of the sort of limits with which we must contend in forming public policy. It might be that an effective prohibition of narcotic drugs would be in the public interest.[7] I favor legalization, however, precisely because it is not within our power to make such a prohibition effective. The social costs of prohibition far outweigh any gains that might come in the form of a slight reduction in the number of users.

I have not tried to defend every scheme of social reform. But I have tried to show that individualism in social theory or in ethics is not automatically opposed to all action taken "in the public interest."

NOTES

1. Experience might show, for instance, that a certain member of the group emits a higher-pitched shriek when the danger is close at hand rather than far away. His habit, we may imagine, was not contrived. It simply reflected his great state of excitement about dangers close at hand. Over time, other members of the group may imitate him. By imitating him, they can quickly communicate something of the proximity of the danger without having to wait for the others to turn and see what that danger is. Eventually, this distinction between the shriek used for dangers nearby and the shriek used for dangers far off becomes institutionalized, a regular part of the group's emerging language. All this without anyone having intended to create the distinction that in fact emerges.

2. This statement is a normative claim, and it does go beyond positive social theory. It presumes, for example, that the well-being of men and that of women count equally, as do members of different races.

3. The point we are making now has nothing to do with the desirability of regularized and predictable schemes of income transfer. Such schemes may have negative incentive effects, but they do not necessarily corrupt the rule of law.

4. I am presuming that social insurance does not promote foolishness or corruption in the selection of individual goals.

5. Conspicuous by their absence are all considerations concerning the presumption against state action that follow from the sort of social theory Hayek espouses.

6. I ignore risk pooling as a side issue.

7. In spite of the fact that narcotics use is an unmitigated evil, we may doubt that even an effective prohibition is in the public interest when we consider the importance of autonomy to the well-being of the representative individual.

BIBLIOGRAPHY

Ferm, Vergilius, ed. 1956. *Encyclopedia of Morals.* New York: Philosophical Library.

Gray, John N. 1983. *Mill on Liberty: A Defense.* London and Boston: Routledge & Kegan Paul.

Hayek, F. A. 1973. *Law, Legislation and Liberty.* Vol. 1, *Rules and Order.* Chicago: University of Chicago Press.

Hayek, F. A. 1976. *Law, Legislation and Liberty.* Vol. 2, *The Mirage of Social Justice.* Chicago: University of Chicago Press.

Mill, John Stuart. 1863. *Utilitarianism.* Reprinted in Samuel Gorovitz, ed., *Utilitarianism with Critical Essays.* Indianapolis and New York: The Bobbs-Merrill Company, Inc., 1971.

Nozick, Robert. 1974. *Anarchy, State and Utopia.* New York: Basic Books.

Smart, J. J. 1956. "Extreme and Restricted Utilitarianism." Reprinted in Samuel Gorovitz, ed., *Utilitarianism with Critical Essays.* Indianapolis and New York: The Bobbs-Merrill Company, Inc., 1971.

Yeager, Leland B. 1984/85. "Utility, Rights, and Contract: Some Reflections on Hayek's Work." In Kurt R. Leube and Albert H. Zlabinger, eds., *The Political Economy of Freedom.* Munich and Vienna: Philosophia Verlag.

———. 1985. "Rights, Contract, and Utility in Policy Espousal." *The Cato Journal* 5, 1: 259–94.

Part II

Relationships between the Corporation and Outsiders

7

Are Anticompetitive Practices Unethical?

D. T. ARMENTANO

INTRODUCTION

Prior to 1975 economists were nearly unanimous that vigorous enforcement of the antitrust laws was in the consumer's best interest. They were convinced that so called "anticompetitive" practices such as price discrimination and tying agreements were all evidence of "market failure" and were likely to harm consumer welfare. Presumably, government regulation of such practices through tough antitrust enforcement was required to keep the economy efficient and keep prices low to consumers.

The unanimity concerning traditional antitrust enforcement no longer exists. The last fifteen years have seen a near revolution in antitrust thinking and some important changes in the administration of antitrust law (Kwola and White 1989). Many antitrust scholars have raised serious theoretical and empirical questions concerning the conventional notion of monopoly power. They have argued that most of the specific practices restricted by antitrust law (i.e., mergers) often can lead to an increase in economic efficiency and result in lower prices for consumers. Indeed these "new learning" theories and arguments (Goldschmid, Mann, and Weston 1974) were ultimately persuasive at the federal level, and specific antitrust enforcement efforts were relaxed somewhat during the 1980s (Langenfeld and Scheffman 1986).

The economic skepticism concerning antitrust enforcement has not, however, carried over into ethical discussions of the law. With some rare exceptions (Pilon 1979; McGee 1989), there is still strong agreement that (1) the private business activities that the antitrust laws condemn are immoral and that (2) it is ethically appropriate for government to enforce antitrust laws to minimize such behavior or punish it should it occur. This chapter will concern itself primarily with a reexamination of these issues.

THE ETHICAL PROCESS

Human activity can be judged "right" or "wrong," "moral" or "immoral" according to specific principles or standards of conduct. Once a particular ethical principle is defined and accepted, then the conduct to be evaluated can be judged either consistent or inconsistent with the standard. Activity consistent with the principle would be "appropriate," "good," "right," or "ethical." Activity not consistent with the standard would be "inappropriate," "bad," "wrong," or "unethical."

Assume, for example, that we accept "selflessness" as an ethical principle. Individual action consistent with selflessness would be morally correct while behavior at variance with selflessness would be wrong. In the ethical process, then, we start with some ethical standard, do some "moral reasoning," and then come to some ethical conclusions concerning human behavior.

There are some serious difficulties involved in any ethical process. The most obvious difficulty is the determination and defense of the ethical principle itself. In our example, for instance, why should "selflessness" be the standard against which we judge all human behavior? Is that principle itself to be derived by a reasoning process or must it simply be accepted a priori? It should be apparent that if there is no agreement on the ethical standard itself, then there is unlikely to be agreement on any ethical conclusion derived from moral reasoning based on that standard.

Even general agreement on one ethical principle would not necessarily provide clear sailing for the moral reasoning process. Assume, for example, that we can "prove" (or get general agreement) that "selflessness" is an appropriate ethical principle. Nonetheless, we would still have to determine which actions are selfless and which are not. What if an action is essentially selfless but not completely so? (How do we measure selflessness?) In addition, is it the intent of the act itself or its consequences that determine whether an act is selfless? How important are "information" and "ignorance" in the moral reasoning process? What about "mitigating circumstances?" Obviously the moral process is fraught with several major and minor difficulties.

Despite the difficulties, ethical reasoning can be applied to any human activity, including business activity. Although the success or failure (correctness or wrongness) of business activity is usually judged by economic standards such as economic profit or cost savings, there is no reason that such behavior cannot be evaluated (and criticized) from a moral perspective. Indeed, one of the most fashionable trends in academic business education is to apply moral reasoning to selected business case situations (Beauchamp 1989).

Business Ethics

The U.S. antitrust laws are concerned with particular activities that occur between discrete business organizations (competitors, suppliers, distributors) and between business organizations and their consumers. Under certain circumstances, the Sherman Act and Clayton Act restrict price and output agreements between competitors, monopolization, price discrimination, tying agreements, and mergers and acquisitions. Moral reasoning can be applied to all of these activities.

The clear consensus in the business ethics literature is that these "anticompetitive" practices are unfair and unjust (Velasquez 1988, pp. 179–216). Price fixing and price discrimination are not only economically inefficient; they are ethically immoral as well. Indeed the strong ethical condemnation of such practices undoubtedly strengthens the economic case for vigorous antitrust enforcement.

To understand the moral condemnation of so-called anticompetitive practices, we must do two things. First, we must determine and evaluate which particular moral standard is being applied in the moral reasoning process. Second, we must critically analyze the reasoning process employed to deduce specific ethical conclusions.

UTILITARIANISM

Utilitarianism is an important ethical standard for judging the morality of human action. It holds that an action is morally correct if it produces more net utility for society as a whole than any other action. Actions that are morally correct promote the greatest good for the greatest number; they tend to maximize society's benefits at the lowest costs. Such a standard can be employed to evaluate private business activity or any specific public policy.

Many of the important ethical criticisms of anticompetitive practices are fundamentally utilitarian. The argument goes like this: Actions are ethically appropriate if they maximize total social utility; anticompetitive practices (such as price fixing) cannot maximize total utility; anticompetitive practices are immoral. Any critical evaluation of business ethics must begin by examining both the major and minor premises of this argument.

Three important lines of criticism can be directed against a utilitarian standard for business ethics. The first is that there are inherent measurement problems in attempting to determine whether society's welfare is maximized by any action or policy. The second is that the simple economic condemnation of anticompetitive practices upon which utilitarians rely is open to serious dispute. The third is that a standard of morality that ignores all considerations of "rights" cannot be entirely satisfactory.

The Measurement Problem

The measurement problem arises because of the fundamental subjectivity of the concepts "utility" and "cost" (Rothbard 1956). Correctly understood, the utility that an individual experiences from any action is personal and subjective; it cannot be added to or subtracted from the utility that another individual experiences. Utility is an internal state of affairs and not an objective (cardinal) magnitude that can be arithmetically manipulated. In short individually felt utilities cannot be totaled into some meaningful aggregate.

Likewise the cost of an action to an individual is the value of the next best opportunity to that individual. Cost is utility sacrificed; it is subjectively felt by each individual and cannot be summed up across different individuals. Thus the concepts of total social utility and total social cost cannot refer to objectively measurable magnitudes. In the absence of such magnitudes, however, it is difficult to understand how the utilitarian ethic can be made operational.

Take the standard ethical condemnation of price-fixing agreements. Utilitarians conclude that price fixing is morally wrong because such agreements are said to lead to a reduction in society's "welfare." Price fixing is widely regarded as unethical because it tends to reduce consumer and social welfare.

Yet such an "easy" ethical conclusion is not strictly warranted. Assume initially that a price agreement between competitors is successful in raising prices to consumers. Because consumers were engaged in exchange prior to the price increase, we reason that they intended to increase their own net utility. Yet any individual gains from trade that they may have realized were subjectively felt and cannot be added together to produce any "total" magnitude. After the price increase, consumers continue to engage in exchange in an attempt to increase their own net utility. Yet again there is no total magnitude of utility that can be compared with the previous state of affairs. Thus in the absence of a constant "unit" of utility, we cannot unambiguously conclude that the price increase lowered "total" consumer utility.

The situation becomes even more ambiguous when we attempt to take producer "welfare" into account. Even if we grant for the sake of argument that price fixing does reduce consumer welfare, we must then accept that the price agreement can increase producer welfare. Economists often conclude that the losses to the consumers equal the gains to the producers but that total social utility is reduced because of a "dead-weight" welfare loss.[1] Yet in the absence of any objective measure of utility, it would always be possible to argue that the producers' utility gains exceed the consumers' utility losses and that total social utility has been increased by price cooperation. This argument is strengthened whenever there are any "cost savings" associated with interfirm price agreements.

The most difficult case for utilitarians would be a price agreement that did not result in any higher prices to consumers. It is all too common to assume that "anticompetitive" practices such as price fixing achieve their intended objective. But this is not necessarily the case. Price agreements can fail to achieve their objectives for a number of different reasons, and several famous conspiracies have been notoriously unsuccessful in terms of enhancing prices or profits (Armentano 1990, pp. 133–66; Asch and Seneca 1976).

From a strictly utilitarian perspective, then, what is morally wrong with a price agreement that does *not* raise consumer prices and may even reduce business costs? Assume, for instance, that the uncertainty of price instability results in lower production and that price stabilization would lead to an increase in market output (Dewey 1979). How would utilitarians morally condemn such a "conspiracy"? Or assume that price stabilization allows steadier employment of labor resources over the business cycle. How can utilitarians be sure that such an agreement, given economic uncertainty and the inherent measurement problems, does not actually enhance net social welfare?

Perfect Competition and Anticompetitive Practices

The most general response to the above criticism is that economic analysis has demonstrated that the business practices under discussion "lower social welfare." In Manuel Velasquez's *Business Ethics*, for example, we get a detailed discussion of the economic model of perfect competition and the relevance of that model to ethical judgments concerning monopoly power (Velasquez 1988, pp. 181–213).

The argument in Velasquez proceeds as follows: (1) Under perfect competition resources would be allocated efficiently and societal welfare would be maximized; (2) the practices that the antitrust laws condemn are elements of monopoly power and demonstrate the absence of perfect competition; (3) such practices must misallocate resources and lower social welfare. Economic analysis, in short, is employed to legitimize utilitarian moral judgments concerning specific business practices.

Unfortunately for utilitarians the economic "analysis" (and moral condemnation) of specific business practices is not nearly so simple. Even assuming for the sake of argument that interpersonal utility comparisons are meaningful, it is now widely recognized by industrial organization economists that perfect competition cannot be employed as a standard to measure resource misallocation in the real business world (Armentano 1990, pp. 13–48). And because it cannot, business practices that deviate from the model cannot automatically be condemned as anticompetitive or as immoral.

To see why this is so, consider that perfect competition is an equilibrium model; it simply assumes conditions to exist (perfect information and costless adjustment, for example) that automatically result in complete "efficiency." It does not explain how those conditions can be brought about nor how long such a process should take. In short, it does not deal with the actual competitive process.

Competition in the real business world is a discovery and adjustment process, not an equilibrium condition (Hayek 1978). The real challenge in allocating resources efficiently is not solving simultaneous equations for price and output, with everything known and constant. The real challenge is in dealing precisely with the problems that perfect competition assumes away, namely, with the process of discovering information and adjusting market supply under conditions of uncertainty (Kirzner 1973).

Economists now argue that many of the practices condemned under antitrust law are attempts by firms to deal with economic change and uncertainty (Shughart 1990). Far from "restraining trade," many of these practices are now seen as enhancing and expanding trade and exchange. Price discrimination, tying agreements, and especially mergers are ways that firms attempt to compete (or cooperate) more efficiently in an attempt to generate lower costs and greater profits. (We have already noted how price agreements might accomplish this result.) Antitrust restrains on such practices tend to hamper the market process, protect rivals from hard competition, and lead to higher prices for consumers.

This revisionist perspective on antitrust is most persuasive with respect to open-market attempts to "monopolize." Rather than reduce output, raise prices, and reduce choices to consumers—behavior predicted by traditional monopoly theory—"dominant firms" have tended to expand output and lower prices and make additional alternatives available to consumers (Armentano 1990, pp. 49–132; Brozen 1982). Indeed, in several of the most important antitrust cases in all business history, the laws themselves were employed by government and private litigants in an attempt to restrict such efficient behavior (Baumol and Ordover 1985). If this is the general reality of antitrust enforcement, utilitarians will have to revise severely their moral evaluation of anticompetitive practices and antitrust law.

Perfect Competition and Morality

Attempting to use the perfectly competitive equilibrium model as a policy tool can lead to economic mischief; it can lead to ethical mischief as well. It is often argued, for instance, that perfectly competitive markets are perfectly "moral" in the sense that consumer welfare is maximized and workers earn exactly what they contribute to production (Velasquez 1988, pp. 187–91). As we are reminded that the real world is never perfectly competitive, business behavior and morality must inevitably be at odds.

But again it must be emphasized that perfectly competitive markets are "efficient" and therefore "just" only because the requirements for complete efficiency are simply assumed. In an equilibrium world, workers would always receive their marginal product and price would always equal "cost." But such a world cannot exist in reality, and the fact that it cannot has nothing to do with business "power." Uncertainty and change imply a disequilibrium world, but one in which important "equilibrating forces" are at work. Legally open markets can be expected to generate an efficient competitive process, but they cannot be expected to produce any perfectly competitive equilibriums. Such conditions are simply not of this world.

It would seem that any reasonable moral process would have to take the realities of the market process into account. The fact that a worker's wage falls short of her "marginal product" or the price a consumer pays exceeds "cost" should not in itself imply immorality or unfairness. After all, the disequilibrium condition may be a function of transactions costs, imperfect information, uncertainty, and change. The correct moral analysis should focus instead on the existence of the competitive process itself rather than on the existence of any equilibrium condition. If we can be reasonably confident that the market process is continually at work to eliminate the discrepancies described, then the process can be said to be moral and fair from a utilitarian perspective. A competitive market process is the best that we can hope for economically; it ought to be the best that we can expect from a utilitarian moral perspective as well.

In conclusion, the standard utilitarian ethical analysis of anticompetitive practices is based on a simplistic theoretical notion that few economists now support; it is also based on an incomplete understanding of antitrust case histories. Without perfect competition as a policy standard and without incontrovertible evidence that business organizations (absent legal protection) can restrain trade, the traditional utilitarian condemnation of "anticompetitive" practices is simply not persuasive.

RIGHTS THEORY AND ANTITRUST LAW

An alternative ethical standard that can be employed for evaluating business practices is a "rights"-based standard. Rights-based standards assume (or demonstrate) that individuals have "rights" and that specific business practices such as price fixing or monopolization violate these rights.[2] Public policy (such as antitrust) could appropriately restrict business activity that violated individual rights and order restitution to victims.

The rights literature is now separated into discussions of "negative" and "positive" rights. A right is generally defined as an individual's entitlement *to* something or to *do* something. A negative right implies that others may not interfere with certain individual actions; positive rights imply that others are obligated to provide resources such that individual rights can be pursued more effectively (DeGeorge 1990; Werhane 1985, pp. 18–20).

An example will attempt to make the differences clear. Assume that we are concerned with an individual who wishes to publish a letter to the editor in a local newspaper. A negative right to free speech would mean that the person should be free to write anything that she wishes employing her own resources in an attempt to get her ideas published. No prior legal restraint on any expression of ideas in a letter would be consistent with negative rights.

Positive rights would imply that an individual who wishes to exercise her right of speech should be supported or aided in her pursuit. Positive rights would impose moral duties or obligations on others to participate. For example, it might be appropriate for the law to require that individuals be allowed to petition and speak in private shopping centers even though the owners disagree. It might also be morally wrong for an editor to refuse a letter that expounded a viewpoint with which the editor (or the owners of the newspaper) disagreed. A law requiring "equal treatment" (and publication) of opposing viewpoints might be appropriate from a positive-rights perspective.

It should be apparent that there may be an inherent conflict between negative and positive rights positions. What might be "right" to do under negative rights could be morally abhorrent under positive rights, for example, the "right" to discriminate. Almost every "duty" imposed under positive rights—especially duties obligated by law—would be in conflict with negative rights. Thus whether a particular business practice does or does not violate "rights" will depend upon which particular rights standard is adopted.

Negative Rights

Do the business practices restrained by antitrust law violate rights? From a strict negative-rights position, it does not appear that they do. Under negative rights, individuals own property and have a right to use it without interference by others. This implies that individual owners (or trustees acting for owners) can legitimately decide to charge any price, produce any output (including no output), make any agreement, and refuse to deal with anyone for any reason whatever.[3] Any outside (nonowner) interference with those decisions would violate the rights of owners of property to determine a legitimate use for their own property.

A negative-rights regime implies that all trades of property must be voluntary. Each owner must consent to have her property employed in a particular manner. The use of anyone's property without explicit consent, or the existence of any laws restraining voluntary agreements between property owners, would constitute a violation of negative rights.

We are now in a position to examine the morality of various "anticompetitive" practices. Assume, for example, that an agreement exists between rival sellers with respect to price and output. Does such an agreement violate individual rights?

If the price agreement is voluntary and is restricted (privity is the legal term) only to the property of the sellers involved, it would appear that it is not rights violating. Each seller has the unlimited negative right to decide his own output either independently or interdependently. Because each seller has the unlimited negative right to produce nothing (i.e., to refuse to deal), each would certainly have the negative right to "restrict" output. As long as the colluders don't forcefully interfere with the output decisions of noncolluding firms or their customers, negative rights have not been violated.

But aren't the "rights" of consumers violated by price fixing? Not really. Consumers have an absolute right to their own property, their income, but no rights whatever to someone else's property, the output of the sellers. Their (negative) rights to their property are fully intact both before and after the price increase. The only rights issue is, Does price collusion, or price discrimination, or a tying contract, represent an interference with their use of their own property? The answer appears to be "No."

Higher prices may reduce utility (although see the discussion above), but that is not a violation of right. In addition, consumers may need and prefer lower prices; but, again, need and preference are not relevant in negative-rights analysis (although they may be in positive-rights analysis).

Similar reasoning can be applied to the ethics of monopolizing. Some writers assert that monopoly markets "embody restrictions on the negative rights that perfectly free markets respect"; sellers are not "free" to enter markets where monopoly exists (Velasquez 1988, pp. 194–95). But whether all of this is true or not depends upon a correct theory of monopoly and how the term "free" is employed.

Government can legally bar entry into markets and establish monopoly as a matter of public policy. Such monopoly does restrict negative rights, because it can prevent consumers and potential suppliers from making voluntary agreements with respect to their own property. Shut-out suppliers and their potential customers can claim, legitimately, that their rights (to trade) have been interfered with—by government.

But free-market monopoly is another matter entirely. A firm that monopolizes existing consumer preferences does not violate the negative rights of rival sellers or potential sellers. Rival sellers are perfectly "free" to enter the market and attempt to compete away the customers of the monopolist. Any barriers to "entry" that may exist all embody economic advantages that the monopolist provides (product differentiation, low price) and that the rivals can attempt to overcome. Thus under a regime of negative rights, potential sellers are free to attempt to displace dominant firms just as existing sellers are free to attempt to keep their customers.

The common mistake here is to use the expression "free market" in two entirely different senses. Negative rights concern the freedom to employ your own property without interference from another. But the employment of that property cannot be "free," that is, costless. Certainly it may be difficult (costly) to enter markets dominated by existing firms and attempt to overcome existing preferences; it may even prove impossible. Likewise, it may be difficult (costly) for existing firms to attempt to hold their monopoly position over consumer preferences. But all of this is only a testament to the fact that economic scarcity creates costs and that costs and prices are relevant as far as consumer preferences are concerned. The negative rights of consumers and would-be sellers are not abridged by scarcity or by economic efficiency.

In conclusion, price fixing, price discriminating, merging, and monopolizing are all voluntary market activities, which cannot violate negative rights. On the other hand, antitrust regulation that interferes with such voluntary agreements must constitute a violation of negative rights. Thus we come to the unorthodox conclusion that the antitrust laws themselves, not the acts which they regulate, are unethical from a negative-rights perspective.

Positive Rights

Positive rights imply that others in society have a positive duty or obligation to provide the holder of a right with whatever she needs to effectuate that entitlement. If consumers, for example, have a positive right to "competitively" priced products, then it would be right to enforce the antitrust laws against collusive agreements. If potential sellers have a positive right to enter markets and compete, then it would be right to subsidize such sellers or penalize existing producers. If consumers have a positive right to be treated "equally" with dignity and respect, then price discrimination is morally wrong and should be prohibited.

The most basic criticism of a positive-rights regime is that it is internally inconsistent. How are the positive rights of consumers to low prices to be reconciled with the positive rights of potential sellers who may be excluded by those very same low prices? Price increases that effectuate entry for potential sellers are the very same price increases that would violate the positive rights of consumers. A positive right to have prices reflect costs—that is, to price-discriminate—can conflict with a positive right to have all consumers treated equally with respect to price. Thus it may be impossible to apply the positive-rights regime equally to everyone in society.

Another criticism of a positive-rights regime is that it imposes unchosen obligations on others and that these unchosen obligations must interfere with negative rights. For instance a negative right to make a price agreement is compromised by a consumer's positive right to "competitive" prices. A negative right to charge consumers different prices is compromised by a positive obligation not to price-discriminate. Thus to fulfill the positive rights of some (consumers, potential sellers) the negative rights of others must be constantly compromised (Nozick 1974).

In addition, the positive-rights notion appears economically unbounded. If each individual has a right to whatever she needs to effectuate an entitlement, then there is really no limit to the economic obligations that some may impose on others. Further, in the name of justice and fairness, any desirable end might be termed a "right," and (other people's) resources would then have to be employed in an attempt to effectuate that end. Thus the theory of positive rights would appear to justify an unprecedented redistribution of income and wealth.

Finally, attempting to apply positive-rights theory to anticompetitive practices would produce economically bizarre results. If less-efficient sellers have a positive right to enter markets, then more-efficient firms (and consumers) could be forced to subsidize such entry. If less-efficient firms have a positive right to more market share, then more-efficient firms should be handicapped by law to effectuate that right.[4] If consumers have a positive right to some specific standard of living, then any price increase (even one that could be cost-justified) could be considered unfair and rights violating. In short, taking positive-rights theory seriously would require a radical restructuring of the competitive market process and the entire social order.

Positive Rights and the Golden Rule

It has been argued that certain anticompetitive practices violate basic rights because they are not consistent with the "categorical imperative" of Immanuel Kant (1724–1804). According to Kant (1964), an action is moral if everyone, at least in principle, could act in the same manner and if the actor would be willing to have others act the same way that she did, even toward herself. The "imperative" can be summarized, Do unto others as you would have them do unto you.

The author fails to see, however, why the activities that the antitrust laws restrict cannot be both universalized and reversed. Assume, for instance, that the author attempts to fix prices with another author. Everyone, at least in principle, could attempt to fix prices for his labor services with a competitor; the behavior could be universalized. Further, as long as the author would be willing to have other labor sellers attempt to fix their prices—and he is perfectly willing to have this activity reversed—then the activity becomes perfectly moral under Kant's imperative. How then would price collusion or price discrimination violate any golden rule?

In addition, it has been argued that activities such as price discrimination tend to treat people as a "means to an end," rather than as an "end in themselves." But this is a strange criticism of any voluntary market exchange. After all, buyers as well as sellers are always motivated by a concern for increasing their own utility and are always "using" the services or output of others for their own purposes. Thus there is nothing uniquely selfish about anticompetitive practices in this regard. If they can be condemned as immoral from a positive-rights perspective, then so can any other exchange, including all of those under competitive conditions.

CONCLUSIONS

Are so-called anticompetitive practices unethical? It all depends upon which ethical standard is adopted and whether that standard and the reasoning process are acceptable or not.

The traditional utilitarian condemnation of anticompetitive practices appears to depend upon very questionable assumptions concerning both the measurability of utility and the actual purpose and effect of such practices. Under a different set of assumptions, as we have argued, it can be argued that the practices restricted by antitrust law may tend to make the economy more efficient. Indeed, the antitrust law itself, not the practices it restricts, may be ethically condemnable from a utilitarian perspective.

Whether anticompetitive practices violate individual rights or not depends upon which rights theory is operative. From a negative-rights perspective, business practices such as price fixing and price discrimination do not violate individual rights. Indeed to compel alternative behavior, as antitrust law does, creates two serious moral difficulties. First, such laws violate individual rights themselves because they represent outside interference with the use of one's own property. Second, as such law removes the element of individual choice itself, it robs the circumstance of any truly moral dimension.

Finally, the application of a positive-rights regime to such practices would conclude that they can be unethical. Yet there are some serious problems for any theory of positive rights. First, the theory may not be internally consistent. Second, the theory of positive rights would appear to clash sharply both with negative rights and with some basic economic principles such as scarcity and efficiency. It is difficult to accept the idea that the positive-rights position is correct when both negative rights and efficiency must be severely sacrificed to pursue it.

The recent revolution in antitrust economics has challenged economists and lawyers to rethink their support of traditional antitrust enforcement. Perhaps the time is also ripe for moral theorists to reevaluate their condemnation of anticompetitive practices and their nearly unanimous support of antitrust law.

NOTES

1. Economists do this by making an illegitimate assumption: that the marginal utility of money is the same for all market participants. This allows them to "measure" consumer and producer "surplus" and conclude that social welfare is reduced by price collusion.

2. The ultimate source of and justification for individual rights is well beyond the scope of this chapter. For a recent comprehensive treatment of the subject see Machan 1989. Some assert that rights are inalienable or natural; some assume that they are God-given; some argue that they can only be rationalized by what government legislates. In the discussion that follows, we are concerned mainly with internal consistency and with some economic and moral consequences rather than with the ultimate foundation of rights theory.

3. Some might argue that while individuals clearly have the rights identified, corporate entities might not have the same rights (Werhane 1985, pp. 61–64). For counterargument see Hessen 1980.

4. There are several bizarre antitrust decisions where efficient dominant firms have been legally handicapped in order to make it easier for competitors to gain market share (Armentano 1990, pp. 112–18, 209–13).

BIBLIOGRAPHY

Armentano, Dominick T. 1990. *Antitrust and Monopoly: Anatomy of a Policy Failure*. 2nd ed. New York and London: Holmes and Meier.

Asch, Peter, and Joseph J. Seneca. 1976. "Is Collusion Profitable?" *Review of Economics and Statistics* 58 (February): 1–13.

Baumol, William, and Janusz Ordover. 1985. "Use of Antitrust to Subvert Competition." *Journal of Law and Economics* 28 (May): 247–65.

Beauchamp, Tom L. 1989. *Case Studies in Business, Society, and Ethics*, 2nd ed. Englewood Cliffs, N.J.: Prentice-Hall.

Brozen, Yale. 1982. *Concentration, Mergers, and Public Policy*. New York: Macmillan.

DeGeorge, Richard T. 1990. *Business Ethics*, 3rd ed. New York and London: Macmillan Publishing Company, pp. 81–82.

Dewey, Donald. 1979. "Information, Entry and Welfare: The Case for Collusion." *American Economic Review* 69 (September): 587–94.

Goldschmid, Harvey J., Michael H. Mann, and Fred J. Weston, eds. 1974. *Industrial Concentration: The New Learning*. Boston: Little, Brown and Company.

Hayek, F. A. 1978. "Competition as a Discovery Process." In *New Studies in Philosophy, Politics and the History of Ideas*. London: Routledge and Kegan Paul.

Hessen, Robert. 1980. *In Defense of the Corporation*. Stanford: Hoover Institution Press, chap. 4.

Kant, Immanuel. 1964. *Groundwork of the Metaphysics of Morals*, trans. H. J. Paton. New York: Harper & Row.

Kirzner, Israel. 1973. *Competition and Entrepreneurship*. Chicago: University of Chicago Press.

Kwoka, John E., Jr., and Lawrence J. White, eds. 1989. *The Antitrust Revolution*. Glenview, Ill.: Scott, Foresman and Company.

Langenfeld, James, and David Scheffman. 1986. "Evolution or Revolution: What Is the Future of Antitrust?" *Antitrust Bulletin* (Summer): 287–99.

Machan, Tibor R. 1989. *Individuals and Their Rights*. Peru, Ill.: Open Court.

McGee, Robert W. 1989. "Ethical Issues in Acquisitions and Mergers." *The Mid-Atlantic Journal of Business* 25 (March): 19–40.

Nozick, Robert. 1974. *Anarchy, State, and Utopia*. New York: Basic Books, chap. 7.

Pilon, Roger. 1979. "Corporations and Rights: On Treating Corporate People Justly." *Georgia Law Review* 13 (Summer): 1245–1370.

Rothbard, Murray N. 1956. "Toward a Reconstruction of Utility and Welfare Economics." In M. Sennholz, ed., *On Freedom and Free Enterprise*. Princeton: D. Van Nostrand.

Shughart, William F. II. 1990. *Antitrust Policy and Interest-Group Politics*. Westport, Conn.: Quorum Books.

Velasquez, Manuel G. 1988. *Business Ethics: Concepts and Cases*, 2nd ed. Englewood Cliffs, N.J.: Prentice-Hall.

Werhane, Patricia H. 1985. *Persons, Rights, and Corporations*. Englewood Cliffs, N.J.: Prentice-Hall.

8

To Whom Does the Corporation Owe a Duty?

GEORGE C. S. BENSON

A common misconception, perhaps unintentionally favored by early court decisions, is that corporations owe their principal, perhaps sole, obligations to their shareholders. But more careful examination of corporate history and circumstances affecting corporate life indicate that there are several other important obligations, some of which may at times be more compelling than the obligation to the shareholder. This chapter will discuss the obligations to the company's reputation, to financial solvency, to shareholders, to customers, to employees, to management, to community, to product liability, to ethnic groups, to distressed areas, to staff and customer safety, to research and development, to foreign countries, and to education. Each of these will be discussed in turn, the last section including a discussion of conflicts between obligations. A few paragraphs on corporate law will serve as introduction.

HISTORICAL INTRODUCTION

The modern commercial corporation was little known in American business life until the beginning of the nineteenth century. Great Britain's unhappy experience with the South Sea Bubble in 1720 led to a British law against private commercial corporations that was applied to the American colonies in 1741 and did not disappear until the Revolution. The remarkable commercial growth of the colonies, which led directly into the Revolution, came in spite of the problems of partnerships and associations. Partnerships were somewhat handicapped by the process of reassignment of assets whenever a partner died or resigned. Associations did not have a clear status in the law until they developed into corporations.[1]

Corporations had a long experience in British common law, but they were confined largely to eleemosynary institutions such as parishes, colleges and schools, monasteries, guilds, city corporations, asylums, and the like. These all served their purposes, the exercise of which was usually reviewed by an appropriate government or religious official; but the problems of finance in those bodies differed greatly from that of the modern commercial corporation. England's great trading corporations for the South Seas, India, and the Americas had a combination of government and commercial functions, which again was only a partial precedent for the modern corporation.

The commercial corporation, which was used very little before 1800, became very useful, in fact essential, in the nineteenth century to meeting the American problem of developing livelihoods in an undeveloped country, with an immigrant population intent on improving its own lot but usually devoid of capital. The corporations brought together funds from a number of shareholders; they were originally chartered for a limited number of years or specific purposes, but state government soon began to realize the folly of ending the life or limiting the activity of a useful body that employed citizens, produced goods, and paid taxes. Early nineteenth-century state governments also failed to realize that corporations would be more useful to the economy if they were competing with each other. In fact, it took several decades for some of the states to realize the advantages of granting corporate charters freely to all responsible applicants.

In addition to the initial failure to realize the value of competing corporations, most state legislatures also failed to realize the need for inserting into corporate charters some provisions protecting shareholders, workers, managers, and customers. Most protections of shareholders were slowly developed by courts and legislatures during the nineteenth and early twentieth centuries.

In some ways corporations were off to a better start in the America of 1800 than they had been in the early 1700s under Great Britain. There was no American equivalent of the South Sea Bubble madness. Many of the late eighteenth-century corporations were organized to perform important public functions like construction of turnpikes or canals. Several early railroads were built as much for public service as for money making. Well into the first half of the nineteenth century, towns and governments bought shares of railroad stock or gave land to railroads to develop needed transportation routes. Many corporations were started for pro bono publico reasons. It was not until the later nineteenth century that some misuses of the corporate structure became so evident as to require statutory or judicial correction, as discussed in a section on obligations to shareholders. Even today, there are still grave disputes about the structure and purposes of corporations.

OBLIGATION TO ITS OWN REPUTATION

Any self-respecting organization that wants to keep customers or staff or maintain good relations with the governments or communities with which it has contact should be basically concerned with its reputation. Reputations vary with the variety of groups that have contacts with the corporation; in modern society that group of contacts may be greatly varied. In the case of corporations the fact that salesmen, personnel officers, purchasing agents, engineering advisers, or other contact groups make up a broad variety of people increases the importance of reputations. Johnson & Johnson spent $30 million to offset a criticism of acts that were not the company's fault in any way. J & J's business reputation today is greater because of the courage shown on that one occasion. On the other side of the table, Drexel, Burnham, Lambert risked its reputation on the sale of large quantities of shaky "junk" bonds and is now in bankruptcy.

Business corporations are absolutely essential to American life. With the possible exception of a few government-owned public utilities, no other organization has been able to take care of the multitude of details involved in feeding, housing, clothing, and other services for over 250 million people. With bewildering rapidity our corporations perform these and other tasks.

But it is important to admit that American business corporations do not have a generally good reputation with much of the American press and public. There must be twenty books critical of corporations in this office, perhaps half of them written by able and more or less objective scholars or reporters. Ralph Nader and his associates fire away at the corporate structure. The popular ratings of industry and of industry leaders are surprisingly bad as reported in *The Confidence Gap*.[2] Able ethical young people frequently shy away from business careers, thus adding to the ethical difficulties of business. Congress and state legislatures in well-meant reform efforts frequently pass laws that unduly limit the freedom of business operations. Governmental administrators often delay or block good enterprises of corporations with "bad reputations," even though the "bad reputation" is not fully deserved. It is true that some politicians use corporations as a whipping horse in their campaigns, but real ethical difficulties often underlie the problems of the corporations that the politicians castigate.

The following items give some ideas of the obligations of corporations; good reputations are sought by efforts to meet these obligations. A strong sense of ethics on the part of management is likely to lead to the proper handling of these obligations.

OBLIGATION TO CORPORATE FINANCIAL SOLVENCY

Deep in the hearts of most corporate executives, boards of directors, principal shareholders, and employees should be a recognition of the necessity of financial solvency. In most cases such solvency can be secured only if there is adequate income to more than balance the expenditures of the business. Employee wages and salaries, management salaries and bonuses, payments to creditors, taxes, fines and court- or government-ordered damages, all require adequate income. Without adequate income all those who have any form of financial dependency on the corporation will suffer heavy damage.

Some economists, notably Milton Friedman, have insisted that profits made by corporations should not be used for social purposes but should be used only to maximize profits for shareholders.[3] Many corporations have refused to accept Friedman's advice. The chairman of a cement company that had a plant with many poor factory workers in a desert area distant from the county hospital reasoned this way to me: "A wealthy man living in that area would be very unpopular if he did not make a significant contribution to that hospital; our company is an equivalent part of that area and must contribute, for both philanthropic and political reasons. The Congress recognizes these same reasons when it allows our corporation a tax deduction up to 10% of corporate taxable income for the year."

Many larger corporations contribute to various charities, public and private, although the average contribution is nearer 1 percent than the allowable deduction of 10 percent of profits today.

OBLIGATION TO SHAREHOLDERS

At first sight the shareholder is the "king dog" of those to whom the corporation has an obligation. Shareholders "own" the company; if it should be liquidated, shareholders are entitled to an appropriate part of the remaining value. Shareholders elect the board of directors, which selects top management and runs the company; shareholders may change the members of the board. Some companies make efforts to cultivate shareholders with attractive printed reports or lunches at the annual meeting. As the company gains assets, shareholders draw larger dividends and find themselves possessors of larger assets. Everyone should strive to be a shareholder.

In actual fact shareholders are sometimes not very potent members of the corporate body. If assets and dividends are to grow, management must make the decisions, with occasional prods from the board of directors or its committees. Only a few large shareholders or directors of large pension funds have any clout over management unless the corporation is very small. Managements are almost never voted out by shareholders, except in takeovers. If a business turns sour for a few years, the shareholders are often the first to suffer; their dividends can be cut legally while wages, purchases, other contracts, salaries, taxes, advertising costs, and consultant fees must be paid before dividends. If the company fails financially the shareholder may have nothing left after creditors are paid off.

The reader is reminded that the commercial corporation is a relatively new institution in history and that the nineteenth-century American legislators and judges who slowly worked out the laws for corporations in the nineteenth century often had little idea what part of the corporate family needed protection. James Willard Hurst, one of the leading students of the history of American law, tells us, "A new phase of public policy towards the business corporation opened in 1896 when New Jersey and soon afterward Delaware adopted general incorporation laws more generous in their terms for the interest of promoters and management."[4] From the same book, he says, "As his distance increased from the working policies of the company, the ordinary stockholder's concern focused simply on assured receipt of dividends and the hope of capital gain."[5] If the shareholder became dissatisfied, he sold his shares. Government was not very helpful to the shareholder. In another book Hurst comments, "Late-nineteenth and early-twentieth-century decisions generally refused effect to agreement of shareholders to pool their voters or to require unanimity on basic matters. . . . Courts also refused effect to corporate articles which conditioned board action on stockholder's consent or which by classifying shares sought to guarantee particular shareholders fixed representation on the board."[6]

Fortunately, as the number of shareholders has greatly increased in the United States, there has been a countercurrent for shareholders. Many states tried, often rather ineffectively, to protect security purchases by "blue sky" laws enacted chiefly in the 1910–1920 period.[7]

During the Progressive period the Boston lawyer who later became Justice Louis Brandeis suggested protection of the shareholder by a policy requiring corporate disclosure of facts regarding corporate income and property. The idea was not fully developed until the establishment of the federal Securities and Exchange Commission (SEC) in 1933 and 1934. The commission initially attempted to regulate security sales by persuasion of stock exchanges. It also sometimes accepted business suggestions that were not especially friendly to shareholders. But later experience has made the stock exchanges friendlier to the SEC; and SEC's rulings of disclosure and other controls have made greater protection for the shareholder.

Joel Seligman[8] gives a very comprehensive account of the SEC development of rules that aid shareholders. Corporate managements must give annual and quarterly reports, the former audited by certified public accountants for the shareholders. The SEC has also pressured companies to have at least a majority of "outside" board members who are considered more likely to value the shareholder's interest over the interest of management. The SEC wants the important committees on auditing and nomination of board members and officers to be made up of outside board members.

New problems have come with the growth of the corporate takeover movement in the last two decades. Prior to the passage of the Williams Act in 1968, it was almost possible that company X could be merged into company Y without the management or share holders of X knowing that it had happened. Clearly management of company X could do little to protect itself or its shareholders. The Williams Act required that initial acquisitions be disclosed to shareholders and that tender offers remain open for twenty business days or more. This disclosure policy did not reduce the number of major mergers at all.[9] Another federal act, Hart-Scott-Rodino of 1976, had little effect on the number of mergers. Several state legislatures have passed acts to delay mergers, but Delaware, the state of incorporation of the largest number of big corporations, is not one of them. It looks as if the merger movement is to continue, although currently at reduced speed.

The movement is not a total loss to shareholders, but it has some disadvantages. They may be offered market or larger-than-market figures for their shares. Incompetent CEOs may be eliminated. However, two-tier tender offers may be unfair to shareholders who are left in the lower tier. The necessity of selling shares on which there is a capital gain may be inconveniently expensive for some shareholders.

Until laws and business habits of thought are changed, little can be done by management of the corporation to help the shareholder in these situations; most shareholders, however, are given an opportunity to sell shares at the price originally set by the takeover company. In some ways the takeover movement has increased management's responsibility to shareholders. John L. Casey, the managing director of a major investment counsel firm has written an account of a study case that emphasizes the importance of giving greater concern to the already existent values of management and workers and shareholders of the target company.[10]

If one follows Casey's thought, the management and board of the target corporation should have a clear-cut obligation to agree to a merger that satisfies the reasonable rights not only of shareholders and management but also of labor and the community.

OBLIGATION TO CUSTOMERS

Corporations and noncorporate retailers know that the operation of the market is the greatest pressure on them to act ethically to customers. If prices are unreasonable or goods are unsatisfactory or unhealthy, the alert customer can shift to another store or market.

There may, however, be obstructions to this simple control. For example, when Iowa Beef started to sell its economical prepackaged beef in the large New York City area in the 1970s, it found that unions controlled the dealers or the retailers and that the unions were controlled by organized-crime personnel. Iowa Beef and other firms had to make very substantial payments to the union or organized-crime representatives before the wholesaler would sell its packaged product to local butcher shops. Costs of this "racket" problem totalled several million dollars. Cost of the bribes was of course passed on to customers. The New York County district attorney's office observed some of the fraudulent transactions and secured several dozen convictions, but the penalties imposed by the New York courts were very light.[11]

The obligation of the corporations selling meat under these circumstances is difficult to define. An attitude of decent corporate citizenship requires effort to inform law enforcement agencies and to cooperate with their efforts. But those dealers knew the power of organized crime in New York, even though it did not dominate the district attorney's office. The only clear obligation was that of trying to secure a better level of government in New York City, a very difficult task.[12]

The corporate obligation in cases like this should rest with joint corporate organizations, like a Chamber of Commerce, a Manufacturers Association, or the Business Roundtable. At different times this writer has served on committees or boards of local, metropolitan, and national Chamber boards and has had other contacts with similar groups; these bodies have all seemed constructive and civic minded, but little or nothing has been said about overcoming organized crime or strengthening prosecution of criminal activities.

An even more complicated obligation of corporations to consumers is in the field of advertising. The obligation to tell the truth in advertising is accepted by all careful writers, although there are important differences of opinion as to the desirable degree of enforcement of the truth requirement by government. Perhaps the strongest enforcement agency is the Federal Trade Commission; but several other agencies, such as the offices working on drug abuse, at times enforce the requirement in their own areas of regulation. State attorneys general and county district attorneys usually have power to enforce a truth-in-advertising requirement but usually lack staff time or staff skill to bring legal action.[13]

There are widely different views as to what constitutes truth in advertising. Nevertheless, this writer believes that the corporate obligation to tell the truth is very important, not only for protection of the consumer but for its general effect on the ethics of the population. Intelligent adults can learn to identify untruths in advertising, but it would not be at all surprising if a child, after reading many interesting advertisements that she or he knew to be untrue, formed the conclusion that truth telling is not important in American society. Yet Sissela Bok has clearly demonstrated that truth telling is an essential base to reasonable operation of our complex society.[14] The many billions devoted to advertising could well have the side effect of teaching us not to expect or want the truth, unless corporations carry out their obligation to advertise truthfully.

An important question for lawyers and courts to struggle over is, how can a corporation prove that its advertisements are telling truths? It would often be difficult or impossible to demonstrate that the claims for the product in the advertisement were true.[15]

A few writers who wish to improve advertising have gone beyond the desire for truth to the more ambitious goal that corporate advertising should give useful information to the prospective customer. This would indeed be a worthwhile purpose. It is realized in some technical journals; probably the advertisements for breakfast cereals that include "fiber" or for cars that include a safety feature like air bags do add to general education about those products. However, many advertisers disregard information on the grounds that they want customers to buy the product, not to know more about it.

It is certainly true that some very worthwhile new products have entered into general use much more rapidly because of advertising. As Porter has reported, "Two studies have found that high levels of advertising are associated with high rates of introductions of new brands."[16] But this bit of evidence does not indicate a corporate ethical obligation to introduce new products when we find that Porter's examples were cigarettes.

It is conceivable that immense advertising could be planned to put competitors out of business; in view of the general American acceptance of antitrust legislation, such advertising could be viewed as counter to corporate legal obligations under the antitrust laws.[17]

Advertising is a field fraught with difficulties in which corporate obligations are not easily described; a related aspect of the corporate-customer relationship has clearer obligations. No responsible corporation should deceive or cheat its potential or actual customers. This writer can remember a day when Sears Roebuck and Montgomery Ward seemed very honest in contrast to local stores, but even they were selling questionable patent medicines at an earlier time (1900–1910).[18] Today most department stores and supermarkets make honest efforts to sell only worthwhile products at an established price. Real progress has been made in mercantile ethics.

But there are still petty tricks of retailing that a good corporation is obligated not to follow. When the Federal Trade Commission penalized a very respectable retailer in Los Angeles for having a "sale" price on products the prices of which had been raised only a fortnight earlier, one wonders. The constant prices of $2.99 and $4.99 are an easy way to confuse customers. One wonders if the slow but steady increase of all prices is respecting an obligation to consumers. In some southern California stores, prices for raincoats suddenly rise on the rare days when they are needed. The obligation of the corporate retailer should be strict honesty to customers, for the sake of the store's reputation as well as the customer's pocketbook.

OBLIGATION TO THE EMPLOYEES

Most corporate leaders realize that their staff is the corporation's "biggest asset" or at least say so for public relations purposes. Indeed, if you look through the most solid and civic-minded corporations of your area, you will find that most of them have employees who have been carefully selected, work hard to keep their jobs, are safeguarded in their work, and often develop an affection for the company. In many areas workers can point to a half dozen or more strong corporations that have a record of steady, safe employment, public service, and careful fiscal policy.

But there are a number of important exceptions that test the duties of these corporations to their community and staff. The recently publicized finding that a fraction of savings and loan executives used their new freedom from regulation in the 1980s to make highly personal loans on very dangerous purchases of new assets leads us to wonder if there was no ethical education of the seductive salesmen who talked themselves into S & L presidencies and then proceeded to embezzle or blunder their way to lost assets and discharged staff. These pseudo-executives were most unfaithful to their employees.

What does a corporation with an uncertain fiscal future do for its employees? The first ethical responsibility is to tell the prospective employee about the hopes and fears for the future of the corporation. The writer was once president of a small, new, pathetically underfinanced educational venture, with perhaps the smallest assets of any college in the United States; yet the college managed, more or less truthfully, to give the prospective employees a vision of hopes for a high-quality enterprise. Two men left tenured professorships at Harvard and Chicago universities to join this new venture in California and continued working there until retirement. However, in late spring of the second year of the new venture came war-reduced enrollment possibilities that led to the expectation of a very dangerous deficit, which made it seem necessary to tell a few satisfactory employees that reemployment for the next academic year was uncertain. Luckily, reemployment later proved to be possible, but there was substantial resentment from the junior faculty whose jobs were in jeopardy and from many of their colleagues. Should the enterprise have taken the chance of a crippling deficit in order to promise employment to these men?

As one reads the financial columns in the 1990s, many corporations experiencing declining business are eliminating older factories or unprofitable retail outlets. Such retrenchment programs raise ethical problems. Where possible, employees are offered similar jobs at other work points; but the cost of moving may be high or family ties may exist with the present workplace. If the company is facing real financial risks, what is ethical? Federal law requires a two-year notice or substantial dismissal payments. Sometimes an attractive retirement package can be offered; likely to be less helpful is assistance in finding new employment. But in the last analysis the useful aspects of a free-enterprise program to a free society may outweigh the possibility of guaranteeing continued employment. At the time of this writing (October 1990) the United Auto Workers, in renegotiating contracts, has secured from General Motors contracts that guarantee large fractions of pay in the event of layoffs as follows: ten years' seniority, three years' benefits, eighteen months for other workers; training of other workers and full pay if laid off for more than thirty-six weeks.[19]

Studies of ethics of businessmen[20] clearly indicate that business executives are more sensitive to employee management problems than to other ethical difficulties. There is still room for the invention of mechanisms that may ease some of those problems.

Casey's *Ethics in the Financial Marketplace*[21] discusses the problem of a financial analyst advising a pension trust controlled by company and union representatives. Should she direct investments in new businesses or local government projects in the area, hoping to build jobs for her clients? Or should she concentrate on investing the funds in a manner that seems most secure for maintaining income to the beneficiaries of the trust? After reviewing both aspects, Casey advises the consultant "to chip away at the problem piece by piece" and to try to make good investments along with local needs.

This kind of advice may be needed by corporations wondering what they should do about areas in which their business is declining.

WHAT THE CORPORATION OWES TO MANAGEMENT

Compensation of middle and higher levels of management at times may present great ethical difficulty. The Congress has required publication of salaries and benefits of presidents of major corporations. Lists of salaries of top executives of the "Fortune 500" or other lists of Chief Administrative Officers are widely published. Such executive salaries may be in the $2 million to $20 million range, very far ahead of salaries of other executives in business or government and well ahead of similar salaries in other modern industrial countries such as Japan, France, Britain, and the Scandinavian region. The financial obligation to management is overemphasized in many American corporations; mergers in which management wins a large percentage of ownership are also questionable.

The main argument for these high salaries is the fact that extremely able executives are hard to find and must be paid many million of dollars. There are other ethical arguments for these high salaries. The high salaries are a small percentage of corporate costs. Much of the high salary is absorbed in federal and state income taxes. If the board of directors is responsible for the company, it should determine the salary of the chief manager. The workload of the top executive is heavy, both in public appearances and in the stretching of mind and will to supervise a large enterprise on which rests the welfare of many workers and shareholders.

There are however, ethical arguments against these huge salaries. Sometimes the amount is sharply increased in spite of declining corporate income or obvious mistakes in management. Chrysler President Lee Iacocca forced a $2 million increase in his salary in a year when workers on the assembly line had their pay reduced. Few actions could have more sharply reduced Iacocca's popularity. There is also often concern about whether the highly paid CEO is really the best executive or whether he occupies this key location because of friendships on the board of trustees.

Luckily many major concerns have put a sharp limit on the length of CEO service, usually a sixty-five-year-age maximum. The unhappy tendency of Congress to legislate against fixed retirement procedure seems not to have disturbed some board decisions on CEO retirement ages.

In many major companies, the CEO determines most of the agenda of board meetings, probably a reasonable procedure. Not altogether happily, the CEO has also been the major leader in the selection of new board members. This often gives him a chance to select friends who will not judge the value of his service as sharply as they should, raising again the question of whether the high salary and perquisites are really of value to the corporate community. Readers of *The Barbarians at the Gate*[22] are reminded of the high salary and perquisites of a CEO who was promptly retired when the new board of RJR Nabisco was chosen. The old board was probably wrong in permitting this high pay level and agreeing to $60 million in "golden parachutes" to a man who was probably overvalued.

The corporation does have an obligation to see that management is reasonably well paid and appropriately taught and that there is a good retirement system for managers and other employees. Quality of management is often the most important factor in determining the success of the corporation. Good bosses are important, but the middle managers do the work.

Management itself has a responsibility that is still frequently overlooked. About 90 percent of Fortune 500 companies have codes of ethics. Almost half of all companies are said to have such codes.[23] If such codes are properly administered by management, they can do much to help meet other obligations of the corporation, for example, problems of ethnic groups, community environment, and employee morale. If the corporation wishes to avoid ethnic rivalries, sex controversies, and other unhappy encounters, a code in which all employees are indoctrinated can be of great value. Most of the hundred-odd corporate codes read by this writer do a very good job of forbidding conflicts of interest but are not successful in teaching employees to avoid the problems of internal organization that Professor Robert Jackal describes in *Moral Mazes*.[24]

OBLIGATION TO COMMUNITY

Corporations have responsibilities to the community in which their work is carried out. Like any other citizens they are subject to standards set by the community on the emission of noise, fire, dust, undue heat or gas, ugly buildings, or ugly environment. They must obey planning and zoning laws and ordinances. Forward-looking corporations welcome these obligations and try to perform in accordance with them. A host of other obligations to the environment could be cited. Alyeska's careful construction of the oil pipeline across Alaska from the North Slope to Valdez is one. The huge cost of the badly steered Exxon *Valdez* is an unhappy result of bad management of a corporate public duty. The elaborate bargains of public utility companies to make appropriate arrangements for operating in endangered areas are another example of obligation to the community.

There are other obligations to the community. A large firm should make its contributions of expense and attentiveness to the community's health and appearance. A corporation should share in but wisely try not to be dominant in community leadership for needed health, planning, or aesthetic programs. Clearly these community-helping activities will benefit the corporation not only in the exercise of its civic responsibility but in aid to the welfare and morale of its employees.

A more difficult part of a corporation's responsibility to the community is the touchy subject of crime control. The recent fast development of very high murder rates, including drive-by shootings, puts America's murder rates to the bloody top of modern industrial nations. It is to be assumed that the normal business cooperates with the local police and prosecutor's office, not hesitating to report crimes of its own staff or customers. But larger business associations have a larger obligation to American society related to the crime problem. The Business Roundtable urges support of the schools in teaching important subjects like mathematics, science, and English, yet it never refers to one of the greatest weaknesses of American public schools—their failure to teach ethics, in which American public schools are probably the most backward of modern industrial democracies.[25] How can one expect millions of uneducated new immigrant children from Latin America and Asia to understand the reasons against indiscriminate use of firearms when no one instructs them or other children on their obligation to respect the lives of their fellow citizens? Organized crime is probably more frequent in America than in other industrialized democratic nations (except possibly its motherland, Italy); but we hear little about Corporate Roundtable efforts to help the FBI in its efforts of recent years to suppress organized crime. The writer still remembers the time when a highly esteemed merchant friend told him about a big order for his business from Murder Incorporated but said nothing of efforts to help control that ultracriminal organization. By the way, many estimable political leaders have also shown a willingness to live with organized crime if it helped deliver the votes.

Corporations that resisted environmental responsibilities two decades ago are now recognizing their duties. Tighter laws or threats of tighter laws have led many major responsible corporations to recognize their obligations to the environment. But there are still discouraging examples. The shift of control of Pacific Lumber Company to Charles Hurwitz in 1985[26] led to partial revocation in that business of the "sustained yield" ethic, which is one way for lumber companies to pay constructive attention to the environment. The unhappy result came in part from inadequate state legislation to protect sustained-yield forests and in part from an executive who refused to recognize environmental responsibilities.

A legal maxim that can be traced through Roman law back to the Code of Hammurabi (eighteenth century B.C.) applies to corporations as well as to other legal "persons." It is in the Latin version of the common law: "Sic utere tuo ut alienum non laedas"; in English, "So use your property that it does not damage the property of others." Hammurabi was concerned that farmers on an upland farm should manage the flow of water on their property so that it would not cause damage to the property below. In Roman law the theory applied to permitting a branch to grow over a neighbor's property. In American nineteenth-century law, however, the cultural drive was to help business, which was permitted to invade environments in many ways. Railroads were initially allowed to send out sparks into farm country and woods; farmers were free to cut down trees that had protected neighboring farmers from wind storms; lumber companies cleared broad acreages of protective trees.

As the population of America expands greatly and uses up more of our geographic area and as scientific knowledge of the environment increases, it is inevitable that corporations operating in certain industries will find that their business or manufacturing methods are dangerous to the safety of their workers or their customers or both. In a comparative observation of corporate adaptation in two industries, land development and mining, Joanna Underwood[27] finds that in both industries companies "injure themselves when they do not grasp the very concept of communication." In land development, AMREP in New Mexico abused the environment and consumers at an ultimate cost to the corporation; and General Development in Florida stayed abreast of new environmental knowledge and communicated with government agencies, modified its policies, and provided steady cooperation. In the smelting part of the copper industry, Newmont Mining refused to share data with interested outside groups; Anaconda (then an ARCO subsidiary) worked closely with outsiders and with worker groups and took care of certain problems. Underwood concludes that "the processes of good communications and the complexities of two-way planning may appear expensive but they generally prove rewarding."

PRODUCT LIABILITY

There is considerable literature on damage suits for product liability that have resulted in millions of dollars of judgments against corporations. Steps that corporations should take to reduce product liability are clearly outlined in Irwin Gray's book on that subject.[28] There is some tendency in courts and legislatures to reduce the highest product-liability awards, but there is still a legislative desire to force corporations to use all possible methods to avoid danger to employees or customers or the general public.[29]

There are a number of cases where corporations have been secretive and uncooperative in discussing their role in environmental problems, although their responsibilities are those of citizens and owners in a total community. Such companies are ignoring an important obligation. Professor James E. Post[30] tells how Reserve Mining Company, a subsidiary of Armco and Republic Steel Corporations, was dumping "large amounts of minute amphibole fibers into Lake Superior" (beginning in 1947). These fibers, somewhat similar to amosite asbestos, were damaging "when ingested as well as when inhaled." Academic and government authorities opposed the dumping. A first injunction against the dumping was secured on May 15, 1974. After numerous court cases, a federal court imposed million dollar fines in 1976 on both parent companies.

Post is not sure why Reserve Mining fought so long in the courts to maintain an obvious danger to the health of many people. He suggests that management either turned the problem over to the lawyers to handle or deliberately decided to keep securing the million dollars a month netted from the operation of dumping against the public health. Clearly, Reserve Mining was not meeting its obligation to the community.

An important obligation of moderately sized or bigger corporations is to urge their employees to participate in elections as voters and, if desired, as candidates. The low level of responsibility of many American citizens in government is deplorable; many of our country's international and domestic troubles come in part from corporate employees' ignoring government and its problems. Perhaps it is better for them as business leaders not to be candidates for major political jobs, but business executives should have a friendly stance towards employee contributions to political life.

OBLIGATION TO ETHNIC GROUPS

As many responsibilities to staff are also responsibilities to community, we are devoting this separate section to equal opportunity for both groups.

There is little doubt that corporations (including educational ones) have serious equal-opportunity problems. America's lax immigration laws permit the immigration of millions of poor, often uneducated, often unhealthy Asians and Latin Americans, in addition to the black Americans for whom we have an obvious long-term responsibility. Once these groups are established in the United States it becomes a legal responsibility to offer them equal opportunities in basic health treatment, education, and in matters of employment.

The difficult problem for personnel management of any corporation is how to offer equal opportunity to ethnic groups of low educational (and sometimes low health) standards without lowering the corporation's administrative capacity. A certain amount of poor management can be endured for the sake of better relations between the business and the community where it is located. Recently this writer heard several business personnel directors concluding that if there is a large minority population with low educational achievement in the factory area, there is much to be said for employing an appropriate percentage of that group in jobs at the lowest educational level. The workers' income helps a poor community, there is steady employment at the lower wage level, and the company will be employing less-educated people at unchallenging jobs. A requirement that janitors or truck drivers be high school graduates would be adding some dissatisfied janitors as well as damaging a poorer community. Welfare and subsequent tax burdens on the business could be lowered if jobs are available for poorer people.

There are many other problems of equal opportunity employment. The legal obligation bothersome to most corporations is that of offering jobs or making promotions without any bias against any ethnic group. So long as this requirement is not backed by quotas that disregard quality of appointments, there is an ethically valid obligation here.

OBLIGATION TO DISTRESSED AREAS

A number of successful businesses have made efforts to help poorer areas or minority groups by bringing people into close touch with work of the company. Control Data Corporation established a plant in a black area of Minneapolis, establishing child-care facilities, part-time job opportunities, and an educational system, "Plato," designed for education of employees who had limited education opportunities. Another program has used modern technology to raise health levels on a South Dakota reservation. With other groups, Control Data has established a nonprofit corporation to find means of helping new companies establish themselves.[31]

Another report[32] quotes executives on reasons that their companies would not follow the Control Data example or be concerned with the plight of poorer, less-educated persons in central city areas. Executives have pointed out that very few factories have been built in central city areas, that "corporate social responsibility" is in "disrepute"; that the cost of doing business in large cities is greater than in less populated areas; that "in states like New York and Ohio, state and local taxes and labor policies are an additional burden"; that "the helpful thing the Federal Government can do for the cities is to avoid actions that interfere with their financial health and impede their natural rejuvenation."

Despite these pessimistic corporate reactions, there has in the last decade been a considerable rejuvenation of downtown office building areas; some of it motivated by federal grants but some built by corporations with partly philanthropic motives. The question for us to face is whether or not corporations should be obligated to help a central city area by rebuilding or with training programs to help uneducated children or workers.

In the four decades since the end of World War II, the majority of free, educated citizens seem to have concluded that a basically free-market system helps more people toward a better life than does a government-controlled price system. Russia's shift to a free market is being followed by most of the former satellite countries; leading European, American, and Asian countries have been encouraging their businesses to venture boldly in free markets. The thought of a government encouraging its corporations to engage in expensive ventures like the Control Data projects seems in some ways counter to our recent recognition of free markets.

However, our postwar society is not lowering its architectural, housing, or health standards for people. If there are things that business can do in cooperation with governments to spend a fraction of their incomes on helping an unfortunate inner-city group improve themselves or a city improve its attractiveness, it is, if not an obligation, at least a charitable act to be encouraged.

OBLIGATION TO STAFF AND CUSTOMER SAFETY

Corporations are "persons" under both federal and state law and are entitled to the privileges guaranteed to "persons" by the Fifth and Fourteenth Amendments to the Constitution and the laws enacted under those amendments and corresponding state constitutional provisions. They are also expected to meet the legal obligations of persons. How a corporation can be punished for personal criminal actions like murder may be subject to some question, but there is no doubt that corporations and their officers may be fined or imprisoned for violation of federal or state statutes. The Ford Motor Company was charged heavily in a damage suit but unsuccessfully prosecuted for murder when two passengers were killed in an accident. Their auto had been manufactured ten years earlier by Ford under a standard of gas tank location known by some Ford executives to be not the safest but the general practice of the industry at the time of manufacture. Executives of a small Chicago factory were convicted and punished for maintaining very unhealthy work conditions.

There can be little doubt that corporations have a responsibility to the community to maintain their work operations in a fashion that is safe for employees and in accordance with law. Both the federal occupational, safety, and health law and corresponding state and local regulations are not challenged because each corporation owes that duty to the community.

Some corporations have led in safety contests, but others have failed dismally.

It is surprising to learn how often corporate management has disregarded the health and safety of employees. The fault was not deliberate intent in any case, but a failure of corporate management to check adequately into employee safety problems. Several railroads failed to adopt the Westinghouse airbrake in the 1880s until Congress forced them to do so, preventing further deaths among a large number of switchmen.[33] Rohm and Haas failed to check carefully into the experience of other firms manufacturing Bis-chloromethyl ether (BCME), permitting the deaths of fifty or sixty employees.[34] The American Apparel Manufacturer's Association (and for a time the Consumer Product Safety Commission) defended the manufacture of children's sleeping apparel using Tris, a chemical derived from World War II chemical warfare studies, until the National Cancer Institute showed that Tris was a carcinogen.[35] Many of the asbestos problems of Mansville and other asbestos firms could have been prevented if the companies or the Public Health Service had checked carefully into a report to the British Parliament in the 1920s.[36]

It is a clear obligation of a corporation to check thoroughly into possible bad effects of any manufacturing process or product on the health of staff or customers. That obligation is more important than making a profit or survival of the company.

OBLIGATION TO RESEARCH AND DEVELOPMENT

Many, perhaps most, large corporations need to conduct active research and development programs. If company A fails to do so, competitive Companies B and C will do it and will make substantial inroads on Company A's business. Even in a mass operation like retailing, there are needs for new methods of packaging, new store arrangements, new ways of training workers, and new methods of display and advertising of sales items. In manufacturing or transportation or public utilities, research could be even more expensive but also could be of even larger importance to continued sales.

Corporations in large-scale finance or major production industries could easily add that research is a patriotic responsibility for them. If America is to continue to operate commercially in the world, its major companies must always be preparing the industrial background for competition.

OBLIGATION TO CITIZENS OF OTHER COUNTRIES

In several instances, American corporations forbidden by law or public health regulation from selling certain drugs or foodstuffs in this country have continued to sell the product abroad. In 1969 the Food and Drug

Administration banned the sale of cyclamates in the United States. Over the next sixteen months, Libby, McNeill, and Libby sold "300,000 cases of cyclamate-sweetened fruit to customers in West Germany, Spain, and elsewhere."[37]

After considerable evidence had shown that the sale of infant formulas to mothers in undeveloped countries was a very real danger to the lives of their infants, companies from several modern countries continued to sell their formulas. The Swiss firm, Nestle, was subjected to a worldwide boycott on this account. Nestle finally dropped the objectionable sales process after the World Health Organization secured an International Code of Marketing of Breastmilk Substitutes. An American firm, Bristol Meyers, was selling baby-food products after their undesirability was generally acknowledged.[38]

These undesirable food or drug products have usually been sold to Third World countries, where the product could legally be sold. But if the product or process is unsalable in the United States, it is unethical for an American corporation to sell it abroad. The Judaic-Christian tradition of loving thy neighbor as thyself and the Kantian maxim of acting as if your actions were subject to universal law both argue against selling an undesirable product to ignorant people.

OBLIGATION OF CORPORATIONS TO EDUCATION

In recent years a number of corporations, prodded in part by the Business Roundtable, have decided to help and persuade poor children to continue their education. According to a recent *Fortune* article,[39] Ashland Oil sends high school students to college for a day in Kentucky and West Virginia (in areas of many potential dropouts).

Firestone endorses a college-bound program for forty poor children a year. The program includes enrichment programs from sixth grade on and payment of university tuition.

A Cleveland corporate program provides counselors to help children through the maze of entering college. New York City, Boston, Miami, and Baltimore have similar programs.

IBM, Exxon, Coca-Cola, RJR Nabisco, and Citicorp have "mounted a virtual crusade to help save the public schools." As one means of helping the schools these big corporations, mostly directed from the top, are urging schools, perhaps a bit illogically, to push authority down to the teacher.

Coca-Cola has developed "mentors," employees who will encourage students in poor minority areas to go further in school. The *Fortune* article also describes a school for the children of an American Banker's Insurance group in Miami; the firm pays for the whole school, but it gives children much more time to be with their parents.

The problem of dropouts from minority groups in central city areas very much needs genuine educational help and prodding, and we should all applaud these corporate endeavors, both for the financial help and for pushing administrative decentralization. Business's need for better-educated high school children justifies this charity both for its public purpose and its business usefulness. It need not exist everywhere. Many suburban cities and wealthy urban areas can afford to and do give a good education. But the idea of special corporate help on this important issue to poverty-stricken areas can easily be viewed as an obligation of the corporation in a particular area. In wealthier areas corporations may find firm opposition from teachers' unions or political groups to suggestions about decentralizing authority in the schools; if so, the obligation disappears. In other areas it may be unwise for a corporation to spend money on public education if the company itself is in serious financial trouble.

OBLIGATION WHEN CORPORATE INCOME DROPS

A successful company should recognize and fulfill most of the obligations discussed in this chapter. However, many companies do not have enough stable income to meet each obligation every year. There are also questions as to how much should be allocated to each of these obligations. Proper appraisal of which expenditures should be reduced or eliminated in the event of substantial reductions in corporate income is important; with the ups and downs of business conditions, a significant percentage of American business has to adapt itself to drops of 20 or 30 percent in income.

Substantial reductions of income almost inevitably result in sharp cuts in purchases and sometimes in employment. In the later nineteenth century the reaction of railroad and steel companies was to cut wages. The future philanthropist Andrew Carnegie led the way. Today newer or less-productive employees are dropped, an action that seems cruel but is partly cushioned by unemployment insurance and whatever dismissal pay the company can afford. The cut may be required by economic circumstances; it may be better for the economy of the community to have a smaller company than to risk losing the entire company. Many people would advise cutting dividends before cutting wages; however, cutting dividends means damage to shareholders and may reduce the possibility of needed new financing.

If one or more factories are closed, as they often are in many large companies, special attention should be paid to discharged workers who live in a town with only one major employer. There may be valid reasons for closing an old factory in a one-industry town, but the company then has a substantial obligation to the discharged workers and perhaps to the town.

Management may be cut back, one hopes with appropriate severance or retirement pay. The millions of dollars in "golden horseshoes" given to executives retired by a forced merger are often unduly liberal rewards, as are some of the very high salaries discussed in the section on obligations to management.

The responsibility to employ ethnic groups should not lead to special retirement benefits for ethnic groups. Those who chose to come to America for its high wage levels should accept, like other Americans, the hazards of employment. But if they are a large group in the area, and work continues, some ethnics should be employed.

A company's obligation to community environment may be lowered by partial withdrawal from a community, but it may not necessarily continue after a total withdrawal. Whenever a company moves from New York City, some officials charge it with disloyalty or lack of patriotism. New York City officials should consider that the company may be fulfilling a greater responsibility to employees who want to live in a less-expensive, less-crowded place; also, the company may fulfill its responsibility to the national economy better by locating its headquarters in a less-expensive and healthier spot. Is there really a patriotic obligation to keep people living in a very expensive city that has a fairly steady record of political corruption adding to costs of living?

The export of unhealthy products to foreign countries should not be developed or continued because of a company's lessened income. It remains an immoral activity, as noted above.

Other comparisons require thought. Although President Iacocca's $2.5 million paid in a year in which employee wages were cut, seems wrong, it would be unwise to cut salaries of executives who are performing effectively on their jobs at reasonable income levels.

Some companies have bravely continued contributions to Community Chests or important community planning activities in times of economic recession; their example is commendable but should not be followed if those costs pose a financial threat to the future of the company, upon which many workers are dependent.

Obligations that should not be eliminated include those activities essential to company reputation, activities essential to financial solvency, and maintenance of adequate safety standards for employees and customers.

NOTES

1. Shaw Livermore, *Early American Land Companies* (New York: Octagon Books, 1968).

2. Seymour Lipset and William Schneider, *The Confidence Gap* (Baltimore: Johns Hopkins University Press, 1987).

3. Milton Friedman, *Capitalism and Freedom* (Chicago: University of Chicago Press, 1962), p. 133.

4. James Willard Hurst, *Law and Social Order in the United States* (Ithaca, N.Y.: Cornell University Press, 1977), p. 214.

5. Ibid., p. 243.

6. James Willard Hurst, *The Legitimacy of the Business Corporation* (Charlottesville: University Press of Virginia, 1970), p. 79.

7. Louis Loss and Edward M. Cowett, *Blue Sky Law* (Boston: Little Brown and Co., 1958).

8. Joel Seligman, *The Transformation of Wall Street* (Boston: Houghton Mifflin, 1982).

9. John Brooks, *The Takeover Game* (New York: Twentieth Century Fund, 1978), pp. 256–88.

10. John L. Casey, *Ethics in the Financial Marketplace* (New York: Scudder, Stevens, and Clark, 1988), chap. 13.

11. Jonathan Kwitny, *Vicious Circles* (New York: W. W. Norton, 1979).

12. Jack Newfield and Wayne Barrett, *City for Sale* (New York: Harper and Row, 1988).

13. Philip Schrag, *Counsel for the Deceived* (New York: Pantheon Books, 1972).

14. Sissela Bok, *Lying* (New York: Vintage Books, 1978), chaps. 1, 2.

15. Richard A. Posner, "Truth in Advertising," in *Advertising and Society*, ed. Yale Brozen (New York: New York University Press, 1974), p. 120.

16. Michael E. Porter, "Optimal Advertising: An Intra-Industry Approach," in *Issues in Advertising*, ed. David G. Tarek (Washington, D.C.: American Institute for Public Policy Research, 1978).

17. Robert Pitofsky, "Changing Focus in the Regulation of Advertising," in *Advertising and Society*, ed. Yale Brozen (New York: New York University Press, 1974), p. 131.

18. Boris Emmet and John E. Jeuck, *Catalogues and Counters* (Chicago: University of Chicago Press, 1990), pp. 67–104.

19. *Business Week*, October 1, 1990.

20. Raymond Baumhart, S.J., *Ethics in Business* (New York: Holt, Rinehart, Winston, 1968), pp. 29–33.

21. Casey, *Ethics in the Financial Marketplace*, chap. 11.

22. Bryan Burrough and John Helyar, *The Barbarians at the Gate* (New York: Harper and Row, 1990).

23. Patrick E. Murphy, "Implementing Business Ethics," in *Journal of Business Ethics* (1988), pp. 907–13.

24. Robert Jackal, *Moral Mazes* (New York: Oxford University Press, 1988).

25. George C. S. Benson and Thomas S. Engeman, *Amoral America* (Durham, N.C.: Carolina Academic Press, 1982).

26. *Los Angeles Times*, August 19, 1990.

27. Joanna Underwood, "Land Development and Working Conditions, and The Copper Industry," in Thornton Bradshaw and David Vogel, *Corporations and Their Critics* (New York: McGraw-Hill, 1981), pp. 171–85.

28. Irwin Gray et al., *Product Liability* (New York: Amacom, American Management Association, 1975).

29. "Cockroaches in Courts," *Forbes*, October 1, 1988, p. 248.

30. James E. Post, *Corporate Behavior and Social Change* (Reston, Va.: Reston Publishing Co., 1978), pp. 168–86.

31. William C. Morris, "Business Opportunities in Addressing Societal Problems," in Thornton Bradshaw and David Vogel, *Corporations and Their Critics* (New York: McGraw-Hill, 1981).

32. Milton Moskarty, "Affirmative Action and the Urban Crises," in Thornton Bradshaw and David Vogel, *Corporations and Their Critics* (New York: McGraw-Hill, 1981), pp. 93–101.

33. Charles Frances Adams, Jr., *Notes on Railroad Accidents* (New York: Putnam's Sons, 1979); Thomas C. Cochran, *Railroad Leaders 1845–1890* (Cambridge, Mass.: Harvard University Press, 1955), pp. 142–45, 206.

34. Willard Randal and Stephen D. Solomon, *Building 8* (Boston: Little, Brown and Co., 1975).

35. Robert H. Doyle and staff of the Environmental Defense Fund (New York: Vantage Books, Random House, 1980), pp. 193–201.

36. Paul Brodeur, *Outrageous Misconduct* (New York: Pantheon Books, 1985), pp. 13–17.

37. Robert L. Heilbroner, ed., *In the Name of Profit* (Garden City, N.Y.: Doubleday and Company, 1972), p. 224.

38. Mark Green, ed., *The Business Reader* (New York: Pilgrim Press, 1983), 353–61.

39. "Education," *Fortune*, Spring 1990.

9

Corporate Social Responsibility

Douglas J. Den Uyl

No good sensible working bee listens to the advice of a bedbug on the subject of business.
—Elbert Hubbard, *The Book of Business*, 1913.

Corporations are polluting our environment, defrauding stockholders, discriminating against women and minorities, arbitrarily casting thousands into unemployment, producing unsafe products, and concerned about nothing other than the "bottom line." Sound familiar? It is a litany we have lived with now for decades. In the past, these accusations were debated primarily by social scientists. Today a new player has entered the game, the ethician. Business ethics has taken on increased importance, and business schools receive large sums of money to instruct students in ethics. Moreover, philosophers are finding new avenues of employment as consultants, textbook writers, and purveyors of the virtues of "applied ethics." In light of the importance now attached to ethics, we shall outline here the most general and basic (and oldest) of the issues in business ethics: corporate social responsibility.

WHAT IS A CORPORATION?

It may seem strange, but the debate over what corporations have as their responsibilities begins with the question, "What is a corporation?" It would seem that everyone knows the answer to that question, yet such is not the case. There are two main and conflicting theories on this issue, and the theory one chooses may have a strong influence on what one would be likely to say about corporate social responsibility (CSR).

The first theory usually goes under the heading of the "legal creator" theory. The person most often associated with this theory is Ralph Nader. The main idea behind the theory is that corporations are creatures of the state—hence the name. This theory is quite common, even commonsensical. Indeed, most business students and businesspersons seem to believe it. The reason the theory fits so well with common sense is that everyone knows that corporations are fictitious legal persons. It seems only a short step from that to saying they are therefore created by the state. Of course, logically it does not follow that, from the premise that corporations are fictious legal persons, we must conclude that they are creatures of the state (as we shall see). But the connection is so natural that it goes some distance toward explaining the popularity of the theory.

The legal creator theory defends its interpretation by referring to the fact that corporations must obtain a corporate charter. Without a corporate charter, so the argument goes, a corporation would not exist. Corporate charters are granted by the state. Therefore, corporations are created by the state. The second main line of defense has to do with limited liability. Corporations possess limited liability in both torts and credit. Relative to other businesses, limited liability is a special privilege granted to corporations by the state. Because corporations would not have this privilege without the state, the state creates corporations; otherwise, these business entities would be of some other form.

The alternative theory about the basic nature of corporations is known as the "legal recognition theory." Here corporations are not creatures of the state, but rather arise and exist independently of the state. All the state does is to give legal recognition to what already exists. Robert Hessen[1] offers a useful analogy on how a cooperative arrangement that has legal status can be meaningfully said to exist prior to the conferral of that legal status. That analogy is marriage. The state may recognize and protect what already exists between two people, but it does not create that relationship in the first place. The same could be said for corporations. They *apply* for legal status; the state does not seek them out or create them initially. In addition, articles of incorporation simply record certain features of corporations (name, purpose, intended duration, etc.) and do not constitute government authorization. Finally, nothing in the charter mandates or obligates a corporation to serve public rather than private interests.

Limited liability would appear to be a more troublesome objection for the legal recognition theory to overcome. However, limited liability for debts is not a special privilege because it isn't guaranteed: Creditors can refuse credit. With respect to torts, limited liability is not necessarily granted to all shareholders: It depends on how active they are in management. The state merely recognizes degrees of involvement, not special privileges. In any case, the assets of most corporations exceed the worth of any shareholder. It's not at all clear that either creditors or victims of torts would be better off if stockholders were all held personally liable.

The main point, though, is that there is nothing corporations do that cannot be found or contracted for in the existing marketplace. It is just that the corporate form combines in one efficient package elements that may exist separately elsewhere.

In some respects, however, the details of the liability question sidetrack us from our main concern.[2] For as far as corporate social responsibility is concerned, the essential issue is whether one views corporations as fundamentally public institutions or as fundamentally private ones. This question, of course, is quite different from the question of whether corporations *ought* to be made public or regulated more by public institutions. It is worth noting that critics of corporations often want to adopt the legal creator theory. Yet if corporations were creatures of the state or fundamentally public institutions and still behaved so badly, critics ought to pause before giving the state even more responsibility over them. But the reason for the attachment to the legal creator theory has little to do with logic. If corporations are creatures of the state, then the moral case for state control is much easier to make. Let us now turn to the issue of CSR directly.

TWO AND ONE-HALF THEORIES OF CORPORATE SOCIAL RESPONSIBILITY

Many labels are attached to theories of corporate social responsibility. These include attempts to define CSR in terms of good citizenship; service to constituencies; obligations to owners, labor, society, or God; the forces of tradition, the market, or world history and the like. Here, however, we are concerned with fundamentals; and from that perspective there are only two basic ethical outlooks. There is also another "half" theory, which we have labeled elsewhere a "functionalist" approach.[3] This approach tries to skirt the ethical question entirely. That is one reason we have labeled it a "half" theory. The other reason is that it does not succeed in avoiding the ethical question. Its experiential or descriptive method goes only "half" the way and needs a value or normative orientation. We shall have a little more to say about this approach later, but we shall not dwell on it. Our main focus will be upon our two approaches: the "individual agreement" theory and the "social permission" theory.

Social Permission Theory

The social permission theory begins with a perspective on business and society best expressed in these words by Keith Davis: "The fundamental assumption of this model is that society has entrusted to business large amounts of society's resources to accomplish its mission, and business is expected to manage these resources as a wise trustee for society."[4] The key elements in this view are that resources belong to society and that corporations exist or are permitted to act only at the behest of society. In a sense, then, society gives businesses permission to operate, and society does so only if business will act in society's interest. CSR is generated, therefore, by something like the following argument:

1. A trustee relationship is one in which one party is obligated to represent the interests of another because the first party has agreed to do so or has been entrusted to do so by another party with the authority to make such an arrangement.

2. Ownership is essentially a trustee relationship between the state and individuals or corporations.

3. As trustees of society's resources, corporations must behave in ways that promote the general welfare (i.e., the interests of society).

4. "Social responsibility" expresses a course of conduct that promotes the general welfare.

5. Therefore, corporations are obligated to act in socially responsible ways.

From this argument it is easy to see why many social permission theorists would be attracted to the legal creator theory. In both cases, corporations are represented as fundamentally public institutions.

Other implications flow from this argument as well. As Thomas Donaldson has suggested, the view implies that there is a social good different from and superior to the goods pursued or agreed upon by individual members of society. In addition, the plans, purposes, and interests of individual members of society can be subordinated to the good of society as a whole.[5] In practice, the state is likely to play an active role in monitoring or regulating business. This is because "society" has no mouthpiece but the state. It does not follow, however, that social permission theorists are necessarily in favor of the way in which the state is now constituted or behaves. It is also logically possible for the state to be "active" by adopting a laissez-faire attitude, provided it regards such a posture as promoting the general welfare. Some might even interpret periods of American history along these lines. Nevertheless, the *structural* subordination of private to public, individual to state, suggests an inevitable departure from laissez-faire as well as the right for the state to be more directly regulatory. The theory is essentially socialistic, without necessarily requiring the national ownership of the means of production.

Social permission theorists are also often fond of speaking in terms of the "social contract" between business and society. Writers such as Donaldson, Anshen, and Norman Bowie all use this language.[6] It is a language familiar to businesspeople because contracts are part of their daily lives and a means by which they understand obligations. In addition, contract language fits neatly with the trustee relationship mentioned in the argument. Yet it is not necessary that this language be employed, because such language is at best a metaphor. Obviously, "business" and "society" made no formalized contract, because no such entities exist. But contract language has the advantage of suggesting that business is in basic agreement with what the social permission theorists are demanding. They appear, then, simply to be calling for business to live up to that agreement. The strategic benefits of this language are evident.

It is clear from the argument that the social permission theory is a *moral* theory. It talks in terms of obligations, of responsibility, and of welfare. As it turns out, this moral theory is also the one dominant in business ethics today—the approach from which the vast majority of articles, texts, and advice are offered. It is not, as we have indicated, the only approach. It is to the other minority opinion we now turn.

Individual Agreement Theory

The individual agreement theory is rooted in an argument given by the well-known economist Milton Friedman almost three decades ago in his book *Capitalism and Freedom*. The appropriate passages from that book, or similar renditions of the argument Friedman gives elsewhere,[7] are often reprinted in business ethics texts. One seldom sees the argument surrounded by more recent variations on its theme, as one finds with the social permission theory.[8] The argument is usually castigated as the now-antiquated traditionalist view, which we can brush aside for more modern approaches. Be that as it may, the argument hangs on as a fundamental alternative to the social permission theory.

The argument is founded upon the idea that the sanctity of the contract is the essence of the capitalist system. Here "contract" refers to agreements between individuals, either in the form of explicit agreements or in terms of agency relationships that may exist between them. On one reading[9] of the argument, if we want to maintain a capitalist economic system then the sanctity of the contract must remain inviolable (deception and fraud violate that sanctity). Of course, we may not want a capitalist system any longer. A stronger reading is to say that there is no morally legitimate reason for violating contractual relationships for the sake of some other social good. Either way, the argument then cashes out as follows:

1. Corporate managers are fiduciaries of the corporate owners (stockholders) (given legal relationship).

2. Corporate owners have only one interest and reason for hiring managers—to maximize profits.

3. Therefore, corporate managers would violate their fiduciary trust by engaging in actions that are unrelated to (or that consciously minimize) profit maximization.

The above argument might be called the *profit maximization argument*. Related to this argument is the *social responsibility argument*, which may be summarized as follows:

1. Acts of corporate charity ("social responsibility") lessen the amount of profits the firm and/or owners receive. (By definition, or there's no point to CSR.)
2. If corporate managers act to lessen profits (as in the preceding statement), they violate their contractual responsibilities to owners.
3. A call for managers to be "socially responsible" is a call for them to violate their contractual obligations.
4. Thus managers should not direct their firms into "socially responsible" activities.

Although Milton Friedman may not be noted for his treatises in moral philosophy, notice that this is a strictly moral argument. It makes no appeal to the economic advantages of the arrangement he calls for, and it uses the language of "trust" and "responsible agency." Notice also that the argument refers to individuals rather than to macro categories such as "business" and "society." The argument is therefore a natural fit for the legal recognition theory that begins with the notion that corporations grow out of individual agreements.

The individual agreement theory is the one we believe to be the correct approach to CSR. But we shall examine it, as well as the social permission theory, after a brief look at our "half" theory.

The Amoralist Approach

It must be admitted that moral argumentation can get messy and even cause conflict. It is tempting to try to avoid it entirely and present a value-free or value-neutral argument for some version of CSR. After all, why bother with controversial moral positions when we can present a position in terms of "objective" facts? There have indeed been many attempts to define CSR in terms that do not make moral judgments. Proponents of these efforts range from those who are against corporations engaging in CSR to those who argue for a strong version of it. The most common sort of approach is to speak of changing social conditions, mores, climates of opinion, financial realities, or the like as requiring a certain posture on CSR. Under this vision we are all caught up in the forces of history and are either in or out of step with the times.

An excellent example of this sort of argument is the famous "Iron Law of Responsibility" offered by Keith Davis and Robert Blomstrom. The "Iron Law" goes like this: "In the long run, those who do not use power in a manner which society considers responsible will tend to lose it."[10] Notice the ineluctability of this so-called law. We need not worry about the morality of CSR because the forces of social opinion will guarantee that "responsible" behavior will win out in the long run. Of course, what "responsible" behavior means is unclear, but presumably it matches Davis and Blomstrom's own prescription for corporate behavior. The rhetorical and strategic advantages of this "law" are not to be denied. If Davis and Blomstrom can convince people they have an insight into the forces of history or social opinion such that they are accurately representing what responsible behavior will be, then they can claim that anyone who disagrees with them is simply "out of step" and won't survive to remain a nuisance anyway. Thus they can avoid all the messy complications of a moral stance while still adhering to a strong version of the social permission perspective on CSR.[11]

The problem, of course, is that social opinion may not reflect the version of CSR outlined by Davis and Blomstrom. If it does not, then they must either admit that they were wrong about what CSR means and thus that it is perfectly responsible to act in ways contrary to what they recommend or admit that businesses *ought* to behave in a certain way. The latter alternative takes them out of the amoralist camp and gives them a moral posture. The former leaves them with an amoral argument but at the cost of making their views irrelevant. For why should we care what Davis and Blomstrom have to say about responsibility, if we'll find out soon enough anyway?

Even if society were to move along the exact lines suggested by Davis and Blomstrom's vision of responsibility, that would not necessarily show they had predicted correctly. It might only show that people in positions of power share their value structure and move (coerce?) society in the desired direction. For the truth is that, however much society may be the unintended result of intended actions or the confluence of unanticipated consequences, human choice still moves the world. If that is true, the way things turn out can be changed, which means at least that they can be evaluated as good or bad, right or wrong. If the term "responsibility" has any content at all, it is not only subject to, but requires, normative evaluation. Otherwise, the "Iron Law" says no more than "whatever will be, will be."

In a related vein, a well-known essay by Theodore Levitt attempts to avoid the moral form of argument by claiming that it is not the function of business to engage in social welfare activities, that that function belongs to government. Levitt's own argument has some twists and complications that go beyond this claim,[12] but it is common enough to hear arguments against CSR that hold it is not the function of business to engage in such activities. Saying it is not the function of business to concern itself with social issues is a nonmoral way of combating those who want more CSR. Unfortunately, this argument turns against itself. For if the government is in charge of social welfare and if business is but a part of society, then the government has every right to tell business what role it must play in the

promotion of that welfare. Instead of a separation between business and
the state, a merger seems more probable.

But even if one were to claim that no institution is responsible for the
overall welfare of society, it would not help. For there is no reason that
the "function" of business cannot change. Indeed, that is precisely the
point of those advocating strong forms of CSR: Business must or ought to
change what it has traditionally seen as its function. One cannot simply
assert that business has a certain function without begging the whole question of CSR. The better approach would be to claim that business should
not engage in CSR and make one's stand a moral one. That leads us back
to where we need to be.

BACK TO ETHICS

As stated above, the individual agreement theory is the superior of the
two positions.[13] For one thing, the individual agreement theory speaks in
terms of real individuals having obligations to other individuals based upon
some agreement they themselves have made. There is little vague and
abstract talk about "society" or "business" or "society's resources," nor
are there a priori and indefinite obligations to "manage society's resources
wisely." The obligations in the individual agreement theory are as clear
and certain as the actual contracts individuals make or the law that governs
them. Although it would be unfair to cast all social permission theorists
as necessarily being economic socialists, their theory is at least drawn to
massive government involvement by the fact that the state is the only
mechanism that is likely to give meaning to what is in "society's" interest.
In this respect, it is correct to say that the social permission theory is at
odds with the tradition of American business in a way that the individual
agreement theory is not, for that tradition is rooted in the values of individual initiative, choice, and private enterprise, not in public policy and
public enterprise.

The "contract" spoken of by the social permission theorists is also no
contract at all. Apart from the point just made that there are no such
entities as "business" and "society" to make the contract, if such entities
did exist, the relationship would still not be contractual. For as "trustees,"
"business" has no independent right to refuse to make the "agreement"
in the first place. As the theory is described by most of its proponents, it
has no bargaining power as to terms either. In its essence, it holds that
business operates by permission, not by right; and we know not only that
permission can be withdrawn, but also that actions must accord with the
wishes of whoever is giving the permission. In essence, corporations are
to act—in the remarkably revealing words of one author—like "good
puppies"[14] towards the self-styled purveyors of social responsibility.

But does it not make sense, as Norman Bowie suggests, to say that those who have the most resources also bear most of the responsibility?[15] Perhaps there is some plausibility in this claim, at least if it means that those with more are in a position to affect more people and therefore need to pay more attention to their conduct. But if a business deals honestly and without fraud and produces a product consumers find valuable, we know of no moral principle that requires that something additional be done. Only if one *assumes* that business has no independent right to exist or to own resources might one be required to claim that there is a moral obligation to do more than to provide the product or service. Of course, envy or the exploitative desire to redistribute might also be motives for saying one's obligations are more extensive than honest dealing, but then those are not supposed to be *reputable* moral motives.

We should, therefore, adopt the individual agreement perspective. But this perspective has not been without critics or beyond interpretation. Christopher D. Stone, for example, tries to argue against Friedman's view by saying that (1) managers are not agents and (2) stockholders are not owners.[16] This is supposed to suggest that Friedman's position is without foundation and that therefore nothing holds back the adoption of the social permission theory. That claim, of course, does not follow, for there may be other ways to arrive at a conclusion similar to Friedman's. Fortunately, we can ignore that move, for Stone's argument does not work on its own merits.

As evidence that managers are not agents, Stone cites a ruling that concluded that managers are not *mere* agents of the stockholders. This is certainly true if it means that stockholders cannot completely ignore or act contrary to the business interests or survival of the corporation, or if it means that managers do not have any leeway to manage and must conduct plebiscites on every issue. So, yes, managers are not mere agents of the stockholders; but the "law of agency" clearly regards them as fiduciaries of the stockholders and describes their obligations in terms of the financial interests of those owners.

As evidence that stockholders are not really owners of the corporation, Stone points to how little control stockholders have over managers. Now there may be legitimate worries, even within the individual agreement theory, about the relationship between ownership and control and the ethics involved therein. But this would not establish that there is no obligation in the sense described by Friedman. It would at most establish that some are not living up to their obligations. But as Friedman's argument is framed in terms of *financial* interest, the bulk of the concern would have to be over whether managers are serving the financial interests of the stockholders, and not whether they are serving some social interest Stone fancies or even whether they are responding to every wish of the stockholders. In any case, it is much harder to show that managers are not concerned about the financial interests of stockholders, especially since

Friedman's critics often cite an "exclusive" concern with financial matters as what stands in the way of CSR.

Stone, however, notes that even if we grant that managers are fiduciaries of the stockholders, there may still be some latitude for "socially responsible" sorts of activities. It is here that Stone is making a point with possible merit. For one criticism to be made of the traditional Friedmanesque version of the individual agreement theory is its assumption that the meaning of "profit maximization" is clear. Apart from the fact that actions taken to "maximize profits" might differ if one's perspective is short or long run, actions that might at first not look as if they contribute to profits might actually do so. In 1914, Henry Ford's decision to pay his workers $5 a day was thought to be eleemosynary when it in fact contributed significantly to a more productive work force and greater sales and profits. Today it might be less expensive to offer plans that rehabilitate drug users than to fire them. What will or will not contribute to profits is not a matter of a priori speculation but of practical thought and action. The point is that one can be open to such possibilities without jeopardizing one's fiduciary responsibility.

It is important in this connection to realize that we are not reducing morality to a means. It is not our contention that when one discovers a "socially responsible" activity that will generate more profits that one "pretend" to be concerned about morality and take the action. It is simply false to suppose that our only choices are actions taken for the sake of "morality" (defined here as "for its own sake" and "without reference to one's self") alone or actions that reduce everything to some selfish end. First of all, the individual agreement theory holds that the act of pursuing profits *is* an act in accord with a moral obligation and that this obligation is primary. If other moral considerations, ones that do not at first appear directly related to the financial, can be incorporated into the pursuit of the primary obligation, so much the better. A recognition of one's primary responsibility does not preclude a genuine concern for nonfinancial matters; one simply needs to be aware of which moral obligation takes precedence.

We would, however, object to those who would take Friedman's argument to be a license to narrow one's vision to the "bottom line" only, as much as to those who want to reject Friedman's argument altogether. The purpose here is not to breed moral skepticism nor provide a rationalization for those who wish to pay no attention to moral matters. It is instead to suggest that motivations can be legitimately diverse without making one element a means to another. Indeed, we would expect that more often than not the successful and respected businessperson knows how to deal with people as well as numbers and integrates both elements well. That individual sees not an unbridgeable gulf separating morality from profits, but rather their unification. Yet the issue of whether a person is of narrow

or broad vision must still be of secondary importance to the obligation to
pursue profits.

One moral concern, however, overrides all others, including profitability.
In the normal rendition of Friedman's argument, businesses should pursue
profits "without deception or fraud" "within the rules of the game." The
latter phrase is rather vague or self-defeating, for the "rules of the game"
could be such that corporations are to act in ways contrary to what Friedman is recommending. We would suggest that corporations must act in
ways that do not violate individual rights and that the nonviolation of
individual rights is the moral principle that supersedes all others. It is true
that the nature of "individual rights" can be controversial and that space
does not permit us the luxury of developing a theory here.[17] But we do
not need a full-blown explanation of rights to point out that rights set the
conditions under which social interaction will take place and that "individual rights" will include as wide a latitude as possible for the individual
to make his or her own decisions, choices, and contracts. Rights, then, are
what Robert Nozick calls "side constraints" on the goals we pursue. Businesses have the goal of pursuing profits, but they cannot do so by any
means and people cannot contract to violate individual rights (e.g., by
forming "Hit Man, Inc."). These side constraints keep us between the
bounds of legitimacy. Of course, having said all this, it is important to
realize that this obligation to respect individual rights is not unique to
business but shared by all of us, both as individuals and as part of institutions or organizations.

WHO HAS A STAKE IN ALL THIS?

By way of conclusion, we should look at the newest way the social
permission theory is being sold, by speaking in terms of corporations having
obligations to "stakeholders" rather than stockholders. Stakeholders turn
out to be "any identifiable group or individual who can affect or is affected
by organizational performance in terms of its products, policies, and work
processes."[18] Corporations owe their allegiance to "stakeholders" rather
than, as under the "old-fashioned" view, stockholders. But as virtually no
one is excluded by this definition of stakeholder, we obviously have socialism with a vengeance! Of course, to make the definition nontrivial we
must make a distinction between primary stakeholders and others, with
primary stakeholders being those groups needed for the corporation's "survival" (e.g., consumers, labor, management, etc.). But this distinction
really indicates only which groups have favored status. There is no non-
arbitrary basis for discriminating between primary and other sorts of
stakeholders.

The main difference between the stockholder theory and the stakeholder

theory is stated nicely by Anthony F. Buono and Lawrence T. Nichols:
The stockholder approach "assumes that the interactions between business
organizations and the different groups affected by their operations (employees, consumers, suppliers) are most effectively structured as marketplace activities."[19] In one simple sentence we have what we have claimed
all along is the essence of the debate over corporate social responsibility—
the market economy versus a command or government controlled economy. The stockholder approach does indeed presuppose a market economy, and the virtues of that system are now being demonstrated daily as
we uncover more and more about what has gone on behind the Iron
Curtain. But this essay is about ethics and related matters. What are the
reasons for adopting the stakeholder model rather than the market economy and its corresponding emphasis upon stockholders? Buono and Nichols offer four reasons:

1. The stockholder model has failed to deal adequately with contemporary societal
   problems and the true complexities of economic transactions and interactions.
2. It is in the long-term interest of business to take a broader view of its responsibilities. If business does not become accountable for its actions on its own,
   growing stakeholder pressures will ensure government-imposed accountability.
3. Understanding and satisfying the needs of stakeholders is important to the well-
   being of the firm. . . . In today's highly competitive economic and social environment, no important stakeholder can be ignored.
4. The stakeholder model is in keeping with our notions of fairness. Employees,
   consumers, communities, and the like are not just instruments for enriching
   stockholders.[20]

How good are these reasons? The first one leaves it unclear what the
supposed failures of businesses are supposed to be. But in any case, either
the view is false or begs the question. It is false if it claims that businesses
do not respond to their environments (businesses don't survive if they're
out of touch with their environment), or if it claims that the stockholder
view was ever supposed to be the complete theory of economic or social
relations of the firm. The first reason begs the question if it implies that
the stockholder view does not easily accommodate a robust engagement
in social charity. Of course it does not, and that is precisely what is at
issue. The second reason is either a restatement of the "Iron Law" or a
threat. It can be ignored. The third reason supposes that the stockholder
model is less interested in competitiveness and survival in "today's" world.
This is obviously false. If businesses are having trouble being competitive,
it is unlikely that it is because of their attachment to the stockholder view;
if anything, the distraction of the flurry of obligations and regulations
businesses are said to have or are burdened with would seem a more likely
candidate. The fourth reason is really the only ethical reason given. But

it trades on there being something called "our" sense of fairness. If our sense of fairness is supposed to look like the social permission theory, then if this chapter has done nothing else it should indicate there is no comfortable uniformity about that. In any case, the stockholder view doesn't transform people into "instruments." What it says is that the primary obligation is the pursuit of profits in an open and free market. People can choose to deal with the corporation or not, and that choice is what indicates that market transactions are *human* endeavors, rather than relations among instruments.

In short, there are no compelling reasons to adopt the stakeholder view and some good reasons not to. Indeed, the groups supposedly qualifying as stakeholders really have no stake in corporations. Apart from any problems associated with thinking in terms of collective entities like "consumers" or "suppliers," the theory confuses "being affected by" with "having an interest in," with "having a stake in." Virtually anyone could be "affected" by a corporation, and large numbers of people could have little or no connection with the corporation but still have an "interest" in it—indeed, even feel strongly about what it does. But only those people have a stake in something who have also invested in it. Other than stockholders and creditors, none of the groups mentioned as "stakeholders" have any investments in corporations, with the possible exception of employees. Why does investment make all the difference? Because without putting some part of oneself into something, one is merely the passive recipient of a benefit or harm, not an active participant. This is why living together calls for less commitment than marriage, why rental property is less well maintained than personal property, why people would rather win the championship as a player than a bench warmer. True, lots of people can be affected by corporate actions both positively and negatively, and we hope to minimize any negative externalities that may result from corporate activities. What should worry us above all else, however, is a society that is confused about the difference between having a stake in something and being affected by it. That is the kind of society that cannot distinguish the moral from the beneficial, leadership from conformity, tyranny from liberty.

NOTES

1. See Robert Hessen, *In Defense of the Corporation* (Stanford: Hoover Institution Press, 1979) for the best and most complete defense of the legal recognition theory.

2. Another side issue often discussed in this connection is the issue of whether corporations are themselves persons or should be regarded as such rather than as collections of individuals. One can easily find the argument that they are persons in Peter French, "Corporate Moral Agency," in the textbook *Business Ethics*, ed.

W. Michael Hoffman and Jennifer Mills Moore (New York: McGraw-Hill, 1990), pp. 194–202. A rebuttal to this view of things is given in the same text in the article by John R. Danley ("Corporate Moral Agency: The Case for Anthropological Bigotry," pp. 202–8). To discuss this question would take us too far afield, but in some respects it doesn't make much difference anyway. For in our view, the obligation to respect individual rights is primary, and whether corporations are individuals or not does not affect that obligation.

3. This is the way we described it in *The New Crusaders: The Corporate Social Responsibility Debate* (Bowling Green, Ohio: Social Philosophy and Policy Center, Bowling Green State University, 1984), chaps. 2–3. Much of the material used here is based on what is said in that book.

4. Originally from "Five Propositions for Social Responsibility," *Business Horizons*, 18, 3 (June 1975): 19–24; but this article, or portions of it, is reprinted in virtually every business ethics text published.

5. Thomas Donaldson, *Corporations and Morality* (Englewood Cliffs, N.J.: Prentice-Hall, 1982), p. 55.

6. See ibid., pp. 36–54, for Donaldson; see also *Ethical Theory and Business*, ed. Norman Bowie and Tom L. Beauchamp (Englewood Cliffs, N.J.: Prentice-Hall, Inc., 1979), pp. 97–105, for Anshen's and Bowie's uses.

7. An equally well-known source is a *New York Times Magazine* article of September 13, 1970, reprinted in W. Michael Hoffman and Jennifer Mills Moore, eds., *Business Ethics* (New York: McGraw-Hill, 1990), pp. 153–57.

8. An exception is the essay on CSR by Fred D. Miller and John Ahrens found in *Commerce and Morality*, ed. Tibor Machan (Totowa, N.J.: Rowman and Littlefield, 1988).

9. I am unclear as to which reading most accurately represents Friedman's view. It may be that both are equally good.

10. Keith Davis and Robert L. Blomstrom, *Business and Society: Environment and Responsibility* (New York: McGraw-Hill, 1975), p. 50.

11. Actually, as we have seen above, Davis's own work is a mixture of moral and amoral arguments.

12. For a more detailed critique of Levitt's argument see Den Uyl, *The New Crusaders*, pp. 10–12.

13. A somewhat more extensive critique of the social permission theory can be found in Den Uyl, *The New Crusaders*, pp. 13–19.

14. Laura Nash, "Ethics without the Sermon," *Harvard Business Review* 59 (1981): 89. See my letter to the editor in response in the following issue.

15. Norman Bowie, "Changing the Rules," in Tom L. Beauchamp and Norman Bowie, eds., *Ethical Theory and Business* (Englewood Cliffs, N.J.: Prentice-Hall, Inc., 1979), pp. 103ff.

16. Christopher D. Stone, "Why Shouldn't Corporations Be Socially Responsible?" in W. Michael Hoffman and Jennifer Mills Moore, eds., *Business Ethics* (New York: McGraw-Hill, 1990), pp. 157–61.

17. If interested in our own view, see Douglas Rasmussen and Douglas J. Den Uyl, *Liberty and Nature: An Aristotelian Defense of Liberal Order* (La Salle, Ill.: Open Court, 1991), chap. 3.

18. Anthony F. Buono and Lawrence T. Nichols, "Stockholder and Stakeholder Interpretations of Business's Social Role," in W. Michael Hoffman and Jennifer Mills Moore, eds., *Business Ethics* (New York: McGraw-Hill, 1990), p. 171.

19. Ibid.

20. Ibid., pp. 174–75.

10

Business Environmental Ethics

ROBERT E. GORDON, JR.

Earth Day, April 22, 1990, brought about a heightened awareness of environmental issues and made more mainstream the attention given to environmental degradation. A clear understanding of what being environmentally responsible means is now essential to successfully operate a business. Not only is it important to businesses on the grounds of ensuring sound stewardship of our natural resources but also for legal reasons, corporate image, and what accountants term "goodwill." Any discussion of business ethics and the environment must begin with the questions, "What is the source of environmental degradation?" and "What can be done to improve the quality and condition of the environment?"

British economist Garrett Harden correctly pointed out the source of environmental degradation as common ownership of a natural resource, something he termed the *tragedy of the commons*. Communal ownership of natural resources—water, wildlife, air, or other—leads to environmental degradation as users are encouraged to reap the greatest possible reward with little concern for their impact on the resource or the environment. In strictly economic terms, resource users will maximize benefits without regard for the externality of environmental degradation, which is borne by the community at large. With this as a basis, we understand that environmental degradation by industry is not a result of market failure but a failure to create markets for and protect property rights over natural resources.

UNFORTUNATE HISTORY

Unfortunately, many early environmentalists regarded industrial pollution as the result of greed and market failure. Rather than creating the needed markets, over the years a complex, often contradictory, and sometimes counterproductive framework of policies and regulating entities has been jury-rigged. The inefficiency and shortcomings of this system have been magnified by three conditions: (1) heavy reliance on centralized decision making, (2) historical erosion of private property rights, and (3) the historically bequeathed massive government estate. In combination with *preservationist* environmental philosophy, the tragedy of the commons and these three conditions have thwarted the development of internalized resolutions to our environmental problems.[1]

THE ERROR OF CENTRALIZATION

Heavy reliance on centralized decision making can be traced at least in part to an inaccurate understanding of the nature of renewable natural resources. Renewable natural resources are, for the most part, the ones that would be of concern in a discussion of business ethics. Few individuals would be distraught over the disappearance of degradation of such non-renewables as fossil fuels on the grounds of aesthetic or philosophical value. These types of resources are generally valued, even in terms of intergenerational equity, only in that they may be expended at some point. Renewable resources include such things as air, water, wildlife, forests, soil, and range. These resources are valued by different individuals and entities for different reasons.

Conventional preservationist wisdom incorrectly holds renewable resources to be essentially static and destined to degradation and decline as a result of interaction with man. From this vantage point, progress, development, and economic prosperity seem at odds with sound environmentalism. Environmental problems are not judged individually as to how serious they are but are seen in the context of a continual and inevitable march toward ecological catastrophe. The recourse for those who hold this perspective of renewable natural resources is to reduce human interaction with them and to pass control of the resources over to a "protective" central authority. Society, economy, and the environment suffer as a consequence of an approach based on this premise. Justifying a business using resources and having plans for an increased level of use in the future (growth) to someone who embraces this perspective is difficult if not outright impossible. In its purest form, this understanding of our environment offers little if any room for human industry beyond the sustenance level.

Industry in general and particularly resource intensive industry will increasingly find itself faced with accusations of unethical conduct by those who hold this modern-day Luddite-style understanding of the world. This world view has gained great strength in the past decade as many environmental problems are billed as "global" and as requiring centralized bureaucratic remedies.

The Clean Air Act of 1990 is a paramount example of a preservationist command-and-control policy. The legislation was developed in part to deal with acid raid, the pollution resulting from the combustion of high sulfur content coals. The problem was portrayed by many as extensive even though the EPA's multimillion dollar National Acid Precipitation Assessment Project showed that there are only 630 acid lakes in the whole eastern United States, which represent less than one-fiftieth of 1 percent of the 200 million acres of water in the Northeast alone. More than half of this acidic water is found in Florida, which does not receive a high level of acidic precipitation. Much of the remainder is attributable to other factors such as regeneration of the northeastern forests and the subsequent increase in acidic runoff from leaf decomposition. A NAPAP study determined that the pH level of all the lakes of the Adirondacks could be lowered for as little as $170,000 annually by adding lime. Yet Clear Air legislation designed to reduce sulfur emissions will cost at least $4 to $7 billion per year.[2]

The cost of this inefficient legislation to the economy will be staggering. The preservationist approach to solve problems such as acid rain is to impose broad and costly command-and-control remedies. No cost is deemed too exorbitant by preservationists, who view it as the collective responsibility of mankind to protect those things that cannot protect themselves, those things that are held in common. The ethical question of whether it is right to impose the costs of a particular environmental protection program on those in society who are not responsible for the environmental degradation the program is designed to alleviate is often ignored.

THE DENUDING OF PRIVATE PROPERTY RIGHTS

Acceptance of the underlying assumptions of preservationism leads one in the direction of sacrificing private property rights so that central command and control structures will be charged with protecting them for the common good. A strong trend in this direction was evidenced by President Reagan's belief in the need for and decision to issue an executive order forcing the government to study the impact of government takings. However, preservationists have fought such private property protections hard. A Senate bill forcing the government to provide equitable compensation for the lost value of lands declared wetlands or subject to endangered species limits failed. The path towards more communal ownership and the resulting environmental degradation is not new. It was paved by a series of nineteenth-century judicial rulings that virtually obliterated more efficient English common law concepts.

Under English common law, parties were responsible for the costs and consequences of damage they caused to others and their property. A factory, for example, which polluted a river and thereby reduced the quality of fish downstream would be liable to a fishing club that had fishing rights over the stream. The club members would be sure to monitor the quality of fishing and take action against a polluter, and the factory owners would strive to keep their costs down, including liability for damage done to other property, such as the fishing club's rights.

Unfortunately, this is increasingly not the situation in which businesses find themselves confronting environmental problems. More and more businesses are responsible to meet regulatory standards rather than contend with stewards of private property. In this situation, businesses are not responsible for the actual costs of rectifying any environmental degradation they cause but for the costs that reflect political vagaries and often arbitrarily set fines and fees. During a recession, political pressures might favor economic growth regardless of its impact on communal resources. In such a situation, businesses might be allowed to cause a great deal of environmental degradation and not bear the cost of damage done. However, as the political climate shifts, businesses may face such ponderous regulation and heavy costs that profitable operation becomes impossible.

The Clean Air Act of 1990 again serves as a good example. This act was born during a period of sustained economic growth, when public attention was not focused on elemental economic questions. The legislation will force as many as 150,000 businesses ranging from large multinationals to mom-and-pop operations to acquire permits for more than 191 pollutants and to secure new permits anytime there is a change in emissions, even a change leading to less pollutants. Failure to meet these standards and strict compliance timetables can result in anything from 450 years of prison to an unlimited $25,000/day fine.[3]

For some businesses, the question will not be how to operate in an environmentally ethical manner under regulations like those mentioned above but how to operate at all. The unfortunate trend towards weaker private property rights and the resulting reliance on centralized decision making will undoubtedly complicate the matter of environmental business ethics.

HISTORY'S INHERITED ESTATE

The tragedy of the commons and environmentally unsound practices by corporations are, in part, a result of history. The U.S. government owns all the waterways of the United States, polices the quality of the air, and is the third largest landholder in the world after the USSR and PRC. Government entities such as the Bureau of Land Management and the Forest Service in combination with state and local governments own nearly 40 percent of the United States. In Nevada, more than 70 percent of the land is in government hands. A tremendous amount of our national timber, mining, oil, and livestock resources are on or dependent on these lands. Industries not dependent upon the federal land base must often use waterways or air that is owned or controlled by the government.

Although most of this state ownership is the baggage of history, some is a result of the push for centralized control of natural resources. For reasons discussed above, command ownership of natural resources lends itself to a bureaucratic command-and-control style of management, with costs of stewardship to be imposed upon the entire community. Preservationists argue that this is the only recourse to ensure the quality of the environment.

In practice state ownership of natural resources does not lead to either a healthy environment or a strong economy. The inefficiency and shortcomings of this approach are evidenced by the poor economies and abysmal environmental records of the Soviet Union and the Eastern European nations. The failure of these nations to provide the framework for a prosperous economy and healthy environment is a systemic failure. It is a failure to provide the incentives for environmentally sound economic growth by using the tools of markets and individual responsibility and is magnified by the degree to which natural resources are owned by the state.

CAN BUSINESSES BE PHILOSOPHICAL PRESERVATIONISTS

The current patchwork of legislation, federal, state, local, and private natural resources holdings, combined with the powerful impact of preservationist philosophy, provide a complicated and confusing framework for operating a business. Preservationist environmentalists have essentially billed business as synonymous with environmental degradation, profit with ecological destruction. The push for state control over resources and commercial enterprises has gone so far that some national legislators see little room for the driving force of economic incentive. For example, contrary elemental market economics, Representative Pat Schroeder believes that "corporate America . . . should run business as a service to the public and not as something to buy and sell for personal profit."[4]

The environmental advocates embracing a preservationist philosophy see the economic incentives created by markets as the root cause of environmental degradation. From this perspective, technology and economic growth are viewed as almost inevitably leading to further degradation of the environment. The extreme proponents of this perspective such as Earth First! favor a world based on "hunter-gatherer tribes" and have a rallying cry of "Back to the Pleistocene."[5] Certainly, there is little room for business with those who embrace this philosophy other than small-scale bartering of flint chips and sharpened sticks. Unfortunately, many in the public have unknowingly adopted environmental views and ethics based on the ideas of the preservationist movement. The strict preservationist philosophy has a profound impact on national policies and the framework under which businesses operate.

The most important step for a business in developing a coherent framework of environmental ethics is choosing an environmental philosophy. The pressure that can be brought to bear by the status quo, heavily preservationism-influenced environmentalists, is powerful. The environmental lobby has as much as $1 billion to push for preservationist-based legislation. If businesses adopt and support preservationist ideas, they are in fact endorsing a position that is diametrically opposed to their *raison d'etre*.

IF NOT PRESERVATIONIST, WHAT?

As the foundations of preservationism and market economics are irreconcilably opposed, does one have to choose between the opportunity for economic growth and progress provided by a market economy and the opportunity to be a sound environmental steward. If such a choice is necessary, one dedicated to business must do so accepting that with every business success, they play an increasingly negative environmental role. The idea that any logical environmental business ethic could be embraced in such a situation is dubious.

Fortunately, the preservationists' catch–22 is avoidable and will be avoided by those who have a clear understanding of the cause of environmental degradation and the principles that are the basis of what may be called free-market environmentalism, wise use or wise management. These principles allow one to manage environmental problems while simultaneously working to foster economic growth, technological development and progress in general. The framework that these principles provide also affords for a consistent and logical ethical matrix.

A SOUND UNDERSTANDING OF
RENEWABLE RESOURCES

The first principle is that renewable natural resources—things such as wildlife and trees—are resilient, dynamic, and lend themselves to active management. In essence, renewable resources are truly renewable; and man can enhance them in quality and quantity by the application of the art and science gathered over centuries. The impact of this statement is powerful. It recognizes that man can use, enjoy, and benefit from renewable natural resources without inevitable environmental degradation. Such an idea is contrary to the precepts of preservationism.

While it is faddish among many preservationist environmentalists to portray all environmental conditions as bad and rapidly getting worse, the trends in the quality and quantity of many natural resources contradict this view. EPA Administrator William Reilly has pointed out that emissions from particulates are down 64 percent, sulfur oxides down 25 percent, volatile organics down 29 percent, carbon monoxide down 38 percent, and lead down 96 percent from 1970 levels.[6] There are positive trends not only in the decreasing level of air pollution but also in water quality, soil conditions, range conditions, and the quality and quantity of trees and wildlife. Black bear, wild turkey, antelope, mountain lion, bald eagles, osprey, giant Canada geese, wood ducks, beaver, bighorn sheep, elk, mule, and white-tailed deer and a plethora of other animals have risen dramatically in number.[7] Although there is not space in the chapter to correct the many misconceptions that the public has about the condition of *renewable* resources, facts such as these should cause one to question the statements of environmental alarmists.

A SITE AND SITUATION SPECIFIC APPROACH

The second principle is that improvements to environmental quality are site and situation specific. The qualitative and quantitative improvements to our natural resources, as illustrated above, are the result of efforts that tap the dynamic and resilient characteristics of renewable resources on a site and situational specific basis. Managing environmental problems on a case-by-case basis ensures that the most appropriate actions are taken and allows for reasonable prioritizing. Such an approach also combats the fear and hype that are often generated for far-reaching bureaucratic schemes.

On the contrary, strongly centralized schemes to manage environmental problems are more often than not insensitive to the particulars of environmental problems and therefore negative in effect. A blatant example of this are federal farm policies, which have induced farmers to engage in practices that have led to erosion so severe it is comparable to the days of the Dust Bowl.[8] Such folly is a universal characteristic of central planning, as is evidenced by the Brazilian policies, which have induced reckless deforestation of the Amazon, and Soviet policies, which have led to severe environmental destruction of the USSR's formerly fertile agricultural belt.

PRIVATE PROPERTY PROTECTION AND
MARKET FORCES

The third principle is that the forces of a free-market economy and the extension of the protection of private property rights hold the most promising new opportunities for improving the environment. As pointed out above, environmental degradation is the result not of market failure but of the failure to create markets and protect private property—the tragedy of the commons. Because the cost of environmental degradation to communal resources has been borne by the community at large rather than the polluter, historically there has been little incentive for the private sector to turn its innovation and technology to reducing the cost and liability of doing damage to others or their property. In a case of resource ownership, the fact that a private entity's current and future welfare is directly related the quality of its resources induces behavior to add to the value of the resource and guard against actions that would detract from its value. With a greater degree of protection of private property comes higher property value and subsequently increased demand for market forces to provide innovations and new technologies for better management.

Many have a difficult time applying the concept of the market to renewable natural resources such as wildlife, but it is done; as usual, the market has proven itself more efficient than command and control systems. This is well-illustrated in the comparison of the healthy wildlife and habitat on the enormous private and profitable Desert Ranch in Woodruff, Utah, and the ecologically declining condition of Yellowstone National Park.[9] In cases of other resources such as air and water, it may be more difficult. These areas call for considerable exploration, but there are immediate steps that can be taken to tap into the environmentally valuable results of incentive. One such step is application of the concept that the polluter pays.

THE POLLUTER PAYS

Making the polluter pay may strike many readers as a foregone conclusion, but in practice it has not been. Reliance on the command-and-control approach that goes hand-in-hand with communal ownership has left those most vulnerable in the political process often footing the bill for cleaning up pollution. In reality this has often meant that taxpayers covered the cost of repairing environmental degradation done to air, waterways, and federal or state lands.

In March 1989, when the Exxon *Valdez* ran aground, the stage was set for an important and positive precedent. Shore near the spill was land administered by the U.S. Forest Service, an agency of the USDA. Agriculture officials quickly realized they had an expensive and timely project at hand. With the urging of the subcabinet officials in the Departments of Agriculture, Interior, and Justice of the Bush administration, then—Secretary of Agriculture Clayton K. Yeutter untraditionally charged the polluter, Exxon, with the responsibility to undertake and pay for most of the cleanup operations. Normal procedure in such cases had been for the taxpayers to cover a large amount of the costs through the budgets of various federal agencies.

Making the polluter pay attaches individual responsibility to actions. Pollution in such cases is not an externality to be borne by the community at large but is rightly an intrinsic cost that must be calculated. Liability in such an instance again encourages innovation and technological development to reduce costs. Although it may currently be difficult to determine the source of some pollutants, there is every reason to believe that new technologies will increasingly simplify the task. For example, some have suggested the "fingerprinting" of factory emissions with environmentally benign tracing substances, as is currently done with shipped oil to determine the source of leaks or spills. In a similar approach, cars can now be tested accurately for the amount of pollution they produce. A system could be devised whereby during safety inspections the owner of a car is charged a fee based on the car's emission level multiplied by the number of miles driven. Such an approach forces drivers to recognize the true cost of driving, creates a demand for cleaner cars, and makes the polluter pay, as opposed to an air-quality program funded by a uniform tax.

THE GOLDEN RULE

Corporations have a responsibility to conduct business in such a manner that they do not destroy the environment, but they also have a legal and moral obligation to investors to employ their assets in the optimum manner to maximize economic returns. The precepts of the environmental philosophy of preservationism hold these responsibilities to be mutually exclusive courses. However, an environmental philosophy based on the three principles outlined above allows a business to strive consistently to meet both the responsibility to be a sound environmental steward and the responsibility to maximize economic returns. The ethical framework under which a business adopting this environmental philosophy operates is based upon the golden rule.

In the example of the fishing club and the upstream factory, the factory strives to maximize economic returns. In a situation where the factory is liable for any environmental degradation to others or their property directly resulting from the factory's operation, prevention of or restitution for pollution becomes an intrinsic cost to be calculated in the effort to maximize returns. The responsibility to maximize revenue and be environmentally responsible become inextricably linked. As success in meeting the responsibility of maximizing returns is dependent to a degree on the success of meeting the responsibility of being a good steward, the preservationist's dilemma vanishes.

PHILANTHROPY AND POLITICAL INVOLVEMENT

Recognizing the profound differences between these environmental schools of thought may also bring another responsibility upon a corporation. It will not be argued here whether or not businesses should engage in supporting charities, political candidates or movements, and other similar programs. However, for reasons of tax concerns, public relations, goodwill, and others, most businesses do support philanthropic or educational causes and often contribute to political causes through PACs or in other manners. If a business does engage in such a venture, it has a responsibility to its investors to ensure that the support does not go to causes, organizations, or candidates that are promoting ideas or programs that work to detract from the concepts that support a framework allowing the business to meet its undeniable responsibility of seeking to maximize economic returns. A corporation, for example, that provided funding to a nonprofit organization dedicated to promoting preservationist environmental philosophy would be irresponsible. In such an instance the business has failed in its responsibility to protect the interests of its investors by furthering ideas contrary to those upon which the business is built. The responsibility not to make such a mistake begets another responsibility, which is to be informed about the ramifications of different environmental philosophies well enough to make sound decisions.

CONCLUSION

Businesses in the 1990s will find themselves faced with complicated environmental issues. Such strong emotional lines have been drawn in environmental affairs that choosing courses of action that offend few will be increasingly difficult. Many difficult decisions will have to be made by business leaders. A strong and consistent philosophy and guiding ethical framework will be indispensable for managing environmental problems and striving to set positive precedents for future situations. Understanding and rejecting the precepts of preservationism and adopting an environmental philosophy based on the three principles: (1) Renewable resources are resilient and dynamic, (2) Improvements in environmental quality are site and situation specific, (3) Extending the protection of private property rights and harnessing free-market forces provide the most promising new opportunities for environmental improvement—combined with an understanding of the root of environmental degradation—will allow business to meet their many responsibilities ethically in these increasingly complex times.

NOTES

1. *Preservationism* is here used to describe a school of thought that will be touched upon in this work rather than the site and situation specific tool or practice of conservation.

2. Edward C. Krug, "Fish Story: The Great Acid Rain Flimflam," *Policy Review* 52 (Spring 1990, The Heritage Foundation, Washington, D.C.).

3. Warren Brookes, "America Dragged Down," *National Review*, 43, 20 (October 15, 1990).

4. Patricia Schroeder, correspondence with a constituent dated April 2, 1989.

5. Betsy Carpenter, "Redwood Radicals," Science & Society section, *U.S. News & World Report*, September 17, 1990, p. 51.

6. William K. Reilly, "Preventing Pollution Won't Hurt the Economy," Guest Commentary section, *Design News*, October 17, 1990, p. 176.

7. Robert E. Gordon, Jr., and George S. Dunlop, "Creature Comfort: The Revitalization of American Wildlife," *Policy Review* 53 (Summer 1990), The Heritage Foundation, pp. 60–64.

8. Richard K. Armey, interview in the "Perspective," *NWI Resource*, 1, 3 (June/July 1990), National Wilderness Institute, Washington, D.C.

9. Dr. Jo Kwong Echard, "Where the Deer and the Antelope Play," Wildlife Management section, *NWI Resource*, 1, 2 (April 1990), National Wilderness Institute, Washington, D.C.

Part III

Responsibilities of the Corporation to Insiders

11

Ethical Issues in Acquisitions and Mergers

Robert W. McGee

This chapter discusses some ethical aspects of acquisitions and mergers. Granted that acquisitions and mergers tend to benefit shareholders, consumers, and the economy in general, is it ethical for management, which is hired to protect shareholder interests, to attempt to thwart a takeover attempt by resorting to poison pills, greenmail, or some other device? Is it ethical for anyone to prevent consenting adults from exchanging their property at some mutually agreed-upon price?

There is ample evidence to suggest that acquisitions and mergers are generally beneficial to a wide segment of society because they shift assets from lower uses to higher uses, from less efficient managements to more efficient managements. Space does not permit a detailed analysis of this point, but many studies have already drawn this conclusion.[1] The old shareholders benefit because they receive a premium for their stock. New shareholders benefit because they are buying into a company that is about to become more efficient and competitive. Nontendering shareholders benefit because their stock increases in value as a result of the tender offer. Society benefits because a restructured, lean and efficient company provides higher quality goods and services at lower prices. Employees benefit because a healthy company provides more job security than a weak, noncompetitive, inefficient company.[2] Even an unsuccessful takeover attempt can cause these groups to benefit because the mere threat of a takeover often causes management to become better managers. The only group that stands to lose as a result of an acquisition or merger is top management, which stands to be replaced if the takeover is successful. Thus, it follows that attempts to prevent takeovers reduce the welfare of all these groups, with the exception of management, which stands to gain by thwarting a takeover attempt.

Many of the ethical problems connected with takeovers relate to top management's attempt to prevent their companies from being taken over. Management has a fiduciary duty to act in the best interest of shareholders, yet a successful takeover will often result in some members of top management losing their jobs and perhaps forcing them into early retirement. Given this scenario, there is tremendous pressure on top management to breach their fiduciary duty and pull out all stops either to prevent a takeover attempt from being successful or to make plans to cushion their fall in the event the takeover attempt is successful. Defensive tactics used by management may include hiding behind the antitrust laws or the Williams Act or some state antitakeover law or making the company less desirable as a takeover target by adopting a poison pill, selling the company's most attractive assets, going into debt, giving a third party lock-up rights that allow it to repurchase in the event of a hostile takeover, repurchasing company stock at a premium, paying a large dividend to deplete cash, merging with a "white knight," or awarding golden parachute contracts to top (and perhaps middle) management.

The business judgment rule is often cited as justification for management to fight tender offers and there is some judicial support for this position.[3] Yet it seems that attempts by management to prevent shareholders from considering offers that could increase their wealth is a breach of management's fiduciary duty and is a conflict of interest as well, as shareholders, if given the opportunity to consider a takeover offer, might decide to accept the offer's terms, thus placing top management jobs in jeopardy.

Some commentators have suggested that laws should be passed to guarantee shareholders the right to receive and vote on tender offers without being subjected to obstacles placed in their path by the management that is supposed to represent their interests.[4] Yet new laws are not really needed if courts would only start recognizing attempts by management to thwart takeovers as breaches of fiduciary duty. Some courts have recognized breaches of fiduciary duty where management attempts to thwart a takeover to protect itself. For example, the Second Circuit Court of Appeals found that management breached its duty of loyalty when it issued new shares to fund a newly created employee stock option plan when the reason for the move was to thwart a takeover attempt.[5] Shareholders could remove many obstacles to takeover attempts (and increase the price of their stock at the same time) by inserting provisions in the company's bylaws or articles of incorporation that include antiresistance provisions. The stock of companies that have such provisions would be more attractive to investors than the stock of companies that do not have any safeguards to prevent management from resisting takeover attempts. Companies that have supermajority consent rules or similar "blocks" will be less attractive to potential raiders than companies having rules that allow raiders to make offers.[6]

Some managements use the excuse that they are fighting a tender offer so that other potential raiders can have the opportunity to make a higher bid. But quite often, the use of delaying tactics gives management the time it needs to make moves that will result in thwarting any offer by any raider. Furthermore, even if the use of stalling tactics does result in a higher bid by another raider, the effect is a net social loss. Even if there were no transaction costs, the increased price the target company shareholders receive would be exactly offset by the increased resources the bidder would have to transfer to consummate the deal, so there is no net social gain. But as transaction costs are increased, there is always a net loss to the general shareholding public as the result of delaying tactics. The only groups that benefit by blocking tactics are entrenched management of the target economy and the lawyers and accountants they hire to help them block the takeover attempt.

POISON PILLS

Poison pills are financial schemes made by management to make the company a less attractive takeover target. Poison pills may take several forms, many of which involve debt restructuring, preferred stock, discriminatory targeted repurchases, or poison pill rights. An important question to ask is who benefits and who loses by the introduction of a poison pill?

The obvious losers are the potential raiders. A raider may decide not to attempt a takeover because of the poison pill. If an attempt is made, it may be unsuccessful and costly. Even if it is successful, the cost of success is higher where there is a poison pill.

The less obvious losers are the target company shareholders. Because the evidence suggests that target company shareholders tend to benefit by a takeover, thwarting a takeover by use of a poison pill (or by any other means) prevents shareholders from earning a premium on their stock. A Securities and Exchange Commission study found that the announcement of a poison pill plan by a takeover target causes the stock price to drop by an average of 2.4 percent, whereas announcement of such a plan by a company that is not a target has no effect on stock price.[7] Ironically, it is management, which is supposed to protect shareholder interests, that makes the poison pill.

Another group that stands to lose by poison pills is consumers. As the raider is prevented from making more efficient use of the assets than the present management, the company is unable to upgrade quality and reduce cost, with the result that consumers will have to pay higher prices to purchase goods or services that are of lower quality.

An even less obvious class of losers consists of the thousands of other industries that would get extra business if the target company was taken over and made to run more efficiently. If the target company's sales were $10 billion before the acquisition and the raider was able to cut costs to the point where the company could reduce prices by 10 percent, an extra $1 billion of customer funds would become available to purchase other goods and services even if the number of units sold did not increase. However, if prices were reduced by 10 percent, it is likely that the number of units sold would increase, so sales would be something more than $900 million. Customer A might decide to use the $10,000 it saves to buy an additional machine for its factory. Customer B might use its $15,000 savings to buy another car for the corporate fleet. Customer C might use its $100,000 savings to invest in employee education or training. Customers A, B, and C all benefit because they are able to buy something they could not have afforded in the absence of the takeover. The company that sold the machine to Customer A, the car to Customer B, and the education and training to Customer C also benefit because of the takeover, as do the Customer C employees who receive the education and training. There is no way to predict what the target company's customers would do with their cost savings, but the fact that they would do something cannot be denied. Even if all they do is let the savings sit in their bank accounts, the fact that the money is there (perhaps earning interest) means that it is available for the bank to use to make loans to businesses or individuals. Because the quantity of money available for loans has increased, there is downward pressure on interest rates, which benefits anyone who might borrow money. The general economic law that "as supply increases, price decreases" applies to the supply of money as well as to the supply of any other commodity.

If all these groups stand to lose by the introduction of a poison pill, why are such pills introduced? Someone must gain by their introduction. Otherwise, the poison pills would never be introduced. An easy way to find who benefits is to look at who introduces them in the first place, as it is usually the advocate that tends to benefit. Management is clearly the foremost advocate of poison pills. It does not take long to see how management stands to benefit by the introduction of a poison pill. Poison pills decrease the chances of a successful takeover. If a takeover is successful, a high percentage of managers stand to lose their jobs.[8] Therefore, management takes action to prevent job losses by introducing a poison pill.

Thus, it appears that management is working against the interest of its shareholders by introducing a poison pill. Yet some courts have upheld the right of management to introduce poison pills. In one case, the Delaware Supreme Court upheld the right of management to restrict the right of its shareholders to sell their stock,[9] an interesting result in light of the fact that management is supposed to be the agent of the stockholders.

As a result of this case, corporations are adopting poison pills in record numbers. Three recent studies found that the mere announcement of such an adoption causes the company's stock price to fall,[10] perhaps because of the decreased likelihood of a successful takeover, which would cause the stock price to rise.

However, not all courts have ruled that management may interfere with shareholder voting rights. New York[11] and New Jersey[12] have crushed some poison pills; and an Illinois court, while dissolving one poison pill, allowed the same company to adopt a different poison pill a few weeks later.[13]

GREENMAIL

Greenmail is seen in the popular press as something that is evil, a bribe that is paid to a raider to prevent a takeover attempt from proceeding. The raider is seen as being unjustly enriched at the expense of the target company and shareholders. Greenmail is a payment top management decides to make to protect shareholders from a corporate raider. It is seen as an evil, but the lesser of two evils.

Greenmail payments do, indeed, stop takeover attempts dead in their tracks. But an economic analysis of greenmail payments raises questions as to their propriety. As the evidence suggests that target company shareholders (as well as consumers and the economy in general) tend to benefit by takeovers, should management prevent a takeover by making greenmail payments? Rather than protecting shareholders, it appears that making greenmail payments harms shareholders, since it prevents them from obtaining the benefits that go with a takeover—primarily, an increase in the price of their stock. Consumers are also harmed, because blocking a takeover prevents the new owners from using the acquired assets more efficiently, which would otherwise lead to offering higher quality products or services at lower prices. Preventing takeovers tends to protect management, many of whom would lose their jobs if the takeover attempt were successful. Thus, it appears that management, unwittingly or not, makes greenmail payments to protect themselves against job loss, to the detriment of shareholders and consumers.

Lew Rockwell sums up the economics of greenmail very succinctly:

Say you owned a small apartment building in a distant city, and you hired a professional manager to run it for you. This person likes the job, and when someone—an apartment "raider"—sought to offer you a good price for the building, the manager does everything possible to prevent you from being able to consider the offer. And he calls the local mayor for a city ordinance to keep the apartment "independent." When all else fails, the manager takes some of your own money and pays the potential buyer greenmail to look elsewhere.

This is exactly what's going on in the unfriendly takeovers we hear about. A takeover attempt is only unfriendly to present management, who risk losing cushy jobs. No offer can be unfriendly to the owners of the firm, the stockholders, who are free to accept or reject the price offered.[14]

Paying greenmail is actually a form of an antitakeover action, a targeted repurchase. It could be construed as being unfair to a large group of shareholders, as it involves an offer to repurchase the shares of one or a small group of shareholders at a premium, an offer that is not extended to all shareholders. Ironically, it is the greenmailer who is offering the other shareholders the opportunity to sell their shares at a premium, an offer the company's management is trying to prevent from being made or accepted.

Recent studies indicate that the stock's price increases between the initial purchase by the greenmailer and the later repurchase.[15] Thus, shareholders benefit rather than suffer harm because the price of their stock is bid up. If management buys off the raider, the shareholders lose the premium.[16] However, the stock price might not go back to its pretakeover attempt position, because the market may anticipate that there will be other future attempts that may prove successful. But if the company's financial position is weakened as a result of having to pay a large sum to thwart a takeover, the stock's price may slide, as the company is perceived as being in a weakened financial condition and thus as being a less desirable investment.

Some commentators have been calling for legislation to prevent or regulate the making of greenmail payments. But legislation is not necessary. All that is needed is a statement in the corporate bylaws that greenmail payments will not be made. If courts would start to recognize greenmail payments as a breach of the business judgment rule, such payments would be stopped dead in their tracks.

GOLDEN PARACHUTES

The subject of "golden parachutes" has become a controversial one in recent years. As takeovers become more sophisticated and "junk" bond financing makes it possible to take over even the largest companies, top management is no longer protected by working for a very large firm. That, plus the fact that about half the target company's top management are no longer with the company three years after the takeover, creates a tremendous amount of anxiety and gives management a strong incentive to seek ways to protect themselves in the event of a takeover.

Briefly, a golden parachute is a severance contract to compensate high-level corporate officials when they lose their jobs if their company is taken over. Most commentators have seen such contracts as shareholder ripoffs because the high-level employee benefits and the shareholders don't get anything for their money. But this analysis is simplistic. There is really much more involved than initially meets the eye. There are circumstances under which shareholders can benefit by having the corporation enter into golden parachute contracts with top management employees.

One beneficial effect of golden parachute contracts is that they can help reduce the conflict of interest that would otherwise exist between top management and shareholders.[17] Management may resist a takeover attempt that would be in the shareholders' interest because they stand to lose their jobs if the takeover is successful. Thus, they are working against the shareholders' interests. Having a properly constructed golden parachute will eliminate or at least reduce this potential conflict of interest because management would be less likely to attempt to thwart a takeover attempt if their incomes were protected by golden parachutes. The evidence suggests that merely having golden parachute contracts raises the company's stock price by about 3 percent when the existence of the golden parachute contracts is announced.[18] This price rise might be due to a perception by the investing public that a takeover attempt is more likely than before, but also it may happen because the market sees that the potential conflict of interest between management and the corporation has been reduced, thus making the stock a better investment. In all likelihood, both of these factors have somewhat of an effect on the increase in the company's stock price.

Because the evidence suggests that takeovers are good for the stockholders of the target company, as well as for the general consuming public, it seems logical that company and government policy should be to encourage top management to negotiate takeovers that seem to be in the shareholders' best interests. Yet some present policies, such as the Deficit Reduction Act of 1984, penalize companies and managers who enter into golden parachute contracts, and state and federal officials are advocating placing further restrictions on golden parachute contracts.[19] As a properly structured golden parachute contract reduces top management's conflict of interest, legislation that restricts or prohibits such contracts actually works against the shareholders' interests and the interests of the economy in general, because takeovers tend to be in the consumers' interest, too. The logical solution would be to repeal legislation that restricts companies from entering into golden parachute contracts with their top management.

However, not all golden parachute contracts resolve the conflict of interest problem. Depending on how the contract is structured, it may serve to make management more entrenched than before, which tends to work against the shareholders' interest. A well-designed contract will reduce this potential conflict of interest, whereas a badly designed contract will do just the opposite. One way to make such contracts work for the benefit of the shareholders is to extend them to the members of top management who would be negotiating the takeover and implementing the later restructuring. However, extending golden parachute contracts to lower-level managers who would not be involved in takeover negotiations would be more difficult to justify on shareholder-interest grounds. Extending too many golden parachutes raises the cost of the acquisitions, thus making it less attractive to potential raiders, while not gaining any corresponding benefits for the corporation. Beneficial Corporation, for example, awarded golden parachute contracts to more than two hundred of its executives, which had to make Beneficial stock less attractive to raiders.[20] It is difficult to justify such actions on ethical grounds if the premise is that top management should be looking out for the interests of shareholders.

Another beneficial effect of golden parachute contracts is that they make it easier to attract top management. Golden parachute contracts are a form of compensation, a salary substitute, an insurance policy against job loss, and potentially a supplemental retirement plan. Absence of a golden parachute provision makes a job offer less attractive to a potential top-level manager; as golden parachutes are a form of compensation, companies that do not have them would probably have to offer higher salaries to entice potential top managers to join the company.

But not all golden parachute contracts are in the best interests of shareholders. While a properly constructed contract reduces the manager's conflict of interest, an improperly structured contract will do just the opposite. If the golden parachute is too "golden," top management might be too willing to sell the company; thus, they might tend to take the first offer that comes along rather than negotiate a higher price for their shareholders. As managers and board members who hold a great deal of stock in the company will have less incentive to take the first offer than those who own little or no stock, the company might provide incentives that encourage top management and board members to own stock in the company. Yet present insider-trading laws provide a disincentive, and some top managers and board members are selling their stock so that they will not be accused of insider trading. Offering stock options and restricted stock appreciation rights that are exercisable only if control changes is one possible solution.

THE WILLIAMS ACT

The Williams Act was enacted by Congress in 1968 to regulate tender offers.[21] To be more specific, the act requires raiders to give advance warning that they are going to attack and requires them to disclose other detailed information as well. Anyone who acquires, directly or indirectly, a 5 percent beneficial interest in a certain security must disclose detailed information outlining his background, identity, source of funds, and acquisition plans. The number of shares owned and any agreements between the acquirer and other persons must also be disclosed. The party acquiring 5 percent must disclose the information to the target company, to the Securities and Exchange Commission, and to the exchange where the stock is being traded. Once the offer is announced, the offeror may not make purchases other than through the tender offer. Open market purchases (at a lower price) are forbidden.

The Williams Act also gives the target company shareholders the right to withdraw their tendered shares within seven days after the tender offer is published or within sixty days from the date the original offer was made. This deadline has been extended by the Securities and Exchange Commission to fifteen business days from the start of the offer and ten business days from the start of any competing offer, provided the original raider knows about the competing offer and has not accepted the shares the shareholders seek to withdraw. If the offer is for less than all the shares of a particular class and the shareholders are willing to offer more shares than the offeror is willing to purchase, the offeror must purchase the shares on a pro rata basis rather than a first-come, first-served basis. Originally, the Williams Act proration requirement applied only to shares tendered within the first ten days of the offer, but the Securities and Exchange Commission later extended the allowable time to the entire offer period. If the raider increases consideration during the offer period, all tendering shareholders are entitled to receive the same deal—the highest price offered. The Williams Act also prohibits any untrue statements or material omission of facts or any fraudulent, deceptive, or manipulative acts or practices.

Because acquisitions and mergers are good for the economy in general and for target company shareholders in particular, it seems logical that government should promote such activity or at least not place artificial hurdles in the way of consenting adults who want to enter into such activity. Yet it appears that the Williams Act is one of those hurdles. The act is aimed at reducing the number of tender offers made and increasing the cost of those that are made. Raiders must give advance warning of their intent, which gives entrenched management the opportunity to thwart the takeover bid. Once the declaration to acquire is made, the raider can no longer purchase shares on the open market, where they are cheaper. A premium must be paid on all shares subsequently acquired. If the shares are acquired at more than one price, the raider must later make up the price differential to those shareholders who willingly sold at a lower price before.

Once the decision is made to acquire the target company, it is in the raider's best interest to acquire as many shares as possible before the word hits the street that the acquisition is being made. The Williams Act limits the number of shares that the raider can acquire before making its intentions known, which both places a chilling effect on acquisition activity and drives up the cost of any acquisition attempt. Both the shareholders and the raider are harmed by this result.[22] The shareholders are harmed because they stand to benefit if the acquisition attempt is successful. The raider loses because the disclosure rule drives up the cost of the acquisition and makes it less attractive. If successful, the raider will make the company operate more efficiently, which is good for the company, the consumers, and the shareholders. Inefficient management that the shareholders cannot get rid of (because they are entrenched) can be replaced by a management team that does a better job. Preventing such events from happening hurts just about everyone except the target company's present management.

Before the Williams Act, potential raiders could gather together to formulate a plan in secret. They would place tender offer ads in the major newspapers over the weekend, and when the newspapers hit the stands they would be ready to buy. They could make the offer good for a very short time, such as a week, and they would know whether their takeover attempt was successful within a matter of days. The high interest charges they have to pay on the borrowed money used for the takeover could be kept to a minimum. But with the extended-offer terms required by the Williams Act, the interest charges keep mounting over a much longer time period, thus driving up the cost of the acquisition attempt and reducing the takeover's chance of success.

The Williams Act caused corporate raiders to change the way they do business. Raiders had to find out how many shares they could acquire at a given price before actually making their intent known to the public, so risk arbitrageurs gave them a helping hand by prepositioning or warehousing blocks of shares before the tender offer was made public. Their actions might have taken place with or without collusion, but the fact that arbitrageurs make the chances of a successful takeover more likely should be noted. These so-called dealers in insider information benefit the economy by helping to make takeover bids successful; and successful takeover bids, as has been demonstrated, are good for the economy. As one critic of the Williams Act has stated: "The tender offer is the most important and beneficial financial invention of the 20th century. Its very existence has probably added hundreds of billions of dollars to American capital values. Without it, noncontrolling shareholders in companies with widely diffused ownership would be nearly helpless in the face of managerial incompetence, self-dealing or inattention to business."[23]

Because the Williams Act protects entrenched management at the expense of shareholders, harms the economy and consumers in general and increases the price corporate raiders must pay, the logical step would be to repeal it. Yet some senators, such as Senator Howard Metzenbaum, want to see tender offer regulations tightened, an action that would make the situation worse. Before Congress starts changing the law, it should be very careful to determine what the possible effects on various groups would be. According to Senator Metzenbaum's position, it appears that Congress (or at least Senator Metzenbaum) has not yet done that.

HIDING BEHIND LEGISLATION

There is ample evidence to suggest that takeover legislation tends to harm, rather than protect shareholders. Several studies confirm this thesis.

Government protection of incumbent management in New Jersey caused the stock prices of eighty-seven affected companies to fall by 11.5 percent. Stock prices for seventy-four companies incorporated in Ohio dropped 3.2 percent, or $1.5 billion, after the legislature passed restrictive legislation, according to a Securities and Exchange Commission study. New York's statute cost stockholders $1.2 billion, or 1 percent of stock value, according to a Federal Trade Commission estimate.[24] Yet there is a push for more such legislation, both at the federal and state levels. Such legislation reduces shareholder wealth and reduces the odds that a takeover attempt will be successful. Thus, by supporting such legislation, management harms the shareholders it is supposed to be working for.

Management often hides behind legislation to protect itself at the expense of shareholders. Fostering and supporting antitakeover legislation is only one way that this task is accomplished. Management can also use the Williams Act and the antitrust laws to slow down or stop a potential raider.

This ploy is not new. Management has been using the force of government to protect itself from competition for hundreds of years, as Adam Smith pointed out in *The Wealth of Nations*. A threatened management need only point out some possible infraction by a raider to the appropriate government agency to put the brakes on a takeover attempt. Just pointing out that a raider might have breached the Williams Act will cause the Securities and Exchange Commission to investigate, thereby raising the raider's costs and slowing down the momentum of the takeover attempt. Whether there is in fact an infraction is not as important to target management as the fact that calling in the SEC can make a successful takeover attempt less likely. Target management is not penalized for using this ploy. In fact, it is often commended for doing so, under the guise of protecting shareholders from a hostile takeover. Yet shareholders benefit from a takeover, so this rationale for hiding behind some law is seen for what it is—using the force of government to protect management at the expense of the shareholders they are supposed to represent.

Another tactic, one that has been used not only to slow down a takeover attempt but also to harass competitors, is to allege that some action by a competitor or raider violates the antitrust laws.[25] By pointing out a "potential" antitrust violation, the target company management lets the federal government slow down a raider at very little cost to the target company.[26] Curiously, the target company cannot successfully sue under the antitrust laws because only those who have been harmed have standing to sue and takeover targets stand to gain rather than lose as a result of a successful takeover attempt.

Defending an antitrust action, or even responding to an antitrust inquiry, is time-consuming and costly. This tactic can be used very effectively to thwart a takeover attempt or at least to increase its cost and reduce the odds that the attempt will be successful.[27] In the Mobil-Conoco merger attempt, for example, the Justice Department's request for information prohibited Mobil from acquiring Conoco stock and also prohibited Mobil from competing with other raiders for control of Conoco, even though Mobil's offer was about $1 billion more than that of the nearest competitor.[28] It is difficult to see how shareholder interests are served by this kind of tactic.

Some companies, such as Marshall Field's department stores, even went so far as to establish locations where competitors already had stores so that any takeover attempt would raise antitrust questions.[29] Yet there is evidence to suggest that most takeovers actually increase competition rather than reduce it.[30] There is also evidence to suggest that the antitrust laws actually reduce competition in many cases rather than increase it, by setting up artificial barriers to market entry and by protecting established firms at the expense of newcomers.[31] This being the case, attempts by target company management to use the antitrust laws to thwart a takeover attempt seems ethically questionable, at best.

PROPERTY RIGHTS

So far, the arguments in this chapter have centered on economic efficiency. Takeovers benefit just about everyone (except entrenched management). Therefore they should be permitted. However, there is another side to the issue of whether takeover attempts should be permitted or regulated—the philosophical aspect of placing restrictions on the rights of consenting adults to do whatever they want as long as they do not violate anyone else's rights. This philosophical side of the question is many-sided and complex. Philosophers over the past twenty-five centuries have been unable to agree on even the basic approach to be taken. Marxists continue to argue that private property should be abolished. Yet wherever serious attempts to do just that have been made, there is poverty, starvation, and economic stagnation.

The other approach is based on natural law theory. Aristotle, Aquinas, Locke, and hundreds of other philosophers through the ages have used variations of this approach to explain reality. From a wealth-generating perspective, as well as from ethical and sociological perspectives, this approach is the only one that holds water.[32] Briefly stated, individuals should be able to create, acquire, sell, and inherit property without interference or obstruction as long as they do so without the use of force. Anyone who interferes with this basic right acts unethically.

One can apply this natural rights approach to the issue of corporate takeovers. Shares of stock in a corporation are property. As property owners, individuals should be able to buy or sell their stock to anyone they want, at any price they can agree on, as long as there is no coercion. If a raider wishes to offer a 20 percent premium to acquire someone's stock, that is no one's business but the parties to the transaction. Philosophically, the question of who benefits and who loses should not even be raised. Both the buyer and the seller have benefitted, according to their own subjective value judgments. Otherwise, the transaction would never take place. The parties to any transaction must necessarily assign different values to the subject matter of the exchange, or there would be no exchange. If the buyer and seller agree on a price of $100 a share, the buyer must prefer a share of stock to $100 and the seller must prefer the cash to the stock. They both gain. The transaction is win-win, not zero-sum.

If shareholders are prevented from acquiring or disposing of this property, the individual who prevents them from doing so is acting unethically. Such an individual is violating the rights of a buyer and seller to enter into an agreement that concerns no one but themselves. If some law prevents the transaction from taking place, the law is unjust and should be repealed. It can even be argued that the person who enforces such a law is acting unethically (unless you subscribe to the Nuremberg defense—I was just following orders), although there is a long-established theory that holds that where there is no choice there is no fault. Likewise, if a corporate officer or director uses such a law to prevent willing buyers and sellers from entering into an agreement, that individual is also acting unethically, as well as against the interests of the shareholders he or she is supposed to protect.

THE RIGHT TO CONTRACT

The right to contract is closely tied to the right to property. Our founding fathers saw this right as inalienable. Individuals who want to enter into a voluntary contract have an absolute right to do so. Article I, Section 10, of the United States Constitution protects this basic right from any infringement by the states. That clause states that "No State shall . . . pass any . . . Law impairing the Obligation of Contracts. . . . " Unfortunately, this prohibition against interference with contract has eroded almost to the point of nonexistence in recent decades, although a number of legal scholars are attempting to revitalize it, with some success.[33]

The thrust of the contract clause argument is that consenting adults should be able to enter into a contractual relationship without interference by the state. The state should protect contractual relationships, not impair them. State takeover laws that restrict the contractual relationship are therefore unconstitutional, or should be.

Henry N. Butler and Larry E. Ribstein develop the contract clause argument in depth.[34] They see a contract as existing among management, shareholders, creditors, and others. If shareholders lose the ability to freely transfer all incidents of ownership, such as the ability to transfer voting rights, because of a state law, their ability to contract is being impaired. The Indiana law is one example where this right is lost, since a 20 percent shareholder cannot acquire voting rights.[35] Also, shareholders who purchased stock before the law was passed with the intent of eventually gaining a controlling interest have that right taken away from them without just compensation, which seems to be a violation of the Constitution's takings clause.[36] Many other states also have passed laws that restrict the right of consenting adults to buy and sell stock in the company of their choice, and it appears that this trend will continue rather than reverse in the near future.

FREEDOM OF ASSOCIATION

The freedom of association is another basic right that is being infringed by corporate antitakeover laws.[37] Basically, the freedom of association is the right to associate (or not to associate) with anyone you want for any reason you want. But courts tend to view corporations as existing by state grant (creatures of the state) rather than as a series of contractual relations that include shareholders, management, employees, creditors, and others. This contractual view goes back to Roman law and at least as far back in American law as Justice John Marshall's decision in *Trustees of Dartmouth College* v. *Woodward*.[38] This view is still considered valid.

A number of authors have pointed out that the "creation of state" view of corporations is a myth.[39] Henry N. Butler and Larry E. Ribstein point out that a state corporate filing no more creates a corporation than a birth certificate creates a baby.[40] The state merely provides a standard form to facilitate contracting parties. Contrary to the Marshallian view (John, not Alfred), the state is not a party to the incorporation contract, just as the state is not a party to a sales contract where the contracting parties follow the terms of the Uniform Commercial Code.

By purchasing stock, individuals become a part of a voluntary association. By selling their stock interest they decide to sever their association with that voluntary organization. Laws that prohibit or restrict the purchase or sale of stock interests violate this basic freedom of association.

CONCLUDING COMMENTS

The evidence that acquisitions and mergers are good for shareholders, the economy, society, business, and consumers is overwhelming. The only group that stands to lose from a successful takeover attempt is top management, which stands a very good chance of becoming unemployed. A number of ethical issues arise because of the inherent conflict of interest that exists with top management in the event of a takeover attempt. On the one hand, management is hired to act in the best interest of shareholders. But if management does act in the shareholder interest, it stands to become unemployed.

Because of this built-in conflict of interest, a number of ploys have been used by management to protect itself at the expense of the shareholders, whose interests they are hired to protect. One such ploy is the poison pill, which can take many forms, but which is always used to thwart a takeover attempt—often in the guise of protecting the shareholders. Greenmail, a form of bribery using shareholder money, is sometimes used as well. Top management often uses the force of government to protect itself at the expense of shareholders by hiding behind laws that actually harm shareholder interests. Golden parachutes can reduce this conflict of interest if used judiciously but may exacerbate the problem if too many managers have them.

Several other, infrequently addressed issues also need to be considered. Aside from the question of who wins and who loses—the economic issues— some philosophical issues need to be considered. Is it ever ethically justified to interfere with an individual's right to buy or sell property, such as shares of stock, especially if no one is aggressed against? If consenting adults want to enter into a contract to exchange shares of stock, is it anyone else's business? America was founded on the principle that individuals should be able to do what they want with their property and their lives without interference from any individual or institution. Government, rather than being the institution that interferes, should be the institution that protects these basic rights.

NOTES

1. The beneficial effects of acquisitions and mergers are pointed out in several studies. See Robert W. McGee, "The Economics of Mergers and Acquisitions," *The Mid-Atlantic Journal of Business* 25:4 (February 1989); Michael C. Jensen, "Takeovers: Their Causes and Consequences," *Journal of Economic Perspectives* 2:1 (Winter 1988): 21–48; Michael C. Jensen and Richard S. Ruback, "The Market for Corporate Control: The Scientific Evidence," *Journal of Financial Economics* 11 (1983): 5–50; Michael C. Jensen, "The Efficiency of Takeovers," *The Corporate Board* (September/October 1985): 16–22; Michael C. Jensen, "The Takeover Controversy: Analysis and Evidence," *Midland Corporate Finance Journal* 4:2 (Summer 1986); Michael C. Jensen, "Takeovers: Folklore and Science," *Harvard Business Review* 62:6 (November/December 1984): 109–21; Michael C. Jensen, "Agency Costs of Free Cash Flow, Corporate Finance, and Takeovers," *American Economic Review* 76:2 (May 1986): 323–29; Paul J. Halpern, "Empirical Estimates of the Amount and Distribution of Gains to Companies in Mergers," *Journal of Business* 46:4 (October 1973): 554–75; Frank H. Easterbrook and Daniel R. Fischel, "The Proper Role of a Target's Management in Responding to a Tender Offer," *Harvard Law Review* 94 (April 1981): 1161–1204; Douglas H. Ginsburg and John F. Robinson, "The Case against Federal Intervention in the Market for Corporate Con-

trol," *The Brookings Review* (Winter/Spring 1986): 9–14; Glenn Yago and Gelvin Stevenson, "Mergers and Acquisitions in the New Jersey Economy," sponsored by the Securities Industry Association and published by the Economic Research Bureau, State University of New York at Stony Brook, May 8, 1986.

2. There is some evidence to suggest that hostile takeovers have a beneficial effect on wages and employment. See Charles Brown and James L. Medoff, "The Impact of Firm Acquisitions on Labor," National Bureau of Economic Research, May 1987.

3. See Easterbrook and Fischel, "The Proper Role of a Target's Management in Responding to a Tender Offer," pp. 1161–1204; Herzel, Schmidt, and Davis, "Why Corporate Directors Have a Right to Resist Tender Offers," *Corporate Law Review* 3 (1980): 107 ff.; Lipton, "Takeover Bids in the Target's Boardroom," *Business Lawyer* 35 (1979): 101ff.; Steinbrink, "Management's Response to the Takeover Attempt," *Case Western Law Review* 28 (1978): 882ff. For a critique of the Easterbrook and Fischel thesis, see David D. Haddock, Jonathan R. Macey, and Fred S. McChesney, "Property Rights in Assets and Resistance to Tender Offers," *Virginia Law Review* 73 (1987): 701–42. For a discussion of the business judgment rule, see Michael J. Keliher, "Anti-Takeover Measures—What Standard Should be Used to Evaluate Them?" *Houston Law Review* 25 (March 1988): 419–39.

4. Gregory R. Andre, "Tender Offers for Corporate Control: A Critical Analysis and Proposals for Reform," *Delaware Journal of Corporate Law* 12 (1987): 865–910; Carl C. Icahn, "The Case for Takeovers," *New York Times Magazine* (January 29, 1989), p. 34.

5. *Norlin Corp. v. Rooney Pace, Inc.*, 744 F.2d 255 (CA-2, 1984).

6. British tender offer rules prevent management from attempting to stop a takeover attempt without approval from the majority of stockholders. For a discussion of the British rules, see *City Code on Takeovers and Mergers*, 6th rev. ed. (Council in the Securities Industry, 1987); Thomas Hurst, "The Regulation of Tender Offers in the United States and the United Kingdom: Self-Regulation versus Legal Regulation," 12 *N.C.J. Int'l. L. & Com. Reg.* (1987), pp. 389–416; Deborah A. Demott, "Current Issues in Tender Offer Regulation: Lessons from the British," *New York University Law Review* 58 (1983): 945ff. For a comparison of takeover regulations in the United States, Britain, Canada, and Australia, see Deborah A. Demott, "Comparative Dimensions of Takeover Regulation," *Washington University Law Quarterly* 65 (1987): 69–129.

7. Office of the Chief Economist, "The Economics of Poison Pills," Securities and Exchange Commission, March 5, 1986; M. Ryngaert, "The Effect of Poison Pill Securities on Shareholder Wealth," *Journal of Financial Economics* (1988); P. Malatesta, and R. Walkling, "The Impact of Poison Pill Securities on Shareholder Wealth," *Journal of Financial Economics* (1988); Jensen, "Takeovers: Their Causes and Consequences," p. 43.

8. Up to 50 percent of top management lose their jobs within three years of a takeover, according to one report. See Jensen, "Takeovers: Their Causes and Consequences," p. 39.

9. *Moran v. Household International, Inc.*, 490 A.2d 1059, *aff'd.* 500 A.2d 1346 (1985).

10. Office of the Chief Economist, "The Economics of Poison Pills," Securities

and Exchange Commission, March 5, 1986; M. Ryngaert, "The Effect of Poison Pill Securities on Shareholder Wealth"; P. Malatesta, and R. Walkling, "The Impact of Poison Pill Securities on Shareholder Wealth"; Jensen, "Takeovers: Their Causes and Consequences," p. 43.

11. *Ministar Acquiring Corp. v. AMF, Inc.*, 621 F.Supp. 1252 (SDNY, 1985); *Unilever Acquisition Corp. v. Richardson-Vicks, Inc.*, 618 F.Supp. 407 (SDNY 1985).

12. *Asarco Inc. v. M.R.H. Holmes a Court*, 611 F.Supp. 468 (DCNJ, 1985).

13. *Dynamics Corp. of America v. CTS Corp., et al.*, U.S.D.C., N.D.Ill., Eastern Division, No. 86 C 1624 (April 17, 1986), *aff'd.* CA-7, Nos. 86–1601, 86–1608, and *Dynamics Corp. of America v. CTS Corp., et al.* (May 3, 1986). For a discussion of the New York, New Jersey, and Illinois cases, see Jensen, "The Takeover Controversy: Analysis and Evidence," reprinted in abbreviated form in John Coffee, Louis Lowenstein, and Susan Rose-Ackerman, eds., *Takeovers and Contests for Corporate Control* (New York: Oxford University Press, 1987).

14. Llewellyn H. Rockwell, Jr., "Green Stripes and Greenmail," *The Free Market* (June 1985): 2.

15. C. Holderness and D. Sheehan, "Raiders or Saviors? The Evidence of Six Controversial Investors," *Journal of Financial Economics* 14 (December 1985): 555–79; W. Mikkelson and R. Ruback, "An Empirical Analysis of the Interfirm Equity Investment Process," *Journal of Financial Economics* 14 (December 1985): 523–53.

16. This result is discussed in M. Bradley, A. Desai, and E. Kim, "The Rationale behind Interfirm Tender Offers: Information or Synergy?" *Journal of Financial Economics* 11:1 (April 1983): 183–206.

17. For more on this point, see Jensen, "The Takeover Controversy: Analysis and Evidence," Coffee, Lowenstein, and Ackerman, eds., *Takeovers and Contests for Corporate Control.*

18. R. Lambert and D. Larcker, "Golden Parachutes, Executive Decision-Making, and Shareholder Wealth," *Journal of Accounting and Economics* 7 (April 1985): 179–204.

19. The Internal Revenue Code (Title 26 USC) limits the amount of golden parachute compensation that may be deducted as salary expense and places a nondeductible excise tax on the excess. See IRC Sections 280G and 4999.

20. Ann Morrison, "Those Executive Bailout Deals," *Fortune* (December 13, 1982): 82–87.

21. U.S.C. §§78m(d)-(e), 78n(d)(f) (1982 & Supp. III 1985). Ostensibly, the drafters of the Williams Act wanted it to be neutral in effect as between target company management and the offerors. Some corporate raiders would disagree with that assessment of the Act. See S. Rep. No. 550, 90th Cong., 1st Sess. (1967).

22. Actually, target company shareholders can benefit if the attempt is successful because they receive the benefit of the higher price the raider must pay for the stock. But by artificially raising the stock price, the Williams Act also decreases the probability of a successful takeover, so target company shareholders stand to lose as a result. For some studies that measure the cost of takeover regulation, see Paul Asquith, Robert F. Bruner, and David W. Mullins, Jr., "The Gains to Bidding Firms from Merger," *Journal of Financial Economics* 11 (1983); Gregg Jarrell and Michael Bradley, "The Economic Effects of Federal and State Regulations of Cash

Tender Offers," *Journal of Law and Economics* 23 (1980): 371–407; Katherine Schipper and Rex Thompson, "Evidence on the Capitalized Value of Merger Activity for Acquiring Firms," *Journal of Financial Economics* 11 (1983); Robert Smiley, "The Effect of the Williams Amendment and Other Factors on Transactions Costs in Tender Offers," *Industrial Organization Review* 3 (1975): 138–45. For a summary of these studies, see Michael C. Jensen and Richard S. Ruback, "The Market for Corporate Control: The Scientific Evidence," *Journal of Financial Economics* 11 (1983): 5–50 at 28–29.

23. Henry G. Manne, "The Real Boesky-Case Issue," *New York Times*, November 25, 1986, A–27, column 1.

24. Doug Bandow, "Delaware's Takeover Law: Curbing Raiders Is Bad for Business," *New York Times* (February 7, 1988); Office of the Chief Economist, "Shareholder Wealth Effects of Ohio Legislation Affecting Takeovers," Securities and Exchange Commission, May 18, 1987; L. Schumann, "State Regulation of Takeovers and Shareholder Wealth: The Effects of New York's 1985 Takeover Statutes," Bureau of Economics Staff Report to the Federal Trade Commission, March 1987; Susan E. Woodward, "How Much Indiana's Anti-Takeover Law Cost Shareholders," *Wall Street Journal* (May 5, 1988); Stephen Labaton, "A Debate over the Impact of Delaware Takeover Law," *New York Times* (February 1, 1988), D1.

25. For an in-depth analysis of this tactic, see Frank H. Easterbrook and Daniel R. Fischel, "Antitrust Suits by Targets of Tender Offers," *Michigan Law Review* 80 (May 1982): 1155–78.

26. Many companies have used this ploy to totally defeat takeover attempts. For a few examples, see *Grumman Corp. v. LTV Corp.*, 665 F.2d 10 (CA–2, 1982); *Marathon Oil Co. v. Mobil Corp.*, 669 F.2d 378 (CA–6, 1981), cert. denied 102 S. Ct. 1490 (1982).

27. For some studies that measure this cost and show how an antitrust action can thwart a takeover attempt, see B. Espen Eckbo, "Horizontal Mergers, Collusion, and Stockholder Wealth," *Journal of Financial Economics* 11 (1983); J. C. Ellert, "Antitrust Enforcement and the Behavior of Stock Prices" (Ph.D dissertation, University of Chicago, 1976); Peggy G. Wier, "The Costs of Antimerger Lawsuits: Evidence from the Stock Market," *Journal of Financial Economics* 11 (1983). For a summary of these studies, see Jensen and Ruback, "The Market for Corporate Control: The Scientific Evidence," 5–50 at 27–28.

28. For more on this case, see Richard S. Ruback, "The Conoco Takeover and Stockholder Returns," *Sloan Management Review* 23 (1982): 13–33.

29. David L. Prychitko, "Corporate Takeovers and Shareholder Interests," Issue Alert No. 13 (Washington, D.C.: Citizens for a Sound Economy, April 16, 1987); Allen Michael and Israel Shaked, *Takeover Madness: Corporate America Fights Back* (New York: John Wiley, 1986); Frank H. Easterbrook and Daniel R. Fischel, "The Proper Role of a Target's Management in Responding to a Tender Offer," *Harvard Law Review* 94 (April 1981): 1202; *Panter v. Marshall Field & Co.*, 486 F.Supp. 1168 (N.D.Ill., 1980); 646 F.2d 271 (CA–7); cert. denied, 454 U.S. 1092 (1981).

30. Goldberg, "The Effect of Conglomerate Mergers on Competition," *Journal of Law and Economics* 16 (1973): 137 ff.

31. Dominick T. Armentano, *Antitrust and Monopoly: Anatomy of a Policy*

Failure (New York: Wiley, 1982); Dominick T. Armentano, *Antitrust Policy: The Case for Repeal* (Washington, D.C.: The Cato Institute, 1986).

32. For a recent philosophical, sociological, and economic critique of natural rights-based property theory, see Hans-Hermann Hoppe, *A Theory of Socialism and Capitalism* (Boston: Kluwer Academic Publishers, 1989). For a detailed philosophical approach to natural rights property theory, see Robert Nozick, *Anarchy, State, and Utopia* (New York: Basic Books, 1974).

33. Henry N. Butler and Larry E. Ribstein, "State Anti-Takeover Statutes and the Contract Clause," *University of Cincinnati Law Review* 57 (Fall 1988): 611–56; Richard A. Epstein, "Toward A Revitalization of the Contract Clause," *University of Chicago Law Review* 51 (Summer 1984): 703–51; E. Mack, "In Defense of 'Unbridled' Freedom of Contract," *American Journal of Economics and Sociology* 40 (January 1981): 1–15; M. Phillips, "The Life and Times of the Contract Clause," *American Business Law Journal* 20 (1982): 139–78.

34. Henry N. Butler and Larry E. Ribstein, "State Anti-Takeover Statutes and the Contract Clause," *University of Cincinnati Law Review* 57 (Fall 1988): 611–56.

35. *CTS Corp. v. Dynamics Corporation of America*, 107 S.Ct. 1637 (1987).

36. Amendments V and XIV. For a thorough analysis of the takings clause, see Richard A. Epstein, *Takings* (Cambridge, Mass.: Harvard University Press, 1985).

37. Nicholas Wolfson, "Civil Liberties and Regulation of Insider Trading," in *Economic Liberties and the Judiciary*, ed. James A. Dorn and Henry G. Manne (Fairfax, Va.: George Mason University Press, 1987), pp. 329–34.

38. 17 U.S., 4 Wheat. 518, 636 (1819).

39. G. Anderson and R. Tollison, "The Myth of the Corporation as a Creation of the State," *International Review of Law and Economics* 3 (1983): 107 ff.; Robert Hessen, *In Defense of the Corporation* (Stanford: Hoover Institution Press, 1979); A. Machen, "Corporate Personality," Part II, *Harvard Law Review* 24 (1911): 361.

40. Butler and Ribstein, "State Anti-Takeover Statutes and the Contract Clause," p. 620.

12

Ethics and Affirmative Action— A Managerial Approach

Rosalyn Wiggins Berne and R. Edward Freeman

The words "affirmative action" have evolved over the past twenty years, from a legal term describing a practice of corrective hiring to a highly emotive term bearing individual ethical and social ramifications. Hardly any American worker or employer can hear or use the term "affirmative action" without an emotional reaction of defensiveness, frustration, or anger. Why is this so? Perhaps the answer lies in matters of perceived fairness, justice, and opportunities gained and opportunities lost; in perceptions of personal harms and goods; and in other issues that lie at the heart of ethics.

In pursuit of the question, "Are affirmative action policies ethical: why or why not?" the study of ethics points to *values* as a means for understanding, and values can best be understood in case analysis. In this chapter, we will trace the historical development of affirmative action and discuss an emerging shift in corporate values that is changing the language of human resource management.

After reading this chapter, one should understand why business developed affirmative action procedures and what may have led to the transition in values that is now apparent. This chapter will also relay important lessons in the integration of bottom-line business interests with notions of respect for the individual. Ultimately, this chapter seeks to identify the key ethical challenges in the philosophy and practice of affirmative action.

A HISTORICAL PERSPECTIVE

Affirmative action and the language of equal opportunity arose in the late 1960s as a political response to the social outcry for racial fairness and equality in access to the workplace. It was an attempt to correct the injustices of the past, in effect, to alleviate inequities in hiring, education,

and economic opportunity. American corporations and educational institutions reacted with affirmative action policies to what had become intense
political, judicial, and social pressures. They implemented such practices
as preferential hiring, "minority recruitment and retention" programs, and
managerial methods for correcting underrepresentation within the
organization.

The governing of racial discrimination first appeared in the case of *Brown*
v. *Board of Education*, the 1954 landmark decision that ruled categorically
that school segregation was unconstitutional. Following *Brown*, the government worked vigorously to correct apparent employment injustices in
the public setting. Simultaneously, tremendous social pressure was rapidly
rising for the onset of corrective programs within private business as well.
Twenty years after *Brown*, the federal government was compelled to take
an aggressive step of intervention into the hiring practices of American
business enterprise. The American Telephone and Telegraph (AT&T) consent decree is a prime example of this intervention and a key case pointing
to the effects of the social and federal pressures of the time. A brief
description of that case follows.

American Telephone and Telegraph. Until 1973, deliberate sex discrimination in employment was a policy at AT&T. Men and women were
recruited and screened by dual standards of measurement and then tracked
into explicitly gender-specific job classifications. Women were offered positions as operators, clerks, secretaries, and inside sales representatives,
while men were given opportunities in skilled crafts and management
tracks. (Blacks were sparsely represented and nowhere to be found in the
company's upper ranks.) AT&T defended its position on gender discrimination with the arguments that women were not qualified for the jobs held
by men; that they think differently than men do; that they weren't mobile
as men were; and, above all, that they weren't even interested in holding
the men's positions. AT&T argued further that the career aspirations of
women were incompatible with male employment tracks. AT&T's blatantly
discriminatory system in those days reveals strongly held company values
regarding the distinctive roles and contributions of men and women. Even
women who in the early 1970s held "male" jobs were compensated with
significantly lower wages.

The work force of AT&T of today barely resembles its payroll of the
1970s. Today the company employs a balanced and thriving culture of
workers and is a leader in work-force diversity. What happened to create
the change? The primary impetus was the threat of extensive litigation,
through a head-on attack launched by the Federal Communications Commission and the Equal Opportunity Employment Commission, which
sought to ratify the company's employment practices. To avoid full and
consequential legal charges, AT&T went into an agreement, under the
supervision of the federal government, to comply with established terms

to change the way they hired and promoted company employees. This 1973 consent decree represents the onset of the acceleration in legal pressure on companies to implement affirmative action programs.

Other examples of litigious pressure are found in the cases of *Local 28, Sheet Metal Workers* v. *Equal Employment Opportunity Commission* and *Local Number 93* v. *Cleveland*, in which the courts upheld plans that required fixed goals and quotas for the hiring and promotion of black workers. Sheet Metal had a long history of continuing discrimination by the union. Justices William Brennan and Lewis Powell found the union had committed such egregious violations of government interest to justify the imposition of a racially classified remedy. As with AT&T, the plan upheld in the Cleveland case was later adopted in a consent decree.

While private employers were being pressed through litigation to correct hiring injustices, the justice of affirmative action as a practice was itself being challenged in the courts. Those who felt they were victims of its effects, white males in particular, were crying "reverse discrimination," believing they had been passed over for opportunities they might otherwise have had. It was exactly this voice that challenged the Supreme Court with the question of fairness. That the injustices of the past and present were to be corrected was not in question. What was in dispute was how it would be done and who would ultimately carry the burden of those corrections. The cases of DeFunis and Bakke asked these questions and raised important dilemmas regarding fairness in affirmative action. The highlights of those cases follow.

DeFunis and Bakke. Marco DeFunis, a white graduate of the University of Washington, had been denied admission to the university's law school. Thirty-six minority applicants with averages lower than his had been offered admission under a special program. DeFunis sued in state court, claiming that the law school admissions committee had discriminated against him on account of his race, in violation of the Equal Protection Clause. The trial court agreed, and DeFunis was admitted to the law school. On appeal in 1974, toward the end of his academic course, the DeFunis case was argued before the U.S. Supreme Court. By then, Marco DeFunis was approaching graduation, and the case was disposed of on mootness grounds.

Of all the "reverse discrimination" claims litigated, Allan Bakke's voice echoed the furthest. In that landmark case against the University of California at Davis, the U.S. Supreme Court upheld the decision of the lower courts that the U.C. Davis minority admissions program arbitrarily foreclosed all competition solely on the basis of race or ethnic origin, thereby violating the equal protection clause. Though the *Bakke* decision meant that Bakke had won admission to Davis medical school, the way was left open for special admissions practices, with the court upholding the validity of well-tailored affirmative action programs.

Legal and Social Transitions

Early in the history of affirmative action, most preferential programs were developed in response to unyielding mounting legal and social pressure. Gradually, affirmative action was discovered to be a valuable tool in the strategy to enhance public relations: It was good for business to project an image of corporate commitment to social issues. For some employers, the quest for fairness in hiring and for a work force representative of the community was in part motivated by a sense of organizational duty to society. The idea was that corporations, as social entities, should play a role in the social issues of the day, taking seriously their "obligations to society" and actively trying to fulfill them.

Since the 1950s, many treatises on the notion of corporate social responsibility have been written and various approaches proposed.[1] Most urged executives and their companies to be good citizens and not to ignore their role in society. Milton Friedman sounded the drum on the other side, by publishing an essay condemning executives who undertook any projects other than maximizing the interests of stockholders. Published in the *New York Times*, Friedman's essay sparked an ongoing debate. In Friedman's view, if corporate social responsibility required expenditures that were without a direct benefit to stockholders, it was tantamount to stealing from stockholders. On the other hand, Friedman argued, if corporate social responsibility was just good public relations and if investing in communities actually produced greater profits in some future economic period, then it was hard to see how any noneconomic responsibility had been fulfilled.[2]

Affirmative action as a response to federal litigation pressures was fairly straightforward in terms of stockholder responsibility and in terms of corporate strategy. However, affirmative action as a stand-alone policy reflecting corporate social responsibility for corrective measures became problematic, replete with moral dilemmas and ethical questions such as: Is it rightly the responsibility of the corporation to correct the injustices of a blighted social history? Is it morally correct to hire preferentially for the sake of correcting social inequities? Who among the employed is harmed and who benefits with a policy of affirmative action? And what about the stockholders? Do the associated costs of affirmative action adversely affect the bottom line and, if so, how can it be justified? Of concern as well are the moral implications of affirmative action when used solely as an image-creating effort for good public relations, or in compliance with legal mandates, where the hire is externally motivated with no regard for the individual good. When individuals are hired, shouldn't they confidently assume that they have been hired as individuals for their personal attributes, skills, and abilities? The moral risks are high when in fact not the individual person but rather the genetic attributes of gender and color are the true impetus for the hire. What is communicated to employees when these new hires join the company under unconventional processes? What kind of personal harms or benefits are experienced by all employees under an externally pressured system of preferential hiring?

According to consultant R. Roosevelt Thomas, Jr., affirmative action was developed thirty years ago on the basis of five premises:

1. Adult white males make up something called the U.S. business mainstream.
2. The U.S. economic edifice is a solid, unchanging institution with more than enough space for everyone.
3. Women, blacks, immigrants, and other minorities should be allowed in as a matter of public policy and common decency.
4. Widespread racial, ethnic, and sexual prejudice keeps them out.
5. Legal and social coercion are necessary to bring about the change.[3]

Thomas suggests that these premises are no longer useful because, he asserts, blacks, women, and other formerly underrepresented persons have gained full access to the workplace. Further, in the face of decreased racism, these persons are now wanting only of mobility and promotion. We question whether it is fully the case that racial, ethnic, and gender prejudices are no longer functioning as a barrier to the workplace. We do, however, find Thomas's premises to be useful in terms of grasping the history of affirmative action and for understanding the subsequent change in language and values in human resource management.

FROM AFFIRMATIVE ACTION TO VALUING DIVERSITY

Thirty years ago judges, social activists, potential employees, and employers were talking about inequality, injustice, fairness, and affirmative action. Today, we witness a major shift in language as well as in strategy, as a dynamic quest for "work-force diversity" emerges. This alteration in language seems to reflect a change in organizational values. It is an anticipation of changing demographics, as well as management's desire to acknowledge the unique contributions made to an organization by a diverse work force. It bypasses such ethical conflicts as the application of dual and lower standards that were problematic in the former practices of affirmative action. Today we find a growing trend towards the judgment of individual ability through the use of varied, race- and gender-neutral tools as opposed to the standard application of culturally insensitive, uniform measures, the results of which were overlooked or the standards of which were lowered when necessary in the past. For example, rather than using a standard written test as a prescreening device for employees and then hiring "protected" races with lower than standard scores, some companies are developing a wider array of supplemental and more revealing employment screening tools (such as open-ended interviewing and essays), which provide for racially unpredictable success.

Work-force diversity as a strategy in the problem-solving mode works well when it is inclusive rather than exclusive. A contemporary example of this type of effort at work follows.

Corning Incorporated. Corning is a large, family-controlled manufacturer of Pyrex, Corning Ware, and Steuben crystal. The company is chaired by Jamie Houghton, great-grandson of Amory Houghton, the glassmaker who moved his operation to Corning, New York, from Brooklyn in 1868. Recently, Corning's efforts in workforce diversification have been touted as one of corporate America's "most ambitious experiments in cultural engineering." The company has enlisted tremendous resources throughout its ranks to hire and retain women and blacks. (They hope to expand their ethnic and racial diversity eventually to increase participation by other groups as well.)

Corning as been working diligently, as have many companies these days, to recruit blacks and women employees. Unfortunately, until recently, the culture of Corning, New York, has not been conducive to retaining these employees, and attrition has cost the company $4 million annually in turnover costs. Today, although attrition is still double that of white males, Corning's efforts have significantly reduced the number of blacks and women leaving the company. How has this been accomplished?

To begin with, company management, specifically the chairman, has declared work-force diversity a company value that makes "good business sense." Additionally, they have developed procedures to incorporate these values throughout the company culture, so that employees will make a personal commitment to change. To that end, executives' raises and bonuses depend largely on recruiting blacks and women and on their success in training and promoting these new hires. Also, the company requires its managers to take company-sponsored courses such as "Men and Women as Colleagues" and "Valuing Racial Diversity." One of Corning's board members recently said, "I was impressed with Jamie [Chairman Houghton] putting diversity right up there with Total Quality and financial performance as one of his top three priorities for Corning." A most innovative aspect of its push for diversity is the creative endeavor and the financial commitment it's made toward changing the culture of Corning, New York. It's built a hotel, encouraged small business development, attracted the black entertainment network to air on the local cable network, and encouraged the local radio station to include more music attuned to black tastes. It even hired black barbers and hairdressers so that black employees would have these services locally. In 1990, Corning hired its first corporate director of diversity to manage and coordinate all the various diversity programs across the company network.

Thomas states,

The reason you want to move beyond affirmative action to managing diversity is because affirmative action fails to deal with the root causes of prejudice and inequality and does little to develop the full potential of every man and woman in the company. In a country seeking competitive advantage in a global economy, the goal of managing diversity is to develop our capacity to accept, incorporate, and empower the diverse human talents of the most diverse nation on earth. It's our reality, we need to make it our strength.[4]

It is in the development of human potential and in the failure to deal with prejudice and inequality that affirmative action as it has been known raises questions of ethical concern.

What are values? A person who values something wants that thing or wants a future state of affairs to come to pass. Values are intrinsically worthwhile to a person, and the effects of values are revealed in behavior. Values explain action, and an intentional action is the product of a certain belief and a set of certain values.

Values are apparent in organizations as well as in individual persons and are central to organizational strategy. The whole point of corporate strategy is to act intentionally in the name of some collective, the corporation. The alternative to corporate strategy is to act randomly or according to the dictates of an outsider. It follows that acting strategically is a matter of acting according to certain values. The values that support a corporate strategy are the most important purposes that we are able to admit to ourselves or to discover by questioning others. They are embodied in our most important projects, which will take them to fruition. The difficulty comes, however, when values conflict.

WHERE ARE WE GOING?

Affirmative action during the last two decades has been an ongoing and tenuous process of balancing notions of fairness with competing values of equality. On a moral level, it has been largely unsuccessful. Employees are particularly sensitive to any hint of unfairness; and when it comes down to individual cases, people rarely understand or tolerate what seems to be a passing-over of themselves. Few persons are willing to make what appear to be personal sacrifices of employment status for "social goods"; herein lies the root of ethical query in affirmative action programs. As long as some employees have a sense of being cheated, employees hired under affirmative action will be made to function in an environment of mistrust and doubt. Despite the good intention, classic preferential programs convey to employees hired under them the message that they are not truly valued as individuals, but rather are viewed as a means to an end. In these programs, they are indirectly made to feel like objects, much the way women have felt when notions of sexuality supersede perceptions of competency.

This is one reason why the concept of affirmative action has in contemporary practice evolved to a new notion—the value of workplace diversity, wherein an attempt is made to replace the language of "minorities" with "colleagues," of "them" with "us." Unfortunately, even this shift in language still fails to resolve the heart of the moral conflict inherent in preferential programs.

A moral decision is a decision connected with moral issues, in the same way a financial decision is connected with financial issues. It is a decision of the moral kind. Strategic decisions are based on a set of values, and these values yield certain projects or purposes which key individuals or groups want to realize. If we want to understand the strategy, we must understand the values on which the decision was based.

There are multiple conflicts in the business of human resource management, and many of them arise because conflicting values are at work. The key question is, how can we link ethics and strategy? How can we allocate benefits to all individuals while also sustaining the profitability of the company? One method is to change the individual and collective attitude (value) about diverse employee representation in the workplace.

The strategy of preferential hiring and promoting is a process that by its nature raises profound ethical issues. The moral concerns that surface will be fewer, however, when management fully embraces the language of ethics in its policies. By using ethical language, discussion is active regarding who is harmed and who is benefitted by each alternative, whose rights are protected and whose are violated.

If managerial strategy (in the programs and language that reflect it) ignores the reality of race and gender, then it will necessarily fail in the creation and sustenance of a productive work force of high employee morale. The consequences of that failure in the current and future international marketplace are obvious.

CONCLUSION

"Start with values, and the profits will follow." This is the only precept that can sustain an ethically sound strategy for the management of a diverse work force in a business enterprise. Only through internally held values will the practices of managing a diverse work force reflect a respect for the individual. The failure to do so is exactly the genesis of the existing ethical problems in affirmative action.

Increasingly, business is viewed as a contract among management, shareholders, employees, and the community at large. If affirmative action/diversity management is to exist as an effective and viable, ethically sound system in business, it can do so only with careful regard to the stakeholder contract of genuine value and respect. This will happen ultimately through a reworking and expansion of existing values that takes hold of a rich new language expressing a validated and deep desire for mutual sharing among races, ethnicities, belief systems, cultures, religions, and genders.

NOTES

1. For a full discussion of the Friedman position, see E. Epstein, "The Corporate Social Policy Process: Beyond Business Ethics, Corporate Social Responsibility, and Corporate Social Responsiveness," in *California Management Review* (1987) 29(3): 99–114.

2. This paragraph on corporate social responsibility is taken verbatim from R. E. Freeman and D. R. Gilbert, *Corporate Strategy and the Search for Ethics* (Englewood Cliffs, N.J.: Prentice-Hall, 1988).

3. R. Roosevelt Thomas, Jr., "From Affirmative Action to Affirming Diversity," in *Harvard Business Review* (March/April 1990).

4. Ibid.

13

Ethical Behavior in Labor Relations

Bevars D. Mabry

THE PROBLEM

A jurisdictional strike occurs at Cape Canaveral, and missile operations grind to a halt at the nation's foremost rocket-testing center. Air controllers strike for higher wages, grounding almost all airline traffic, and President Reagan discharges them. Longshoremen "hit the bricks" along the Eastern Seaboard and in Gulf Coast ports, and the nation's maritime activities are drastically curtailed. A national walkout is threatened by over-the-road truck drivers, jeopardizing the major arteries along which flows much of the country's commerce.

The National Football League is cited by the National Labor Relations Board for an unfair labor practice by not allowing players who ended their strike to participate in the next scheduled set of Sunday games, almost fifty years after the law has declared such employer behavior to be unfair and illegal. A utility dispute erupts in the dead of winter, and during subzero weather a gas line is maliciously destroyed so that essential services are denied to the public at a most critical moment. Yet both labor and management attempt to blame each other for the incident, and either party could be the culprit.

A company attempts to operate its plant during a labor dispute, which it has a legal right to do, and a worker is abused by a mob of picketers as she attempts to gain entry into the plant. A company hires a private-detective agency or labor relations consultant to spy on its employees to determine if a union is in the process of being established, who is sympathetic to or instrumental in the formation of a labor organization, and what can be done to prevent the workers from exercising their legal right to establish such an organization. A paper products company closes its plant in a small Michigan town and moves to another state, because the labor organization chosen by its employees in an NLRB certification election will not bargain for a wage decrease that would allow the plant to become cost competitive, and paper workers of the town's major industry all become unemployed.

These and similar events in the practice of labor relations are reported daily by the news media of the country. Depending on the degree of the reader's involvement in, or knowledge of, the event, such reports elicit sentiments of approval or disapproval, of outrage or of sympathy with the reported behavior. One's approval is forthcoming when one feels that the behavior is appropriate in the situation described, that, somehow, the action taken is justified and correct under the circumstances. Disapproval is manifested when the behavior is judged to be incorrect, inappropriate, or excessive in response to the set of events surrounding the action. In effect, the observer of the account of the labor-relations event makes a moral judgment with respect to the behavior of the participants in the event. One sympathizes with (perhaps supports) or condemns the actions of the labor union in accordance with one's impression of the rightness or wrongness of the behavior ascribed to the labor organization. Similarly, one concurs with or rejects the propriety of the employer's activities on the basis of one's sentiments of right and wrong. The observer, in effect, makes a moral judgment by applying a set of ethical standards to the behavior in question.

THE ETHICAL FOUNDATIONS OF CAPITALISM

One might argue with good merit that the ethical code implicit in Adam Smith's *Wealth of Nations* set the tone for the individual morality practiced under capitalism. In an earlier philosophic work, published in 1759, Adam Smith[1] explained his ethical system more explicitly. In this work, he attempted to show that the pursuit of self-interest is justifiable, not only from an individual point of view, which is understandable, but also from the standpoint of society's interests as a whole. He assumed humans to be social creatures whose need for social interaction requires them, as well as all other individuals, to consider the feelings of others in their actions; from this essential consideration of others they develop a moral system that defines rights and duties for all. As humans do not possess clairvoyance, they cannot possibly know the consequences of all their actions or their effect on society's welfare. For this reason, Smith acknowledged that social morality cannot be a planned product, but instead evolves from the milieu of multitudinous human interactions.[2]

The Roles of Mankind

Smith assumed that mankind has the ability to empathize, to share another's feelings vicariously, to a very great degree. A person also needs the empathy (Smith used the word "sympathy") of others. The need for empathy and the ability to empathize are essential elements in the development of a "conscience," the internal moral judge. As a participant in society, a person has four roles to play: (1) One is an initiator of action (A). (2) One is the object of, and responds to, the actions of others (B). (3) One observes the interactions of others (C). (4) One observes one's own actions (D). As an external observer of human interactions (C) or as an internal observer of one's own actions (D), a person passes judgment on behavior. This judgment can be either a spontaneously empathetic response or a deliberate one. In the A role, a person commits an act motivated by self-interest and another (B) is affected. If other individuals, functioning in the C role, agree that A's act is appropriate, but that the effect on B is too severe—that is, if C's sentiments are favorable to B even though the propriety of A's act is recognized—the act is morally unacceptable. Similarly, if A's act cannot be deemed appropriate by C, although the act may indirectly lead to effects on B of which C approves, the act is not morally acceptable. An act becomes ethically permissible only if the act of A is deserving of approval and the effect on B is not offensive, as seen by C. The sentiments of C are communicated to A, who, because of his or her empathetic need, is susceptible to them. A perceives these sentiments and either accepts or rejects them. He or she may attempt to influence C's sentiments through education or propaganda in order to make them favorable to his or her act. Thus, communications are exchanged between A and C. Through this continuous process, the actions of A and the sentiments of C are modified and brought into a harmony, an equilibrium. The acts of A are adjusted to earn the approval of C, and/or the sentiments of C are prevailed upon to change or to recognize and support the compulsions behind A's acts. The degree of movement from the initial position of A or C depends on the strength of the sentiments of each.

Mankind's ability to empathize enables a person to develop a "conscience" (D), which internally takes over the role of C. As a part of the individual, D is not likely to be deceived or misinformed, as C can be. Because one's conscience seeks truth and must be satisfied—one must, after all, live with oneself—one is compelled to adapt one's behavior in line with what one has been led to believe is right and proper, which in turn has developed from the C role one occupies in observing the behavior of others.

An individual is an actor, an object of the action, a judge of others' actions, and a judge of his or her own actions. As one experiences the effects of others' actions, one accumulates a set of beliefs and impressions about what is right and wrong in terms of self-interest. Generalizing from one's own experiences, one sympathizes with or criticizes the actions of others, and their impacts, by substituting oneself in the role of A or B. In this way, one develops a personal ethical system from which one's conscience (D) formulates moral judgments about one's own acts. The conscience is strengthened in its role by its intimate knowledge of the realities surrounding the person's own acts. When behavior is spontaneous, so that the conscience is not given time to exert its inhibiting or controlling influence, it must function belatedly, after the act. But function it does, through reflection; and sentiments of remorse or success serve to mold future behavior that is consistent with the ethical system. Guilty feelings are assuaged through a determination to correct one's behavior or to remedy its effects; feelings of pride and accomplishment reward and strengthen "correct" behavior.

Moral Sentiments as a Social Phenomenon

Self-interest motivates a person to act, but his inherent sensitivity to the feelings of others compels him to modify his behavior in order to elicit favorable sentiments from others; and his conscience operates in such a way as to enable him to associate his behavior with predictable favorable responses from others. Nevertheless, mankind functions in a limited group in a state of incomplete knowledge, and the interplay of sentiments within that group develops a rather narrow concept of morality. Individuals tend to develop a group morality rather than a universal morality. Whatever favors the group becomes the standard by which the internal observer (D) is able to judge behavior. But, just as the individual depends on the favorable sentiments of others in his group, so his group depends on the acceptance of other groups in a larger society. The interactions of the individual with the group and of the group with other groups diffuse a moral code common to all.

Smith attempted to show that the pursuit of self-interest is adjusted and directed into behavior that conforms to the moral standard of the group and of society. The automatic regulators are (1) the dependence of the individual on favorable sentiments, (2) her ability to empathize, (3) the judgments of others with respect to her behavior that are communicated to her, and (4) the formation of a conscience, by means of which she evaluates her own behavior in the light of her accumulated experience and the continuing communication of sentiments from others. It is self-interest that motivates action, and it is self-interest that brings about changes in behavior, in response to the sentiments of others.

The preceding ideas suggest that morality is as much a social phenomenon as it is an individual one. As an individual, a person places a moral value on actions in terms of whether they enhance or reduce her self-interest. Yet, she cannot be the final arbiter of what actions are proper or improper, because her self-interest cannot be perfectly consistent with the interests of all members of the society. The social mores, or social morality, reflect what has been interpreted as being good for society. If an individual's moral code does not agree with that of society, she may seek to change the social code. If she is unsuccessful and continues to practice her personal morality, other individuals in society whose personal codes are consistent will reject her code and, through various means, attempt to alter her behavior. Indeed, society is at least a collection of individuals; if there exists such a thing as a social code, it must reflect the value judgments of the influential (in terms of quantity and/or quality) members of the community. Humans as moral agents may choose to contravene their group's consensus regarding the proper behavior of members of the group, but this behavior will be judged as being right or wrong in terms of how it affects the basic interests of the society as a whole.

The Social Network of Moral Sentiments

It should be noted that there are many societies and that these societies stand partially in a nested relationship to one another, partially in an overlapping relationship, and partially in an interdependent relationship. A member of one society may be a member of several societies, particularly where the nested relationship holds. For example, a member of a family may also be a member of the city, county, and state; a sibling in one family may be a parent or grandparent in another; and so on. A worker may be a member of a family, an employee, a union member, and a citizen, and accordingly, be a member of several distinct social groups. Each of these groups will have a code of conduct, formal or informal, which may or may not be consistent with those of the others. An act viewed by one group as correct and proper may have no moral significance to another group, or it may be condemned as being against the best interests of the other group. Each group, as a composite of individual sentiments, tends to regard both internal and external behavior in terms of its impact on the interests of the group—moral if the impact is favorable, immoral if the impact is unfavorable, and nonmoral if the impact is neutral. For example, it is possible for a businessman to "wheel and deal" or to "cheat" a customer and not violate the ethics of his commercial group; yet, in so doing, he may violate the ethics of his religious group. The latter may represent more closely the ethical norm of the total society; and the very same businessman may share these moral sentiments when evidence of the similar behavior of others are revealed via the news media, without being aware of any inconsistency in his moral structure. He meets the standards imposed on him by his commercial group, which is sufficient to assuage his conscience. Yet, if society focuses attention on the moral code of the commercial group that condones this behavior, is it likely that his unawareness of the inconsistency will persist?[3]

THE CONCEPT OF A RIGHT

Definitions and Distinctions

So far, the question of morality has been discussed in terms of right and wrong, but no explanation has yet been offered of the concept of "right." If moral behavior is "right" behavior—that is, if a moral person is one who has a right to act as he does—what is meant by a "right"? There are legal rights and moral rights, and this distinction is important. A legal right is a claim, title, or interest in anything whatsoever that is enforceable by a proceeding in a court of law or equity. In this sense, an individual who possesses a right may act in accordance with that legal right; and if he is prevented from so acting, he may utilize the power of the state to protect his liberty of action. He is free from interference in following the particular line of conduct that constitutes his right. Corresponding to his right is the legal obligation of others to comply with his right. They may not like it, but they must accept it. If his right involves a claim to the performance of another, the state will assist him in compelling performance if such a response is not forthcoming. For example, a child has a right to be educated; if a parent fails to send the child to school, the state may intercede to protect that child's claim against its parents. The parents, therefore, have a legal obligation. Similarly, the right of freedom of speech conveys to the individual an obligation on the part of others not to interfere with that right, and the state will enforce that obligation.

Moral rights similarly bestow on individuals freedoms of action that are claims on the conduct of others that they, in turn, are obligated to respect. These claims may call for performance or noninterference by others. The basic difference between a moral right and a legal right is the nature of the sanctions that can be applied to secure these rights. Moral rights are enforceable through individual or group (private) sanctions, whereas legal rights may use whatever sanctions the state is capable of marshaling to ensure performance of obligations. Thus, both moral and legal rights carry claims against others and require corresponding obligations; only the source of authority to compel fulfillment of responsibility is different. Obviously, moral rights *may* be legal rights and legal rights *may* be moral rights, just as moral responsibilities and legal responsibilities may coincide. However, the coincidence is not a *necessary* relationship.

Might and Right

An interesting question is posed by the above definition of a right: Does a right exist if there is no power to enforce it? Viewed somewhat differently, if an action requires a corresponding duty or obligation to be fulfilled in order to make the action effective, what is the status of the action if no means exist whereby performance of the obligation can be compelled? Does the party engaging in the activity possess a right? This is related to the familiar question, Does might make right? Although it does not necessarily follow that might always produces right, it is certainly true that sufficient power to enforce fulfillment of the obligations imposed by a right is a necessary concomitant. As Pascal has observed, "Law without force is impotent." As an illustration, it might be asked with respect to our Civil War: Would slavery have become morally, as well as legally, acceptable if the South had won? In the realm of labor relations, if an employer wins a protracted strike, does this prove that his bargaining position was the ethically correct one and that the labor organization was necessarily in the wrong in not fulfilling its "obligation" to accept the employer's "just" offer? An implication that can be drawn from answers to these questions is that, although the exercise of power is not always morally correct, no right can be achieved without the exercise of power.

The Order of Rights

Another characteristic of rights is that they are of varying denominations. There are orders of rights: Some are of higher rank; others are of lower rank. Thus, certain state rights are subservient to certain federal rights (and vice versa); venial sins violate rights that are less important than those rights violated by mortal sins; the right to life is superior to property rights; and so on. Just as there are orders of rights, there are corresponding orders of obligations. One is a citizen of a city, state, and country, but to which level of government is his sense of obligation the strongest? He is obligated to be "good" to others, but is this obligation superior to or inferior to his obligation to protect his own interest? If he is a labor leader, is he more obligated to serve the interest of the membership, of the employer, or of the public? The significance of the order of rights becomes apparent when the problem of moral dilemmas is posed.

Conflict of Rights

Humans tend to direct their actions according to their concept of self-interest, and this concept modified by conscience serves as a criterion for individuals by which to judge the correctness of their actions. Acts that perpetuate a person's own interests are regarded, at least initially, as correct. Whether or not the acts constitute rights, however, depends on that person's ability to get others to accept the obligations imposed on them. If others do not wish to acknowledge such obligations because to do so would violate their own interests, they are apt to question the person's right to engage in the actions. In fact, the others may wish to impose on the person a conflicting set of obligations, in order to perpetuate actions they consider to be part of their rights. This is illustrated by the desire of a union to be consulted by management regarding work assignments when a technological change is being introduced. The union may feel that it has a right to be consulted and that management is obligated to discuss such changes with it. Management may not wish to accept this obligation; instead, it may seek to exercise what it considers its right to initiate technological changes independent of the union's wishes, and it may feel that the union is obligated to respect (not interfere with) the exercise of this right. The self-interest of both the labor organization and management is obviously affected by a technological change. Whose self-interest shall prevail? It is apparent that self-interest alone cannot determine who is right in the example. The ability to compel acceptance of the obligation is essential; and, where a conflict of interests such as the above exists, the stage is set for a power contest.

When two or more parties, each pursuing their own interest, find that their goals cannot simultaneously be achieved without impairing the interests of one another, will a power struggle decide who is right? In one sense, the answer is "Yes." If each party can justify her action to herself, and if through an exercise of strength a particular party wins the dispute and compels acceptance of the obligations corresponding to her action, that party's concept of right has been validated. The others have been *forced* to acknowledge the preeminence of that party's claim. For the moment, a particular concept of what is right has been determined. However, if the question should be raised again, and the balance of power in the meantime shifts in favor of a second party, the outcome of the subsequent power struggle will validate the second party's concept of what is right. As long as the standard of what is right is determined by (1) the individual valuations and (2) the relative power of individuals, such rights will be transitory and change whenever the power balance changes.[4] A degree of permanence in the concept of a right requires stability in the power equation, which, in turn, normally requires a standard of morality of broader scope than that of the individual's self-interest.

The Ethical Process in Labor Relations

Let us examine the process through which the broader standard of morality is developed. Suppose, for example, that we look at an attempt to form a union in, say, the 1920s. The workers in a particular company may feel that their interests are being thwarted by personnel practices of their employer. Let us suppose that, as individuals, they have been unable to persuade the employer to alter his behavior toward them to fit their concept of proper personnel policies. To meet their demands would impose higher cost, reduced authority, and greater operational inflexibility on the employer and thereby thwart his self-interest. Thus, a conflict of interest develops. The workers, individually at a power disadvantage and unable to force their concept of right on the employer, then begin to attempt to band together and form a union. If they are successful in forming a union, the employer recognizes that his superior power position, which protects his interests, will be threatened; therefore, he rationalizes that the formation of a union is, to him, an evil act. It does him harm. Consequently, he undertakes policies to prevent the emergence of a force designed to change the existing structure of rights. He may engage in industrial espionage to discover the ringleaders of and sympathizers with the union plot; he may thereupon discharge those suspected of an alliance with union organizers; and he may cooperate with other employers by placing the discharged employees' names on a blacklist to protect the employer group from the infiltration of employees who seek to promote industrial subversion. These devices, at the time under consideration, were not illegal; consequently, the employer had the right, under law, to engage in these practices. In addition, as a condition of employment, he could exact from workers a pledge to refrain from becoming union members while they remained employees of the business. This so-called yellow-dog contract was enforceable at law, and organizers who sought to induce workers to break this agreement could be enjoined from such activity.

In spite of these tactics available to the employer to inhibit the formation of a labor organization, let us suppose that a union is established and presents the workers' demands to the employer. The workers, let us assume, have voluntarily established the union in the face of numerous obstacles and, therefore, must believe that such an organization is moral and right. It protects their interest, it gives meaning to their activity, and it meets their needs for social intercourse. Nevertheless, the employer is, at the period of history under consideration, not obligated to recognize the union, to negotiate with it, or even to receive its demands presented on behalf of the workers. Believing it has the right to speak for the workers and attempting to illustrate that it possesses the workers' loyalties, the union thereupon attempts to compel the employer to recognize his obligation to treat with it by calling a strike. The union uses power to establish its right to be recognized and the workers' right to participate actively in the determination of the terms of the employment contract. The employer can respond to this exercise of power by attempting to neutralize the impact of the strike. The employer may choose to exercise his legal right to operate the business in the face of the strike by attempting to replace the striking workers. New employees may be hired, and their role becomes one of strikebreaking.

So far, in this sequence of events, no one has violated a law. Every act on the part of the workers, the union, and the employer has been legal. Each has been acting in accordance with his or her concept of what is right. However, as the strikebreakers attempt to gain access to the plant, the striking union members recognize that their jobs are in jeopardy. The strikebreakers represent a threat to the interests of the strikers, and to allow the former to gain entry would be contrary to the "rights" of the latter. To the strikers, the actions of the strikebreakers are immoral. As a result, it is to be expected that the strikers will attempt to prevent, by force if necessary, the strikebreakers from crossing the picket line. Legally, however, the strikers have no such right; and a violation of the law now occurs.

The company can counter the power play of the picketing workers against the new employees by obtaining an injunction against the union members. If the injunction nullifies the union's weapons of direct action, it may seek to utilize indirect weapons. Through affiliated and sympathetic organizations, it may promote a secondary boycott, utilize secondary picketing, or encourage secondary strikes and in this manner broaden the conflict by involving parties outside the immediate employer-employee relationship. Such action, however, renders the union liable to charges of restraint of trade by the employer or by the outside parties and subjects the union to the antitrust laws. Through a series of moves and countermoves, each party attempts to force acceptance by the other of the obligations that would make effective the rights it believes it possesses. During the sequence of moves, both parties are motivated by moral sentiments.

It must become apparent to the union, which is attempting to survive in the 1920s, that existing legal doctrines and instruments of law developed earlier in a rural, nonindustrial society provide employers with the superior power. Industrial unions at this time are a comparatively recent phenomenon. To survive, the union must somehow neutralize or change what it feels is the bias of law. But to change the content of the law requires a series of legislative acts, which in turn requires changes in public sentiments toward organized labor. Somehow the public must become convinced that the goals, values, and interests of union members are consistent with those of the majority of society, and that repression of those goals, values, and interests by employer groups somehow is detrimental to the interests of the majority of the individuals in society.[5] Specifically, the union needs to (1) obtain public acceptance of the principle of unionism, (2) restrict the use of the injunction, (3) broaden the concept of a legitimate labor dispute to include indirect forms of union pressure, (4) nullify the yellow-dog contract, (5) declare unfair and illegal the techniques of opposition utilized by the employer, and (6) compel the employer to recognize the right of workers to choose a bargaining representative and require the employer to examine with an open mind the appropriateness of the claims of the workers as presented by their representative.

It is significant that the type of public sentiment desired by the union was not forthcoming until the advent of the Great Depression. Not until then could other people put themselves in the place of the workers and thereby understand the types of insecurities employees face and their help-lessness as individuals to control the sources of these insecurities. Not until the Great Depression was there an identification of the interests of society with the interests of the workers sufficient to favor the workers' concept of morality in labor relations. Not until then were unions accepted as moral institutions whose rights imposed corollary obligations on employers. The bias of the law was changed, and the Federal Anti-Injunction Act of 1932 and the National Labor Relations Act of 1935 codified and validated the rights of employees in labor relations. The bias of law was changed once the necessary public sympathy was forthcoming, and the alliance of soci-ety's interests with those of employees provided the latter with sufficient power to compel employers to acknowledge the rights of employees. Just as in the period prior to the 1930s employers enjoyed an alliance with society, passive though it might have been with respect to attitudes toward labor organizations, so did labor develop an alliance with society from the 1930s through much of the 1940s.

Moral values are slow to change, however. A declaration of law does not automatically change the sentiments of everyone. Those parties sym-pathetic to attitudes shared by employers have continued to regard activ-ities of labor organizations as immoral because those activities are detrimental to important interests common to the former. Consequently, among the group favoring employer sentiments, continued practice of tech-niques to oppose unions has not been considered to be immoral, even though society has declared the techniques to be "not right." Many em-ployers have continued since 1947 to utilize with good conscience unfair labor practices to oppose unions and will continue to do so as long as they regard unions an institutions detrimental to their interests. This is why conflict of group norms with social norms is an ever-present phenomenon, and this is why practices of individuals or groups that violate social norms must be controlled and suppressed by the combined power of the society. When one can use the massive power of the agencies of the society to protect his or her interests, which society has legitimatized, he or she has indeed acquired a right. In recognition of this, there is a continuing contest among competing groups to influence public sentiments in order to win public support for a particular position. The right-to-work movement, as an illustration, cannot be fully understood except in this context, for it uses propaganda to sway public sentiment about the goodness or badness of unions.

A similar analysis can be applied to explain the modifications in labor-relations legislation that have occurred since World War II. Sentiments of the public with respect to certain activities of labor unions and labor leaders have changed. In effect, society has agreed with certain persons—both employers and employees—that the interests of the majority can be pre-served by imposing specific obligations on labor leaders. These obligations limit the activities of the labor leaders, restrict their power, and as a result advance the interests of those who heretofore were subject to the unregulated behavior of the labor officials. Union sanctions, particularly with respect to secondary activities, have been restricted because society can sympathize with neutral third parties on whom the union has tried to impose obligations that restrict the third parties' freedoms of association and contract. Society agrees that unions have no "right" to involve the third parties, and thus impede their interests, in a dispute with which the third parties are not primarily concerned.

In the era of free trade in the 1980s, with domestic industry facing the competition of cheap labor from less developed countries, the monopoly power of unions in raising wages and restricting productivity gains has motivated employers to move production facilities either to areas of the country where unions are constrained by hostile social sentiments that regard them as alien and antisocial or to other regions of the world where unions are weak or almost nonexistent. This flight of industry in response to strong economic pressure created by unions has motivated U.S. workers facing loss of jobs to reevaluate the question of whether unions do in fact serve the workers' self-interests; whether unions are in fact moral institutions for them. Is it any wonder that union membership in the 1980s has declined and that actions of employers in resisting unions have been reevaluated by society with regard to their propriety.

Summary

To summarize, then, morality is a social phenomenon as well as an individual one. When two or more parties have conflicts of interests, society lets them exercise power against one another in order to establish their concept of "rights," as long as the power struggle does not jeopardize the interests of other, major elements in the society. When such other interests are sufficiently endangered, society begins to "take sides," to define the rights and obligations of the parties and to apply sanctions in order to protect rights and enforce obligations. In the process, alliances among individuals develop and groups are formed that possess a community of interest sufficient to bind the individuals together in common action. However, as new groups appear within society as a whole, old roles and old patterns of interaction are changed. Pursuing their own interests, the members of the group are subject to, and may themselves apply, standards of morality that were valid in the structure of society existing before the formation of the group. If these standards are inadequate, other components of the society will begin to feel that the standards are no longer appropriate—that they need to be changed to reflect the changing structure and needs of the society—and they will seek by various propaganda and publicity devices to bring about new standards in keeping with their concept of what the standards of right and wrong ought to be. This is a gradual process, and in a dynamic society it is a continuing one.[6]

SOCIAL RESPONSIBILITY

Its Nature

A prominent economist once argued that, if the United States is to perpetuate its system of economic liberty, based on the principle of voluntary action, it has become absolutely necessary for organized groups to assume voluntarily a high degree of responsibility—to develop an enlarged sense of ethical conduct—for the "exercise of the degree of power and discretion which they possess."[7] How valid is this argument? Can individuals functioning in groups develop and practice a sense of social responsibility? In fact, just what does it mean to be socially responsible? One definition of "social responsibility" is the exercise of private authority in one relationship in such a way as to be consistent with rights and responsibilities in other relationships."[8] Simply put, this means that an activity of one group within the framework of that group's set of rights, which includes the corresponding set of obligations of those with whom the group interacts, should not impair the basic rights of other important groups in the society. Viewed in a somewhat different manner, socially responsible behavior is that behavior of a person or group that fulfills basic commitments to other important groups within society and for which the individual or group can be held accountable by other elements of the society.

Its Requirements

What is necessary in order for socially responsible behavior to be practiced? Certainly, the party must have some prior knowledge of the impact of the activity on the welfare of society. If an action occurs and the well-being of important groups is adversely affected, the action cannot be declared to be irresponsible if the results could not have been predicted by a reasonable person. Not only must one know of possible adverse results, but the probability of the occurrence of the undesirable consequences must be sufficiently high to modify the behavior of a reasonable person. Additionally, the consequences must be so severe if a low probability of their occurrence exists that the weighted impact of the action still generates great harm to society; that is, if a party engages in an act that is highly unlikely to produce undesirable effects and if the undesirable effects are highly unlikely to be serious, such an act cannot be declared to be irresponsible even if severe harm happens to result to other parties. Of course, if society specifically identifies types of behavior as being socially undesirable, then participation in such behavior may be declared to be an act of social irresponsibility, but the party is presumed to know about the nature of that act.

A second condition necessary for the practice of social responsibility is the application of sanctions sufficiently severe to repress socially undesirable behavior. In effect, a dichotomy is established so that all behavior that is not socially irresponsible is automatically socially responsible. Sanctions are intended to ensure the practice only of socially responsible behavior by suppressing socially irresponsible behavior. As Chamberlain has stated, "social responsibility must be enforceable to have any significance. An unenforceable responsibility remains a matter for one's private conscience."[9]

Finally, in order to declare an act socially irresponsible, it must be apparent that the primary group does not generate greater moral pressure to commit the act than society as a whole generates not to commit the act. If, for example, an individual is under great group pressure to commit an act that may have undesirable overtones outside the group but that meets little or no outside organized resistance, commission of the act by the person represents fulfillment of, to her, a higher morality.

If the present ethical system in the economic world parallels that described by Adam Smith, then the nature of this system tends to produce a rather narrow concept of responsibility. For example, a firm may have the ability to meet a union demand, say, for a new fringe benefit. The union may be willing to strike to obtain that benefit. If a strike occurs, important interests in the society will be harmed. Even though it is within the capacity of the firm to grant the demand, it may refuse to do so and thus force a strike to occur. The firm here may feel compelled to reject the union demand in order not to establish a precedent for the industry of which it is a part. Social pressure by the business associates of the firm determines the firm's actions. To grant the demand would violate the moral precepts of the business group, although not to grant the demand may harm society. Under the circumstances, the firm is compelled to obey the code of the group. As Clark observes, "if an individual wants to serve all humanity, he still has a primary obligation to the sector of humanity closest to him."[10]

The Moral-Dilemma Problem

A commitment to follow "the higher morality" is necessary if one is to resolve situations involving moral dilemmas. When behavioral decisions are limited to choosing between a moral and an immoral act, no problem is presented. However, when one is forced to choose between two or more acts each of which is moral, but to a different degree, a problem is posed because one is obligated to choose the act involving the higher morality. The most serious problem, of course, occurs when one is *forced* to choose between two or more immoral acts. In such a case, a moral dilemma is posed because the choice is limited to two or more acts that produce undesirable consequences. The moral obligation in this case is, of course, to choose the least immoral of the acts. An an illustration, suppose the director of a vocational-rehabilitation program is offered assistance by a local building contractor who promises to employ twenty of the graduates of the rehabilitation program. The director accepts. Now suppose that subsequent to the acceptance she learns that the building contractor employs nonunion personnel and that a craft union objects to the action of the contractor. Suppose, in addition, that the craft union threatens to use its political influence against the rehabilitation agency if the contractor's employment assistance is accepted. Finally, suppose that the craft union offers to admit two hundred graduates of the rehabilitation project into its apprenticeship program. A dilemma is posed for the director. If she rejects the contractor's offer, she risks the alienation of other businesses whose cooperation she must have if she is to find jobs for her graduates. However, if she accepts the contractor's offer, she incurs the wrath of the craft union, whose political power might be used to undermine the rehabilitation program. Whatever she does produces an undesirable result for the program. She faces a moral dilemma. What would she do?

To summarize, an act cannot be said to be socially irresponsible if (1) its results or the degree of impact of its consequences cannot be known, (2) it has not been declared illegal, (3) the declaration of illegality is not buttressed by sufficiently strong sanctions, and (4) the party is acting in pursuit of a higher morality (in terms of moral sentiments).

SOCIAL RESPONSIBILITY IN LABOR RELATIONS

A number of questions were raised initially in this chapter about the propriety of certain practices in the business world. A variety of practices exist in the field of labor relations about which questions of social ethics have been raised and to which the criteria of socially responsible behavior developed above can be applied. Through such an examination, a perspective may be developed within which the propriety of such practices can be analyzed.

Opposition to Technological Change

The railroads in 1959 claimed that featherbedding practices were costing them $500 million, and various commissions have confirmed that unnecessary personnel had been employed by the railroads. A more productive machine is introduced into a plant, and the union resists a piece-rate modification or a reduction in the size of the operating crew. A new tool (or technique) is developed that converts a highly skilled occupation into a semiskilled one, and the affected craft union prohibits its members from using the innovation. All of these practices either impede the substitution of more efficient techniques for less efficient ones or else negate the benefits of the superior technique. Is the union being socially irresponsible by depriving society of the benefits of improved technology? The union might argue that use of the new technique may not benefit society as a whole but only the employer, who reduces his cost but may not lower his price. Unless the price is reduced or a superior product is clearly the result, the innovation need not benefit society. Its social effect is not clear. Except in Colorado, it has not been illegal to require the employer to enter into an agreement to mitigate the impact of the technological improvement. Union leaders also have argued that their primary responsibility is to represent the interests of their constituents, and these interests require them to pursue featherbedding or make-work policies. The unemployment that will result from the new technique will weigh most heavily on the union's members. The obvious needs of the workers take precedence, insofar as the union is concerned, over the somewhat nebulous impact on the welfare of society. Yet, obviously, the interests of employers are clearly impeded if they are not allowed to use the most efficient methods available to them.

On the other hand, if employers are free to close down or move those production facilities that are not cost effective, will unions be under pressure to modify their opposition to technological change? If the union refuses to reduce its opposition to technological change and if the employer moves the plant to Malaysia, has the union served the interests of its members?

Jurisdictional Disputes

A union pulls its member off of a job because another group of workers, affiliated with another union, is assigned work the first union's members believe belongs to them. The nature of the work may, in fact, fall under the broad language of the "exclusive" jurisdiction assigned to each by its AFL-CIO charter. Such disputes are common when new industries develop rapidly, as in the aerospace industry, because entirely new tasks are created. Also, such disputes are common when technological innovations alter either the content of the job or the materials and processes used. For example, both the Carpenters and the Metalworkers unions might legitimately claim jurisdiction over the installation of aluminum siding on buildings. A jurisdictional strike certainly harms the interests of the opposing union, the employer, and the customer. The range of interests that are impeded is quite large. In addition, federal law declares such disputes to be unfair labor practices. Yet, the legal sanctions imposed on offenders are mild; in most cases, a simple injunction is obtained. Nevertheless, of the unions participating in a jurisdictional strike, each regards the performance of the task as a property right. Each, in effect, claims that it owns the job by virtue of its charter. Unfortunately, this claim is based on a charter that does not have contractual validity with employers and cannot be enforced in a court of equity.[11] Thus, to protect its "rights," the union seeks to exercise whatever power it may possess. A type of "law of the jungle" is practiced. To fail to protect its "rights" may deprive its members of future valuable work opportunities over which the union feels it has at least some degree of claim. For a union leader not to act to protect the members' right subjects that leader to a charge of being irresponsible to the interests of the union.

Strikes in Strategic Industries

In February 1965, the East Coast dockworkers ended a thirty-three-day strike, which, on the basis of the shipping industry's estimates, deprived the nation of $2 billion in gross national product. Industry spokesmen also declared the strike "to be senseless—a needless power play." Yet it occurred, and it undoubtedly depressed the economy of the nation's East Coast and Gulf Coast ports. The strike was essentially over economic issues. The national-emergency provisions of the Taft-Hartley Act were not invoked, so the strike was not illegal. But even if the eighty-day injunction had delayed the strike, the International Longshoremen's Association could legally have struck after the injunction had expired. When strikes occur over economic issues and are opposed to important public interests, who is being socially irresponsible, if, indeed, anyone is? Is the union being irresponsible because it seeks to improve the economic lot of its members? Is the management being irresponsible because it wishes to protect its "ability to manage," its solvency, or the interests of its stockholders? Indeed, who is responsible for the strike—the union, because it presents unreasonable demands, or the employer, because he refuses to grant reasonable demands? What is reasonable? If responsibility cannot be attached to any one party, can any one party arbitrarily be selected as the irresponsible party?

The Wage-Price Problem and Inflation

The Union. Formulating a guidepost to deter inflation, the government first in 1962, later in 1971, and again in 1979 admonished labor not to seek wage increases proportionally greater than the nation's average annual increase in productivity.[12] If wage rates advance at the same pace as productivity improvements, costs need not rise and firms will not be under pressure to raise prices—so the reasoning goes. Yet, if a union seeks a 5 percent increase in wages when national productivity has improved only 3 percent, is the union negating its social obligations?

First of all, the admonitions, except in 1971, were not in the form of a statute. Failure to heed the advice violated no existing law. Second, let us suppose that this union—call it "A"—does not heed the advice, but all other unions do. Unless union A is a very large union, it is unlikely that the wage increase in and of itself will generate much upward movement in the general level of prices. Conversely, if union A does abide by the policy and seeks only moderate wage increases but all other unions ignore the admonition, union A's responsible show of restraint will not keep prices from rising significantly. Third, even if union A seeks only moderate wage increases, this does not guarantee that the industry will not raise prices. (Such a situation occurred in the steel industry in 1962 and greatly embarrassed the USW President.) Demand-pull forces work perhaps more strongly to bring about price increases than do cost-push forces, and union A certainly has no control over industrial price policy or aggregate demand. Thus, the union cannot alone assume responsibility for maintaining price stability. Price stability depends on many factors, and union A may regard itself as one small part. Consider also the possibility that, whereas the national productivity increase might be 3 percent, it is possible that, in the company or industry with which union A negotiates, productivity may have increased 5, 6, or 8 percent. To forego a wage increase of like magnitude may swell the company's profits and subject the union president to the charge that he is allowing the company to evade its obligation to share its prosperity with its employees. Such a charge not only damages the union official's status in the labor movement, it may also permit the rise of political opposition. Can a union leader in such a situation fail to press for as much as he can get?

The Employer. The government wage-price policy applies also to businessmen, by imposing upon them a moral obligation to maintain existing price levels if union demands are moderated. Is management irresponsible if it raises prices in the face of union wage demands consistent with government policy? Business may well regard the admonition with greater suspicion than does organized labor, for such an admonition in peacetime may constitute a serious breach of the principle of laissez faire. Is it proper for the government to take this first step in regulating private economic behavior? The answer is not obvious.

Suppose that the demand for a company's product is increasing. A normal consequence is for prices to be bid up as buyers seek to obtain a limited supply. To ask the firm to refuse to acknowledge price pressures is to nullify the rationing effect of prices and the automatic signaling and allocating functions of the price system. In effect, the government would be asking firms to forego the opportunity to earn profits whenever the opportunity occurs. What effect would this have on the dynamic character of the American economic system? Would the government in subsequent years reimburse industry for losses incurred during lean years? If not, does the government have the right to ask business (and unions) to moderate wages and prices?

It may be demonstrated that a single firm's price policy is generally insignificant in the determination of the overall price level. In addition, wages are not the only costs to which firms are subject and, if the other costs are rising, independently of what happens to wage rates, firms may be under cost pressures to raise prices. If, however, firms in an oligopolistic industry are reluctant to do this for fear of a charge of collusion by the antitrust agencies of government, they may welcome a scapegoat on which to lay the blame for a price increase. One economist has argued that this is why price increases occur so frequently in ologopolistic industries after wage negotiations on which the public's attention has been focused.[13]

Finally, what about the responsibilities of management to the solvency of the firm, to its stockholders, and to its members' own needs for status and survival? Would not a price policy pursued for national interests contradict the interests of those who most directly rely on management's good judgment?

The Union Shop

Why should a union compel even a minority of workers who do not desire to affiliate with it to join it in order to maintain their employment status with a company? As Clark has observed, "a value of vital importance to a minority may deserve to outweigh a less important majority value."[14] In most states, the union shop is not illegal. Nevertheless, before it can be secured, it must be bargained for and the employer must agree to it. If the majority of workers subject to the union shop become dissatisfied with it, they may vote in an NLRB election to deauthorize the union shop. Thus, a union-shop clause that persists is a contractual obligation to which the union, the employer, and the majority of the members of the bargaining unit are parties. The vital question here is whether the interests of the minority are of sufficient strength to outweigh the interests of the majority. In terms of social responsibility, union-shop clauses cannot be held to be against the public welfare unless they violate some basic civil right by which certain minorities are protected; to the contrary, the principles of contract and of majority rule are consistently utilized to obtain the union shop.

In Western European countries, much less emphasis is put on union security provisions in labor agreements. However, the industrial environment in these countries is much less hostile to the union movement; and European unions, therefore, do not experience the threat to survival to which American labor organizations are subject. Given this hostile environment, American unions argue that they cannot effectively represent their membership unless the employer guarantees his acceptance of the union through such a provision. Unions argue that a minority component of the bargaining unit today may become a majority tomorrow if employers are able to practice selective hiring, for then they will be able to employ personnel unsympathetic to the union cause. Labor feels that only when union membership becomes automatic does the issue of union sympathy become unimportant; otherwise, it may be a major criterion of employment. Only if unions have security, their leaders claim, can they function as responsible organizations. Thus, unions regard union-shop clauses as morally correct and in the social interest. Of course, at the same time, union-shop clauses strengthen the union and, therefore, relatively weaken the bargaining position of the employer. Would this influence the moral sentiments of employers in their attitude toward the union shop?

If worker sentiments in the 1980s and 1990s have changed sufficiently to consider the presence of unions in a firm as a greater threat to their job security than the absence of unions, would union-shop clauses continue to serve the self-interests of the majority of the firm's employees? Is this why unions in the 1980s have lost the majority of elections where they have sought to obtain exclusive collective bargaining rights?

Violations of Labor-Relations Law

Undoubtedly, many violations of the law are based on ignorance. However, willful violation of any law, it may be argued, weakens the respect for the law and thus serves to undo the links that permit our society to function as an integrated whole. Willful violation of the law is contrary to good citizenship; therefore, is not such a violation clear evidence of social irresponsibility? Union officials and members, management, and labor consultants have all been guilty of legal transgressions with full knowledge of what they were doing and of the implications of their acts. Why do these violations occur? In some cases they are committed by persons who well may be morally motivated to breach the law. Suppose a statute has been enacted that an employer believes to be unconstitutional. May she not challenge the constitutionality of the law by means of a test violation? It is done. Suppose the law is constitutional but is regarded as being in conflict with basic values of the individual and of the group that renders her moral support. Compliance with the law may, as a result, be regarded as more immoral than violation of the law. Examples abound outside the labor-relations realm and include the actions of segregationists who opposed the civil rights movement, as well as the objections of pacifist groups to military service during the Vietnam war era. Violations of the law by people with these sentiments represent to them conformance with a higher morality.

An employer steeped in the traditions of "management's rights" and "laissez faire" may not be able to accept the idea that unions have legal rights. Freeman and Medoff have collected substantial evidence to indicate that the primary reason for the relative decline in the U.S. union movement in the decades of the 1970s and 1980s has been the willingness of employers to violate the unfair labor practice prohibitions imposed by federal law.[15] Union officials, outcasts and oppressed for so many years, may not be able to accept that they themselves may now be oppressing basic rights of others, for example, when they pursue policies based on the premise that all workers should be union members even though the workers of some companies simply do not want or need union representation.

Violations of laws also occur when legal sanctions are inadequate. Mild antitrust fines with no accompanying imprisonment of violators induce, rather than suppress, price fixing and other collusive practices. Anticipated profits from collusion greatly exceed anticipated fines. It simply is good business to violate the antitrust laws. Similarly, it may be good business to oppose unions if an order to cease and desist is the only penalty for committing an unfair labor practice.

CONCLUSION

Even though questions of whether an action is moral and whether an action is socially irresponsible cannot easily be answered, perhaps some insights into the ethical nature of behavior are possible. In making a moral judgment about a particular type of behavior, the observer should consider a number of factors before he or she reaches a conclusion. First, is one biased? Does one identify with some group that is either adversely or favorably affected by the behavior? Second, is the act legal? If it is legal, may it nevertheless be immoral, or socially wrong? In analyzing the behavior, the observer should consider the range of alternatives available to the acting party in the situation to which he or she is exposed. Perhaps the action was the lesser of several evils. Perhaps a moral dilemma forced the party to follow a course of action that he or she would not have followed if the choices had not been so limited. Finally, what were the sources and the types of the group pressures that were operating to direct the behavior along its pattern? How strong were these pressures, and were they of such nature that a normal person could resist them? Was ignorance of the result of the behavior a factor? It may be helpful to experiment with this approach the next time one finds oneself assuming the role of judge and jury.

NOTES

1. *The Theory of Moral Sentiments*, 6th ed. (1790; reprint, New Rochelle, N.Y.: Arlington House, 1969).

2. For an excellent summary of Smith's ethical system, see Overton H. Taylor, *A History of Economic Thought* (New York: McGraw-Hill Book Co., 1960), chaps. 2–4.

3. Joseph McGuire believes it is impossible to develop a code of ethics for businessmen that they would accept. He states, "In real-life business situations there are imponderable factors which are too complicated for simple ethical codes of behavior." *Business and Society* (New York: McGraw-Hill Book Co., 1963), p. 286. Does this mean that there exist no standards of right or wrong that apply to business conduct?

4. The alternating views of the National Labor Relations Board, as its composition is changed through presidential appointments, towards the legality of labor relations practices under Section 8 of the National Labor Relations Act is an apt illustration. Similarly, the composition of the Supreme Court is important to each side of a wide range of social issues—capital punishment, obscenity, abortion, and state's rights.

5. It is for this reason the worker protests against management tend to assume political overtones. For example, Richard A. Lester presents this argument in *As Unions Mature* (Princeton, N.J.: Princeton University Press, 1958), pp. 14–20.

6. As John Maurice Clark has argued in *Economics, Institutions and Human Welfare* (New York: Alfred A. Knopf, Inc., 1957), p. 182, "in a new activity, bringing people into new relationships, appropriate standards take time to develop."

7. Ibid., p. 32. The Chicago Board of Trade, in response to the federal government's indictment and unsuccessful 1990 prosecution of its "pit traders," has instituted an "ethics seminar" that all traders in commodity and foreign exchange future markets must attend.

8. Neil W. Chamberlain, *Social Responsibility and Strikes* (New York: Harper & Row, 1953), p. 16.

9. Ibid., p. 17.

10. Clark, *Economics, Institutions and Human Welfare*, p. 206.

11. In fact, the union has legal representational rights over job positions only if the NLRB has certified that those positions are contained within the "appropriate bargaining unit."

12. From August 15 to November 15, 1971, wages were actually frozen under the Nixon Wage–Price Guidelines. A second phase was then instituted until January 1973, during which wage increases in key industries were monitored by a Pay Board that restrained such increases to those matched by increases in productivity. George Schultz and Kenneth Dam, *Economic Policy beyond the Headlines* (New York: W. W. Norton & Co., 1977), pp. 65–85.

13. John Kenneth Galbraith, *The Affluent Society* (Boston: Houghton Mifflin Co., 1958), pp. 219–20.

14. Clark, *Economics, Institutions and Human Welfare*, p. 30.

15. Richard D. Freeman and James L. Medoff, *What Do Unions Do?* (New York: Basic Books, Inc., 1984), pp. 230–45.

14

Insider Trading

ROBERT W. MCGEE AND WALTER E. BLOCK

Insider trading has gotten a bad name in recent years. News commentators and government officials often disparage inside traders as greedy, sinister people who would cut their own mother's throat if she got in the way of a deal. But while that may be true in a few cases, it is the exception rather than the rule. In fact, many of the transactions that might be considered insider trading result in no "harm" to anyone and may actually be beneficial to society.

Many commentators who disparage insider trading do so because they do not understand how it works, and they do not see that it can be beneficial. It should be pointed out that we are not trying to defend all forms of insider trading, because some kinds of insider trading are unethical. What we are attempting to show is that blanket statements like "insider trading in unethical" are not always true.

What determines whether insider trading is ethical or unethical? Basically, one must look to whether someone's rights have been violated. One example of insider trading resulting in a rights violation occurs when someone misappropriates property of another. But that does not mean that anyone who does something that results in economic harm to another has done something unethical. If a supermarket chain opens a new store across the street from a mom-and-pop grocery, Mom and Pop might lose business and thereby suffer economic harm, but that does not mean that the chain store people have done anything unethical. Mom and Pop have a right to sell groceries, but so does the chain store. Although Mom and Pop may be harmed economically, their rights have not been violated because there is no one preventing them from offering their goods for sale. If customers decide to do business with the chain store rather than with Mom and Pop, that is their business and their right.

Misappropriation is a different story. When someone misappropriates the property of another—and insider information is property—the misappropriation is a violation of the rights of the property owner. But when individuals use for their own benefit information that they have honestly acquired, there is nothing unethical about that. Let's take a look at some examples.

Let's say that Joe quits his low-paying job so that he can take advantage of another job opportunity a few blocks away. Does he have any obligation to tell his coworkers about the position first, before he applies for the position? Does it make any difference whether he learned about the position from a newspaper ad or from his brother-in-law? Regardless of how he learned of the job opportunity, he has the right to apply for the position without telling others about it first. Indeed, it is to his advantage to keep his mouth shut until he has the position locked up.

All Joe is doing is taking advantage of a position of superior knowledge, which is not much different than what a stock trader who spends fifty or sixty hours a week searching for information does. People who spend a great deal of time studying the market can gain information that others do not possess, not because they have stolen it but because they worked to acquire it. The information they gain is their property, and they should be able to do with it as they see fit—sell it, trade on it, give it away, or sit on it. They have no moral obligation to announce their findings to the world, just as Joe had no obligation to tell anyone about the job opportunity he discovered.

The method by which such information is acquired is irrelevant for purposes of determining whether using it is ethical or not, as long as it was acquired honestly, that is, without fraud or coercion. Whether Joe learned about the job by digging through want ads, by placing phone calls or going on numerous job interviews, or by receiving the information from an employment agency makes no difference. The fact that his brother-in-law might have dumped the information in his lap does not change anything. The brother-in-law has, in effect, given him a gift of property—information—that Joe is free to use as he sees fit. The only way that Joe could use this information unethically is if he obtained it from an employment agency under the stipulation that he not tell anyone else about the job. If he sells the information to another under this circumstance, he is misappropriating the employment agency's property. If he gives the information away rather than selling it, he is still acting unethically even though he might not have benefitted personally, because he is breaching his contract with the employment agency not to tell others what he has learned. This situation is not unlike that of individuals who breach their fiduciary duty to their employer or client not to tell anyone that a merger (or bankruptcy) is right around the corner.

Is insider trading fraudulent? St. Thomas Aquinas said that fraud can be perpetrated in three ways, either by selling one thing for another or by giving the wrong quality or quantity.[1] A more modern definition is "intentional deception to cause a person to give up property or some lawful rights."[2] A more general definition is that fraud is perpetrated when a person knowingly or intentionally makes a false representation of fact to another with the intent that the other party rely on the representation and when the other party actually did rely upon the false statement to his loss, detriment, or damage.[3] Some courts have extended liability to include negligent or inadvertent misrepresentation.[4] According to this theory, there is no fraud if there is no loss. And since much so-called insider trading does not involve any identifiable loss, the practice is not fraudulent. Even in cases where there is loss, it still has to be proven that all the elements of fraud are present before an inside trader can be found guilty of the offense.

A typical case of insider trading occurs when a buyer with inside information calls his stockbroker and tells him to buy, knowing that the stock price is likely to rise as soon as the inside information becomes public. In this case, the buyer does not deceive the seller into giving up property. Indeed, the buyer does not even know who the seller is, and the seller would have sold anyway, anonymously. The seller's action would have been the same whether an inside trader was the other party to the transaction or not. If the inside trader had not purchased the stock, someone else would have. Yet this "someone else" would not be accused of reaping unjust profits, even if the identical stock were purchased for the same price the insider would have paid. Consequently, insider trading does not seem to fit the definition of fraud. Furthermore, according to Aquinas, there is no moral duty to inform a potential buyer that the price of the good you are trying to sell is likely to change in the near future.[5]

In the case Aquinas discusses, a wheat merchant

carries wheat to a place where wheat fetches a high price, knowing that many will come after him carrying wheat . . . if the buyers knew this they would give a lower price. But . . . the seller need not give the buyer this information . . . the seller, since he sells his goods at the price actually offered him, does not seem to act contrary to justice through not stating what is going to happen. If however he were to do so, or if he lowered his price, it would be exceedingly virtuous on his part: although he does not seem to be bound to do this as a debt of justice.[6]

A similar example is discussed by Cicero, in which a merchant is bringing grain from Alexandria to Rhodes, whose residents are starving. He knows that other grain merchants will arrive shortly. If he discloses this fact, the price for his own grain will fall. Should he disclose?[7]

An insider who knows the stock price is likely to change in the near future has no "moral" duty to inform potential buyers of this fact. Where there is no moral duty, certainly there should be no legal duty either. In fact, the U.S. Supreme Court has ruled at least twice that those in possession of nonpublic information do not have a general duty to disclose the information to the marketplace.[8] The Fourth Circuit Court of Appeals in 1988 held that a corporation has no duty to disclose tentative merger plans to stockholders before it buys their stock.[9]

In *Chiarella*, the Supreme Court held that "one who fails to disclose material information prior to the consummation of a transaction commits fraud only when he is under a duty to do so."[10] Chiarella was an employee of a printing company. Part of his job was to print confidential documents for corporations. In the course of his employment, he was able to determine that certain companies were going to be the target of takeovers, and he bought stock in those companies. He did not have any fiduciary relationship to the company's stockholders. The Supreme Court held that he was not guilty of violating Rule 10b–5 because he did not commit any fraud against the party who sold him the stock.[11]

In *Dirks*, the Supreme Court held that insiders have a fiduciary duty to the shareholders and must either disclose material inside information or not trade in the securities of the corporation.[12] It also held that a tippee who receives material nonpublic information from an insider and trades on it violates Rule 10b–5 if the insider breaches any fiduciary duty by disclosing the information, provided the tippee either knew or should have known that there was a breach. But an insider is deemed to breach a duty only if he personally benefits from the disclosure, either directly or indirectly. Dirks was a securities analyst. He got his inside information from a company's employees, who told him that the company was engaged in massive fraud. Dirks told his clients to sell their stock in the company. The employees who told Dirks the insider information did not act for personal gain. They wanted to expose the fraud. Since the employees did not breach a fiduciary duty to any shareholders, Dirks could not be found guilty of violating Rule 10b–5.

Chiarella and *Dirks* represent a major split with the SEC because these cases held that there is no general duty to disclose nonpublic information. The SEC had been contending that the law required information between traders to be equal, based on the flawed decision in *Texas Gulf Sulphur*.[13] In *Taylor* v. *First Union Corp. of So. Carolina* the fourth circuit held that neither the acquiring nor the selling corporation has a duty to tell shareholders that they are engaging in merger discussions.[14]

WHOSE RIGHTS ARE VIOLATED BY INSIDER TRADING?

Although the transaction of buying and selling stock by an insider does not meet either the dictionary's or Aquinas's definition of fraud, the question of justice still remains. If no one's rights are violated, the act is not unjust; if someone's rights are violated, the act is unjust. The obvious question to raise is: "Whose rights are violated by insider trading?"

The most obvious potential "victims" of insider trading are the potential sellers who sell their stock anonymously to an inside trader. But they would have sold anyway, so whether the inside trader buys from them or not does not affect the proceeds they receive from the sale. If the sellers are hurt by having an inside trader in the market, it is difficult to measure the damage, and it appears that there is no damage. In fact, the academic literature recognizes that insider trading does not result in any harm to any identifiable group.[15] As those who sell to inside traders may actually be helped rather than harmed because they received a better price, it appears illogical to allow them to sue for damage if in fact there are no damages. In any event, there appears to be no violation of anyone's rights in such instances of insider trading.

It has been argued that employers are harmed by insider trading because employees misappropriate corporate information for personal gain.[16] Yet employers whose employees misappropriate information for personal gain have a remedy at law already. If anyone sues, it should be the employer that sues the employee. Government should not be a party to such a lawsuit, since it is a private rights violation rather than a public harm that has been committed, if in fact any rights violation has been committed at all. Yet there has been little private restriction on trading on insider information,[17] and some authors have gone so far as to state that the gains derived from insider trading are equivalent to compensation that a corporation would otherwise pay to corporate officers for their entrepreneurial expertise[18] and that employers are not harmed at all by insider trading.

WHAT ARE THE BENEFICIAL EFFECTS OF INSIDER TRADING?

Insider trading serves as a means of communicating market information, which makes markets more efficient.[19] When insiders are seen trading, it acts as a signal to others that a stock's price will likely move in a certain direction. If a director of General Motors purchases a large quantity of General Motors stock, that act reveals evidence that the stock's price is likely to rise in the near future. Likewise, if the director sells, it is likely that the price will soon fall. A chain reaction will take place as the brokerage firm handling the transaction alerts other brokers and clients, and the stock price will start moving in the correct direction, closer to its true value. There is no need to make a public announcement, because the market reacts almost immediately. Even if the insider is anonymous, an increase (or decrease) in demand for a particular stock will be noticed by the market, and the price will move accordingly. Placing prohibitions on insider trading has the effect of blocking this flow of information. Insiders will attempt to hide their trades or perhaps not make them at all, thus preventing the market from learning this valuable information.

The potential acquirer in a takeover attempt may also benefit by insider trading. The investment banker hired by the acquirer may leak information to arbitrageurs, who then accumulate shares in the target company with the intent of tendering them shortly thereafter. The result is that the take-over's chances of success are increased, and the acquirer may actually benefit as a result of the investment banker's alleged misconduct.[20]

The necessary separation of management from owners inherent in all large corporations has caused corporate management to be unresponsive to the wishes of corporate stockholders. Management can make decisions based on self-interest rather than shareholder interest with little fear of reprisal because it is easier for shareholders to sell their stock than to fight management decisions. This fact of corporate life is not new. It has been true ever since owners became separated from managers.

The (relatively) free market economy of the United States has found a way to pierce the protective veil that insulates unresponsive management from the wrath of small shareholders—the takeover. The corporate take-over is practically the only way that entrenched management can be shaken up and either forced to be responsive to shareholder interests or fired. This market for corporate control does not exist to any great extent in any other country, which gives the United States a competitive advantage because the threat of takeover gives U.S. corporate management an extra incentive to work for shareholder interests rather than their own. Thus, shareholders of U.S. companies receive a higher return on investment than can investors in companies that are not subject to a takeover threat, all other things being equal.[21] The attack on Drexel Burnham Lambert, and the threat of an attack on anyone else who tries to facilitate the market for corporate control with junk bonds, is bound to harm the market for corporate control and thus to decrease the already weak voice that shareholders have. Man-agement of companies that do not have to fear a takeover will have less incentive to be efficient, and that hurts employees and consumers, too.

The shareholders who sell at the time the arbitrageurs are buying may also benefit. The increased demand generated by the arbitrageurs increases the price the sellers receive when they sell. Without the leakage of the insider information to the arbitrageurs, the demand for the stock in ques-tion would have been lower, thus the sellers (who would probably have sold anyway) would have received a somewhat lower price for their stock. Shareholders who do not sell also benefit, as the price of their shares rises as a result of insider trading.

A goal of most corporate managements is to increase shareholder wealth, in other words to increase the stock's price. As insider trading has a ten-dency to increase the stock's price, inside traders assist management achieve its goal. Inside traders may benefit the corporation in another way as well.

A decision by the board or its delegates to "tip" inside corporate information to certain outsiders, to facilitate trading by them, could also be in the best interests of the corporation. For example, where the corporation has received valuable services from an outsider, one way of providing indirect compensation for those services is by providing the outsider with the authorized use of inside information owned by the corporation. Thus, if one accepts the notion that inside information is property of the corporation, even the tipping of that information to others ought not be regarded as improper, if the board of directors or other authorized corporate decision maker has determined that such tipping is in the best interests of the corporation.[22]

WHO IS HARMED BY PROHIBITIONS ON INSIDER TRADING?

Who is harmed by prohibitions on insider trading? The obvious answer is the inside traders themselves. If insider trading is not viewed as "immoral," then punishing insiders by preventing them from using their knowledge becomes an unjust act in itself.

There is a case to be made that the company's shareholders may be harmed by placing prohibitions on insider trading.[23] For example, the Williams Act, the part of the Securities Exchange Act of 1934 that requires anyone contemplating a tender offer to announce the intention well in advance (Sections 13d and e, Sections 14d, e and f), makes it easier for target managements to thwart a takeover. Several authors have argued that shareholders tend to benefit by takeovers, so that making it easier to thwart a takeover may be against the stockholders' interest.[24]

Outlawing or restricting insider trading may have long-term adverse effects on the economy. The market certainly will operate less efficiently, because insider trading increases market efficiency.[25] As hostile takeovers will be more difficult to make, shareholders will lose, as shareholders tend to benefit by hostile takeovers.[26]

Insider trading laws result in compliance and escape costs. The legal and accounting fees involved in complying with or circumventing the law can be fairly expensive, an expense that would not be incurred in the absence of insider trading laws. Using indirect means to accomplish what could otherwise be accomplished directly also leads to unnecessary costs.[27] The delay in disclosure that results from using indirect means of accomplishing the goal also increases market inefficiency. There may also be other transaction costs, such as using an obscure mutual fund or a foreign bank or broker, when a more direct purchase would be less costly.

Taxpayers are adversely affected by insider trading laws, as enormous resources must be placed at the disposal of the police power to do any kind of policing. The resources used to police the insider trading laws might be better used to prevent some real criminal activity from being committed. For any use of government resources, there is a cost and a benefit. Because insider trading can be regarded as a victimless crime, if indeed it is a crime at all, an argument can be made that the resources government uses to enforce the insider trading laws can be better employed elsewhere.

PROPERTY RIGHTS

Information can be an asset. Where the owner of an asset uses that information for gain, there should be no complaint, as long as there is no fraud or coercion. But where such asset is used for gain without the owner's permission, any gain belongs to the owner.

Financial analysts generally obtain information about a company by analyzing public information and interviewing company officials, who are often all too eager to provide whatever information is requested. In such cases, it can hardly be said that the financial analyst misappropriated information belonging to the company, and there should be no prohibition on using the information for profit. Such property is in the public domain, and the company therefore has relinquished whatever claim it once had. Whatever information a financial analyst obtains in this manner is earned by considerable effort, and the analyst acquires a property right in that information, which can then be sold to clients, published in a newsletter to clients, or used for personal gain.[28] There is no ethical duty to give this property to the world, just as there is no ethical duty to give any other property to the world. The property can be kept for personal use or given to any persons of the owner's choosing, either for profit or for free. Forcing an analyst to give this information to the world before being allowed to trade on it would eliminate the incentive to develop the information in the first place, and the market would suffer as a result.[29] Such coercive actions would also be unjust to the analyst, whose property rights are being impinged upon.

CONCLUDING COMMENTS

Insider trading has been viewed as evil, and inside traders have been seen as unethical individuals. As we have tried to point out, these views are often incorrect. Insider trading can be beneficial to a number of groups. Whether or not the practice is unethical depends not on the effects—who is "harmed"—but on property rights and fraud (or the absence of fraud). If the transaction is not fraudulent and the inside trader is not violating anyone's property rights in information, there is nothing unethical about the practice. The fact that an inside trader can make millions of dollars, seemingly with little effort, is completely irrelevant as far as determining whether the practice is unethical.

NOTES

1. G. Dalcourt, *The Philosophy and Writings of St. Thomas Aquinas* (1965), at 105; St. Thomas Aquinas, *Summa Theologica*, II-II, Q.77.

2. *Webster's New World Dictionary of the American Language*, college edition (1964).

3. *Kaufman Inv. Corp. v. Johnson*, 623 F.2d 598 (9th Cir. 1980), *cert. den.* 450 US 914; *Meader v. Francis Ford, Inc.*, 286 Or. 451, 595 P.2d 480 (1979); *Metal Tech. Corp. v. Metal Techniques Co., Inc.*, 74 Or. App. 297, 703 P.2d 237 (1985); 2 *Restatement* 55, et. seq., Torts Second § 525 ff., cited in Foley, "Insider Trading: The Moral Issue," *The Freeman* 37 (November 1987): 409, at note 7.

4. *Weiss v. Gumbert*, 191 Or. 119, 227 P.2d 812, 228 P.2d 800 (1951); 3 *Restatement* 126-45, Torts Second §§ 552-552C, cited in Foley, "Insider Trading: The Moral Issue," *Freeman* 37 (November 1987): 409, at note 8.

5. St. Thomas Aquinas, *Summa Theologica*, II-II, Q.77, art. 3(4); Barath, "The Just Price and the Costs of Production According to St. Thomas Aquinas," *New Scholasticism* 34 (1960): 420; Bartell, "Value Price, and St. Thomas," *The Thomist* 25 (July 1962) at 359-60.

6. St. Thomas Aquinas, *Summa Theologica*, II-II, Q.77, art. 3(4).

7. Cicero, *De Officiis* Bk. III, ch. xiii (W. Miller trans. 1968). G. Lawson discusses this passage in "The Ethics of Insider Trading," *Harv. J.L. & Pub. Pol'y* 11 (1988): 727, at 738-39. This passage is also mentioned in Barry, "The Economics of Outside Information and Rule 10b-5," *U. Pa.L. Rev.* 129 (1981): 1307, at 1361 n. 206. For a critique of the Lawson article, see J. R. Macey, "Comment: Ethics, Economics, and Insider Trading: Ayn Rand Meets the Theory of the Firm,'" *Harv. J.L. & Pub. Pol'y* 11 (1988): 785.

8. *Chiarella v. United States*, 445 U.S. 222 (1980); *Dirks v. Securities and Exchange Commission*, 463 U.S. 646 (1983). Also see Jonathan R. Macey, "The SEC's Insider Trading Proposal: Good Politics, Bad Policy," *Policy Analysis*, 101 (Washington, D.C.: Cato Institute, March 31, 1988), 2. In *Chiarella*, at 230, the Court held that silence in connection with the purchase or sale of securities may operate as a fraud only where there is a duty to disclose that arises from a relationship of trust and confidence between the parties to the transaction. For a discussion of these two cases, see Aldave, "Misappropriation: A General Theory of Liability for Trading on Nonpublic Information," *Hofstra L. Rev.* 13 (1984): 101; Heller, "Chiarella, SEC Rule 14e-3 and Dirks: Fairness Versus Economic Theory," *Bus. Law* 37 (1982): 517; Morgan, "Insider Trading and the Infringement of Property Rights," *Ohio St. L.J.* 48 (1987): 79. For other discussions of *Chiarella* and the misappropriation theory, see Anderson, "Fraud, Fiduciaries, and Insider Trading," *Hofstra L. Rev.* 10 (1982): 341; Branson, "Discourse on the Supreme Court Approach to SEC Rule 10b-5 and Insider Trading," *Emory L.J.* 30 (1981): 263; Langevoort, "Insider Trading and the Fiduciary Principle: A Post-Chiarella Restatement," *Calif. L. Rev.* 70 (1982): 1; Macey, "From Fairness to Contract: The New Direction of the Rules against Insider Trading," *Hofstra L. Rev.* 13

(1984): 9; Martin, "Insider Trading and the Misappropriation Theory: Has the Second Circuit Gone Too Far?" *St. John's L. Rev.* 61 (1986): 78; Morgan, "The Insider Trading Rules after Chiarella: Are They Consistent with Statutory Policy?" *Hastings L.J.* 33 (1982): 1407. For a summary of the literature on the "wrongness" of insider trading, see Rider and Ffrench, *The Regulation of Insider Trading* (1979). Other discussions on the subject may be found in Brudney, "Insiders, Outsiders and Informational Advantages under the Federal Securities Law," *Harv. L. Rev.* 93 (1979): 322; Dooley, "Enforcement of Insider Trading Restrictions," *Va. L. Rev.* 66 (1980: 1; Scott, "Insider Trading, Rule 10b–5, Disclosure and Corporate Privacy," *J. Leg. Stud.* 9 (1980): 801.

9. *Taylor v. First Union Corp. of So. Carolina*, 857 F.2d 240 (4th Cir. 1988).

10. 445 U.S. at 228.

11. Id. at 234–35.

12. 463 U.S. at 653.

13. 401 F.2d 833 (2d Cir. 1968), cert. denied 394 U.S. 976, 89 S. Ct. 1454, 22 L.Ed.2d 756 (1969).

14. 857 F.2d 240 (4th Cir. 1988).

15. Henry Manne, "Insider Trading and Property Rights in New Information," *Cato Journal* 4 (Winter 1985): 933 reprinted in Dorn and Manne, eds., *Economic Liberties and the Judiciary* (1987) at 317–27; Morgan, "Insider Trading and the Infringement of Property Rights," *Ohio St. L. J.* 48 (1987): 79.

16. Scott, "Insider Trading: Rule 10b–5, Disclosure and Corporate Privacy," *J. Legal Stud.* 9 (December 1980): 801; Martin, "Insider Trading and Misappropriation Theory: Has the Second Circuit Gone Too Far?" *St. John's L. Rev.* 61 (1986): 78; Morgan, "Insider Trading and the Infringement of Property Rights," *Ohio St. L.J.* 48 (1987): 79.

17. Dooley, "Enforcement of Insider Trading Restrictions," *Virg. L. Rev.* 66 (February 1980): 1; Easterbrook, "Insider Trading, Secret Agents, Evidentiary Privileges, and the Production of Information," *Sup. Ct. Rev.* (1981): 309.

18. Manne, "Insider Trading and the Stock Market," JSD diss., Yale University, 1966; H. Manne, *Insider Trading and the Stock Market* (1966); Carlton and Fischel, "The Regulation of Insider Trading," *Stan. L. Rev.* 35 (May 1983) at 858, 876; Easterbrook, "Insider Trading, Secret Agents, Evidentiary Privileges, and the Production of Information," *Sup. Ct. Rev.* (1981): 309, at 332; Scott, "Insider Trading: Rule 10b–5, Disclosure and Corporate Privacy," *J. Legal Stud.* 9 (December 1980): 801, at 808.

19. Wu, "An Economist Looks at Section 16 of the Securities Exchange Act of 1934," *Colum. L. Rev.* 68 (February 1968): 260; Kelly, Nardinelli, and Wallace, "Regulation of Insider Trading: Rethinking SEC Policy Rules," *Cato J.* 7 (Fall 1987): 441, at 442; Carlton and Fischel, "The Regulation of Insider Trading," *Stan. L. Rev.* 35 (May 1983): 857; Morgan, "Insider Trading and the Infringement of Property Rights," *Ohio St. L.J.* 48 (1987): 79, at 105.

20. Herzel and Katz, "Insider Trading: Who Loses?" *Lloyds Bank Review* 15 (July 1987).

21. Manne and Ribstein make this point in "The SEC v. The American Shareholder," *National Review*, November 25, 1988, at 29.

22. Morgan, "Insider Trading and the Infringement of Property Rights," *Ohio St. L.J.* 48 (1987): 79, at 98.

23. Carlton and Fischel, "The Regulation of Insider Trading," *Stanford Law Review* 35 (May 1983).

24. A number of authors have addressed this point in recent years. See Johnson, "Antitakeover Legislation: Not Necessary, Not Wise," *Cleve. St. L. Rev.* 35 (1986–87): 303; Manne, "The Real Boesky-Case Issue," *New York Times* (November 25, 1986), A–27, col. 1; Bandow, "Curbing Raiders Is Bad for Business," *New York Times* (February 7, 1988); D. Prychitko, "Corporate Takeovers and Shareholder Interests," *Issue Alert* no. 13 (Washington, D.C.: Citizens for a Sound Economy, April 16, 1987); Coffee, Grundfest, Romano, and Weidenbaum, "Corporate Takeovers: Who Wins; Who Loses; Who Should Regulate?" *Regulation* 88 (1988): 23; Bubb, "Hostile Acquisitions and the Restructuring of Corporate America," *The Freeman* 36 (May 1986): 166; Romano, "The Political Economy of Takeover Statutes," *Virg. L. Rev.* 73 (1987); Jensen, "Takeovers: Folklore and Science," *Harv. Bus. Rev.* 109 (November-December 1984); Jarrell, Brickley, and Netter, "The Market for Corporate Control: The Empirical Evidence Since 1980," *J. Econ. Perspectives* 49 (Winter 1988); Buttarazzi, "Corporate Takeovers: What Is the Federal Role?" *Backgrounder* 606, The Heritage Foundation (September 29, 1987); and Woodward, "How Much Indiana's Anti-Takeover Law Cost Shareholders," *Wall Street Journal* (May 5, 1988).

25. Finnerty, "Insiders and Market Efficiency," *Journal of Finance* 31 (September 1976): 1141.

26. Jarrell, Brickley, and Netter, "The Market for Corporate Control: The Empirical Evidence Since 1980," *J. Economic Perspectives* 49 (Winter 1988).

27. H. Demsetz, "Perfect Competition, Regulation, and the Stock Market," in H. Manne, ed., *Economic Policy and the Regulation of Corporate Securities* (1969); H. Manne, "Insider Trading and Property Rights in New Information," *Cato J.* 4 (Winter 1985): 933 reprinted in Dorn and Manne, eds., *Economic Liberties and the Judiciary* (1987), 317–27.

28. Fleischer, Mundheim, and Murphy, "An Initial Inquiry into the Responsibility to Disclose Market Information," *Univ. Pennsylvania L. Rev.* 121 (1973): 798.

29. Fama and Laffer, "Information and Capital Markets," *J. Business* (July 1971): 289; Ronen, "The Effect of Insider Trading Rules on Information Generation and Disclosure by Corporations," *Accounting Review* (1977): 438.

Part IV

Responsibilities of Employees and the Corporation

15

Conflicts of Interest

GEORGE C. S. BENSON

The historical part of this chapter will indicate that for many centuries ethical persons have had to face situations in which two or more interests are legitimately present and competing or conflicting. The individual (or firm) making a decision that will affect those interests may have a larger stake in one interest than in the other (or others), but he or she is expected, in fact obligated, to serve each, regardless of that stake.[1]

Both government and commerce have made efforts to reduce the number of conflicts or to forbid the crimes that may result in conflicts or are derived from conflicts, but such efforts are often misunderstood or unenforceable.

Conflict situations may result in criminal action, but they also may come from criminal action. Bribes given a legislator to vote for the wishes of an industry become a crime themselves, but it is a clearer case of crime when the conflicting interest causes the legislator to vote against the public interest in favor of the briber's requests. The act of "insider trading" means that the employee values money for himself above the interests of his employer and the law. A large percentage of savings and loan failures in recent years were a result of executives making large risky loans in the interest of a firm or friend other than the institution that was their primary fiduciary responsibility. Governmental awards of work to an industry or a group of citizens are made in return for political rewards, again expressing an evaluation of personal interest above a conflicting official responsibility.

Some conflicts are hard to control. Most members of Congress have received gifts for campaign expenses from corporate or union "political action committees." Clearly these gifts are intended to keep the congressman favorable to the interest of that group. Some may view such gifts as bribes. Yet the senator or representative is commonly supposed to represent all the needs of his area, which certainly include those of the corporations, unions, and other associations of people in his district or state.

His vote, when he must decide on issues affecting his constituents or contributors, is made on the basis of his presumably honest judgment. It is
almost inconceivable that one could ban all conflicts of interest on the part
of legislators without altering the nature of representative government.
Senator Robert Kerr of Oklahoma once commented that a real effort to
ban conflicts in Congress would result in no votes on some issues. For
example, all congressmen need bank accounts; should they then be banned
from voting on bank legislation that may affect the interest rates on or
security of their bank deposits? To give another example, former Senator
"Cotton Ed" Smith of Mississippi was accustomed to give vigorous support
to higher federal payments on cotton crops, including his own large holdings. If charged with conflict of interest, he could answer that he had an
overriding responsibility to represent Mississippi's principal industry—the
growth of cotton. There are bad conflicts of interest in politics, but the
term "conflicts" is overused in political campaigns.

There are also many unescapable conflicts in commercial life. Does the
bank director vote to protect his deposits or his shares or to enhance his
fees when he votes on a budget? Before analyzing the efforts to reduce
conflict of interest, it may help to review their history.

HISTORY OF THE CONCEPT OF CONFLICTS

Bribes are a common means of creating conflicts of interest. The historical judgment against judge bribing is undeniable. The Code of Hammurabi in the eighteenth century B.C. in Babylon provides that a judge
who alters his judgment, presumably for a bribe, shall pay twelve times
the cost and be barred from the judge's position forever. The Instruction
of Amen-Em-Opet in Egypt in the sixth to tenth centuries B.C. specifically
tells the judge not to accept the bribe of a powerful man.[2] There is a
generalized injunction against taking bribes in Exodus 23:8. Plato says that
it is forbidden for a public servant to accept bribes, and one who is convicted
in court for doing so should be executed.[3] The briber should also be prosecuted under Athenian law. William Blackstone[4] says that Roman law had
many penalties against bribery of public officials or judges, but curiously
left it possible for the magistrate to receive one hundred crowns a year.
In medieval England inferior officers were subject to fines and imprisonment, as was the briber. The case of judges accepting a bribe was so serious
that Chief Justice Thorpe was hanged for it in the reign of Edward III. A
statute (II Henry IV), set a forfeit of treble the bribe and discharge from
the king's service.

But there are many conflicts of interest other than those resulting from
bribing. Alexander Hamilton had problems about conflict of interest. When
in 1789 he became Secretary of the Treasury, he owned some stock in the
Bank of New York with which the U.S. government had dealings, so he

ordered sale of the stock.[5] Yet his previous connection with the Bank of New York was probably one of the reasons for his protest against the installation of a branch of the first Bank of the United States in New York City, a branch that would compete with the Bank of New York.

Transferring attention to later commercial history, we find the concept recognized but no more clearly. In the nineteenth century, early state laws governing corporations paid little or no attention to conflict of interest. Black's Law Dictionary (1979) curiously defines conflict of interest only as involving public officials. Adolph A. Berle and Gardener C. Means[6] speak of an "adverse interest" in commerce, another term for conflict. They point out, correctly, that representation of conflicting interests on a board of directors may provide a channel of communication to help solve difficulties but also may raise conflicts. For example J. P. Morgan and Company in 1901 organized a syndicate to float a bond issue of $100 million for U.S. Steel. Fifteen of the twenty-four members of the board of directors of U.S. Steel were members of the syndicate. A New Jersey court held that the transaction was voidable but commented that the interconnecting directorship helped the new company.[7] Berle and Means think the charge that directors are on both sides of such transactions has been overused. But they point out that as early as 1893, then Circuit Court Judge Taft sharply criticized a contract made by a corporation, a majority shareholder of which exercised undue influence over the directors.[8]

LATE NINETEENTH-CENTURY ETHICAL PROGRESS

While the courts have been slowly pondering the problem of conflicting interests on corporate boards, the ethical consciousness of businessmen on the subject apparently increased. Cochran's study of nineteenth-century railroad executives' correspondence concludes that between 1850 and 1900 the executives became more aware of the disadvantages of a frequent conflict, the creation of a construction corporation by railroad directors, often with a clear intent to profit personally from their own railroad's need to extend the railroad line.[9] The price for construction of the new line, usually paid in railroad securities, could be adjusted to increase the profit possibilities for railroad executives. Several excuses were offered: The difficulty of finding contractors and the possibility of construction profits as an added reward to those who bought railroad stock in difficult times were two.

Explaining actions like the Erie Railroad bribes, Friedman[10] points out that the post–Civil War period "was an unregulated market; no SEC kept it honest, and the level of promoter morality was painfully low."

However, by the 1870s this practice was being condemned by railroad executives and by financiers like John Murray Forbes. Forbes was angry when he found in 1875 that the Chicago, Burlington and Quincy Railroad's president Graves was paying himself as president of the construction company without accounting to anyone.[11]

Engelbourg writes, of a later trend, perhaps a shade too optimistically, that "by 1880 most of these unfair practices had declined in frequency or diminished."[12] As time went on, railroads became more careful about allowing their executives or directors to invest in other auxiliary companies or in making sales to the railroad. In 1888 the Atchinson railroad's annual report was proud that the company had built all its new lines itself.[13] This consciousness of conflict came slowly. President Erastus Corning of the New York Central was an investor in railroads from the 1830s and put together the New York Central consolidation in 1853, while his iron-and-steel company largely supplied the rails, running gear, and other iron and steel used by the New York Central Railroad, of which he was a nonsalaried president. Engelbourg points out that the Vanderbilts did not have such a conflict when they took over the New York Central in 1867. John Murray Forbes, the Boston financier who had opposed conflicting-interest construction companies, worked closely with Corning while the latter was selling iron and steel to the Michigan Central and other railroad lines on whose board he served.[14] In 1855, a New York Central investigating committee did not find Corning's prices to be above the market rates but did object to paying him a commission for importing railroad iron; they believed the practice of buying from shareholders could lead to "abuses of great magnitude."[15]

WERE ALL CONFLICTS BAD?

Conflicting interests are generally dangerous, but some may have been practically useful. An example of a partially constructive conflicting interest was that of Moses Taylor, a New York merchant, investor, and bank founder from the 1840s to the 1870s. He was a large shareholder in the Delaware and Lackawanna Railroad, the Lackawanna Iron and Coal Company, and other companies in the area that were constantly dealing and competing with each other.[16] These conflicts were perhaps useful; Taylor was used on committees negotiating between these companies. Hodas cites only one real problem related to Taylor's conflicts of interest. His stock interests in the closely connected Lackawanna Railroad, the Central Railroad of New Jersey, the Morris and Essex Railroad, and the Jersey Shore Improvement Company led him to serious conflict between those companies, which eventually bankrupted the Central of New Jersey.[17]

Andrew Carnegie's business career often gained from conflict of interests. He would push to secure loans for a new bridge (at a fee to himself) if he owned substantial shares of the railroads on either side and if his Bridge Company was to be used for construction; the company would secure steel from Carnegie Steel. Thus he secured four conflicts of interest, each of which could have been the occasion for favoring an overcharge. If the prices for each service were reasonable, was it not better to have the multiple gain inducing him to get the bridge built than not to have a bridge? Carnegie did, however, criticize conflict of interest in one company's president J.G.A. Fishman when he found his president speculating in Minnesota iron ore stock.[18] He also criticized his president Henry Clay Frick when the latter sold some land to Carnegie Steel. Apparently conflicts were bad if they benefitted someone other than Carnegie; but most people were glad when Carnegie, with his conflicting interests, built the bridge.

J. Edgar Thompson, the first engineering president who built the strong Pennsylvania Railroad in the 1840s and 1850s, had unusual scruples for his time. Initially he would not invest in companies that sold their products to railroads. After years of associating with Carnegie, however, he gave up some of his scruples and invested in companies that were developing new technologies that would be useful to railroads. Again, one wonders if this use of his professional knowledge to favor new professional developments were not a good reason for allowing this degree of conflict of interest.[19]

Mid-nineteenth-century businessmen were not very conscious of the danger of unethical actions resulting from conflicting interest. It may also be the case that the demand for capital overrode any criticism of conflict. Lackawanna valley businessmen and officials were probably so happy to receive economic benefits from Moses Taylor's investments that they were not worried about conflicting interests among his railroad, iron ore, and iron fabrication companies. Such conflicting interests do not have to be damaging; yet even in Taylor's case, as noted above, they sometimes proved embarrassing.

CONTROL OF CONFLICTS IN GOVERNMENT

As indicated in the introduction to this essay, some of the Founding Fathers were well aware of the danger of some conflicts of interest. But, as in business, appropriate precautionary action came slowly. The Constitution prohibited bribery of officials by any king, prince, or foreign state (Article I, section 9, clause 8); the clause also forbade receipt of titles. The common law could be construed to cover some kinds of corruption, but an act prohibiting congressmen and federal officials from accepting bribes was not passed until 1853.[20] A great many conflicts of interest, including bribes, appointments to official posts, and other acts of favoritism were to be found in both federal and state governments in the nineteenth century. The Thirteenth Amendment, forbidding slavery in the United States, was passed in the Congress by offering a position to a congressman's brother, but withholding undesired legislation in a congressional committee, and by having a railroad ask its pledged Democrats to stay away from congressional sessions.[21] These conflicts were well justified by the result of abolishing slavery in the United States.

Few of the states avoided periods in the nineteenth century when bribery and other conflicts controlled their governors or legislatures. The Yazoo land scandal in Georgia's legislature, the chartering and support of railroads in Wisconsin and other western states, the free railroad passes to state legislators, and the purchase of U.S. Senate seats by bribing legislators are only some of the many unhappy examples of conflicts of interest in nineteenth-century state and local governments. There were common-law provisions in some states that could have been used to prosecute these conflicts, but the provisions were very rarely used.

The federal government has had a similar slow growth of attention to conflicts. A good analysis was made in the late 1950s by the Association of the Bar of the City of New York.[22] A particularly difficult federal problem is that, as administrators often need specific knowledge of particular industries, lawyers or executives from that industry are appointed. All too frequently these persons have conflicts of interest between their former employers' objectives and the government's objectives. After various trials and errors, the Conflict of Interest Statute (18 U.S. Code, 202–209) has been enacted and appropriate regulations drafted to forbid almost a score of specific actions that are likely to lead to illegal conflicts of interests. All federal departments and agencies must draft supplementary codes, and work with the U.S. Ethics Office. The federal enforcement of codes of ethics is much stronger and, of course, much more expensive than those of state and local government.

In the twentieth century, especially in the last two decades, most states have passed laws forbidding actions causing conflicts of interest by either state or local officials. Almost all these statutes also include "disclosure" provisions requiring all elected officials and candidates and the better-paid appointed state and local officers to file statements of income and property holding with city clerks or with a state ethics or election commission. The purpose of the disclosure act is to discourage or prevent obvious conflicts of interest. The attention paid to these laws is varied; in more than half the states the use is small, but in some it is substantial.[23] It is this writer's estimate that the enforcement of these laws is improving.

CONFLICTS PUBLICIZED AND CRITICIZED

In the early twentieth century, as a result of discussion by Progressive leaders, the dangers of some conflicts became more fully apparent. As we have seen above, railroad executives and financiers became aware of a part of the dangers and were much less likely to establish self-profiting construction corporations paid by their railroad. Two government investigations illumined other financial situations in which a not yet illegal conflict of interest had damaging results on some economic groups. The Armstrong life insurance investigation committee of the New York legislature in 1904–1906 found a wide variety of conflicting interests, some of which were clearly damaging to corporations and to policy holders. For example, George W. Perkins was vice-president and chairman of the finance committee of New York Life and a Morgan partner, a conflict recognized by J. P. Morgan himself, as New York Life bought Morgan-sponsored securities regularly. Perkins made many millions of such transactions, apparently without personal profit. Morgan suggested that Perkins resign from New York Life before becoming a Moran partner, but Perkins persuaded him otherwise when the president of New York Life did not object to his holding the two posts. Perkins did try not to use the Morgan–New York Life connection for personal gain, but he found his position uncomfortable when Hughes queried him in the Armstrong investigation.[24]

The Armstrong investigation also showed that life insurance company directors often participated in investment syndicates, sometimes rescuing companies whose securities could not be sold by investment bankers. Sometimes officers and directors of the companies personally participated in security purchases that they were arranging for their companies. Some insurance companies kept funds in subsidiary trust companies, largely controlled by insurance company directors, whose funds were at times used to make collateral loans for personal stock purchases of insurance company officials, enabling the latter to use their insurance company position for personal gain, a clear conflict of interest. The Armstrong committee and its general counsel, Charles Evans Hughes, objected to these practices. The Armstrong report resulted in passage of New York laws, later copied in other states, that forbade the underwriting of security issues by life insurance companies and also made illegal the personal interest of an official of any life insurance company in the purchase, sale, or loan of corporation securities.[25] This kind of prohibition of conflict of interest became generally accepted in laws regulating insurance companies and in the practice of the companies.[26] The lesson was not completely lost on other businessmen; Kuhn, Loeb and Company in 1906 had several of its partners resign from directorships of railroads that Kuhn, Loeb was financing.[27]

The same problem was raised by the Pujo committee, a subcommittee of the House Banking and Currency Committee that in 1912 and early 1913 investigated the "Money Trust." The committee, with the leadership of counsel Samuel Untermyer, was trying to demonstrate a concentration of monetary power in large investment banking houses. This effort was not very successful, but some of its examples of conflicting interests apparently pricked both political and business consciences. The committee's report influenced later legislation; one example was the Clayton Act of 1914, which outlawed interlocking directorates among larger banks and trust companies, which frequently must deal with each other, thereby facilitating conflicts of interest. It also forbade common carriers from having any dealing in securities with trust companies that had interlocking directorates. Recognizing the public sentiment against such interlocking directorates, and following Kuhn and Loeb's earlier example, in January 1914, J. P. Morgan, Jr., announced that he and some of his partners would resign from the boards of twenty-seven corporations where the House of Morgan served as underwriter.[28] However, the skeptical *New York Times* pointed out that he left one partner on most of the boards of such companies, where the banker may have served a very useful purpose but could also help create a conflict.

Corporate misadventures with conflicting interests did not end in pre–World War I times. In the 1920s John D. Rockefeller, Jr., led a successful proxy drive to remove President Stewart of Standard Oil of Indiana, who had organized a company to buy oil elsewhere and then sell it to Standard of Indiana, with a profit to Stewart and his associates, a conflict of interest that verged on stealing directly from Standard of Indiana shareholders.

In 1933 Russell Brown, chairman of American Commercial Alcohol, participated in a syndicate that raised the price of Alcohol's stock. The company created new shares to pay for "valuable processes on properties which it already owned." Chairman Brown admitted to Pecora, in charge of the Senate investigation, that he would not do it again. The action would be illegal today.[29] In 1933, there was no law separating security affiliates from banks and no law requiring disclosures or purchases by insiders.

Even more questionable were the actions of National City Bank under the presidency of Charles E. Mitchell. In 1928, the stock of the bank was delisted from the New York Stock Exchange, but this was a cosmetic gesture. An affiliate, the National City Company, was the largest trader in the stock of the parent bank. From 1927 to 1931, it sold almost two million shares of stock, driving the price up to a "fantastic" price of $2,925, against a book value of $70. After the crash of 1929 these high values disappeared, costing the public $650 million. Mitchell profited along the way, but lost in the crash.[30] In 1927, 1928, and 1929, Mitchell received $3,481,732 from "management funds" of the company, over and above his regular salary. The stockholders were not informed about these management funds. Bank officers shared in the gains but not the losses of the company.[31]

The use of funds of a bank, which is supposed to be a solid, reputable institution, to create speculative gains for its officers, who are largely speculating on securities of their employer, is a clear form of conflict of interest. Mitchell, however, did not seem at all ashamed of the transactions. His action and similar conflicting-interest actions of Albert H. Wiggins of the Chase National Bank were major reasons for the Glass-Steagal Act of 1933, which separated banking from investment banking. When the Pecora

Committee of the U.S. Senate revealed these activities in 1933, Mitchell lost the confidence of directors and was forced to resign. Wiggins, under similar pressure, renounced a generous pension from his bank. The whole tradition against conflict, from biblical times on to the criticisms of the Armstrong and Pecora committees, had been ignored by these bank officials. The ethic of respectable corporations today would frown severely on the Stewart or Mitchell or Wiggins type of conflict, but undesirable commercial conflicts have not disappeared.

Holding companies or some kind of "investment trusts," widely used in the 1920s, were sometimes designed to create conflict of interest. Though its investment is relatively small, the dominant force in the holding company can control subordinate companies for its purposes, often in direct conflict with the purposes of other shareholders of the subordinate company. Existence of such companies increases the conflict problem, although in some instances the conflicts may serve useful economic purposes.

The most widely discussed area of conflict of interest is that of securities markets. In the early years (1934–1941) of the Securities and Exchange Commission, relatively strong commissioners were appointed and real efforts made to control abuses, which included some conflicts of interest. However, the procedures of the commission were sharply criticized, and there were real doubts as to the best means of reducing conflicts of interest. The idea of separating dealers from brokers, as was then the case in Great Britain, was proposed but vehemently opposed. Brokers who act as dealers buying and selling stock on their own accounts as well as for their customers are under temptation to put personal interests foremost. The discovery of past-president Richard Whitney's embezzlements weakened the effort of stock exchange members to keep their privileges. The SEC established a program for self-regulation by an Association of Security Dealers. However, American participation in World War II resulted in almost complete deemphasis on securities problems; President Truman was not interested in the SEC and made poor appointments to it; President Eisenhower was also not much interested. In the late 1950s the bull market was accompanied by frauds the suppression of which took most of the SEC's attention.[32]

In an interesting 1976 comparative study, Professor Alfred E. Conard of the University of Michigan Law School noted several reasons why conflict of interest in security matters has been allowed to linger in America. As we have noted, state corporation laws generally failed to condemn conflicts specifically, although separate later securities legislation attempts to do so. But weak state securities commissions have often been slow to enforce laws against conflicts. In France, under a 1966 law, conflicts between personal and official interests of an administrator must be reported to a whole board of administrators, which reports such conflicts to auditors and shareholders; the latter may disapprove. In England directors must

disclose conflicts and are excluded on voting from matters where they have
a conflict. In Germany, transactions with board members can be made
only by a supervisory committee. A Model Corporate Act for American
States decrees that a conflicting contract will be approved if affected directors disclose their interests and abstain from voting.

The fact that laws affecting conflicts of interest on security matters have
moved slowly in America is in part due to the circumstance that Congress
and fifty state legislatures all have a role in laws affecting commercial
conflicts of interest.[33]

TWENTIETH CENTURY FUND STUDY

Abuse on Wall Street: Conflicts of Interest in the Securities Market,[34] a
study financed by the Twentieth Century Fund, is the most thorough recent
study of conflicts known to this writer. It includes not only conflicts in the
sale of securities, but also conflicts in the administration of commercial
bank trust departments, real estate investment trusts, state and local pension fund management, union pension fund management, investment banking, broker-dealer firms, and nonprofit institutions. The supporting studies,
made by law professors and financial writers, were based on studies in the
1970s, which frequently include historical views.

This careful scholarly review portrays a wide variety of conflicts of interest in our modern fiscal machinery. When the investment banker prices
and maintains for a time the price of a new security issue, does he act in
behalf of the corporation offering the securities or in behalf of the customers
buying them? Yet, the services of the investment banker are valuable.
When the union deposits its dues in a union managed bank, is it thinking
of its dues-paying members or of the fees of the union leaders on the board
of the bank? Should banks loan funds to company A and buy securities of
company A for the funds held in trust by the bank? If the loan department
finds company A is not doing well, should it tell the trust department to
sell company A's stock out of trust funds? Should banks buy and sell
securities only through brokers who maintain large deposits in the bank?
Many fiscal interrelationships, which may be unfair to competitive customers, have been simply taken for granted in the business world. "You
scratch my back and I will scratch yours."

However, one cannot read the Twentieth Century Fund study without
realizing that many people are aware of the problem; the confusion of the
late nineteenth century about conflict of interest has been replaced in many
quarters by a thoughtful interest in seeing how the worst conflicts can be
reduced. The staff of the Fund agrees, in some worthwhile conclusions,
that pressures for individual honesty, concern for reputation, fear of complex legal intervention, and pressure of competitive forces tend to reduce
the number of conflicts. This writer would add that court decisions begin-

ning in the last century, the antitrust laws, legislative investigations like the Armstrong committee in New York, the Pujo committee in the House, and the Pecora committee in the Senate have all helped to build an ethic against conflict of interest. In the hundreds of college and philanthropic and government meetings in which this writer has participated, he has rarely known a charge of conflict of interest not to be considered carefully.

The study staff, does not believe that all conflicts can be eliminated, but it does believe that together regulators could be "tougher than most of those in the security industry might consider necessary."[35] It hoped that industry would voluntarily respond before further legislative pressure appears. Sound "fiduciary practice" should help rather than damage the financial industry. Guidelines and standard practices should replace "word of mouth training."

Following further from the Twentieth Century Fund report are several conclusions. Legislators should have thought about the dangers of conflict of interest; in drafting the legislation for real estate investment trusts Congress enacted "features that virtually invited abuse."[36] Congress encouraged expensive conflicts when it broadened the savings and loan areas without increasing regulations and when it authorized real estate investment trusts. Procedures required of regulated firms should be reviewed systematically to reduce conflict of interest. Collective self-regulation may overnight become a regulatory agency. Security and Exchange Commission work with the stock exchanges and over-the-counter markets is probably good; associations of businesspeople may be helpful in suggesting standard procedures to reduce conflicts. It would be better to allow more competition rather than keeping trust business largely in the hands of banks; however, nonbanking trust institutions should meet banking requirements of staffing and capital; in most cases legal requirements of disclosure of financial provisions to customers would help competition.

The Twentieth Century Fund summary is strongly against "hidden compensation for fiduciaries." Bank trust departments should not use excuses to "hold clients idle cash without paying interest." Trustees of nonprofit institutions should not use their positions to secure accounts for banks or brokers or investment managers. Boards of directors should include non-management members as "an essential safeguard against conflict abuses in both business and not-for-profit organizations.[37] Some of this has been accomplished by SEC requirements that auditing and nominating committees be composed of independent trustees. The staff recommends that in corporations or nonprofit agencies where there has been abuse through conflict there be a requirement of a certain proportion of independent directors.

The mechanism that the staff most strongly urges to reduce conflict of interest is disclosure, for which recommendation the chief supporting argument is what four (now five) decades of SEC experience with disclosures has accomplished.[38] Disclosure does not lead to governmental obstacles to action or reduce innovation or flexibility, yet it does deter illegal and unethical conduct. It is conceded that disclosure may be expensive in preparation of brochures for new issues, but it is much less costly than the unfair practices that it helps to prevent. Every organization that provides investment management should disclose its financial results at least once a year. Facts disclosed should include market evaluations, as well as income, and comparisons of results in companies with similar investments. Disclosure should include who provides financial services, what kind of services are provided, and what payments were made, how investments are allocated between units, and how "inside information" is handled. In the case of legitimate transactions that happen to involve conflict of interest, the staff recommends full disclosure to interested parties. Enforcement procedures on both federal and state levels should be enhanced.

The Twentieth Century Fund study and its recommendations are to be commended. They show a desire for steady reform but also recognize that detailed statutes against conflicting interests may often lead to many enforcement troubles. A recommendation of this writer is that corporations should add ethics to their education of employees. The staff is correct in avoiding detailed laws that try to control all bad conflicts of interest. The attention paid to self-regulation, with a stick of government action to keep prodding it, is good. Laws requiring disclosure of conflicting operations are probably desirable but, like any disclosure, will require considerable time to assure results.

JUDICIAL DECISIONS

A glimpse into the voluminous legal literature on conflict of interest leads to the conclusion that, although judges find many conflicts to be undesirable, they have not been able to lay down firm rules. In 1880, not the happiest time in American business ethics, Justice Field was firm in deciding against directors of a railroad company who voted to let a second company exploit coal reserves in the railroad's land but soon secured property of the second company themselves.[39] Miller reports on other cases that conclude that if conflicting interest has been disclosed, the contract may be valid if it passes judicial scrutiny. Delaware, New York, California, and other corporate codes provide that transactions between a director and his corporation may be valid if there was proper disclosure to and approval by a majority of disinterested directors or shareholders and if the transaction was fair to the corporation.[40] Directors have discretion in voting dividends; minority stockholders would have to prove bad faith, fraud, or dishonesty in opposing a dividend policy that favored the financial interests of the director or directors, for example, a desire to keep dividends down in order to reduce his own income taxes. Such a limit would not normally exist in a larger corporation where failure to pay dividends might result in a proxy fight or tender offer.[41] The court was divided in a case where a board rejected a venture and a director or a group later undertook it themselves.[42] Courts are more likely to find directors guilty of negligence if there is a conflict of interest involved in the negligent action.[43] The federal Securities Exchange Act of 1933 and the SEC regulations, especially Rule 10 b–5, have added considerably to the likelihood of prosecution for conflict of interest.[44]

The effect of law on other conflicts of interest in corporate life is discussed by Jacobs.[45] He finds that a higher standard of conduct is imposed upon a higher-ranking official. Conflicts that here are mostly breaches of fiduciary trust to the corporation include delivery of a trade secret to a competitor, taking a position with a competitor under circumstances that convince the court that disclosure is planned, interference with the company's business relations, or establishing a competitive business of one's own while working as a corporate employee. All these conflicts may be met by injunctions or damages.

Judicial attitudes against certain conflicts have been tightened by the Securities and Exchange Acts, where most decisions are made by federal courts. Both Congress and the courts have supported the movement against use of insider information. The decision of the Supreme Court in the Texas Gulf Sulphur case of 1965[46] was criticized sharply by one book,[47] but the result of that and other cases has been to strengthen the laws against insider trading.

The impact of the law, especially the securities legislation and administration, has been to alert many people to some of the conflict of interest that should be classified as unethical. Discussions at the level of boards of directors frequently take possible conflict into mind. This writer has, however, been unable to find any clear statement of what kinds of conflicts are legal and what are not; many businesspeople are still much in doubt.

There has recently been a great deal of interest in an outburst of very large insider trading in conjunction with mergers and leveraged buyouts. An investment banker with a reported income of over a million dollars sold insider tips for millions; that banker is serving a two-year term for the offense. Several others are charged with similar offenses. The former board chairman of a large conglomerate was sent to prison for passing out inside information to friends.[48] Some of the convicted and accused are graduates of excellent institutions of higher education, leading to doubt as to whether higher education is overlooking one of its main tasks, that of showing its students how the world is held together by morality and how conflicting interests speedily become immoral.

CONCLUDING REMARKS

The wide variety of examples discussed in this chapter certainly suggests that there is no quick ethical formula for evaluating and limiting conflict of interest. It would be very difficult to devise a law that would abolish all conflicts in either business or government and yet be flexible enough to permit reasonably desirable business and government transactions.

Yet history shows the gradual evolution of ethical judgment against many types of conflict of interest. American railroads learned some ethical principles after the Civil War; investment bankers and insurance executives learned in the Progressive period; bankers in the post-Crash period.

In recent years approximately 90 percent of Fortune 500 companies have adopted codes of ethics that specifically prohibit most major conflicts of interest. My guess is that half of these companies make a genuine effort to educate and enforce these codes. The federal government and almost all the states have also adopted codes of ethics that prohibit the major conflicts of interest; unhappily, many of the state codes are legalistic and lack widespread dissemination and enforcement.[49]

Kent Druyvesteyn, Vice-President, Ethics, of the General Dynamics Corporation, has given permission to quote from his thoughtful letter:

Here is a thought on conflicts which grows out of my own wrestlings in practical terms with this issue. It's useful to view conflicts as situations, arrangements, or relationships rather than as deeds. One does not commit a conflict of interest. Rather, one acts in a conflict situation for either good or ill.

We daily encounter conflict situations where no wrongdoing has occurred or is likely to occur. Nonetheless, we often seek to break up these situations in order to avoid problems of fact or appearance down the road.

This act of break up is often viewed by the parties involved as discipline for some act of misconduct. This is simply not the case however. The conflict situation itself was not bad (morally speaking) and the persons who found themselves in it were not bad (morally speaking). Often the conflict situation was not even made by the parties involved.

Several useful conclusions stand out in the morass of conflicts of interest. As an aid for analysis, we might divide conflicts of interest into three major categories, each with its own degree of ethical difficulties. A first group would be those very blatant conflicts that are clearly illegal and damaging: kickbacks, bribery of public officials, and insider trading. The actions embodied in this first group have been and should be forcefully discouraged, as few would dispute their harmful ramifications.

A second classification would include those conflicts that ought to be prohibited for the sake of appearance, regardless of the fact that their effects may be unclear or subject to varying interpretations. Conflicts in the sphere of public affairs would be most apt to fall in this category. Avoidance of these practices is best, as the external and internal suspicion surrounding a "questionable" activity may be more deleterious to an organization than the activity itself. Caesar's wife should be above suspicion.

Finally, the third group consists of conflicts that are beneficial and therefore worthy of being cautiously permitted. Such practices may hurt few while providing benefits to a certain region or industry. Roles like that of the investment banker, who determines a price suitable for both his customer and for the corporation issuing the securities, are too valuable to eliminate.

Laws, such as SEC regulations concerning insider trading are best brought to bear against conflicts in the first group. For the second and third groups, however, industry, corporate, and department codes of ethics could be more efficacious, for the reason that those most familiar with the issues involved are best equipped to set standards. It should be noted that enforcement of industry codes would be rather difficult, as problems would inevitably arise involving antitrust laws that prohibit collusion among firms. Corporate codes, however, could be actively enforced, as they would apply only within a particular firm; many corporations are now trying to develop enforcement mechanisms to aid their codes. Codes are being enforced in federal administration, not Congress, and in a slowly increasing number of state governments.

Education of executives and other significant workers is the most important element in the achievement of ethical progress. This educational prerequisite is best served through company or bureau-sponsored ethical education for executives, internal guidelines, and better ethical instruction in schools, from elementary schools, to university programs of business administration.

Such education should allude to various types of conflicts, the results proceeding from them, and the slow historical development of civilized man's sanctions against misuse of conflicts of interest. It should also refer to the Golden Rule, to Kant's categorical imperative, and to the various religious traditions that help to govern American life. All these lines of thought would find evil conflicts of interest to be repulsive.

NOTES

1. Twentieth Century Fund, *Abuse on Wall Street: Conflicts of Interest in the Securities Market* (Westport, Conn.: Quorum Books, 1980), pp. 4–6.

2. James B. Pritchard, *The Ancient Near East*, vol. I (New York: Harcourt Brace, 1972), pp. 138–242.

3. Plato, *The Laws*, Book 12, Section I 12–113.

4. William Blackstone, *Commentaries on the Laws of England*, Book 4, Chap. 10 (Oxford: Oxford University Press, 1769), p. 139.

5. John C. Miller, *Alexander Hamilton and the Growth of the New Nation* (New York: Harper & Row, 1964), p. 274.

6. Adolph A. Berle and Gardener C. Means, *The Modern Corporation and Private Property* (New York: Macmillan, 1932), p. 230.

7. Ibid.

8. Ibid., p. 235.

9. Thomas C. Cochran, *Railroad Leaders, 1845–1890* (Cambridge, Mass.: Harvard University Press, 1953), pp. 110–25.

10. James Friedman, *A History of American Law* (New York: Simon & Schuster, 1973), pp. 447–59.

11. Arthur M. Johnson and Barry E. Supple, *Boston Capitalists and Western Railroads* (Cambridge, Mass.: Harvard University Press, 1967), p. 267.

12. Saul Englebourg, *Policy and Morality* (Westport, Conn.: Greenwood Press, 1980).

13. Ibid., p. 323.

14. Irene Neu, *Erastus Corning* (New York: Macmillan, 1979), pp. 73–87.

15. Edward Hungerford, *Men and Iron* (New York: Arno Press, 1976), pp. 91 ff.

16. Daniel Hodas, *The Business Career of Moses Taylor* (New York: New York University Press, 1976), p. 97.

17. Ibid., pp. 144–48.

18. Joseph Frazier Wall, *Andrew Carnegie* (New York: Oxford University Press, 1970), pp. 278–94.

19. James A. Ward, *J. Edgar Thompson* (Westport, Conn.: Greenwood Press, 1941, 1980), pp. 186–88.

20. John T. Noonan, Jr., *Bribes* (New York: Macmillan, 1981), p. 451.

21. Ibid., pp. 456–57.

22. New York City Bar Association, *Conflict of Interest and Federal Service* (Cambridge, Mass.: Harvard University Press, 1960).

23. Council of Governmental Executive Laws, *Blue Book, 1988–1989*. A 1990–91 edition can be procured from the Council of State Governments, Lexington, Kentucky.

24. John A. Garraty, *Right Hand Man* (Westport, Conn.: Greenwood Press), pp. 84–88, 169–79.

25. Vincent P. Carosso, *Investment Banking in America* (Cambridge, Mass.: Harvard University Press, 1970), pp. 116–27.

26. Morton Keller, *The Life Insurance Enterprise* (Cambridge, Mass.: Belknap Press of Harvard, 1963), pp. 254–59, 269–74.

27. Carosso, *Investment Banking*, p. 180.

28. Ibid., p. 179.

29. J. A. Livingston, *The American Stockholder* (Philadelphia: J. B. Lippincott Co., 1958), pp. 45, 191–92.

30. Ferdinand Pecora, *Wall Street under Oath* (Fairfield, N.J.: Augustus Kelly, Publisher, 1968), pp. 108–12.

31. Ibid., pp. 116–20.

32. Joel Seligman, *The Transformation of Wall Street* (Boston: Houghton Mifflin, 1982), pp. 265–89.

33. Alfred F. Conard, *Corporations in Perspective* (New York: Foundation Press, 1970), pp. 18–30.

34. Twentieth Century Fund, *Abuse on Wall Street*.

35. Ibid., p. 565.

36. Ibid., p. 566.

37. Ibid., p. 573.

38. Ibid., pp. 577 ff.

39. *Wardell* v. *Railroad Co.* 103 U.S. 651, 1880; see Cleveland D. Miller, "Judiciary Duties of a Corporate Director," *Baltimore Law Review* 4: 262.

40. Ibid., p. 263.

41. Ibid., p. 244.

42. Ibid., pp. 267–68.

43. Ibid., p. 269.

44. Ibid., pp. 273 ff.

45. Leslie W. Jacobs, "Business Ethics and the Law; Obligations of a Corporate Executive," *The Business Lawyer* (July 1973), pp. 1063 ff.

46. Twentieth Century Fund, *Abuse on Wall Street*, p. 84; 404 U.S. 1005 (1971).

47. Kenneth G. Patrick, *Perpetual Jeopardy* (New York: Macmillan, 1972).

48. *Time*, May 25, 1987, pp. 22–23.

49. George C. S. Benson, "Codes of Ethics," *Journal of Business Ethics* 8 (1989): 305–19; Patrick E. Murphy, "Implementing Business Ethics," *Journal of Business Ethics* 7 (1988): 907–15.

16

Ethical Dilemmas of Management Accountants

WILLIAM K. GROLLMAN AND JOAN L. VAN HISE

Though there have been many articles and studies relating to the ethics of management accountants, few have focused on specific dilemmas that management accountants face. With the assistance of the National Association of Accountants (NAA), we undertook a survey designed to find the answers to these and other questions:

1. What types of ethical dilemmas have management accountants observed in their current or past positions? How often did they occur?
2. How severe are the dilemmas? If faced with such dilemmas, would accountants choose to resign from their companies or change jobs within their companies?
3. How would answers to the first two questions be affected by demographic characteristics such as age or sex of the respondent, or size or type of the organization?

SURVEY METHODOLOGY

We developed a questionnaire in which management accountants would check off answers to thirty questions concerning both the frequency and severity of specific ethical dilemmas. In addition, the questionnaire contained eleven questions in which the respondents could freely express their observations.

Controllers and divisional controllers were selected for the survey because, having risen to a high level in their chosen field, they were considered likely to have had a wide range of experiences at all levels of the hierarchy during their careers. The questionnaire specifically asked participants to indicate how often they have observed certain ethical dilemmas in their "current or past positions in management accounting."

The questionnaire was first tested by being mailed to a sample of 50 controllers and divisional controllers from among the National Association of Accountants' membership. Nineteen of the 50 controllers in the test group responded, and the survey was revised based on their responses. The survey was then remailed to 1,000 of the 16,354 controllers and divisional controllers in the NAA membership. The selection for both the test sample of 50 controllers and the actual mailing of the questionnaire to 1,000 controllers were made by the NAA's random selection program. Both the test survey and the actual survey were mailed under the auspices of the NAA with a cover letter from a managing director.

The response rate to the final questionnaire was 24.8 percent, as 248 controllers sent back their completed responses. The results were then tabulated and are the basis for this chapter, which summarizes the results.

SPECIFIC ETHICAL DILEMMAS

Eight general types of ethical dilemmas were outlined in the questionnaire:

1. Smoothing income by shifting expenses, shifting revenues, adjusting revenues, capitalizing versus expensing assets, or misclassifying product vs. period costs

2. Improperly approving expenses by padding personal expenses, exceeding authorizations, or accelerating expenses to use up budget

3. Changing, distorting, or stretching the rules in reporting accounting data to meet budget, qualify for bonus, or reach targets reported to the investment community or to facilitate an acquisition

4. Materially distorting budgets by underestimating to assure achievement or overestimating to avoid paying bonuses

5. Leaking information for insider trading by others, to affect competitive bidding, or to affect the purchase price of a prospective acquisition or to curry favor with a suitor

6. Using or leaking privileged information for insider trading

7. Withholding information from auditors concerning lawsuits; illegal payments, gifts, or contributions; tax matters; or liability for environmental cleanups

8. Distorting or falsifying tax returns by omitting an item, misclassifying an item, shifting income between periods, shifting income between jurisdictions, or underreporting sales volume to avoid sales tax.

An additional line marked "other" enabled participants to identify situations unique to their backgrounds.

Each area surveyed had two sections, one relating to frequency of the occurrence and the other to its severity. Frequency was defined as "how often" respondents observed particular situations in their current or past positions in management accounting. Severity was defined as "how severe a dilemma the situation presents. You might want to consider the financial, legal and ethical impact on both the individual and the organization in assessing the severity of the situation."

The possible responses for frequency, ranging from lowest to highest response, were: never = 0 points, occasionally = 1 point, and often = 2 points. For severity, there were three choices: might change job = 0, would change job = 1, and would resign = 2. The overall ratings for frequency and severity of all respondents to the survey are shown in Table 16.1.

Smoothing Income

The frequency ratings in this category were the highest in the survey. Judging by the responses, the frequency with which smoothing of income occurs is very high. The most common technique for smoothing income, as evaluated by the respondents, was by adjusting reserves (.83 rating), followed closely by shifting revenues (.75), shifting expenses (.71), capitalizing versus expensing assets (.64), and misclassifying product versus period costs (.63).

Although the frequency ratings in this area were the highest, the severity ratings were among the lowest. Only the areas of shifting expenses and capitalizing versus expensing assets drew a mid-range severity rating.

Improperly Approving Expenses

The frequency ratings in this category were the second highest in the survey. The situation in which management improperly approved expenses by exceeding authorizations scored the highest frequency rating (.55), followed closely by accelerating expenses to use up budget (.45) and padding personal expenses (.42). The severity ratings for all three situations in this category were near the lowest in the survey. Therefore, though this situation occurs with a great degree of frequency—55 percent of all responding controllers indicated that they had occasionally observed management improperly approving expenses by exceeding authorization—they did not consider these offenses to be severe.

Two respondents graphically described overspending when no budget variance was available. In fact, one said that his company had "no cost conscience." Six respondents noted specific expense account violations. They ranged from the "corporation paying for personal items for a stockholder and using corporate assets without recognition" to a superior "using association affiliation to get free travel from the company." Two responses indicated that there was a personal use of corporate funds in a private company.

Table 16.1
Overall Frequency and Severity Ratings

		Frequency	Severity
1.	Management changed, distorted or stretched the rules in reporting accounting data to:		
	A. meet budget	.39	56
	B. qualify for bonus	.26	.68
	C. reach targets reported to the investment community	.17	.88
	D. facilitate an acquisition	.11	.90
2.	Management withheld information from auditors concerning:		
	A. lawsuits	.01	.79
	B. illegal payments, gifts, contributions	.02	1.21
	C. tax matters	.10	.68
	D. liability for environmental cleanups	.23	1.08
3.	Management leaked information:		
	A. for insider trading by others	.08	1.13
	B. to affect competitive bidding	.17	.43
	C. to affect the purchase price of a prospective acquisition or to curry favor with a suitor	.09	.22
4.	Management used privileged information for:		
	A. insider trading	.11	1.10
5.	Management smoothed income by:		
	A. shifting expenses	.71	.23
	B. shifting revenues	.75	.19
	C. adjusting reserves	.83	.11
	D. capitalizing vs. expensing assets	.64	.40
	E. misclassifying product vs. period costs	.63	.05
6.	Management improperly approved expenses by:		
	A. padding personal expenses	.42	.21
	B. exceeding authorizations	.55	.06
	C. accelerating expenses to use up budget	.45	.06
7.	Management materially distorted budgets by:		
	A. underestimating to assure achievement	.28	.29
	B. overestimating to avoid paying bonuses	.10	.34
8.	Management distorted or falsified tax returns by:		
	A. omitting an item	0	1.12
	B. misclassifying an item	0	.80
	C. shifting income between periods	.11	.93
	D. shifting income between jurisdictions	.06	.99
	E. underreporting sales volume to avoid sales tax	.02	1.01

Adherence to Rules in Reporting Accounting Data

The overwhelming majority of respondents indicated that they had rarely observed specific transgressions in this area. However, 39.2 percent of the respondents noted that they had observed management changing, distorting, or stretching the rules to meet budget occasionally and 26.1 percent indicated the same with respect to qualifying for a bonus. Very significantly, no respondents said that they had observed any of this happening often.

The controllers considered changing, distorting, or stretching the rules in order to facilitate an acquisition to be the most severe infraction, followed closely by using the same methods to reach targets reported to the investment community. Changing, distorting, or stretching the rules to qualify for a bonus or to meet budget were not considered to be as severe offenses. However, for all situations in this category, at least 25 percent of the controllers indicated that they would resign if they knew management had in fact changed, distorted, or stretched the rules in reporting accounting data.

Respondents noted the following additional reasons for violations in reporting accounting data: to satisfy lenders, to please regulatory authorities, and to influence the equity section of the balance sheet.

Materially Distorting Budgets

The responding controllers had rarely encountered management materially distorting budgets by overestimating to avoid paying bonuses, but 28 percent of those responding had encountered management underestimating budgets to assure achievement.

Several respondents noted specific reasons for materially distorting budgets. Three controllers noted that budgets were overestimated to receive more favorable banking relationships or to raise more capital. Two others indicated that a focus on the budget causes pressure to distort interim results. Another stated that his company created "unrealistic revenue numbers to balance expenditure budgets."

Management Leaking Information

The frequency ratings for all items in this category—for insider trading by others, to affect competitive bidding, to affect the purchase price of a prospective acquisition, or to curry favor with a suitor—were very low. However, the severity rating for management leaking information for insider trading by others was a very high 1.13, with 48 percent of the controllers indicating they would resign if such a situation occurred in their company. However, participants did not judge the possibility of management leaking information to affect competitive bidding, to affect the purchase price of a prospective acquisition, or to curry favor with a suitor to be nearly as severe.

Using Privileged Information for Insider Trading

Although the frequency with which respondents observed management using privileged information for insider trading was very low at .11, once again the severity rating was high at 1.10. Somewhat surprisingly, the severity rating for management using privileged information for insider trading by themselves was judged to be marginally less severe than their leaking information for insider trading by others (1.10 vs. 1.13).

Withholding Information from Auditors

The frequency ratings for management withholding information from auditors concerning lawsuits or for illegal payments, gifts, or contributions were among the lowest for any situation observed by controllers in the survey. However, the severity rating for management withholding information from auditors concerning lawsuits or illegal payments, gifts, or contributions was the second highest for all questions tested in the survey, indicating that respondents considered any transgressions that did occur in this area to be very serious. In fact, 50 percent of all controllers responding to this item indicated they would resign if such a situation occurred in their company.

More than 25 percent of the respondents had occasionally observed management withholding information from auditors concerning liability for environmental cleanups, and the severity rating was high at 1.08. Again, 50 percent of the controllers indicated they would resign if they knew such a situation had occurred in their company. Both the frequency and the severity ratings for withholding information with respect to tax matters were considerably lower at .10 and .68 respectively.

Additional information withheld from auditors, as cited by respondents, included the likelihood of selling obsolete machinery, realistic inventory levels for a small private company, information on contracts, and a large number of accounts payable that would require adjusting journal entries.

Distorting or Falsifying Tax Returns

There was virtually no observation by the respondents of any distortion or falsification of tax returns in their present or former companies. The only item that had any significant response related to distorting or falsifying a tax return by shifting income between periods, in which 11 percent of the respondents had occasionally noted this happening in their companies.

However, as one controller noted with respect to taxes, "If it even looks gray, take it."

Intentionally omitting an item on the tax return was considered to be the most severe transgression, with a 1.12 severity rating. In fact, 42 percent of respondents indicated they would resign if this occurred within their company. Underreporting of sales volume to avoid sales tax (1.01) was judged the next most severe infraction, followed by shifting income between jurisdictions (.99) and shifting income between periods (.93). Misclassifying an item was judged to be the least severe violation (.80) in this category.

Other Ethical Dilemmas

In addition to ethical dilemmas specifically delineated on the questionnaire, respondents cited several other problems. Three respondents referred to situations between related entities. These included intentional over- and underallocations between related entities and holding companies. All of the additional dilemmas cited can best be described as company-specific situations. For example, one respondent indicated that his company did not report information on toxic chemicals used at the workplace, as required by the state's Department of Environmental Quality and OSHA. Another cited a supplier's gifts to employees. Another referred to sales prices being negotiated to facilitate financing or credit arrangements. Another indicated that there were violations with respect to internal control expenditure approval. Yet another cited a "kickback" from investment bankers. Another violation involved keeping duplicate payments and extending vendor payment terms.

Classifying Frequent or Occasional Occurrences

The controllers were asked to classify the majority of the situations they had identified as either frequent or occasional occurrences. The three classifications suggested in the survey were the following:

1. Personal ethical dilemmas with little impact on the organization
2. Corporate ethical dilemmas with significant current or financial impact on the organization
3. Violations of law

According to the respondents, the greatest number of occurrences were personal ethical dilemmas with little impact on the organization, and legal violations were considered to be the fewest in number. Corporate ethical dilemmas with significant current or potential financial impact on the organization were ranked second in frequency by the controllers.

DEMOGRAPHIC DATA

The demographic data relating to respondents and their companies was as follows:

89 percent were males and 11 percent were females.

23 percent of the respondents were in their twenties, 33 percent were in their thirties, 30 percent were in their forties, and 14 percent were age fifty or older.

14 percent were age 50 or older.

65 percent of the respondents worked in private for profit corporations, 25 percent worked in public for profit corporations, 7 percent worked in not-for-profit organizations, and 3 percent worked in the government.

45 percent of the controllers worked in organizations with less than $20 million in sales; of the rest, 21 percent worked in organizations with $20 million to $50 million in sales, 14 percent worked in organizations with $50 million to $100 million in sales, and 20 percent worked in organizations with over $100 million in sales.

Almost two-thirds of the participants (63 percent) have been members of the NAA for ten years or less: another 26 percent have been members for eleven–twenty years; and only 11 percent have been members for more than twenty years.

While 68 percent of the respondents were familiar with the NAA Code of Ethical Conduct for Managerial Accountants, only 40 percent were familiar with the Treadway Commission Report.

COMPARISON OF FREQUENCY RATINGS BY ORGANIZATION TYPE

There were several large differences in frequency ratings grouped by organization type. These are summarized in Table 16.2.

Controllers in private corporations had significantly higher frequency ratings with respect to shifting revenues and shifting expenses (.91 and .77 respectively). The comparable ratings for governmental, not-for-profit, and public companies were much lower with respect to shifting revenues and, except for public corporations, they were also much lower with respect to shifting expenses. Controllers in private corporations had observed the lowest incidence of adjusting reserves. Governmental organizations ranked substantially higher with respect to smoothing income by misclassifying product versus period costs. Based solely on these results, one could conclude that all types of organizations resort to smoothing of income with some degree of frequency; however, they use different methods to achieve this result.

With respect to improperly approving expenses, governmental organizations ranked the highest for all three methods: exceeding authorizations, accelerating expenses to use up budget, and padding personal expenses.

Table 16.2
Comparison of Frequency by Organization Type

		Public	Private	Not-for-Profit	Gov't
1.	Management changed, distorted or stretched the rules in reporting accounting data to:				
	A. meet budget	.42	.39	.40	.57
	B. qualify for bonus	.27	.27	.20	.29
	C. reach targets reported to the investment community	.17	.13	.14	.29
	D. facilitate an acquisition	.03	.13	.14	0
2.	Management withheld information from auditors concerning:				
	A. lawsuits	0	.01	0	0
	B. illegal payments, gifts, contributions	0	.03	0	0
	C. tax matters	.08	.12	0	0
	D. liability for environmental cleanups	.17	.26	.29	.14
3.	Management leaked information:				
	A. for insider trading by others	.02	.10	.21	0
	B. to affect competitive bidding	.20	.18	0	.29
	C. to affect the purchase price of a prospective acquisition or to curry favor with a suitor	.09	.09	0	.29
4.	Management used privileged information for:				
	A. insider trading	.03	.13	.21	0
5.	Management smoothed income by:				
	A. shifting expenses	.68	.77	.38	.43
	B. shifting revenues	.47	.91	.50	.43
	C. adjusting reserves	.88	.64	.80	1.0
	D. capitalizing vs. expensing assets	.62	.66	.53	.71
	E. misclassifying product vs. period costs	.57	.63	.64	.86
6.	Management improperly approved expenses by:				
	A. padding personal expenses	.25	.46	.36	.57
	B. exceeding authorizations	.48	.58	.50	.71
	C. accelerating expenses to use up budget	.44	.44	.54	.71
7.	Management materially distorted budgets by:				
	A. underestimating to assure achievement	.33	.26	.17	.57
	B. overestimating to avoid paying bonuses	.10	.10	0	.29
8.	Management distorted or falsified tax returns by:				
	A. omitting an item	0	0	0	0
	B. misclassifying an item	0	0	0	0
	C. shifting income between periods	.06	.12	.21	0
	D. shifting income between jurisdictions	.12	.04	.14	0
	E. underreporting sales volume to avoid sales tax	0	0.2	.07	0

Conversely, public corporations achieve the lowest ratings in all three areas, especially with respect to padding personal expenses.

Governmental organizations also achieved the highest frequency ratings concerning material distortion of budgets, while not-for-profit organizations achieved the lowest ratings. It should be noted, however, that preparation of budgets in many not-for-profit organizations is substantially more inaccurate, as there is often a heavy dependence on voluntary contributions and/or governmental grants.

COMPARISON OF SEVERITY RATINGS BY ORGANIZATION TYPE

Severity ratings by type of organization are shown in Table 16.3. Among the most significant variances in severity ratings were those concerned with the distortion or falsification of tax returns. Respondents in governmental organizations clearly considered this to be a very serious transgression. As these situations can be illegal acts and governmental employees are often responsible for enforcing laws, this is a logical result. While the ratings for the other three types of organizations were comparable in most areas, those working in private organizations did not consider misclassifying or omitting an item on a tax return to be nearly as severe a violation as those in the other types of organizations.

There were very large differences among the types of organizations with respect to changing or distorting reported accounting data for any reason. There were also significant differences in the severity ratings concerning withholding information from auditors. Those working in governmental organizations considered these actions to be among the most severe violations, while those working in not-for-profit organizations rated them substantially lower. Governmental employees were particularly concerned about withholding data on environmental cleanup liabilities; indeed, all who responded to this question indicated they would resign if they knew of this action. Once again, the law enforcement angle may be involved in these cases.

There were also significant differences with respect to the use of privileged information for insider trading. Those working in public and governmental organizations considered management using privileged information for insider trading to be a much more severe transgression than those working in not-for-profit or private corporations. Leaking information for insider trading by others was considered to be a less serious violation than the direct use of privileged information for insider trading by management by those working in public corporations.

There were other wide swings in severity ratings with respect to smoothing of income. Those working in not-for-profit organizations considered smoothing income by shifting expenses to be the only serious transgression

Table 16.3

Comparison of Severity by Organization Type

		Public	Private	Not-for-Profit	Gov't
1.	Management changed, distorted or stretched the rules in reporting accounting data to:				
	A. meet budget	.31	.35	.57	1.0
	B. qualify for bonus	.56	.65	.83	1.33
	C. reach targets reported to the investment community	.68	1.01	1.0	1.5
	D. facilitate an acquisition	.66	.99	1.0	1.5
2.	Management withheld information from auditors concerning:				
	A. lawsuits	.86	.71	.75	1.33
	B. illegal payments, gifts, contributions	1.14	1.21	1.12	1.67
	C. tax matters	.76	.57	.88	1.33
	D. liability for environmental cleanups	1.17	1.03	.88	2.0
3.	Management leaked information:				
	A. for insider trading by others	.82	.95	.71	1.67
	B. to affect competitive bidding	.32	.46	.62	.67
	C. to affect the purchase price of a prospective acquisition or to curry favor with a suitor	.20	.24	.62	.33
4.	Management used privileged information for:				
	A. insider trading	.91	.88	.71	1.67
5.	Management smoothed income by:				
	A. shifting expenses	.40	.37	.57	1.00
	B. shifting revenues	.34	.35	0	.80
	C. adjusting reserves	.06	.14	0	0
	D. capitalizing vs. expensing assets	.35	.41	0	.80
	E. misclassifying product vs. period costs	0	.08	0	0
6.	Management improperly approved expenses by:				
	A. padding personal expenses	.06	.26	0	0
	B. exceeding authorizations	0	.08	0	0
	C. accelerating expenses to use up budget	0	.09	0	0
7.	Management materially distorted budgets by:				
	A. underestimating to assure achievement	.19	.36	0	0
	B. overestimating to avoid paying bonuses	.26	.35	0	.60
8.	Management distorted or falsified tax returns by:				
	A. omitting an item	1.09	.83	1.14	1.33
	B. misclassifying an item	1.0	.82	1.14	1.33
	C. shifting income between periods	1.03	.89	1.14	1.33
	D. shifting income between jurisdictions	1.05	.99	1.14	1.33
	E. underreporting sales volume to avoid sales tax	1.09	.96	1.29	1.33

in this area. Governmental employees considered the following three means of smoothing income to be far more serious than did those working in any of the other types of organizations: shifting expenses, shifting revenues, and capitalizing vs. expensing costs. The ratings for those working in both public and private organizations were roughly the same for all categories involving smoothing of income. All four types of organizations had extremely low severity ratings for adjusting reserves and misclassifying product versus period costs.

The final area of significant differences was with respect to improperly approving expenses. For all three categories, those working in private corporations considered this to be a much more serious violation than those working in other types of organizations.

COMPARISON OF FREQUENCY RATINGS BY ORGANIZATION SIZE

Frequency ratings by organization size are summarized in Table 16.4. Controllers working in smaller organizations, that is, those with less than $20 million in sales, assigned substantially higher frequency ratings to several items in the survey than those working in larger organizations. Smoothing income by misclassifying product versus period costs and padding of personal expenses were considered far more frequent occurrences in the smaller organizations. In contrast, the largest organizations found smoothing of income by shifting expenses to be a far more frequent occurrence than other organizations, in particular when compared to midsized companies in the $20–$100 million range. However, both the smallest and the largest organizations had the highest overall frequency ratings with respect to smoothing income by shifting reserves. As a general rule, the frequency ratings were higher for both the smaller and the larger organizations in the survey than they were for organizations in either the $20–$50 million or $50–$100 million categories.

COMPARISON OF SEVERITY RATINGS BY ORGANIZATION SIZE

As Table 16.5 clearly shows, there is no significant pattern with respect to severity ratings by organization size. However, in general, the largest organizations considered the falsification of tax returns to be the most serious area of transgression. Withholding information from auditors concerning illegal payments, gifts and contributions, or liability for environmental cleanups was another area rated very highly by the largest organizations, although the severity ratings for the smaller organizations were also high in these two areas. Management's use of privileged information for insider trading was looked on more severely by the larger

Table 16.4
Comparison of Frequency by Organization Size

		Less than $20 Million	$20-50 Million	$50-100 Million	Over $100 Million
1.	Management changed, distorted or stretched the rules in reporting accounting data to:				
	A. meet budget	.42	.35	.37	.45
	B. qualify for bonus	.27	.26	.18	.32
	C. reach targets reported to the investment community	.17	.11	.13	.15
	D. facilitate an acquisition	.14	.11	.03	.12
2.	Management withheld information from auditors concerning:				
	A. lawsuits	.02	0	0	0
	B. illegal payments, gifts, contributions	.03	.02	0	0
	C. tax matters	.09	.11	.09	.10
	D. liability for environmental cleanups	.32	.17	.13	.23
3.	Management leaked information:				
	A. for insider trading by others	.12	.07	.03	.07
	B. to affect competitive bidding	.16	.16	.15	.22
	C. to affect the purchase price of a prospective acquisition or to curry favor with a suitor	.10	.07	.06	.09
4.	Management used privileged information for:				
	A. insider trading	.16	.09	.09	.06
5.	Management smoothed income by:				
	A. shifting expenses	.73	.61	.61	.82
	B. shifting revenues	.61	.47	.48	.52
	C. adjusting reserves	.92	.72	.74	.90
	D. capitalizing vs. expensing assets	.69	.57	.55	.62
	E. misclassifying product vs. period costs	.73	.58	.48	.57
6.	Management improperly approved expenses by:				
	A. padding personal expenses	.52	.36	.27	.36
	B. exceeding authorizations	.58	.50	.52	.54
	C. accelerating expenses to use up budget	.53	.40	.47	.39
7.	Management materially distorted budgets by:				
	A. underestimating to assure achievement	.31	.22	.29	.32
	B. overestimating to avoid paying bonuses	.12	.08	.07	.11
8.	Management distorted or falsified tax returns by:				
	A. omitting an item	0	.0	0	0
	B. misclassifying an item	0	.0	0	0
	C. shifting income between periods	.17	.11	.10	.10
	D. shifting income between jurisdictions	.06	.09	.07	.07
	E. underreporting sales volume to avoid sales tax	.05	.0	0	0

Table 16.5

Comparison of Severity by Organization Size

		Less than $20 Million	$20-50 Million	$50-100 Million	Over $100 Million
1.	Management changed, distorted or stretched the rules in reporting accounting data to:				
	A. meet budget	.39	.31	.27	.44
	B. qualify for bonus	.67	.64	.75	.57
	C. reach targets reported to the investment community	.96	1.04	.95	.78
	D. facilitate an acquisition	.96	1.00	.86	.77
2.	Management withheld information from auditors concerning:				
	A. lawsuits	.75	.70	.71	.82
	B. illegal payments, gifts, contributions	1.18	1.33	1.08	1.18
	C. tax matters	.66	.62	.52	.76
	D. liability for environmental cleanups	.98	1.21	1.06	1.08
3.	Management leaked information:				
	A. for insider trading by others	.91	.96	1.00	.86
	B. to affect competitive bidding	.54	.24	.46	.41
	C. to affect the purchase price of prospective acquisition or to curry favor with a suitor	.33	.15	.19	.26
4.	Management used privileged information for:				
	A. insider trading	.80	.92	1.05	1.08
5.	Management smoothed income by:				
	A. shifting expenses	.42	.34	.33	.52
	B. shifting revenues	.33	.27	.30	.48
	C. adjusting reserves	.12	.04	.10	.18
	D. capitalizing vs. expensing assets	.40	.29	.46	.41
	E. misclassifying product vs. period costs	.04	0	0	.15
6.	Management improperly approved expenses by:				
	A. padding personal expenses	.26	.08	.22	.14
	B. exceeding authorizations	.04	0	0	.15
	C. accelerating expenses to use up budget	.05	0	0	.17
7.	Management materially distorted budgets by:				
	A. underestimating to assure achievement	.38	.12	.32	.25
	B. overestimating to avoid paying bonuses	.38	.16	.25	.41
8.	Management distorted or falsified tax returns by:				
	A. omitting an item	.89	.85	.84	1.11
	B. misclassifying an item	.87	.82	.84	1.03
	C. shifting income between periods	.94	.85	.95	1.03
	D. shifting income between jurisdictions	1.04	.93	1.05	1.03
	E. underreporting sales volume to avoid sales tax	1.02	.92	1.00	1.11

organizations than the smaller ones. In contrast, the smaller organizations assigned higher severity ratings to management changing, distorting, or stretching the rules in reporting accounting data to assure achievement or qualify for bonus.

COMPARISON OF RATINGS BY GENDER

Table 16.6 summarizes frequency and severity ratings for both males and females. With respect to frequency, the largest single difference related to smoothing of income. Males indicated a much more frequent observance of this practice than females. The most substantial differences were with respect to shifting revenues (.79 for males and .40 for females) and misclassifying product versus period costs (.65 for males vs. .33 for females). The second biggest difference was with respect to improperly approving expenses. The frequency ratings for males were substantially higher with respect to approving expenses by exceeding authorizations and by accelerating expenses to use up budget. One other area in which males achieved much higher frequency ratings was with respect to reporting of accounting data. Males had much higher frequency ratings in this area, particularly with respect to meeting budget and reaching targets reported to the investment community by changing, distorting, or stretching the rules in reporting accounting data.

In fact, in only three of twenty-seven categories did females achieve a higher frequency than males. The most significant item was with respect to distorting or falsifying tax returns by shifting income between jurisdictions, in which the frequency ratings for females (.14) was somewhat higher than males (.05). The other two categories with slightly higher frequency ratings for females were with respect to underestimating budgets to assure achievement and in reporting accounting data to facilitate an acquisition.

It's entirely possible that these lower frequency ratings, which indicate that females have not observed as many ethical violations as males, are due to the fact that females have only recently risen to management positions comparable to those of males. Consequently, they may not, until recently, have been in the position to observe these practices.

Somewhat surprisingly, in only two of twenty-seven categories did females achieve a marginally higher severity rating. This indicates that males considered ethical violations to be much more serious than did females, judging by their willingness to resign or change jobs if such ethical violations were to occur. The most significant differences were with respect to changing, distorting, or stretching the rules in reporting accounting data, particularly with respect to facilitating an acquisition, reaching investment community targets, or qualifying for bonus. Other significant differences, in which males considered the ethical violations to be more serious, were with respect to leaking information for insider trading by others or with-

Table 16.6

Comparison of Responses by Gender

		Frequency		Severity	
		Male	Female	Male	Female
1.	Management changed, distorted or stretched the rules in reporting accounting data to:				
	A. meet budget	.42	.23	.40	.17
	B. qualify for bonus	.26	.21	.72	.15
	C. reach targets reported to the investment community	.18	.04	.99	.36
	D. facilitate an acquisition	.10	.13	.98	.27
2.	Management withheld information from auditors concerning:				
	A. lawsuits	.01	0	.80	.50
	B. illegal payments, gifts, contributions	.02	0	1.20	.67
	C. tax matters	.11	0	.69	.50
	D. liability for environmental cleanups	.25	.14	1.12	.64
3.	Management leaked information:				
	A. for insider trading by others	.09	.04	.97	.36
	B. to affect competitive bidding	.17	.14	.44	.29
	C. to affect the purchase price of a prospective acquisition or to curry favor with a suitor	.10	0	.25	.17
4.	Management used privileged information for:				
	A. insider trading	.11	.04	.94	.54
5.	Management smoothed income by:				
	A. shifting expenses	.71	.52	.44	.33
	B. shifting revenues	.79	.40	.39	0
	C. adjusting reserves	.86	.75	.11	0
	D. capitalizing vs. expensing assets	.65	.54	.44	0
	E. misclassifying product vs. period costs	.65	.33	.06	0
6.	Management improperly approved expenses by:				
	A. padding personal expenses	.42	.36	.21	0
	B. exceeding authorizations	.57	.36	.06	0
	C. accelerating expenses to use up budget	.48	.26	.06	0
7.	Management materially distorted budgets by:				
	A. underestimating to assure achievement	.28	.33	.31	0
	B. overestimating to avoid paying bonuses	.10	0	.33	.25
8.	Management distorted or falsified tax returns by:				
	A. omitting an item	0	0	.94	.93
	B. misclassifying an item	0	0	.92	.93
	C. shifting income between periods	.11	.08	.98	.93
	D. shifting income between jurisdictions	.05	.14	1.05	.93
	E. underreporting sales volume to avoid sales tax	.02	0	1.05	1.09

holding information from auditors concerning illegal payments, gifts, and contributions and concerning liability for environmental cleanups. The illegal payments and environmental cleanup areas had the highest severity rating for males of any items in the survey.

NAA CODE OF ETHICAL CONDUCT

It is interesting to note that a significantly larger percentage of the respondents were familiar with the NAA Code of Ethical Conduct for Managerial Accountants than were familiar with the landmark Treadway Commission Report. One question on the survey asked the following question, "Has the NAA Code of Ethical Conduct helped you resolve any ethical dilemmas in your organization? If so, briefly describe." Sixteen of the controllers who answered this question did so in the affirmative.

One respondent indicated that she had copied the NAA Code for all of her employees. Several indicated that it served as a general guide in their work. Another indicated that it "forces us to consider our responsibilities and provides us with a foundation we can rely on in making ethical decisions." Yet another indicated that "it tells ownership what rules I'll be guided by—thereby taking pressure off me." Another respondent indicated "If a dilemma appears, we review the Code and take an appropriate response." One other respondent indicated that with the Code there was "more awareness of ethical considerations" and "better reporting of expenses."

On the negative side, one respondent indicated that the Code does not realistically address the ethical climate that exists in small to medium-size companies.

ETHICAL CLIMATE IN ORGANIZATION

Another question asked "How would you describe the ethical climate in your organization?" The write-in responses were tabulated and entered into four categories: excellent, good, fair, and poor.

An overwhelming majority, 81 percent of those answering the question, indicated that the ethical climate in their organization was either excellent or good, with 47 percent rating it excellent and 34 percent rating it good. Just 11 percent identified the climate as fair, and only 8 percent rated it poor.

Several respondents provided additional insight into their organizations. Seven of the responses indicated that, even though the ethical climate was sound, their organization took advantage of all ethical loopholes. One indicated that the ethical climate in his organization was "poor—although legally correct." Another indicated that "management wants to be ethical, but also tried to get away with as much as they can and go to the very edge of the gray areas." Yet another indicated that his company had an "everybody is doing it attitude."

The most frequently cited factor affecting the ethical climate was the people running the company. Five respondents specifically noted the positive contributions of management. One indicated that the ethical climate was excellent and that it started from the top with the CEO. Another indicated that the ethical climate was "very good" after some management changes.

Five other respondents specifically noted how the negative influence of individuals affected the ethical climate. One specifically mentioned that it was "not good since the new President joined."

A few respondents noted that the relatively small size of their organization, with all policy dictated by one individual, negatively influenced the ethical climate. One respondent noted that, "after several clashes with the President, my services as controller were no longer required by him."

RECENT ETHICAL CHANGES

When asked, "Have you noticed any ethical changes in your organization recently? To what would you attribute this?" six respondents cited the positive effect of top management. One cited tighter controls by the CFO. Another cited the example of the CEO, and another mentioned the "philosophy of the new CEO."

On the negative side, five respondents indicated that recent changes in management had caused an undesirable effect. One cited a change for the worse (sons of shareholders). Another said that the new owners were "not entirely above board." And yet another indicated that the situation had gotten worse ("it will only improve with new management").

WHISTLE BLOWING

Respondents were asked the following questions concerning whistle blowing: Are you aware of any whistle blowing in which punitive action was taken against the culprit? If so, how did the ethical climate affect this?

Twenty-two respondents indicated that they were aware of whistle blowing. While many were not sure of the final resolution of the situation, twelve stated that they were aware of punitive action being taken against the culprit. One respondent indicated that the punitive action "reinforced high standards." Another indicated that his company "believes in honesty and prosecution of violators." Another indicated that "staff was aware that management takes such breaches seriously." Yet another indicated that the violation was "so blatant that action was required by management." Another employee stated, "Peer pressure from good employees tends to influence the bad employees." One more employee, referring to the firing of the culprit, indicated, "Everyone in management believed it was the correct thing to do."

Not all situations had such a happy ending for the whistle blower. In six situations cited, the whistle blower himself was discharged. In the words of one respondent, the action "destroyed any pretense of ethical business conduct." Another indicated that he was fired twelve years ago: "Six months after my firing, I was proved right, but was never formerly apologized to." Another respondent indicated that the individual responsible for blowing the whistle was then avoided by other employees, because he was "not trusted." In another situation, a respondent indicated that the allegations were not proven and the whistle blower was dismissed. Finally, there was an additional situation cited in which both the guilty and the innocent managers were fired.

SUMMARY AND CONCLUSIONS

The results of the survey indicate clearly that the ethical climate in the responding controllers' organizations was either excellent or good. In fact, 81 percent of those answering this question indicated just that, and only 8 percent rated the climate poor. The most frequently cited factor affecting the ethical climate was the human factor. In relatively small organizations policy could be dictated by, and negatively influenced by, just one individual.

It is interesting to note that the ethical situations that were considered to be most serious were not very frequently encountered by the controllers. Although this finding might appear to be very positive and encouraging, it might also be symptomatic of a cause and effect relationship. Perhaps those areas considered to be least severe for ethical violations were the most fertile areas for taking "unethical" action. Or perhaps some situations considered to be ethical dilemmas in the survey, such as smoothing of income, were not considered to be unethical by those taking such actions.

The ethical dilemmas most frequently observed by respondents were with respect to smoothing of income and improperly approving expenses. On the other hand, the most severe ethical violations, as judged by the controllers, were the following: changing, distorting, or stretching the rules in reporting accounting data to facilitate an acquisition or to reach targets reported to the investment community; withholding information from auditors concerning illegal payments, gifts, and contributions or liability for environment cleanups; leaking information for insider trading by others or by oneself; distorting or falsifying tax returns by omitting an item; underreporting sales volume to avoid sales tax; and shifting income between jurisdictions or shifting income between periods.

There were several large differences in frequency ratings by organization type. Controllers in private organizations observed smoothing of income by shifting revenues and shifting expenses, while these ratings were substantially lower for governmental, not-for-profit, and public companies. Government organizations rated substantially higher with respect to smoothing of income by misclassifying product versus period costs. With respect to improperly approving expenses, governmental organizations rated substantially higher than the other types of organizations, with public corporations achieving the lowest ratings in this area. Governmental organizations also achieved the highest frequency ratings concerning material distortion of budgets.

Respondents from governmental organizations considered situations with a legal impact to be the most serious. These included the distortion or falsification of tax returns, withholding information from auditors, withholding data on environmental cleanup liabilities, and using privileged information for insider trading.

With respect to smoothing of income, those working in not-for-profit organizations considered shifting expenses to be the only serious transgression, while government employees considered shifting expenses, shifting revenues, and capitalizing versus expensing costs to be more serious ethical violations than did those working in other organizations. Conversely, those working in private corporations considered the improper approving of expenses to be a much more serious violation than did those working at other types of organizations.

The frequency and severity ratings were inconclusive by organization size. As a general rule, the frequency ratings were higher for both the smaller and larger organizations in the survey than they were for organizations in either of the two middle categories. In addition, there was no significant pattern with respect to severity ratings by organization size.

When considering gender differences, in almost every category males achieved a higher frequency rating than females. In fact, in only three of twenty-seven categories did females achieve a higher frequency rating than males. A possible conclusion is that females have not observed as many ethical violations as males because they have only recently risen to management positions comparable to those of males and, as a result, may not have been in a position to observe these practices. Somewhat surprisingly, males also achieved a significantly higher severity rating in almost all categories. In only two of twenty-seven categories did females assign a higher severity rating to specific ethical violations.

Almost 10 percent of the respondents indicated that they were aware of whistle blowing in their current or past organization. Though many respondents were not sure of the final resolution of the situation, over half stated that they were aware of punitive action being taken against the culprit. However, half as many respondents indicated that the whistle blowing resulted in the whistle blower himself being discharged.

17

The Ethics of Computer Activities

RIVA WENIG BICKEL

INTRODUCTION

As the twentieth century draws to a close, business organizations face a host of ethical issues that have never before been considered. Yet despite the fact that commerce has been a human concern for millennia, many businesspeople are still wrestling with issues that were old at the turn of the last century, issues such as conflicting responsibilities and the handling of unethical competitors.

Unlike business, computers have been with us less than a century and have been commonplace for approximately half a century. During this brief yet potent revolution, a myriad of new ethical dilemmas has sprung into existence. Already beleaguered by problems such as competition, government regulation, and consumerism, businesspeople may find it tempting to ignore the problems of computer ethics.

They are for philosophers. They are for theoreticians. They are for nerds who swim in the sea of computers. Yes, we use computers—but for us they are mere tools. They are like typewriters or calculators. What ethical concerns do businesspeople have with typewriters and calculators? True, it is possible that computers may be used in unethical ways. But those uses, those issues, are really no different than ethical issues that have been of concern for centuries."

Would that this were so. Like it or not, in their brief ascendancy computers have generated and continue to generate a whole new coterie of ethical issues. Some are merely high-tech variations on preexisting ethical themes. But others are unique or, because of the characteristics of computers, have novel implications.

Take, for example, hacking, at its most virulent definition—the entry without authorization into the computer system of another. Many of the activities that constitute hacking are now illegal, including snooping in computer systems, changing information in data bases, and planting worms or viruses. Such acts have been made illegal because of the amount of damage that can be caused. Nonetheless, many people perform such acts routinely. What kind of people are they? Some of them fit traditional criminal patterns; others do not.

Hacking differs in many respects from activities such as bank robbery or embezzlement. Bank robbers work in the open, use or threaten violence, and face their victims. Hackers work in the privacy of their own homes, sit peacefully before a computer terminal, and rarely see their victims. Bank robbers may get shot in the attempt—a very real and immediate hazard. Hackers operate in a world remote from reality, where the only actualities are characters marching across a screen. The computer provides insulation between hackers and the results of their activities.

Yet another problem relating to computer ethics is a variant of a problem long since recognized with respect to scientific ethics. Those who become extraordinarily interested in computers are frequently "problem people" rather than "people people." Their goals tend to be the short-term ones of solving computer problems, and they do not relate the achievement of the goals to the needs and problems of others in particular and society in general. The eternal problem of the responsibility of scientific tinkerers for the use to which others put their products is also a problem of computer professionals.

Finally, some of the ethical issues involving computers are not clearly understood by many people. Why not copy some software your friend brought? You couldn't afford to buy your own copy, and you're not taking anything tangible away from the software company. Why not call some other computers and see if you can get into their database and poke around a bit? You aren't going to hurt anything and if they meant it to be secret they would have protected it better. Why not sell your software with no guarantees whatsoever? You can never create a perfect program anyway.

SOFTWARE AS INTELLECTUAL PROPERTY

Perhaps one of the most unsettling areas of computer ethics involves the copying of software. To better understand the issues involved, it is important to first differentiate among three kinds of copying. The first, frequently termed "pirating," involves the mass reproduction of software with the intention of reselling it. The second, which I will term "soft stealing," involves the copying of a single software program for personal use. The third, which I will term "concept copying," involves the copying of one or more concepts of a computer program in the production of an otherwise different computer program.

Pirating is now clearly illegal in the United States. A violation of the U.S. copyright law, it may result in the copier having to pay a fine and do jail time as well as paying compensation to the victim. Interestingly enough, pirating was not always considered illegal; in early cases some judges had difficulty dealing with certain types of computer programs, especially those that were stored as firmware or that did not interface directly with humans. If a computer program did not fall into the category of something that was legally protected, then copying it, or even pirating it was clearly legal. However, common sense and perhaps a sense of ethics prevailed. It would be grossly unfair to let a competitor spend a trivial amount of money to copy a program (created at a cost of substantial time and money) and then undersell the creative party in the marketplace.

Concept copying presently concerns the hotly debated "look and feel" issue that is still being decided by the courts. The earliest cases involved the audiovisual portions of popular arcade games. The equities in these cases were more clear-cut; not only were the games quite innovative, but also the purchase of the underlying equipment and subsequent game purchases were all tied to whether the initial purchase was of a popular game or its play-alike copy. Currently, both legal and ethical questions have become more blurry. Three parties assert the right to equity. The creators of the base software state that the choices they made in designing their packages required thought and effort to product the best possible programs. Copiers claim that the thought was minimal and the choices either arbitrary or forced, due to the very nature of the package. And the public claims that the originators are charging outrageously high prices and attempting to achieve a monopoly based not on a superior product, but on the reluctance of many users to have to learn an entirely different set of keystrokes for using a package. The ethical question hinges upon the underlying issue of intellectual property protection and how it affects the rights and equities of the parties involved. How little protection is insufficient, and how much protection is excessive?

The issue that is most difficult to handle, however, is the one of soft copying. Under the U.S. copyright laws, this activity is clearly illegal. The law, however, never prevented anyone from merely slowing for a stop sign when driving at 2 A.M. on an empty road. Unless people feel that an activity is unethical, most will have little compunction about performing that activity. When doing so also is convenient, involves almost no chance of being caught and prosecuted, and carries a negligible penalty, mass illegal activity is almost inevitable. Thus, the task at hand becomes how to convince someone that it is wrong to copy a $300 program that he or she can't afford and wouldn't buy, when he or she is not taking anything tangible from anyone else.

Soft copying is especially common in educational circles. Students are loathe to spend their restricted funds on something educational that they might otherwise obtain for free. Teachers, on tight personal and professional budgets and accustomed to copying documents for educational purposes under the fair-use doctrine, do not realize that this exception does not apply to copying entire programs. Thus, bad habits are formed, despite the efforts of many computer science/information systems departments and instructional computing centers to inform users about copyright law and to enforce rules to prevent illegal copying.

To further confuse the issue, software companies frequently act in ways that demonstrate lack of ethical concern for others. Companies that produce poor-quality products, use shrink-wrap licenses to entirely eliminate purchasers' warranty rights, engage in cutthroat competition, base their protected products on the work of others, and charge outrageous prices after eliminating competition will have a hard time convincing members of the public to behave ethically by purchasing two copies of a software package when they can buy one and make one copy for free.

This is not to say that lapses on the part of some software companies serve as justification for illegal copying or, as many a parent has stated, "Two wrongs don't make a right." If everyone copied, software houses could not survive. When a large number of people copy, the cost tends to be borne by legitimate purchasers. Neither of these results is acceptable. Yet so much rationalization abounds that those who would decry copying often find themselves on the defensive, arguing a very difficult position.

This position may become even more tenuous when argued outside the United States. Some countries still do not have laws providing copyright protection for computer software. Still other countries offer a far more limited form of protection than is available in the United States. Many people in Third World countries feel that they have little enough in the way of opportunity to better themselves. As they are not breaking any of their own laws and as the act is such a small, innocuous one compared with the daily injustices and inequalities they see, why not copy a program? What importance has this intangible thing known as an intellectual property right as compared to the success of a small business, when that success may result in the feeding of dozens of hungry mouths?

PRIVACY: A RIGHT UNDER SIEGE

Privacy is a nebulous right, whose borders are constantly being reshaped. If it is a threatened right in our society, then one of the greatest threats is the computer or, to be more precise, the sophisticated database management system.

What rights we do have to privacy originate from a number of different sources. Common-law developments have given us the right to be free of intrusive snooping and to be safe from those who would disseminate embarrassing private information concerning us or who would portray our actions so as to put us in a false light. Nor can our persons be unwillingly exploited for someone else's commercial benefit.

We have, however, no explicit right to privacy under the U.S. Constitution, although such a right is granted by a number of state constitutions. Whatever federal rights we have to privacy are granted either by judicial interpretation or by legislative fiat.

Although Supreme Court pronouncements on privacy were fairly expansive under *Griswold* v. *Connecticut* and *Roe* v. *Wade*, cases such as *Whalen* v. *Roe* showed that they are not without limit. Further, retrenchment under a conservative court and a powerful antiabortion movement has already resulted in a backing away from broad privacy rights under *Webster* v. *Reproductive Health Services*, a trend that is likely to continue.

Federal laws, too, have provided some privacy rights under the Fair Credit Reporting Act, the Privacy Act, and the Computer Matching Act. These laws, however, give rather limited protection, either against government agencies only or with respect to specific information, such as credit data. Loopholes and exceptions also weaken the protection given by these acts.

Nor are such privacy rights as do exist unlimited. Other laws and other interests are weighed against them. Thus, the First Amendment privileges of the press allow a fair amount of journalistic privacy invasion, especially with respect to public figures. At the same time, the practical pressures of living in modern society force us to disclose personal and financial information to various institutions. When we must make such disclosure to rent an apartment or buy a house, obtain a job, be allowed the privilege of driving on the roads, educate our children, or secure the benefit of medical insurance, what choice do we have but to conform?

From cradle to grave, information concerning our daily lives is collected, processed, and disseminated. The collection takes place with or without our permission or even our knowledge. The processing proceeds as we expected or in ways we never imagined, the dissemination may benefit us or may benefit others at our expense. Grouping and matching information in different databases allows all types of associations and assumptions to be made. Poor Joe Q. Public. Dialing a wrong number may put him on a law enforcement list of associates of known criminals, a notation by his wife's third-grade teacher may make her ineligible for federal employment, and a single purchase can make his family the target of dozens of eager retailers.

All this and far more can be the result of correctly entered database information. Imagine, then, the mischief that can be caused by incorrect information. The spectrum of problems caused by incorrect database entries ranges from incorrect billing through denial of jobs, credit, and mortgages and all the way to arrest and incarceration.

Considering the harm that can be done by computer-based information, it is smaller wonder that its collection, processing, security, and dissemination are all cause for ethical concern. Yet perhaps laws can play an especially important role here. Laws concerning computer crime and software copying may not always be very effective protection against individuals who deliberately set out to break them, knowing there is little chance of detection and prosecution. However, laws concerning the creation, use, processing, storing, and security of databases are geared to organizations, both business and governmental, and not so much to individuals. Organizations do not always comply with applicable laws; however, their chances of being detected or reported are fairly high and the penalties for noncompliance may be quite severe. Again, the law has and will follow ethical concerns. As to privacy, it may do so to extremely good effect.

RESPONSIBILITY FOR PRODUCTS

Our society has come a long way from the old commercial chestnut, Caveat emptor. We have come to expect that our money will purchase fair value in the marketplace, whether in goods or services. In the area of computer systems, however, the old buyer-beware standard has been more necessary than not. Consumers have been helped not so much by law and ethics as by marketplace and competitive factors. The perception of vendors has thus not been too flattering. The problem is finally being addressed by some of the major vendors, but they have a long way to go before their image is cleaned of some of its tarnish.

Some of the origins of the existing problems are understandable. Until recently, computer systems were sold as expensive custom or customized packages. Hardware was not totally reliable, and one-of-a-kind software was even less so. Building a system was something of a gamble. Neither the purchaser nor the seller could afford the time and money it would take to insure a high degree of perfection. In fact, as buyers were often purchasing state-of-the-art systems in the hope of achieving a competitive edge, there was always a possibility that the system would not perform at all in the way planned. Pressures to innovate, to experiment, and above all to produce products on time and within budget all exacerbate the problems of creating systems that, if not totally defect-free, operate at an acceptable level of performance.

Given this milieu, it is not surprising that vendors were reluctant to warrant the performance of their systems. And given the scarcity of vendors, the eagerness and lack of technical sophistication of buyers, and the fact that sellers frequently had their attorneys drawing up the contracts, it was smaller wonder that so many of these documents offered no real remedy should the system turn out to be useless.

There is an ethical difference, however, between selling a sophisticated company a system that it knows to be experimental, when it fully understands the possible problems and is able to assume and guard against the attendant risks, and selling an unsophisticated company a system that it believes to be turnkey—plug it in and all problems will be solved. The case law is replete with transactions of the latter variety and with sad tales of successful companies that have failed because of defective computer systems.

Unfortunately, one effect of this history has been to provide a lesson for vendors' attorneys in drawing up tighter contracts. Now those provisions that once allowed a court to find some relief for suffering purchasers are gone from the standard contract forms. Now off-the-shelf software, sold in sufficient volume and at sufficient cost to require extensive and thorough testing before sale, is sealed in shrink-wrap packages which, when opened, reveal a "warranty" that essentially states that the purchaser is receiving, for his money, something that is guaranteed to be a disk, free of disk-type errors. That is, the medium is guaranteed, not the program it carries. If there is a defect in the medium, the remedy is limited to replacement of the disk, often at a small charge to the customer. There is no remedy for a defect in the program, whether it merely does not run properly or whether it damages other files on the computer or the computer itself. In other contexts such contractual provisions would be unconscionable; in a computer software context, they are standard.

It should be mentioned that contract law is not the only law that pertains to software sales. Tort law is also applicable. Sellers of defective goods, such as automobiles, have not been able to contract their way out of responsibility. Despite their very carefully drawn self-protective disclaimers, courts have found them liable on theories of negligence or strict liability in tort (otherwise known as product liability). However, historically these theories have been applied only where the injury results in physical harm to humans. The theories rarely apply to physical harm to objects, and almost never to mere economic injury. Given the problem that courts have with intangibles, it is questionable whether the destruction of files by a virus, for example, would give rise to tort liability. Thus, these nonwarranty warranties are likely to prove effective.

To date, the most effective restraint on the unrestricted exploitation of the consumer has been market pressure. Software companies producing low-quality products have failed. Copy protection, which proved more of a nuisance to legitimate buyers than a deterrent to illegal copiers, has been removed. Popular high-priced application programs are being offered at deep discounts for educational purposes. Consumerism, viewed as a form of demand for more ethical treatment, appears to be a practical way to draw vendors' attentions to ethical issues. Perhaps the heinous shrink-wrap license will be the next to disappear.

COMPUTERS AND CRIME

If crime can be defined as society's expression of the acceptable limits of unethical behavior, then the accelerating passage of computer crime laws tells the story of society's changing perspective on computer ethics.

Historically, the law has always had to grapple with new technology, often achieving rather bizarre results in the process. In the end, however, new technology becomes commonplace and well understood and the law once again achieves some rationality. So it has been in the field of computers.

From the start, judges and juries had little problem dealing with commonplace criminal acts that had been committed using the computer as a tool. Embezzlement, forgery, and theft of tangible property are all recognized crimes with statutory penalties. The problems arose with some fuzzier activities. Is the employee who uses the employer's system during lunch break in order to run his own small business committing a criminal act? Is the student who uses his friend's account to do some research committing a criminal act? Is the teenager who obtains some unused PIN numbers and uses them to make long-distance phone calls committing a criminal act? Is the hacker who accesses a credit bureau's database and browses around, to see if he recognizes any names, committing a criminal act? And if any of these activities are criminal acts, to what extent will the perpetrator be punished?

The answer to these questions depends not only upon the act itself, but also upon the circumstances surrounding it, the exact wording of any applicable laws, the intent and status of the person performing the act, and, of course, the proclivities of those people involved in the criminal justice system—investigators, prosecutors, judges, and juries.

If the perpetrator is a trusted adult employee who is acting out of vengeance or for personal gain, the penalties are likely to be severe. If, on the other hand, the perpetrator is a juvenile who is exercising his computer skills, the penalty is likely to consist primarily of community service. There seems to be a lingering perception in the portrayals of the media, in the minds of the public, and especially in the self-image of hackers themselves that hacking is a romantic activity. The mass media do little to dispel the myth. From the fiction of the movie *War Games* to the facts of the Robert Morris, Jr., trial, the hacker as hero or misguided genius perpetuates the impression that hacking is little more than the high-tech version of joy riding. In computer trade publications, though editorial policy decries hacking, letters to the editor and quotations from some computer professionals take a more sympathetic view of hackers. But just as a carefree joyride can end in the disaster of a fatal accident, so too can hacking result in tragedy. Just consider some of the systems it has compromised, such as hospital databases and emergency 911 systems.

Society is beginning to realize the scope of damage that can be caused by certain computer-related activities. Businesses are becoming increasingly aware of security threats and security needs; legislators at both the state and the national level, having already passed computer-crime laws, are considering whether these laws are broad enough and tough enough.

Awareness and concern have improved the situation. Early in the history of computer crimes, corporate victims feared publicity to the extent that the perpetrators were able to further victimize them by threats of going public. The classic parable is of the computer criminal hired by his victim as a highly paid consultant to make the system safe against other criminals. Now, however, victims are more likely to go public and prosecute. Headlines concerning computer crimes make the daily papers and appear almost weekly in computer literature. A recent public television production, "The Computer, the KGB and Me," showed the computer detective, rather than the computer criminal, as hero.

But computer crime still occurs, and the underlying problem still remains one of ethics. It could be the computer-infatuated adolescent who is entranced with breaking into various computer systems or the trusted employee who wreaks havoc with his employer's system as an act of vengeance. It could be the spy who attempts to gather sufficient unclassified information from military systems to add up to classified intelligence, or the passionate proponent for some cause who falsifies data or programs to bolster his point of view. Whatever the activity, the threat of criminal penalty will serve as little deterrence (especially when that threat is not very immediate). Ethical self-restraint will.

WHISTLE BLOWING VERSUS FOLLOWING ORDERS

Computer professionals tend to fill positions where they are part of the technical staff or of lower- or middle-level management. They rarely are found in the stratum of upper-level management. Their training does not prepare them to deal with the kinds of ethical dilemmas that are faced by executives; the problems they know how to handle involve software and hardware. Thus, it becomes very tempting to ignore possible ethical issues and to concentrate on the technical ones.

Computer professionals frequently start out as programmers—order takers. They are told what programs to write, and they write those programs. They are not asked to consider whether or not these programs will affect all or part of society in a beneficial or adverse way. They may not be asked to consider whether the program operates in a proper way, with sufficient auditing controls or safeguards against errors. The decision of when to market the product is not theirs to make. Questioning management may result in their being ridiculed or, in some cases, unemployed.

Researchers have documented an alarming propensity of students to follow orders or otherwise to act out their assigned roles, regardless of the moral implications of their behavior. Knowledge of some of these studies is widespread; particularly unsettling is the one in which subjects pressed switches when told to do so, despite believing that the result was sending electric current through the bodies of others. Nonetheless, a large majority of computer students still are loath to question orders, whether from their instructor or from hypothetical supervisors. The latter is revealed in responses to job-related ethical dilemmas—"It is not my job to question my supervisor; he has more information than I do," is a frequent response. This attitude was revealed in two programming courses I taught, when the students were asked to write programs associated with increasingly invasive substance testing. By the last programming assignment they were handing over results of testing on everything from AZT to birth control to police. Yet, only one student dared the most delicate question about the propriety of the situation. The rest responded with blank stares when, at the end of the semester, they were asked if there had been anything disturbing about the nature of the programs they'd been been required to write.

This lack of thought—a lack, almost, of ability to think—about underlying questions is a common one in students and does not relate exclusively to ethical questions. Every instructor frequently receives answers that are, on their very face, totally impossible. Analytic thought is a sorely lacking skill, yet without that basis how can anyone analyze complex ethical dilemmas?

Computer professionals are frequently faced with such problems. Because of market pressures, they may be asked to sign off on products with suspected or known defects. They may be forced to produce software under such tight deadlines that adequate testing is not possible. They may be asked to provide products that contain inherent unethical or illegal properties, such as financial packages whose accounting safeguards can be circumvented. The excuses of "Well, I'm just doing my job" or "I just make the product—if someone else uses it for improper means that's not my concern" are ethical cop-outs and should be recognized as such.

CONCLUSIONS

Computers are ethically neutral. There is no more good or evil in this most sophisticated of tools than there is in the most primitive of tools. The good or evil is in what we, as mankind and as individuals, do with our tools.

Nonetheless, sophistication does add a complication to the ethical equation. The complexity and seeming intelligence of computer systems allows us the illusion of avoiding responsibility. We can use immaturity to excuse hacking. We can use custom to excuse invasion of privacy. We can use complexity to excuse shoddy products. We can use our roles as employees to excuse our own actions. We can do all these things, but ultimately the responsibility for our actions must rest upon ourselves. It is we who, upon being given some metal, decide whether to form it into a sword or into a plowshare.

Twenty years ago society understood very little about computers. That is changing. As society better understands this tool, it will be less tolerant of ethical lapses. States and nations have adopted laws concerning computer crimes and protection of intellectual property. Privacy laws have been passed, and more are under consideration. Computer systems are now a necessary part of society, and those who create and use them will answer to society.

What we must do is learn to think not just about the mechanics of using computers but about the ethics of our related actions. "I used to copy software," said one student, "until I took a job programming. Now that I know how much work programming is, I don't copy anymore. I would hate the thought of someone ripping off *my* efforts." The most ancient golden rule applied to the most modern technology. Not a bad start.

BIBLIOGRAPHY

Bickel, Riva W., Maria M. Larrondo-Petrie, David F. Bush, and Fred G. Harold. "Ethical Issues in Computing: Student Responses." *Proceedings of Information Systems Education Conference*, Chicago, October 1990.

Bickel, Riva W., Maria M. Larrondo-Petrie, and David F. Bush. "EDICT: A Tool to Assist Computer Ethics Education." *International Business Schools Computer Users Group Quarterly*, Winter 1990.

———. "Computer Related Ethical Issues Affecting Employees: A Student Perspective." Forthcoming.

Forester, Tom, and Perry Morrison. *Computer Ethics: Cautionary Tales and Ethical Dilemmas in Computing*. Cambridge, Mass.: MIT Press, 1990.

Frenkel, Karen A. "Women & Computing." *Communications of the ACM* 33, 11 (November 1990): 34–46.

Griswold v. Connecticut, 381 U.S. 479 (1965).

Haney, C., C. Banks, and P. Zimboardo. "Interpersonal Dynamics in a Simulated Prison." *International Journal of Criminology and Penology* 1 (1973): 69–97.

Johnson, Deborah G. *Computer Ethics*. Englewood Cliffs, N.J.: Prentice-Hall, 1985.

Johnson, Deborah G., and John W. Snapper. *Ethical Issues in the Use of Computers*. Belmont, Calif.: Wadsworth Publishing Co., 1985.

Leibowitz, Sue L., and L. H. Ludlow. "Measuring Ethical Sensitivity in Computer Use." *American Education Research Association Annual Conference*, Boston, April 16, 1990.

Milgram, S. "A Behavioral Study of Obedience." *Journal of Abnormal and Social Psychology* 67 (1963): 371–78.

Parker, Donn B. *Ethical Conflicts in Computer Science and Technology*. Berkeley, Calif.: AFIPS Press, 1981.

Parker, Donn B., Susan Swope, and Bruce N. Baker. "Ethical Conflicts in Information and Computer Science, Technology and Business." Los Angeles: SRI International, August 1988.

Pearl, Amy, Martha E. Pollack, Eve Riskin, Becky Thomas, Elizabeth Wolf, and

Alice Wu. "Becoming a Computer Scientist." *Communications of the ACM* 33, 11 (November 1990): 47–57.

Rest, J., D. Cooper, R. Coder, J. Masanz, and D. Anderson. "Judging the Important Issues in Moral Dilemmas: An Objective Measure of Development." *Developmental Psychology* 10, 4 (1974): 491–501.

Roe v. Wade, 410 U.S. 113 (1972).

Webster v. Reproductive Health Services, 106 L.Ed.2d 410 (1989).

E. A. Weiss. "Self-Assessment Procedure IX: A Self-Assessment Procedure Dealing with Ethics in Computing." *Communications of the ACM* 25, 3 (March 1982): 181–95.

Whalen v. Roe, 429 U.S. 589 (1977).

18

Codes of Ethics

Leo V. Ryan

EARLY CODES IN HISTORY

Richard DeGeorge once observed that "the history of ethics in business is a long one" but that "the history of business ethics by contrast would be very brief" (1987, p. 201). We can make a similar observation about professional codes of ethics. Codes of conduct enjoy a long tradition from the Code of Hammurabi (1728–1686 B.C.) to the present, but the history of codes of ethics is much more recent.

The Code of Hammurabi contained almost 300 paragraphs of rules governing business, moral, and social life reaching back into the 3d millennium B.C. to the earlier codes of Ur-Nammu (c. 2060–2043 B.C.), the code of Lipit-Ishtar (c. 1983–1733 B.C.), and the code of Eshnunnia (c. 1950 B.C.). These codes were essentially compilations of customs, laws, and rules of ancient Mesopotamia, mostly going back to Sumerian times (cf. Huseman 1967, p. 911).

J.P.M. Van Der Ploeg observes that 'there is no evidence that the codes which have survived were universally applied in the juridical practice of the territories for which they had been given. The law givers proclaimed *their ideals in their codes hoping that these would be put into practice everywhere*" (1967a, p. 547, italics added).

The period of Hammurabi corresponds roughly to the period of the Israelite patriarchs. The concept of law plays a major role in Hebrew tradition. The nature of Old Testament law differs from ancient oriental law in its character of having been revealed. "Tora" etymologically means "instruction." "Tora" in the Greek Septuagint is translated as "law." That translation has become universal. However, "the Hebrew languages possess many synonyms for 'Tora' which . . . came finally to include the meaning (word, prescription, commandment, custom, testimony, etc.)" (Van Der Ploeg, 1967b, pp. 554–55). In the various collections of Hebrew laws there are two that are truly codes, containing both causistic laws and moral principles, that is, a call to higher codes of ethical conduct. The Book of the Covenant (Ex. 20, chapters 22–23, 33) and the Book of Deuteronomy (chapters 12 to 26) are codes.

We know that we can define and examine ethics from several perspectives. The current literature discussing ethics approaches the field from four general perspectives. Two approaches examine moral and ethical issues without presuming to take a moral stand. These approach ethics from a descriptive outlook and do so from either a scientific or a conceptual view. The two other approaches are prescriptive in nature and constitute general or applied normative ethics. Codes of ethics are prescriptive in nature, involving either general or specific norms or a combination of both approaches.

CODES OF ETHICS DEFINED

Steven Weller contends that "Codes of Ethics are similar to laws in that both contain certain rules to guide future behavior. Our experience with law provides an analogy upon which to draw in analyzing the effectiveness of Codes of Ethics" (1988, p. 389).

Modern-day codes of conduct offer an admixture of philosophical statements, commitments to legal observance, and high ideals often combined with admonitions to employees to avoid specific illegal actions and to adhere to certain moral principles, especially those that elevate standards of personal conduct and in particular those with an emphasis on relationships of one person with another. Today we refer to these efforts variously as Codes of Ethics or Codes of Conduct, or Corporate Directives and Administrative Practices, Standards of Business Ethics and Conduct, Conflict of Interest Statements, or some similar designation. An abbreviated history of U.S. corporate codes has been presented by George C. S. Benson (Benson 1989a, pp. 4–7; Benson 1989b, pp. 306–7; cf. White and Montgomery 1980, pp. 80–81).

DeGeorge notes that

the standards to which members of a profession are to hold themselves is usually expressed in a professional code—most often called an ethical code—of conduct promulgated and enforced by a professional organization. Those groups wishing to gain the status of a profession frequently organize into a professional association and promulgate a code of professional ethical conduct. (1982, p. 225)

There are many categories of codes. There are corporate codes developed by a particular company, usually a domestic corporation; but some corporate codes such as Caterpillar and Levi Strauss & Co. are international in their intention and application. There are efforts to develop international codes through private groups such as the Carnegie Center for Transnational Studies, through trade associations such as the U.S. Council of the International Chamber of Commerce, through the United Nations as in its Commission on Transnational Corporations (1975), or through agencies like the Organization of Economic Cooperation and Development (OECD) (1976). There are codes developed for members of learned societies, codes of conduct for individual trade associations, and industry-wide codes. There are codes of practice governing professional groups, including public-service professionals.

Molander further refines the definitions of "ethics" and "ethical codes" that expresses more precisely our approach. "Ethics," he writes,

refers to "the principles of right and wrong conduct which guide the members of a group, profession, or society"... an "ethical code" is defined as "part of that middle ground between internalized societal values on the one hand and law on the other where *formal* social and economic sanctions of a social group—a profession, an industry, a firm, etc.—act to ensure conformity with acceptable standards of behavior and penalize deviance." (1987, pp. 619–20)

Codes of ethics have long been considered a primary means of institutionalizing ethics in the corporation or in a trade association, professional group, or learned society. Weber suggests that "the term institutionalizing ethics is academic and may sound ponderous but it has value" (1981, p. 47). Purcell agrees that "institutionalization may sound like a ponderous word ... but its meaning is straightforward. It simply means setting up new structures to get ethical concerns formally and explicitly introduced into daily business life" (1982, p. 361; Hanson 1984, pp. 185–91).

As George C. S. Benson observes,

if the reform actions of today are to be continuously helpful they must be institutionalized, through writing basic codes, through enforcement of those codes, through sensitive administrative leadership and example, and appropriate actions of participative management, and informed public criticism. (1989b, p. 306)

Benson recognizes implicitly what Mark Frankel says explicitly when he writes that "the code must be viewed as only one part of a larger system intended to promote ethical conduct and to provide a supportive environment for professionals" (ibid., p. 114).

THE EVOLUTION OF CODES

Let us examine the operational development or evolution of codes. David Niken observes that "there can be many reasons for introducing codes, not all of them altruistic. Having managers and workers understand the language of ethics and apply those principles, however, is what the usefulness of Codes in terms of morale and profits is all about" (1989, p. 60).

"A profession's code of ethics is perhaps its most visible and explicit enunciation of its professional norms," writes Mark Frankel, as, "A code embodies the collective conscience of a profession and is testimony to the group's recognition of its moral dimensions" (Frankel 1989, p. 110).

DeGeorge is emphatic that

unless the code is understood in terms of moral principles, it will tend simply to be an expression of rules learned by rote, or even worse, of ideals never to be attained. If a member of a profession is to internalize the rules of his profession, he must understand how they are derived, how they implement moral principles, and how he can use similar reasoning to cover situations of conflict and those situations not handled explicitly in the code. (1982, p. 231)

Frankel proposes that "along a continuum, three types of codes can be identified." They are (1) "an *aspiration* code" ... "a statement of ideals to which practitioners should strive ...," (2) "an *educational* code, one which seeks to buttress understanding of its provisions with extensive commentary and interpretation," and (3) "a *regulatory* code, which includes a set of detailed rules to govern professional conduct and to serve as a basis for adjudicating grievances" (ibid., pp. 110–11).

William C. Starr catalogs reasons proffered for establishing codes:

Codes have been justified on grounds of efficiency, as a binding ideal for a profession, as in the public interest, as consistent with rational self-interest and as an effective tool towards self-regulation. In a more negative manner, codes of ethics may be an effective substitute for increased government regulation which neither business nor its professions generally find attractive. They may help regulate both employee and employer as well as assist in developing some sort of ethical consistency in business and the professions. (1983, p. 99)

What are the functions of codes, especially professional codes?

One of the most compelling reasons for the Code is that management wishes to conduct all its relationships with government, with shareholders, with employees, with supplies and with the public in congruence with the ethics which any civilization must follow to maintain harmony among its members. (Benson 1989a, p. 33)

Mark Frankel introduces his cataloguing of the various functions that may be performed by codes of professional ethics by a quotation from Corrine Gibb:

Not all planks of a professional association's code of ethics are meant to be taken in the same spirit. Some are merely costumes the profession puts on to impress outsiders. Some are preachments to be honored, but not necessarily obeyed. Some are tactical moves in controversies with outside groups. Some are really seriously intended. (quoted in Frankel 1989, p. 11)

Frankel then proposes eight functions of professional codes which "taken collectively . . . reveal a great deal about the relationship between a profession, and the members, its clients and the larger society" (ibid.).

The eight functions of professional codes as perceived by Frankel are comprehensive. They are (1) enabling documents; (2) sources of public evaluation; (3) professional socialization, that is, "codes foster pride in the profession and strengthen professional identity and allegiance"; (4) enhancement of a profession's reputation and public trust; (5) preservation of entrenched professional biases; (6) a deterrent to unethical behavior; (7) a support system, and (8) a basis for adjudication (ibid., pp. 111–12).

Donald Robin and coauthors offer an interesting observation:

Organizational codes of ethics are 1. very different; 2. often similar; 3. not connected with ethics; 4. perceived as an important tool for fostering ethical conduct; and 5. not very effective in a broad ethical sense. A welter of contradictions? Indeed, all the above statements are true—and this fact makes an analysis of ethical codes extremely difficult. (1989, p. 66)

Simon Webley, on behalf of the Institute of Business Ethics (London), has developed a manual that includes a guide to drafting company philosophies and corporate codes of business ethics, complete with a model statement and codes (1988, Part III, Model, pp. 11–13; Part IV, Production and application of Statements and Codes, pp. 14–16). Molander suggests a four-part model for the content of codes that embraces (1) societal values; (2) ethical codes: general purpose; (3) ethical codes: specific practices; and (4) law (Molander 1987, Fig. 1. Guides for conduct, p. 620). He further notes that

The objective of an ethical code fall into three broad categories. First, a code is designed to eliminate or preempt practices that are clearly unethical and inimical to the best interests of the firm. Second, a code establishes the legitimacy of disciplinary actions if the code is violated. Third, a code helps individual employees relieve "ethical dilemmas"—situations in which there are conflicts between the opponent interests of the organization and the ethical beliefs of the individual managers, or between one of these factors and the ethical beliefs of the manager's peers, important corporate client groups, or the society at large. (Ibid., p. 623; cf. Fig. 2, The Business Argument for Ethical Codes)

DeGeorge suggests that

codes should have the following characteristics: 1. The code should be regulative; 2. The code should protect the public interest and the interests of those served by the Profession; 3. The code should not be self-serving; 4. The code should be specific and honest; and 5. The code should be both policeable and policed. (1982, p. 229)

Codes of ethics can be various types according to their intended functions. Codes of ethics tend to contain both general and specific components. Usually the introduction, preface, or preamble outlines the basic philosophy of the organization. Content can vary widely depending on whether the organization is a corporation, a trade association, or a professional group. "General precept codes tend to be, but are not exclusively, of an approbatory nature—made up of 'thou shalts.' Specific practice codes tend to be, but not exclusively, of a prescriptive nature—made up of 'thou shalt not's' " (Molander 1987, p. 620).

Many listings have been developed by an analysis of the typical content of corporate codes of conduct (Benson 1989a, pp. 9–22; Cressey and Moore 1983, Table 9, p. 56; Robin et al., Table 2.6; Nitkin 1989, pp. 57–58; Robin et al. 1989, p. 68; White and Montgomery 1980, Table 3, p. 84). One of the most comprehensive listings of corporate code content has been published as Appendix Two of the Hammaker, Horniman, and Rader study of *Standards of Conduct in Business* for the Center for the Study of Applied Ethics at the Colgate Darden Graduate School, University of Virginia (1977, pp. 55–58). Their listing contains seventeen categories of topics covered in the codes of Fortune 500 firms, along with specific prohibitions within each category ranging from three to thirty-eight examples each.

The pattern of providing for general and specific elements in codes of the future will remain rather constant, but the content will vary considerably depending on the professional group or organization developing the code.

EXPECTATIONS AND LIMITATIONS

What should be our expectations of codes? Are codes really effective? What are their limitations? Do we expect too much? Kenneth Arrow warns that "one must not expect miraculous transformation in human behavior. Ethical codes, if they are to be viable, should be limited in scope" (1973, p. 135). Mark Pastin is quoted as observing that, in searching through thousands of pages of management journals, he has uncovered no evidence that codes of ethics have a positive effect on responsible conduct (Nitkin 1989, p. 58).

"One difference between proponents and the critics (of Codes) has revolved around whether codes of ethics, as opposed to other forms of self-regulation, are or even could be effective in controlling behavior" (Weller 1988, p. 389).

White and Montgomery concluded from their analysis of a random sample of thirty codes (10 percent) from three hundred corporate codes reported in a survey of CFOs in the Fortune 100 and from a random sample of members of the Financial Executives Institute that

The most pressing question to be explored concerns the effectiveness of codes of conduct. Do they have an impact on behavior? Which code design, administrative procedures, and other practices yield the highest levels of effectiveness in terms of behavioral objectives? Existing literature has little to say on these important questions. (1980, p. 86)

The highly critical Cressey and Moore study of 119 corporate codes reached the "overall conclusion that corporate codes of conduct have not done much to provide such assurance" that "the private sector" is dedicated to protecting and promoting the public interest" (Cressey and Moore 1983, p. 75). However, they comment, their "study did not address the question of effectiveness" because "interviews . . . convinced us that there is no practical way of measuring any effects the codes might have on the conduct of corporate personnel" (ibid., p. 73).

In a detailed analysis of corporate codes in terms of organizational behavior and misbehavior, M. Cash Mathews concludes, "From the analysis, it becomes clear that the relationship between codes of ethics/conduct and corporate violations are minimal" (1987, p. 126). Later, he notes that "the findings from this study indicate that it cannot be concluded that codes of ethics demonstrate either (1) social responsibility, (2) a corporate culture which promotes anti-criminal behavior patterns or (3) self-regulation. While the codes hold the promise of aiding us in the accomplishment of all three objectives, it is up to corporate leaders to implement the means by which these objectives can be attained" (ibid., pp. 127–28).

Even Benson concedes that "while the scholarly critics have vastly underestimated their usefulness, it should be admitted that the ethical usefulness of codes has limits" (1989a, p. 30).

What, then, are the perceived limitations? Some critics are simply skeptical about all codes. Bowie reports that some codes are mere "window dressing and a smokescreen to head off more stringent methods of self control" (Bowie 1979, p. 143). Starr points out (1) that codes "can have language so vague that it is not going to be particularly helpful in assisting professionals and businesspersons in ethical decision making"; (2) "Codes of Ethics can be self-serving to the profession or industry involved"; (3) Codes "can be used as a 'PR gimmick' "; and (4) "Some sort of enforcement procedure is going to be required if the code of ethics is to work successfully" (1983, pp. 104–5).

Some "fear codes cannot be properly interpreted, or if properly interpreted, cannot or will not be rigorously enforced. There is a fear that in the final analysis codes of ethics will take a lower priority to maximizing profits" (Starr 1983, p. 99; Molander 1987, p. 630). Others believe that, at a minimum, authors of corporate codes have permitted federal rule-makers to dictate the prevailing ethical concerns. These critics express the need for an ethical regeneration based not on laws, but on the many implications of long range profit responsibilities. For the public service professional, that concept should be translated as long-range public service opportunities.

Cressey and Moore are convinced "that any improvements in business ethics taking place in the last decade are not a consequence of business leader's calls for ethics or the codes themselves." Rather they believe that "any changes have stemmed from conditions imposed by outsiders." More-over, they further believe, based on their analysis of codes, that codes "tend to imitate the criminal law and thus contain few innovative ideas about how the ethical standard of a firm, let alone business in general can be improved" (Cressey and Moore 1983, pp. 73–74). Robin and coauthors conclude: "Codes may communicate specific rules . . . but they have little impact on what might be considered the *important* problem of business" (1989, p. 71).

"A typical defect of Codes," observes Richard DeGeorge, "is that they give the professional or worker no insight into how the code was formu-lated, what moral principles it exemplifies, or how to resolve issues of interpretation or of conflicts not covered by the code" (1982, p. 230).

Other data suggest a somewhat more promising view. The Center for Business Ethics at Bentley College undertook a study relating to corporate efforts "to incorporate ethical values and concerns into daily operations. . . ." It reported that 80 percent of 279 respondents said they had taken such steps and that 93 percent indicated that codes of ethics were used to accomplish their efforts (1986, p. 86). A Touche Ross study revealed that their respondents cited the adoption of codes of ethics as "its most effective measure for encouraging ethical business behavior" (1988, p. 3). Thirty-nine percent of the Touche Ross respondents cited codes as "most effec-tive," which confirms the fact that many managers still see codes as the most valuable tool for dealing with ethical problems. Whatever their per-ceived effectiveness, codes of conduct still prevail as the leading means of institutionalizing ethics in the corporation.

Even so, almost everyone will agree with Hyman, Skipper, and Tansey that "Ethical codes are not enough" and that "managers need more than codes of ethics; they need to ask themselves a few questions to make sure every decision is ethical" (1990, p. 15).

Starr notes that "it is true that codes of ethics by themselves are not a panacea to insure honesty, integrity and ethical behavior in a given profes-sion or industry; only the most naive individual could possibly think that" (1983, p. 105).

Saul Gellerman makes a special plea for administrators and managers to acknowledge the role of personal conscience:

It is only reasonable to note that each individual's conscience plays an indispensable role in keeping an organization ethical. Indeed, if there were too many members of an organization to whom the "still, small voice" that the Bible equated with God did not speak, then no codes of ethics or other human contrivances could save that organization from disrepute. As a practical matter, organizations must appeal to the consciences of their members, because they have no better way to defend the organization's honor. Moreover, such appeals usually work. (1989, p. 73)

In concluding his argument that senior management bears responsibility for creating the environment in which people are likely to behave ethically, Gellerman reflects further on conscience as a primary individual guide that functions best when supported by an ethical secondary support system that he calls a "second line."

Gellerman concludes his reflection with a challenge:

If we could not rely on conscience as a steadfast guide for most of us, most of the time, nothing could save us. Nevertheless, we will not be saved solely through passive trust in each other's conscience. We need ways of helping the best in each of us to prevail against the worst. The individual conscience is our first line of ethical defense; but, like any such defense, it functions much better when backed by a strong, alert, well-managed second line. Our challenge is to erect that second line. (1989, p. 75)

It is the properly developed, carefully articulated, clearly understood, widely promulgated, and sympathetically enforced code of ethics that preserves individual conscience, promotes an ethical environment, and permits a code of ethics to be efficacious. Not only private sector managers have this need, but public sector managers do as well.

David Nitkin offers three arguments favoring the introduction and rigorous application of codes:

First, they involve the realm of the preferred and not merely the possible or probable. . . . Concise, relevant statements of acceptable norms can serve as welcome causes for individual and corporate direction setting. Second, codes of conduct assist in helping recruit and retain the kind of staff (especially at the entry level) that a company participating wants to attract . . . profits can reward those competitive business environments which coordinate mission statements, operational standards and narrative behavior. (1989, p. 59)

THE ENFORCEMENT OF CODES OF CONDUCT

The enforcement of codes of conduct requires that they have been promulgated and implemented and that they incorporate systems to insure compliance. Molander observes that "the most problematic aspect of implementing an ethical code is code enforcement" (1987, p. 629). Like a law, the code should be an ordinance of reason promulgated to all those who are affected by its adoption. Any code adapted by a corporation or a trade or professional association must be widely distributed; the code must be communicated to all pertinent publics. "Promulgation is intended to deter unethical conduct and to educate managers as to the expectation they can legitimately impose on subordinates and client groups" (ibid., p. 629). Codes should also be widely distributed to the larger public.

As Kenneth Arrow notes, "An ethical code is useful only if it is widely accepted" (1973, p. 136). That opinion applies to both internal and public acceptance. "The implementation of ethical codes, the same ethical codes argued for by economists and lawyers, is one means available to business to relieve ethical dilemmas, minimize overtly unethical practices, and restore public confidence in the business community" (ibid., p. 623).

Compliance with the general "spirit of the code" and 'the letter of the code" is a challenge. Some codes are primarily hortatory; other codes are deeply embedded with specifics. Some codes may be ambiguous, permissive, and poorly defined for purposes of compliance. Other codes will be much more precise, legalistic, and replete with provisions for penalties for infraction. A single code may include a statement of ideals, a set of disciplinary rules, and standards of professional etiquette (DeGeorge 1982, p. 229).

"Generally speaking compliance comes about in two fashions: internally by supervision, board review and individual personal integrating; and externally, by independent auditions, government regulations, and the court" (Nitkin 1989, p. 59).

Nitkin identifies some common compliance and review procedures:

the obligation of the individual to follow the guidelines and, if in doubt, whom to approach for advice,

mechanisms for reviewing and discussing the guidelines at both the time of hiring and annual performance appraisals,

how to recognize and address conflicts of interest,

how, and to whom, to complain if your manager is him/herself the problem,

a "speak-up," "open-door" or "ombudsman" program with guaranteed protection against retaliation through a superior's misuse of position of authority, and

an employee's obligation to be alert and report instances of possible code violation. (*ibid.*)

Compliance, to be effective in the case of trade associations and professions, must apply to all members of the industry and to all members of the profession, whether or not they belong to the appropriate association or professional society. Frankel comments that "it would be a strain on the association's credibility for them to promote their profession's moral dimension for the good of society, but then limit their activities and resources only to those who can demonstrate membership in their ranks. The associations' ethical activities must be accessible to all who follow a profession's traditions regardless of their organizational affiliation" (1989, p. 115).

Benson concludes after reviewing the research that "enforcement data is inadequate" (1989b, p. 23). The usual penalties for failure to enforce seem to be reprimand, termination, suspension, or demotion. These penalties, especially the more severe, do not seem to be applied widely, but there are enough cases of enforcement every year to support the seriousness of the policy.

BIBLIOGRAPHY

Arrow, Kenneth J. 1973. "Business Codes and Economic Efficiency." *Public Policy* 21 (Summer 1973). In *Ethical Theory and Business*, 3rd ed., ed. T. L. Beauchamp and N. E. Bowie. Englewood Cliffs, N.J.: Prentice-Hall.

Benson, George C. S. 1989a. *Codes of Ethics: Business and Government*. Claremont, Calif.: The Henry Salvatori Center.

———. 1989b. "Code of Ethics." *Journal of Business Ethics* 8: 306–7.

Bowie, N. E. 1979. "Business Codes of Ethics: Window Dressing or Legitimate Alternative to Government Regulation?" In *Ethical Theory and Business*, ed. T. L. Beauchamp and N. E. Bowie. Englewood Cliffs, N.J.: Prentice-Hall.

Center for Business Ethics, Bentley College. 1986. "Are Corporations Institutionalizing Ethics?" *Journal of Business Ethics* 5 (April): 86.

Cressey, Donald R., and Charles A. Moore. 1983. "Managerial Values and Corporate Codes of Ethics." *California Management Journal* 25, 4 (Summer): 73–44.

DeGeorge, Richard T. 1982. *Business Ethics*. New York: Macmillan Publishing Co., Inc.

———. 1987. "The Status of Business Ethics: Past and Future." *Journal of Business Ethics* 6 (1987): 201.

Ethics Research Center. 1979. "Codes of Ethics in Corporations and Trade Associations and the Teaching of Ethics in Graduate Business Schools." Princeton, N.J.: Opinion Research Corporation. ORC Study 65302. June.

———. 1980. "Implementation and Enforcement of Codes of Ethics in Corporations and Trade Associations." Princeton, N.J.: Opinion Research Corporation, ORC Study 65334, August.

Frankel, Mark. 1989. "Professional Codes: Why, How and with What Impact?" *Journal of Business Ethics* 8 (1989): 114.

Gellerman, Saul W. 1989. "Managing Ethics from the Top Down." *Sloan Management Review* 30, 2 (Winter): 73, 75.

Hammaker, Paul M., Alexander B. Horniman, and Louis T. Rader. 1977. *Standards of Conduct in Business*. Charlottesville, Va.: Center for the Study of Applied Ethics, pp. 55–58.

Hanson, Kirk, 1984. "Institutionalizing Ethics in the Corporation." In *Corporate Governance and Institutionalizing Ethics*, ed. W. Michael Hoffman, Jennifer Mills Moore, and David A. Fedo. Lexington, Mass.: D. C. Heath, pp. 185–91.

Huseman, J. E. 1967. "Hammurabi (Hammurapi). King of Babylon." *New Catholic Encyclopedia*, vol. 6. New York: McGraw-Hill Book Company, p. 911.

Hyman, Michael R., Robert Skipper, and Richard Tansey. 1990. "Ethical Codes are not Enough." *Business Horizons* 33, 2 (March/April): 15.

Mathews, M. Cash. 1987. "Codes of Ethics: Organizational Behavior and Misbehavior." In *Research in Corporate Social Performance and Policy*, ed. William C. Frederick and Lee E. Preston, vol. 9. (Greenwich, Conn.: JAI Press, Inc.).

Molander, Earl A. 1987. "A Paradigm for Design, Promulgation, and Enforcement of Ethical Codes." *Journal of Business Ethics* 9 (1987): 619–20.

Nitkin, David. 1989. "Corporate Codes of Ethics." *The Corporate Ethics Monitor* 1, 4 (July): 6.

Purcell, Theodore V. 1982. "The Ethics of Corporate Governance." *Review of Social Economy* 40, 3 (December): 361.

Robin, Donald, Michael Giallourakis, Fred David, and Thomas E. Moritz. 1989. "A Different Look at Codes of Ethics." *Business Horizons* 32, 1 (January/February): 66.

Schachter, Hindy Laura. 1989. *Frederick Taylor and the Public Administration Community: A Reevaluation*. Albany: State University of New York Press, p. 111.

Starr, William C. 1983. "Codes of Ethics: Towards A Rule-Utilitarian Justification." *Journal of Business Ethics* 2 (1983): 99.

Touche Ross. 1988. *Ethics in American Business*. Detroit: Touche Ross, January.

Van Der Ploeg, J.P.M. 1967a. "Ancient Near East Law." *New Catholic Encyclopedia*, vol. 8. New York: McGraw-Hill Book Company, p. 547.

———. 1967b. "Mosaic Law." *New Catholic Encyclopedia*, vol. 8, New York: McGraw-Hill Book Company, pp. 554–55.

Weber, James. 1981. "Institutionalizing Ethics in the Corporation." *MSU Business Topics* 29, 2 (Spring): 47.

Webley, Simon. 1988. *Company Philosophies and Codes of Business Ethics: A Guide to Their Drafting and Use*. London: Institute for Business Ethics.

Weller, Steven. 1988. "The Effectiveness of Corporate Codes of Ethics." *Journal of Business Ethics* 7 (1988): 389.

White, Bernard J., and B. Ruth Montgomery. 1980. "Corporate Codes of Conduct." *California Management Journal* 23, 2 (Winter).

Index

About the Editor and Contributors

DOMINICK T. ARMENTANO is a professor of economics at the University of Hartford.

GEORGE C. S. BENSON is senior research associate at Salvatori Center and president emeritus of Claremont McKenna College.

ROSALYN WIGGINS BERNE is executive director of the Olsson Center for Applied Ethics at the Darden School, University of Virginia.

RIVA WENIG BICKEL is an associate professor of computer and information systems at SUNY College at Oswego.

WALTER E. BLOCK is a professor of economics at the College of the Holy Cross.

JAMES E. CHESHER is a professor of philosophy at Santa Barbara City College.

DOUGLAS J. DEN UYL is a professor of philosophy and chair of the philosophy department at Bellarmine College.

ANTONY FLEW is emeritus professor of philosophy at the University of Reading, England.

R. EDWARD FREEMAN is Olsson Professor of Business Administration and director of the Olsson Center for Applied Ethics, University of Virginia.

ROBERT E. GORDON, JR., is director of the National Wilderness Institute.

WILLIAM K. GROLLMAN is a professor of accounting at Fordham University and president of the Center for Video Education, Inc.

JERRY KIRKPATRICK is an associate professor of marketing at California State Polytechnic University, Pomona.

ROGER KOPPL is an assistant professor in the department of economics and finance at Fairleigh Dickinson University.

BEVARS D. MABRY is a professor of economics at Bowling Green State University.

ROBERT W. MCGEE is a professor of accounting at Seton Hall University.

TIBOR R. MACHAN is a professor of philosophy at Auburn University.

DOUGLAS B. RASMUSSEN is a professor of philosophy at St. John's University.

LEO V. RYAN is a professor of management at DePaul University.

JOAN L. VAN HISE is an accounting instructor at Fordham University.